RESEARCH IN
FINANCIAL SERVICES
PRIVATE AND PUBLIC POLICY

BANKING, FINANCIAL MARKETS, AND SYSTEMIC RISK

Volume 7 • 1995

EDITORIAL BOARD

RESEARCH IN FINANCIAL SERVICES

PRIVATE AND PUBLIC POLICY

BANKING, FINANCIAL MARKETS, AND SYSTEMIC RISK

Editor: GEORGE G. KAUFMAN
School of Business Administration
Loyola University of Chicago

VOLUME 7 • 1995

JAI PRESS INC.

Greenwich, Connecticut *London, England*

55 Old Post Road, No. 2
Greenwich, Connecticut 06836

JAI PRESS LTD.
The Courtyard
28 High Street
Hampton Hill, Middlesed TW12 1PD
England

ISBN: 1-55938-244-9

Manufactured in the United States of America

BANKING, FINANCIAL MARKETS, AND SYSTEMIC RISK

Papers presented at a conference in Washington, DC on December 2, 1994
Sponsored by the Office of the Comptroller of the Currency

CONFERENCE ORGANIZERS AND SPECIAL EDITORS

Philip F. Bartholomew
Office of the Comptroller of the Currency

George G. Kaufman
Loyola University of Chicago

CONTENTS

LIST OF CONTRIBUTORS ix

DEDICATION xi

INTRODUCTION xiii

PART I. OVERVIEW OF SYSTEMIC RISK

FUNDAMENTALS OF SYSTEMIC RISK
Philip F. Bartholomew and Gary W. Whalen 3

SYSTEMIC RISK AND THE MACROECONOMY
Anna J. Schwartz 19

COMMENT ON SYSTEMIC RISK
Frederic S. Mishkin 31

COMMENT ON SYSTEMIC RISK
George G. Kaufman 47

PART II. SOURCES AND CONSEQUENCES OF SYSTEMIC RISK

SYSTEMIC RISK: BANK DEPOSITS AND CREDIT
Robert A. Eisenbeis 55

PAYMENT AND SETTLEMENT SYSTEMS:
TRENDS AND RISK MANAGEMENT
Claudio Borio 87

DERIVATIVES AND SYSTEMIC RISK: ISSUES,
VIEWS, AND ANALYSIS
Robert J. Mackay 111

COMMENT ON SOURCES OF RISK
James R. Barth 171

PART III. TRANSNATIONAL ASPECTS

INTERNATIONAL ASPECTS OF SYSTEMIC RISK
Morris Goldstein 177

SYSTEMIC RISK WHEN DEPOSITORS BEAR LOSSES: FIVE CASE STUDIES
Herbert Baer and Daniela Klingebiel 195

COMMENT ON TRANSNATIONAL ASPECTS
Daniel E. Nolle 303

PART IV. ADDRESSING SYSTEMIC RISK

IS SYSTEMIC RISK DEAD?
Richard S. Carnell 311

SYSTEMIC RISK AND THE REGULATORY AGENCIES
Susan M. Phillips 317

REGULATORY RESPONSES TO THE POTENTIAL FOR SYSTEMIC RISK IN THE FINANCIAL SECTOR
Mark J. Flannery 323

MISSING ENTAILMENTS IN PUBLIC-POLICY DEFINITIONS OF SYSTEMIC RISK
Edward J. Kane 337

PART V. KEYNOTE ADDRESS

RETHINKING SYSTEMIC RISK
Eugene A. Ludwig 349

LIST OF CONTRIBUTORS

Herbert Baer	Financial Economist World Bank
Philip F. Bartholomew	Director of Bank Research Office of the Comptroller of the Currency
James R. Barth	Lowder Eminent Scholar in Finance Auburn University
Claudio Borio	Monetary and Economic Department Bank for International Settlements Basle, Switzerland
Richard S. Carnell	Assistant Secretary for Financial Institutions U.S. Treasury Department
Robert A. Eisenbeis	Wachovia Professor of Banking University of North Carolina at Chapel Hill
Mark J. Flannery	Barnett Banks Professor of Finance University of Florida
Morris Goldstein	Senior Fellow Institute for International Economics
Edward J. Kane	James F. Cleary Professor in Finance Boston College

George G. Kaufman
John F. Smith Professor of Economics and Finance
Loyola University of Chicago

Daniela Klingebiel
Doctoral candidate
Albert-Ludwigs Universitae
Freiburg, Germany
and World Bank, Washington, DC

Eugene A. Ludwig
Comptroller of the Currency
Washington, DC

Robert J. Mackay
Director
Center for the Study of Futures & Options Markets
Virginia Technical Institute

Frederic S. Mishkin
Executive Vice-President and Director of Research
Federal Reserve Bank of New York

Daniel E. Nolle
Bank Research Division
Office of the Comptroller of the Currency

Susan M. Phillips
Member
Board of Governors of the Federal Reserve System

Anna J. Schwartz
Research Associate
National Bureau of Economic Research

Gary W. Whalen
Deputy Director of Bank Research
Office of the Comptroller of the Currency

DEDICATION

HERBERT L. BAER, JR.
1956-1995

This volume is dedicated to Herbert Baer, who passed away on February 27, 1995 after being struck by an automobile in the suburbs of Washington, DC while bicycling home from work. At the time of his death, Herb was an economist at the World Bank, which he joined in 1993 after a long career at the Federal Reserve Bank of Chicago, where he headed up the banking research group. Herb received his Ph.D. in economics from Northwestern University and his B.A. from Ohio University.

Herb was known to most of the authors of the papers presented at the OCC Conference on Systemic Risk in Washington in December 1994, which are published in this volume. Herb's paper, "Systemic Risk When Depositors Bear Losses: Five Case Studies," coauthored with Daniela Klingebiel, who was a summer intern at the World Bank, is included among the papers published. Like most of Herb's papers, this is an exciting analysis that sheds new light on a number of important issues and attempts both to derive commonalities among events and to identify the underlying economic incentives. As is true with most papers presented at conferences, they are not quite ready for publication, so was Herb's. Herb was in the process of revising the paper for publication in this volume. Unfortunately, he was unable to complete this task and some rough edges and incomplete thoughts and analyses may remain.

Herb will be remembered by those of us who knew and worked with him as a friend and valuable professional colleague. He not only made the world more enjoyable for us, but through his research he helped to further our knowledge of financial economics and banking. In the process, he did much to improve the structure and regulation of financial institutions in the United States. Herb was just starting to apply his analytical and institutional skills to the reform of banking systems in other countries when he died. He will be missed.

INTRODUCTION

The nature and likelihood of systemic risk or contagion in banking and financial markets is one of the most important unresolved and challenging issues in public policy today. Indeed, much of current banking regulation is based on the belief that banking is highly contagious and that the failure of one major bank or other important financial institution is likely to cause sufficient uncertainty and loss of confidence by depositors and other creditors in other similar institutions that the adverse effects will spread in domino fashion throughout the industry. The cumulative failures will be accompanied by increasing losses, depressing aggregate wealth in the economy. In addition, given the importance and pervasive use of money and credit throughout the economy, problems in the financial sector are likely to spillover to the real sector and depress aggregate income and employment. Thus, much of prudential banking regulation is directed at trying to prevent such catastrophes from occurring.

But, in the process of attempting to prevent contagion, the regulators need almost of necessity to impose restrictions that reduce competition and efficiency. That is, increased safety is often pursued at the cost of greater competition and efficiency. As a result, the question arises whether such a tradeoff is worth it. The answer in large measure is dependent on one's belief whether systemic risk is a serious problem in banking in terms of either its probability of occurring or the magnitude of any damage to third parties and economy. The exploration of this issue was the topic at a conference held in Washington, DC on December 2, 1994.

The papers presented and published in this volume examine the issue from a variety of perspectives. As a result, our knowledge of systemic risk has been significantly enhanced. The conference brought together experts, who have devoted many years of their professional career to examining systemic and other risks in financial institutions and markets both theoretically and empirically and both domestically and internationally and are among the most knowledgeable persons in the area. The paper givers and discussants represent academe, regulatory agencies, commercial banks, and international organizations. Thus, they also represent researchers, practitioners, and policymakers.

It is altogether fitting that this conference is sponsored by the Comptroller of the Currency. As the oldest bank regulatory agency, the Comptroller has given thought to this topic the longest. As Administrator of National Banks, the Comptroller has responsibility for protecting the safety and efficiency of the nation's largest banks. The conference was organized by Philip Bartholomew, Director of the Bank Research Division at the Comptrollers Officc, and Gcorgc G. Kaufman, John Smith Profcssor of Banking and Finance at Loyola University of Chicago. They were ably assisted by many other staff members at the Comptroller's Office.

PART I

OVERVIEW OF SYSTEMIC RISK

FUNDAMENTALS OF SYSTEMC RISK

Philip F. Bartholomew and Gary W. Whalen

INTRODUCTION

Among the major concerns of banking regulation and supervision are the containment of systemic risk and the treatment of systemic events. Considering the extensive economic and financial literature on banking and related monetary topics, and the various public policy discussions that have followed the notable financial calamities of the past two centuries, it is rather incredible that few authors have offered an actual definition of the term "systemic risk" and that there is little consensus on what comprises a "systemic event." Though closely related, systemic risk is not synonymous with terms such as banking panic, widespread bank runs, contagion, financial crisis, or financial collapse. In fact, there is some disagreement as to the meaning of these familiar terms. This paper offers a definition of systemic risk, discusses alternative theories of its causes, provides a brief summary of current views concerning its significance, and evaluates the policy options that are available to deal with it.

A key conclusion of the paper is that there is an additional regulatory tool, other than federal deposit insurance and the provision of liquidity by the central bank, that can structurally reduce systemic risk and address the moral

Research in Financial Services Private and Public Policy, Volume 7, pages 3-17.

ISBN: 1-55938-244-9

hazard problem. Given that the existence of central bank liquidity and deposit insurance has the potential of creating a moral hazard, a fixed and well-known early intervention and closure rule reduces uncertainty among players in financial markets and reduces the likelihood that the failure of even the largest financial institutions will increase systemic risk. Knowledge that bank supervisors will act when confronted with a bank failure to impose discipline on those responsible for the failure creates an enormous incentive for owners, managers, and directors to manage risk prudently.

I. DEFINING SYSTEMIC RISK

One of our primary goals in this paper is the relatively modest one of arriving at a broadly acceptable definition of systemic risk. We describe that as a modest goal because, in principle, the act of definition is inherently arbitrary. As long as everyone understands and uses the same definition, it should be possible to communicate clearly and unambiguously; no question of substance is involved in the definition of terms *per se*. On the other hand, some definitions are more useful than others in that they allow greater economy of communication. In the case of systemic risk, for example, it is desirable to define it to include all, or at least a large proportion, of the situations in which emergency actions by the financial regulatory agencies are called for, since this is the context in which systemic risk is usually discussed.

In practice, unfortunately, definition is not the neutral, value-free exercise that is it in principle. Because of the importance of linguistic convenience in dictating the bounds of the discussion, the act of definition may itself influence the outcome of the discussion. In the case of the term "systemic risk," there are actually two distinct concepts that are being defined: the particular set of events or occurrences that are considered to be "systemic" and the precise definition of what is meant by "risk." The problems associated with their definition will be discussed in order below.

Defining "Systemic"

Presumably, the term "systemic" refers to an event having effects on the functioning of the entire banking, financial, or economic system, rather than just one or a few institutions. However, it remains to be determined just how large a proportion of the system must be affected and how severe the effects must be to quality as "systemic." Take the following example, which is a fair description of the situation obtaining today. However fuzzily or inconsistently the concept of systemic risk may be defined, there is abroad agreement that is involves potential adverse effects on the financial system or the economy that go well beyond the failure of one or a few banks. There is a similarly broad, if less than universal, consensus that the moderation or elimination of systemic risk is the primary justification for safety and soundness regulation of depository institutions and the only justification for regulatory intervention to protect uninsured depositors from loss or to provide open bank assistance.

One who has concluded that such extraordinary interventions, broadly characterized as bailouts, should be kept to a minimum—a position that is widely, though not universally accepted—may argue strongly for a narrow definition of a systemic event with the idea of limiting intervention to the relatively few cases that meet that definition. Once such a narrow definition has been adopted, someone favoring more frequent regulatory intervention could still argue for intervening not only in cases of systemic risk but also in an additional set of cases characterized by other risks or conditions. However, that line of argument would encounter greater resistance because of the initial consensus that intervention is justified only to contain systemic risk. If, at the opposite extreme, a systemic event was defined broadly to include any occurrence that affected two or more banks, the same consensus would argue against limiting intervention to a narrower set of cases. Thus it is that definitions and choice of language combine to dictate the substance of public debate over many issues. In this paper, an effort is made to arrive at a definition of a systemic event that both accords as closely as possible with common usage and avoids predisposing one towards either a narrow or a broad view of the class of situations in which government should intervene.

It is important to emphasize that, for many students of systemic risk, the magnitude or pervasiveness of an event is not the key factor in determining whether it should be considered systemic. Relying in part on a medical definition of systemic that emphasizes the "successive" infection of additional parts of the body, George Kaufman (1994) would restrict the term systemic risk to situations involving the transmission of effects from one institution to another that is, to cases of contagion. Thus, Kaufman would exclude from his definition of a systemic event an economy-wide supply shock that dramatically raised interest rates and adversely affected all banks simultaneously. Others, such as Friedman and Schwartz (1963) would define a systemic event narrowly as a sudden contraction of the money stock or bank credit, although this is less a matter of doctrine than an empirical judgment that major financial disturbances are always, or virtually always, associated with such contractions. In contrast, we would be inclined to include in our definition of a systemic event, any event that, potentially, could bring about a severe mulfunctioning of the entire system, regardless of how it originated or was transmitted.

Defining "Risk"

The other key ingredient of a definition of systemic risk focuses on the stochastic, or probabilistic nature, of the systemic events. One of the commonest defects of the existing literature on systemic risk is that, largely because of the absence of an explicit definition, it confuses systemic risk with the events by which that risk manifests itself. It is common for authors to mention the term systemic risk and then to proceed, without a formal definition, to describe such events as a crop failure or sharp downturn in the economy and how these events precipitate runs on banks or other phenomena associated with a banking or financial crisis. Such discussions omit a major component of risk as that term is used in modern finance theory.

First of all, a "risky" event is one whose occurrence within any given period of time is not completely certain in advance, although it may be possible to assign it a numerical probability. Knight (1921) referred to events whose probability of occurrence cannot be determined, usually because they are unique or rare events whose past behavior cannot be observed, as "uncertain" to distinguish them from "risky" events whose probability could be calculated. But, assuming that we could characterize each possible systemic event not only by its probability of occurrence but also the dollar loss associated with its occurrence, we could then talk about the probability of a loss of a given size occurring. In other words, we would have the probability distribution of losses. Multiplying each possible dollar loss by its probability of occurrence and adding the resulting numbers yields the average or "expected" value of the losses occurring during the period. For some purposes, this might be an adequate measure of the "risk."

There is a big difference, however, between a situation in which the loss during a period is known in advance to be a billion dollars and one in which there is a fifty percent probability that the loss will be zero and a fifty percent probability that is will be two billion dollars, even though the average loss in both cases is one billion dollars. In the first case, there is a large loss but no risk, since the outcome is known with certainty in advance. In the second case, there is clearly risk but also a fifty percent probability of no loss at all. The average or expected loss during a period is analogous to the average depth of the water in a river; as many people have pointed out, it is possible to drown in a river whose average depth is only six inches. The difference, clearly, is how much the potential losses, or the depths of the river at various locations, vary around their averages. A common measure of this variation about the average is the variance, which is calculated by taking the difference between the loss associated with each event and the average loss, squaring it, multiplying by the event's probability of occurrence, and adding the resulting numbers for all possible occurrences, Thus, one could define systemic risk as the variance of the distribution of the losses to the deposit insurance funds associated with all possible systemic events over a given period of time.

For some purposes, even the variance is an inadequate measure of risk. For example, if the social costs that superivision and regulation are designed to prevent are associated with the phenomenon of bank failure, the definition and measure of risk should take into account the fact that the probability of failure is a function not only of the variance of bank income, but also of its average or mean level. In the case of individual banks, so-called Z scores have been calculated that combine the mean and variance of income in a single measure that is inversely related to the probability of failure. A measure—and/or definition—of systemic risk might then be the probability that the number of failures, or associated costs, within a given period would equal or exceed a given threshold. The level of this threshold might be determined by empirical analysis of historical episodes and would be the number, or range of numbers, at which serious malfunctioning of the system, and specifically a widespread collapse of confidence, has been observed to occur in the past.

Taking all of these arguments and considerations into account, we propose to define systemic risk as "the likelihood of a sudden, usually unexpected, collapse of confidence in a significant portion of the banking or financial system with potentially large real economic effects." Though stated as a probability, this definition—which has been used previously by Bentsen (1994), and Carnell (1994)—implicitly takes the size of the losses into account by assuming that they exceed some unspecified threshold necessary to bring about a "collapse of confidence." The definition remains somewhat ambiguous, in that the qualitative adjectives, "sudden," "significant," and "large" are all subject to a wide range of interpretations. Nonetheless, it would not seem wise to incorporate specific numbers into what is intended to be a general definition.

II. SOURCES AND SIGNIFICANCE OF SYSTEMIC RISK

The controversy surrounding the sources and significance of systemic risk is not surprising in view of the many competing theories explaining and describing the closely associated phenomenon of financial crises. In his comprehensive review of the literature on systemic risk, Davis (1992) offers eight different theories of financial crises. These include: excessive debt accumulation (Kindleberger, 1978; Minsky, 1967, 1977); bank panics (Friedman and Schwartz, 1963; Schwartz, 1988, 1992; Benston et al., 1986; Benston and Kaufman, 1988, forthcoming; Goodfriend and King, 1988; Todd, 1988); speculative bubbles attributable to rational expectations, the existence of uncertainly (Keynes, 1931); sudden credit rationing (Guttentag and Herring, 1988); asymmetric information (Calomiris and Gorton, 1991; Mishkin, 1991); vulnerabilities associated with dealer markets (Glosten and Milgrom, 1985); and, excessive competition due to deregulation and the erosion of entry barriers in financial markets (Davis, 1992). Given the variety of views on the theory of financial crisis, it is obvious why there is confusion about the definition, cause, and treatment of systemic risk. Moreover, some would argue that policymakers should maintain a degree of ambiguity regarding the circumstances under which they will intervene in order to limit the moral hazard problem associated with bailouts.

Assessing the Seriousness of Systemic Risk

A precise assessment of the significance of systemic risk at any given time is difficult because it inevitably hinges on a number of complex judgments on which knowledgeable individuals may differ. Judgments about the prevailing level of systemic risk depend on assessments of the probabilities or likelihoods of the following developments:

- The failure or near-failure of a large player or simultaneous failures of large numbers of players (bank or nonbank) in the financial system.
- That an initial failure or failures will impose large losses or will result in severe liquidity problems at a considerable number of other market participants.
- That contagious runs will spread severe liquidity pressures through the system.
- That bank illiquidity and/or insolvencies will significantly increase the costs or decrease the availability of credit to a meaningful number of borrowers or severely impair the functioning of payments systems or financial markets.
- That exogenous factors will amplify any initial disturbance
- That supervisors will respond in a timely, effective manner.

Factors Affecting the Seriousness of Systemic Risk

In general, these likelihoods, and therefore the severity of systemic risk, will depend upon a small number of critical factors. One is the type and incidence of any precipitating shock. At one extreme, a single large institution might be adversely affected by some external shock due to idiosyncratic risk. Alternatively, numerous institutions of varying sizes might simultaneously become impaired due to some shock generated externally or endogenously within the financial system.

A second key factor is the extent of connectivity—the number and strength of linkages among firms and markets—in the financial sector. Greater connectivity implies larger secondary effects from some initial financial market disturbance and so greater systemic risk. The classic example is losses suffered by correspondent banks in the event of the unanticipated failure of a larger respondent. Another is settlements failure in payments systems. Linkages between institutions (banks and nonbanks (which some claim are harder to evaluate)), markets (e.g., cash and derivative, securities and forex) and countries (higher legal and regulatory risks) are considerable and growing. This growth is market-driven and so cannot and should not be limited. But the more numerous and increasingly complicated firm and market linkages, together with increased speed of information transmission and processing, imply greater potential exposure and shorter reaction time (for both market participants and regulators) to developments in particular markets (Promisel et al., 1992). Market participants report increasing concern with counterparty credit risk because the volume and size of transactions are increasing, and because counterparty credit quality is becoming increasingly difficult to assess due to the increase in linkages and the growing use of derivative and other off balance sheet instruments. As connectivity increases, risk exposures of counterparties become more complicated and less transparent.

A third critical factor influencing systemic risk is the extent to which the portfolios of financial (and to some, extent nonfinancial) institutions are concentrated. Greater concentration implies a higher risk of failure should an unfavorable shock occur. Asset concentrations are hard to assess for several reasons. Some concentrations may reflect desirable market outcomes. For example, some concerns have been raised about the extent to which a relatively small number of highly rated institutions that play a leading role in multiple markets have increased their concentrations in the derivatives business. This may be the result of inherent advantages possessed by these large institutions, but it does expose them heavily to any kind of disturbance in the derivatives markets. More traditional loan-type concentrations are inherently difficult for bankers, supervisors, and market outsiders to measure and can change relatively quickly. Partly as a result, there may be insufficient disincentives (e.g., a hard-wired capital charge or supervisory penalty) to asset concentration. A complicating factor is the tendency of financial institutions to exhibit "herd mentality." Financial institutions and other financial market participants, rationally pursuing what appear to be attractive investment opportunities, simultaneously and jointly channel credit to particular sectors and/or regions. This can result in an over-concentration in the aggregate, even though individual institutions do not exhibit imprudent portfolio imbalances. If the over-concentration fuels a speculative bubble that subsequently collapses, all creditors to this sector suffer.

A fourth critical factor is actual or perceived financial institution homogeneity—the extent to which the asset and liability porfolios of institutions are similar. Greater homogeneity, in conjunction with portfolio concentrations stemming from herd mentality and/or high leverage, implies greater industry susceptibility to shocks. It also increases the likelihood of contagion because it makes it increasingly difficult for depositors to differentiate banks accurately according to risk.

The fifth and possibly the most important factor affecting the seriousness of systemic risk at any given time is the quantity, quality, and distribution of information available to market participants and regulators. Indeed, the probabilities of the other crucial determinants of the seriousness of systemic risk depend heavily on information quality and asymmetries. When significant information asymmetries exist and/or the quality of information is low, there is a greater danger of inadvertent risk exposures or concentrations, contagion, credit crunches, and inadequate policy responses, and systemic risk is correspondingly greater. Unexpected bank failures are likely to be more frequent and numerous and will tend to inflict larger losses on a larger number of bank and nonbank creditors, perhaps precipitating additional failures. Creditors, unable to assess accurately the condition of apparently similar institutions, might elect to "run" on both truly troubled and truly healthy depositories (Diamond and Dybvig, 1983). This is rational behavior for insufficiently informed creditors whose deposits are not federally guaranteed or collateralized and creates a liquidity crisis. Unless affected institutions can borrow to cover the claims of "running" creditors, otherwise solvent firms may suffer losses from selling illiquid assets at "fire-sale" prices. Although recent research suggests that contagion has been less pervasive than has often been assumed (Kaufman, 1994), there is considerable evidence that it was present during the banking panics of the free banking era (Gilbert, 1988; Hasan and Dwyer, 1988).

The availability and quality of information also influences the speed or effectiveness of any supervisory response to systemic events. The increased speed of information flow, operating through a greatly expanded number of linkages, compresses the amount of time supervisors have to analyze and respond to any given shock (Promisel et al., 1992). Presumably, supervisors have a compensating advantage in the form of information on the risk profiles of affected institutions (obtained through the examination process) that is as good or better than that possessed by the market. However, it is possible (albeit unlikely) that supervisors might be confronted with a situation where some significant portion of the banking industry becomes troubled quickly.

These arguments suggest that the collapse of a bank perceived by the market to be well capitalized, well managed, and not unduly risky could reduce the public's confidence in other banks and lead to cascading bank runs. On the other hand, closure of a bank widely known to be in financial trouble should have relatively little impact on the public's general confidence in banks. Such as closure should not lead to systemic problems because creditors of the troubled bank, recognizing its condition, appropriately adjust their risk exposure prior to the failure. Thus, the state of information is a major, if not the key element in understanding how to deal with systemic problems and how to reduce the degree of systemic risk in the financial system.

III. HOW BEST TO DEAL WITH SYSTEMIC PROBLEMS

There are a number of different strategies to deal with systemic risk. One is to attempt to decrease the likelihood of potential precipitating shocks. Another is to reduce the likelihood that some initial disturbance is transmitted widely and becomes fatal to significant numbers of financial institutions, markets, or the system as a whole.

Disclosure

Systemic risk can be triggered by a wide variety of events originating either inside or outside the banking system. In general, these events are the result of some sort of precipitating economic shock (e.g., unexpectedly volatile commodity or asset price movements or changes in economic activity). In a significant number of cases, the shock appears to stem from a material policy surprise that results in a rapid, persistent change in actual or expected interest or foreign exchange rates, inflation, and real economic growth or some combination of the above. Stable policies and adequate disclosure of current and future policy changes might help reduce systemic risk.

Supervision and Regulation

Another way to limit and manage systemic risk is to attempt to decrease the likelihood that individual financial institutions fail. Bank supervision and regulation play a critical role in limiting risk-taking by individual institutions. Given information asymmetries, the examination process may provide supervisors with a comparative advantage in monitoring and preventing excessive credit concentrations, which may be the best defense against risks stemming from shocks related to herd mentality and speculative bubbles. Another important supervisory role is to establish capital and solvency requirements and verify adherence to these rules through the examination process. Supervisors can also facilitate market access to information on risk and solvency and so enlist the aid of market discipline.

Lender of Last Resort

The two widely recognized means for controlling systemic risk in the current system are designed to reduce the likelihood of damaging runs. Perhaps the most powerful tool available to central banks for limiting the losses associated with systemic events is their ability to serve as a lender of last resort. The existence of a credible lender of last resort, as the Federal Reserve has proved to be in recent years, structurally reduces systemic risk. The appropriate central bank response to systemic crises is to supply liquidity through open market operations, discount window lending, or some combination of the two (Garcia, 1988). These tools prevent runs from precipitating a sharp contraction of bank loans and deposits and associated increases in interest rates as well as the failure of solvent institutions (Schwartz, 1988).

Some experts argue that because the Federal Reserve has neither the incentive nor the ability to limit discount window lending to illiquid but solvent banks, its lending policies may be either too restrictive—resulting in the failure of otherwise solvent institutions and exacerbating real economic declines—or too lenient—keeping insolvent institutions afloat and creating future moral hazard problems. These critics argue that the Federal Reserve could—and should—rely primarily on open market operations to deal with systemic events (Shwartz, 1992; Todd, 1988; Calomiris, 1991; Goodfriend and King, 1988). In the case of open market operations, the Federal Reserve relies on the market to allocate the liquidity supplied. Theory and evidence indicate that the market is effective in channelling funds to illiquid but solvent entities. Essential feedback is available in the form of movements in market rates. The effectiveness of this approach has been demonstrated in a number of recent cases (e.g., the 1987 stock market break and the Drexel bankruptcy).

Deposit Insurance

Government guarantee of some or all bank liabilities, such as is provided by a deposit insurance scheme, is another device used by governments to reduce systemic risk. Deposit insurance structurally reduces the threat of systemic risk by limiting the amount of liabilities exposed to loss at depositories, reducing the incentives of depositors to run. But, both of these tools come with a cost. Deposit insurance creates a moral hazard, reducing the incentive to manage risk prudently.

Thus, both of the tools most commonly used by governments to control systemic risk produce undesirable side effects: in exchange for economic stability, individual banks or other financial institutions benefit from the safety net by receiving better credit terms from the market, precedents are set that may inappropriately constrain future policy, and the sharing of losses with taxpayers induces some institutions to assume more risk. This moral hazard problem is inseparable from the existence of the safety net and strengthens the need for supervision and regulation. Unfortunately, the desire to avoid systemic risk has become so ingrained that government has developed a strong tendency to overreact, by placing excessive reliance on policies that preclude the closing of large banks or other significant financial institutions (Hetzel, 1991; Baer, 1994).

Prompt Corrective Action

There is an often overlooked, but very important supervisory mechanism that can limit the damage associated with bank failures, thereby mitigating systemic risk, that does not entail increased moral hazard. This is a well-known, consistently enforced set of early intervention and closure rules (Benston and Kaufman, 1988). Clear articulation of these rules decreases uncertainly; reduces the chances of a sudden, large, failure with heavy losses to unsecured creditors; and reduces the likelihood that recognition of the failure of even the largest of financial institutions will cause systemic problems. Moreover, assuming the closure rule does not incorporate a too-big-to-fail policy, it should mitigate the moral hazard incentives associated with the existence of the safety net. Knowledge that bank supervisors, when confronted with a bank failure, will act promptly to impose discipline on those responsible for the failure creates an enormous incentive for owners, managers, and directors to manage risk prudently (Carnell, 1994). In addition, regulators now have the bridge bank and final settlement payment options to deal with large bank failures. These devices allow regulators to impose manageable losses on uninsured depositors and unsecured creditors in large bank failures without restricting access to their funds.

IV. CONCLUSION

This paper has developed a definition of systemic risk that takes account of both the magnitude and pervasiveness of losses necessary to qualify an event as systemic and its probability of occurrence. Given this definition and the ensuing discussion, several questions come to mind: How serious has systemic risk been in the past? It is likely to be a greater or lesser problem in the future? What, if anything needs to be done? An analysis of financial market events indicates that, while financial market disturbances have been quite common in the post-Depression era, very few have risen to a systemic level (Carron, 1982). For example, only two events in recent memory, the Continental Bank failure and the 1987 Stock Market Crash, appear to have approached systemic proportions. The other notable financial institution failures, as well as many of the situations involving troubled nonbanking entities that occurred during this period—for example, Bank of New England, First Republic, First Pennsylvania, Franklin National, the ODGF Thrift failures, and Drexel-lacked one or more of the characteristics of a systemic event. Most of them were not sudden or unexpected and so investors and markets generally had ample time to react. Generally, it was readily apparent that the failures were the result of institution- and/or region-specific problems and so there was a low probability that the failures would have caused a collapse of confidence at other solvent institutions. In these and other cases involving nonbanks—for example, the Hunt silver incident and the Penn Central bankruptcy—the potential real economic impact was small. Past experience suggests that the standard remedies for the typical sort of systemic risks—the lender of last resort and deposit insurance—work well.

What is less clear, however, is the appropriate policy for dealing with the systemic risk associated with significant or substantial bank or financial institution insolvencies stemming from exposure to a common external or endogenously generated shock. Fortunately, such as eventuality is probably unlikely. Proactive supervision, including attention to concentrations, is perhaps the best available remedy. Forbearance or inflation are risky and potentially costly alternative solutions to such situations. Bank regulators or policymakers face the temptation to rely on these sorts of solutions since they provide visible short run benefits.

Going forward, what is the likelihood of the most probable precipitating event—the unanticipated failure of a large bank with large losses for numerous creditors? For the immediate future, it appears to be low. The largest institutions appear to be in relatively good shape. In particular, both their asset quality and capital levels are very good. Regulators and banks involved in payments systems have worked to shape agreements assuring the legality of netting, reducing settlement lags and providing for loss sharing (Summers, 1991). Such agreements mitigate systemic risk, because they ensure that the parties involved in such systems understand their risk exposure in the event of a default by one participant, sharpen their incentives to control risks, and institutionalize methods for maintaining the operation of the system in times of stress. For example, the CHIPS system now has a procedure in place to facilitate settlement finality. Bridge bank authority and improved techniques for resolving failed depository institutions allow supervisors to resolve bank failures, particularly large failures, in ways that permit losses to be imposed on uninsured parties without a significant reduction in the liquidity of their funds and so should reduce resolution costs to the FDIC.

The Federal Deposit Insurance Corporation Improvement Act (FDICIA) of 1991 contained a number of provisions that should reduce systemic risk. For example, the section of FDICIA on prompt corrective action tied the intensity of supervision to an institution's capital position and established an explicit closure rule. Some provisions of this section facilitate supervisory actions to limit risk-taking and encourage remedial actions by bank management. Other provisions generally require regulators to close institutions when their capital ratio falls below 2 percent. Although supervisors can make exceptions to this rule, they must justify and document their reasons. Ideally, the provisions of this section will reduce the likelihood and costs of failure. Section 308 of FDICIA required supervisors to impose restrictions on the extent of a bank's exposure to the failures of other banks through correspondent or other types of relationships. This restriction is designed to limit the risk exposure and losses of smaller banks in the event of a large bank failure. This is one way to prevent a failure from having extensive systemic effects. Section 305 of FDICIA required federal bank and thrift regulators to develop some mechanism to adjust risk-based capital requirements for interest rate, credit concentration, and non-traditional activities risks. These risks were not explicitly included in the Basle Accord risk-based requirements. Done correctly, these adjustments should reduce both the probability of failure and the cost of those that do occur.

Assuming that a large unanticipated failure does occur, what is the likelihood of contagion? The likelihood of contagion does not appear to be high, particularly in a world of deposit insurance. It is somewhat difficult for depositors to determine whether their bank is solvent. However, considerable financial information is disclosed by banks and the market does appear to be relatively efficient in processing information about bank risk, particularly if it has the incentives to do so. Thus, contagious runs appear unlikely. In the event that they do occur, the evidence suggests that solvent banks should be able to withstand temporary liquidity pressures due to contagion as long as the Federal Reserve supplies sufficient reserves to the system, either through the discount window or open market operations.

All things considered, systemic risk appears to be at a relatively low level as of late 1994. Even if a systemic event should occur, it appears that the requisite tools and knowledge for limiting its effects are in place and ready for use. Nonetheless, financial markets and the banking system are continuously evolving in unpredictable ways and risk exposures have a way of building up without being detected by traditional supervisory approaches. That is why our definition of systemic risk incorporates the language "sudden, usually unexpected." And that is why regulators and students of banking need to devote continued attention to the analysis and control of systemic risk, however negligible it currently appears to be.

ACKNOWLEDGMENT

The views expressed are the authors' and not necessarily those of the Comptroller of the Currency or the Department of the Treasury. The authors thank especially Ed Ettin and Myron Kwast, who, in several intensive discussions on the subject of systemic risk, helped define the concept and construct the framework for analyzing it. The authors also thank Konrad S. Alt, George Benston, Richard S. Carnell, Frank Edwards, James Kamihachi, George Kaufman, Thomas J. Lutton, Hyman Minsky, Larry Mote, and David VanHoose for significant insights on the subject. An earlier draft of this paper was presented at the annual meetings of the Southern Economic Association in Orlando, Florida on November 21, 1994.

REFERENCES

Baer, Herbert and Daniela Klingebiel, "Does Systemic Risk Make Bank Bailouts Necessary? Five Case Studies," Unpublished Manuscript, Stember 22, 1994.

Bensten, Lloyd, "Statement Before the Committee on Banking, Housing, and Urban Affairs," U.S. Senate, March 1, 1994.

Benston, George J. and George G. Kaufman, *Risk and Solvency Regulation of Depository Institutions: Past Policies and Current Options.* Monograph Series in Finance and Economics, Monograph 1988-1, Salomon Brothers Center for the Study of Financial Institutions, New York University, 1988.

________. "Is the Banking and Payments System Fragile?" *Journal of Financial Services Research* (forthcoming).

Calomiris, Charles and W. Gary Gorton. "The Origins of Bank Panics." In *Financial Markets and Financial Crisis.* Edited by Glenn Hubbard. Chicago: University of Chicago Press. 1991.

Carnell, Richard S., "Systemic Risk." Paper presented at the *Conference on the Financial System in the Decade Ahead: What Should Banks Do?,* The Jerome Levy Economics Institute of Bard College, April 16, 1994.

Carron, Andrew S. "Financial Crises: Recent Experience in U.S. and International Markets." *Brookings Papers on Economic Activity*, No. 2, 1982.

Davis, E. P. *Debt, Financial Fragility, and Systemic Risk.* New York: Oxford University Press, 1992.

Diamond, Douglas W. and Philip H. Dybvig. "Bank Runs, Deposit Insurance, and Liquidity." *Journal of Political Economy*, 91(3) 1983.

Friedman, Milton and Anna J. Schwartz. *A Monetary History of the United States: 1867-1960.* Princeton: Princeton University Press, 1963.

Garcia, Gillian. "Lessons from the Crash of '87: Systemic Issues." *Bank Structure and Competition.* Federal Reserve Bank of Chicago, 1988.

Gilbert, Alton B. "A Re-examination of the History of Bank Failures, Contagion, and Banking Panics." *Bank Structure and Competition.* Federal Reserve Bank of Chicago, 1988.

Glosten, L. R. and P. R. Milgrom. "Bid, Ask and Transactions Prices in a Specialist Market with Heterogenously Informed Traders." *Journal of Financial Economics*, 14, 1985.

Goodfriend, Marvin and Robert G. King. "Financial Deregulation, Monetary Policy, and Central Banking." Working Paper 88-1, Federal Reserve Bank of Richmond, 1988.

Gorton, Gary. "Public Policy and the Evolution of Banking Markets." *Bank Structure and Competition.* Federal Reserve Bank of Chicago, 1989.

Guttentag, Jack and Richard Herring. "Prudential Supervision to Manage Systemic Vulnerability." *Bank Structure and Competition.* Federal Reserve Bank of Chicago, 1988.

Hasan, Iftekhar and Gerald P. Dwyer, Jr. "Contagion Effects and Banks Closed in the Free Banking Period." *Bank Structure and Competition.* Federal Reserve Bank of Chicago, 1988.

Hetzel, Robert L. "Too Big to Fail: Origins, Consequences, and Outlook." *Economic Review.* Federal Reserve Bank of Richmond, November/December 1991.

Kaufman, George G. "Bank Contagion: Theory and Evidence." *Journal of Financial Services Research*, April 1994.

Keynes, John Maynard. "The Consequences to the Banks of the Collapse in Money Values." In *Essays in Persuasion, Collected Writings of J. M. Keynes*, Volume 11. London: Macmillan, 1931.

Kindleberger, Charles P. *Manias, Panics and Crashes.* New York: Basic Books, 1978.

Knight, Frank H. *Risk, Uncertainty, and Profit.* Boston: Houghton Mifflin Co., 1921.

Minsky, Hyman P. "A Theory of Systemic Fragility." In *Financial Crises: Institutions and Markets in a Fragile Environment.* Edited by Edward I. Altman and Arnold W. Sametz. New York: John Wiley, 1977.

________. "Financial Stability Revised: The Economics of Disater." In *Reappraisal of the Federal Reserve Discount Mechanism.* Vol. 3. Washington, D.C.: Board of Governors of the Federal Reserve System, 1967, pp. 95-136.

Mishkin, Frederic S. "Asymmetric Information and Financial Crises: A Historical Perspective. In *Financial Markets and Financial Crisis*. Edited by Glenn Hubbard. Chicago: University of Chicago Press, 1991.

Promisel, Larry J. et al. *Recent Developments in International Interbank Relations*. Basle: Bank for International Settlements, 1992.

Schwartz, Anna J. "Financial Stability and the Federal Safety Net." In *Restructuring Banking & Financial Services in America*. Edited by William S. Haraf and Rose Marie Kushmeider. Washington, D.C.: American Enterprise Institute for Public Policy Research, 1988.

———. "The Misuse of the Fed's Discount Window." *Review*. Federal Reserve Bank of St. Louis, September/October 1992.

Summers, Bruce J. "Clearing and Payment Systems: The Role of the Central Bank." *Federal Reserve Bulletin*, February 1991.

Todd, Walker F. "Lessons of the Past and Prospects for the Future in Lender of Last Resort Theory." *Bank Structure and Competition*. Federal Reserve Bank of Chicago, 1988.

SYSTEMIC RISK AND THE MACROECONOMY

Anna J. Schwartz

INTRODUCTION

In recent years a spate of studies dealing with systemic risk has appeared. Conferences on the subject such as the one now in progress here have been popular. The National Bureau of Economic Research sponsored one in October 1989 (Feldstein, 1991), another one in March 1990 (Hubbard, 1991), and devoted one session to the subject in a conference on the 1980s (Feldstein, 1994). Other organizations like the Federal Reserve Bank of Kansas City and the Brookings Institution have also been active in promoting investigations of systemic risk.

What has been learned about systemic risk in the existing studies? Two impressions of their content predominate. One is that there is no consistency in the use of terms by different writers. The other impression is that each writer's explanation of the phenomenon is partial and overlaps with another writer's explanation. They are like blind men trying to describe an elephant, when one feels the tail, another the tusk, another the trunk. The aggregate animal somehow eludes them.

Research in Financial Services Private and Public Policy, Volume 7, pages 19-30.

ISBN: 1-55938-244-9

With respect to the terms that a reader encounters in the literature, financial fragility, financial crisis, and financial instability are as common as systemic risk, but the terms have different meanings for different writers. Financial fragility, for example, may mean the fragility of the financial services industry or the fragility of nonfinancial entities like corporations and households. Financial crisis may be used interchangeably with economic crisis or systemic risk or may be limited in scope to a particular sector of the economy. Financial instability may be an intermediate point on the way to financial crisis or may be synonymous with financial crisis.

The recent literature on systemic risk, in my view, is alarmist. It regards losses that may be incurred by individual financial institutions or an industry or participants in derivatives markets as potentially capable of engulfing the economy. Public policy, according to the literature, must be prepared to deal with this threat, yet the threat may be a fabrication of the overheated imaginations of academics and regulators.

In my view concern for potential systemic risk in the domestic economy has been overblown by these members of the clerisy. It rests on the assumption that, upon the appearance of weakness anywhere in the economy, however limited in its initial manifestation, market participants will behave as if they cannot distinguish an unsound from a sound condition everywhere else.

Let me cite an example that is generally regarded as vindication for Federal Reserve intervention (Brimmer, 1989; Calomiris, 1993). In June 1970, when Penn Central went bankrupt, it defaulted on $82 million of commercial paper it had outstanding. The Federal Reserve assumed that lenders would not discriminate between a troubled issuer and other perfectly sound issuers of commercial paper, so that the latter would be unable to roll over their issues, generating a financial crisis. To avert the presumed threat of this financial crisis, the Fed announced the availability of discount window assistance to banks meeting the needs of such businesses.

However, commercial paper issuers that faced difficulties did so not because of the condition of the market as such but because of conditions peculiar to themselves. It was not a sign of a liquidity crisis that the market charged more for commercial paper of Chrysler Financial and Commercial Credit Corporation than for paper of sound issuers. Nevertheless, the Penn Central episode fostered the view that bankruptcy proceedings by a large firm created a financial crisis and justified assistance to insolvent nonbanks and banks.

To cite another example of market discrimination between intermediaries that had problems and those that were not so afflicted: the United States stock market price-earnings ratios of money-center banks with the largest portfolios of nonperforming LDC loans fell more after 1982 than did price-earnings ratios of other banks.

The terms systemic risk could be dispensed with, with no loss to the analysis of putative disruptions of the payments and settlement system, the essence of a financial crisis. The term adds nothing to our understanding of a financial crisis. Economic history has familiarized us with two situations that betoken the possibility of a financial crisis. One is occasioned by contagious runs on banks when depositors flee from deposits to currency. Neither runs nor contagion have been observed since World War II. The other situation is occasioned by stock market crashes when borrowers fear that they will be unable to obtain loans. Stock market crashes still occur, but monetary authorities are well schooled in the steps they can take to calm market fears. There have been no genuine financial crises in recent decades, only pseudo-financial crises. I shall say more about this at a later point.

This said about my view of overblown concern for systemic risk in the domestic economy, it is still necessary to ask whether there is potential for systemic risk imported from abroad, as some have averred (Corrigan, 1992). Would failure of banks in one country having connections with banks and customers in other countries be contagious and lead to a collapse of the banking systems of all the countries involved? A similar concern has been expressed with respect to the transmission of a stock market crash and payments disruption in one country to other countries.

In the rest of the paper, I first examine the approach of those who see systemic risk as an ever-present contingency that must be guarded against. I shall then present my assessment of this approach. In the next section In state my own views on the reasons apprehensions of systemic risk in the domestic economy misunderstand the past and misinterpret the present. I also examine the likelihood of systemic risk as an international phenomenon. A brief conclusion follows.

I. STUDIES INVOKING SYSTEMIC RISK

Nine different aspects of behavior of nonfinancial and financial markets are highlighted in studies invoking systemic risk.

1. The title of one monograph by Davis (1992)—the author also lists approaches to systemic risk by others—suggests the links the writer has in mind: Debt, financial fragility, systemic risk. Emphasis on the role of debt as responsible for the problem of systemic risk is fairly widespread (B. Friedman, 1991; H. Kaufman, 1986). The process may begin with debt accumulation by corporations and households. As a result nonfinancial firms become financially fragile. Individual banks may get into difficulties due to financial fragility in the nonfinancial sector but, in one version, based on experience since the 1970s, contagious runs and systemic risk do not necessarily ensue. In another version, based on the Great Depression experience, there is a direct link from overindebtedness and financial fragility in the nonfinancial sector to financial

crisis and, in turn, as a feedback to nonfinancial activity. Financial crisis in this context is defined as "a major collapse of the financial system, entailing inability to provide payments services or to allocate capital; realization of systemic risk" (Davis, 1992, p. 281).

2. Systemic risk has also been linked to scenarios other than overindebtedness. One scenario is banking panics caused by attempts to convert deposits into currency that force bank closures and contraction of the money stock, in the absence of the preventive provision of adequate amounts of high-powered money by the central bank (Friedman and Schwartz, 1963). The consequence is deflation and contraction of economic activity that are deemed by some writers—not by me—to exemplify systemic risk. Proponents of financial fragility who emphasize rising vulnerability of debtors may incorporate in their approach runs on banks and financial markets as potential for contagion and systemic risk.

3. Another scenario links systemic risk to financial market behavior along rational expectations lines, with applications to events susceptible to probability analysis (Flood and Garber, 1982; Blanchard and Watson, 1982). Bubbles can arise in this approach when the expected rate of price change influences the current market price. The bursting of the bubble can produce systemic risk. Similarly, runs can be explained along rational expectations lines as terminating a price-fixing scheme, in the sense that rational speculators will draw down bank reserves backing the price-fixed deposit scheme if they doubt the adequacy of the backing, or foreign exchange reserves backing a fixed exchange rate.

4. A scenario alternative to the rational expectations approach links systemic risk to economic uncertainty. Under conditions where the future cannot be anticipated or hedged against, an increased level of uncertainty may trigger shifts in confidence and runs (Meltzer, 1982).

5. Financial crises are said to result in still another scenario from an increase in credit rationing following a period of relaxation of credit standards (Guttentag and Herring, 1984). Lenders' perceptions of credit risk may be impaired owing to competition among lenders, or because of psychological mechanisms and institutional factors. Lenders may underestimate risk after a period free of shocks and then following a shock may overestimate risk. If shocks are frequent, they will be priced into the risk premium on loans. Accordingly, there is either price rationing following frequent shocks or quantity rationing of credit where borrowers have incentives to take risks. Absent shocks, borrowers' capital positions may decline and creditors become more vulnerable to shocks. Confidence, however, does not decline until a shock occurs, causing a sharp increase in credit rationing. A financial crisis on this approach is a condition in which borrowers formerly able to borrow freely are unable to borrow at any rate, while others who were prime borrowers face heavy default premiums.

6. Asymmetric information is also cited as a mechanism that can cause systemic risk (Mishkin, 1991). Lenders are said to be less informed than borrowers about the merit of projects to be financed. A rise in interest rates may increase adverse selection leading to a decline in lending. Heightened uncertainty that makes screening of borrowers more difficult can worsen adverse selection problems. A widening of credit-quality spreads is an indicator of such problems. Lower collateral values will also increase adverse selection for lenders. Agency costs rise when borrowers have low net worth, attributable to a stock market crash or disinflation, since they have less to lose by default. Contagious runs on solvent banks are said to be another example of asymmetric information that effects credit availability.

7. An approach that is complementary to the asymmetric information mechanism applies it to a widening of spreads in securities markets, reducing the willingness of dealers to make markets. The liquidity of claims declines and price rationing of credit results (Glosten and Milgrom, 1985).

8. An application of industrial organization to financial markets relates it to financial instability (Davis, 1992). Changes in conditions for entry to financial markets that heighten competition may result in reduced prudential standards of credit extension leading to instability.

9. A final invocation of systemic risk relates it to international factors (Krugman, 1991). Currency crises are said to occur when investors under inflationary conditions lose confidence in the currency of a country and seek to rid their portfolios of assets denominated in that currency and other assets subject to exchange controls. The macroeconomic effects are recessionary. Contagion crises are said to occur when a financial crash in one country leads to crashes in other countries and worldwide deflation.

II. ASSESSMENT OF SYSTEMIC RISK STUDIES

Each of the mechanisms that have been identified in studies of systemic risk may play a role in creating problems in a particular financial service firm or industry. But why do the problems involve systemic risk? That question is not addressed in the literature.

In addition, it is not self-evident that all the specific mechanisms intensify vulnerability. Accumulation of debt by households or corporations, for example, may be matched by asset accumulation. True, overindebtedness that cash flow cannot sustain may lead to bankruptcy of such entities and pose difficulties for their creditors. Bankruptcy is a fact of economic life. It occurs to some market participants every day. Again, a link with systemic risk from these circumstances needs to be demonstrated but the studies fail to provide it.

The spin that systemic risk proponents place on bankruptcies is that inherent instability resides in market participants. For them, animal spirits govern entrepreneurial decisions, sometimes exuberant, sometimes restrained. The conditions in which market participants make decisions are not invoked. The critical condition in my view is the price level environment in which they operate. In an inflationary environment, they may be exuberant. In a deflationary environment, they may be restrained. Only monetary authorities can deliver price level stability, but the systemic risk literature ignores this conditioning influence on the behavior of market participants.

The asymmetric information approach overlooks the possibility that both borrowers and lenders evaluate the prospects of projects by extrapolating the prevailing price level or inflation rate. A subsequent decision by monetary authorities to pursue contractionary policies will undermine the price level assumptions of both borrowers and lenders. That is why borrowers default and lenders become distressed.

Bursting of bubbles, heightened uncertainty, credit rationing, asymmetric information, breakdown of markets, excessive competition among lenders can explain financial distress for selected sectors of firms. They do not explain why local strains cause the economy to implode. The writers who develop the importance of each of these explanations acknowledge that individually they do not suffice to account for systemic risk. A synthesis, it is said, is required. But why should all the different pathologies of financial markets come together at one time and place?

One way of dealing with this question is to see whether bank failure contagion might be more serious than in other industries. A recent study (G. Kaufman, 1994) asks whether contagion occurs more rapidly and spreads more broadly within the banking industry, whether it results in a larger number of failures and larger losses to creditors and depositors, and whether it spreads beyond the banking industry. On examining theory and evidence, the author concludes that bank contagion does not "bring down solvent banks, the financial system, and even the entire macroeconomy in domino fashion" (G. Kaufman, 1994, p. 143). Losses to depositor-creditors at failed banks are smaller on average than in nonbank industries. Banks may be "special" relative to other firms with respect to failure, but only slightly so. The long and short of it is that bank failures are neither more contagious nor more injurious than the failures of nonbank firms.

What is special about banks is the effects of deposit insurance on them, the author of the study demonstrates. It was the failure of the Federal Reserve to act as a credible lender of last resort in 1930-1933 that led to deposit insurance. For a long time after the 1930s, deposit insurance was hailed as the outstanding reform of the New Deal. It seemed to have succeeded in preventing banking panics by removing the reason for runs—loss of confidence in the ability to convert deposits into currency. However, in recent decades it has become clear that deposit insurance far from enhancing safety reduces market discipline with deleterious results for the financial services industry.

It is for this reason that the author of the study of bank contagion concludes that banking is unique not "primarily because of potential for contagion but because of federal deposit insurance." By increasing capital requirements for banks and enforcing prompt regulatory corrective intervention when banks get into difficulties, he argues, it is possible to mimic market discipline. No contagion need occur.

It is common in the literature to describe each of the so-called crises that have occurred since 1970: failure of particular nonfinancial and financial firms (Penn Central, Herstatt, Continental Illinois); the Latin American debt defaults; the thrift industry debacle. Each of these had unique features. Contagion between domestic financial markets was not observed.

So a further reason for skepticism about the significance of domestic systemic risk is that there is no episode since World War II that one can cite as an example. Those who tout systemic risk will claim that in each case it was averted by timely actions of public authorities. They endorse the authorities' self defense that, even if no financial crisis would have developed, had no intervention occurred, intervention still was justified because of what might have been. In my view the intervention in each episode since 1970 was a form of bailout that was economically inefficient or inflationary in effect.

The attention to systemic risk that has captured the minds of many economists ultimately reflects the continuing fascination for them of the Great Depression. If systemic risk happened then, what rouses their concern is the likelihood of a recurrence. So it is necessary to discuss why systemic risk occurred in the Great Depression but not since.

In addition, crisis problems arising from international interdependence, it might be argued, are different in kind and degree from strictly domestic problems. Systemic risk might be a true phenomenon in this case when it is not in the domestic case.

I shall turn to these issues in the next section in which I detail my views on what is a genuine case of financial crisis, the term I prefer rather than systemic risk, and when it is not.

III. WHY FEARS OF SYSTEMIC RISK MISAPPREHEND FINANCIAL EVENTS

Let me begin by defining terms as I shall use them (Schwartz, 1986).

Financial crisis. It is fueled by fears that means of payment at any price will be unobtainable. A stock market crash may trigger such fears. (Note that it is not the loss of wealth that makes a stock market crash significant as a possible financial crisis. Its significance resides in its effect on the demand for loans.) A financial crisis is precipitated by desperate actions of the public in a flight to currency that suddently squeeze the reserves of the banking system. In a futile attempt to restore reserves, the banks may call loans, refuse to roll over existing loans, or resort to selling assets.

Such a sequence of events is to be distinguished from what happens during a disinflation or deflation. A deflation or disinflation is a consequence of restricted growth of bank reserves, but it is not precipitated by the public's behavior. Only the monetary authorities determine the growth of bank reserves. The essence of a financial crisis is that it is short-lived, ending with a slackening of the public's demand for additional currency, or additional loans, as authorities demonstrate their readiness to satisfy the demand. A disinflation or deflation may be long drawn out. Nominal wealth may decline, real debts may rise, but these are not financial crises.

The failure of a bank that leads depositors and creditors to shift their funds to what they perceive to be a sound institution is not a financial crisis.

Financial distress. The condition of an individual, a nonfinancial firm, an individual bank, or an industry that has assets with realizable value in money that is less than the amount of its indebtedness.

Financial fragility. The ability of the financial system to withstand economic shocks is weak.

Pseudo-financial crises. Phenomena such as a decline in asset prices of equity stocks, real estate, commodities, art works; depreciation of the exchange value of a national currency; financial distress of a large non-financial firm, a large municipality, a financial industry, or sovereign debtors are pseudo-financial crises. The loss of wealth that is characteristic of investments with negative returns does not undermine the economy at large, no more than does the devastation of a hurricane or flood, because no interruption of payments is involved.

The last episode of systemic risk in the United States occurred from 1930 to 1933. The Federal Reserve during those years did not recognize a sequence of flights to currency and the need for it to provide liquidity to the fractional reserve banking system that was confronted with surges of repeated runs. Contagion then occurred in an environment in which the Federal Reserve permitted the money supply to decline drastically, rendering banks insolvent not because of their own actions but because of the collapsing economy. The lesson of the Great Depression is that contagion need not arise if open market purchases are adequate both to reassure the market and to prevent a collapse of the quantity of money. The stock market crash of October 1929 did not create a financial crisis because the Federal Reserve responded by providing liquidity to the market.

The interpretation of the episode from 1930 to 1933, however, instead of focusing on the failure of the Federal Reserve, has shifted to focus on the behavior of market participants. Bank runs in this light are a quintessential feature of a fractional reserve banking system. According to the influential Diamond-Dybvig model (1983), runs need not depend on any loss in value of the assets that underlie fixed-claim deposits. They can occur even on a sound bank if the cost of liquidating assets reduces the value of the loan portfolio.

Focusing on the behavior of market participants, I believe, is one of the antecedents of systemic risk apprehensions. Contagion becomes something easily liable to happen. And, of course, the importance of intervention by authorities is enhanced. The model builders also wrongly conclude that federally-sponsored deposit insurance is the most, if not the only, effective device for preventing runs, when, in fact, an effective lender of last resort is sufficient to prevent runs.

So I regard to Diamond-Dybvig model as pernicious. The bank in the model has no capital—an obvious source of reassurance to depositors. Furthermore, recurrent banking panics have not been a feature of the economies of advanced countries with an effective lender of last resort.

There has been no recurrence of financial crisis since World War II because the authorities have learned well the lesson of earlier experience. A flight to currency is preventable. A response to a stock market crash by the monetary authorities is appropriate. Assure that deposits can be converted at will into currency and that the demands of all sound debtors for loans will be met. Whatever the difficulties banks may encounter, the solution does not preclude the failure of mismanaged banks.

Demands for conversion of deposits into currency, however, are not typically the response of holders of bank liabilities to current bank difficulties. Instead they shift their deposits and purchases of CDs to other institutions or to safe securities (G. Kaufman, 1988). There are no longer bank runs in the traditional sense of anxious depositors lining up at bank offices to obtain currency. A flight to currency has not been observed as a concomitant to bank failures since World War II. (Runs on savings and loan associations in 1985 in Ohio and Maryland would not have occurred had authorities acted promptly to assure depositors that their demands for cash would be met.) Yet instead of limiting intervention since this basis for doing so has been obviated, and doing what needs to be done, namely, closing insolvent institutions, U.S. authorities since 1970 have acted as if contagion is the problem and proceeded to shore up such institutions. Examples are Franklin National Bank (1974), Continental Illinois (1984), and the hundreds of CAMEL 4- and 5-rated banks (1985-1991) that received extended accommodation, presumably also because the FDIC had limited resources to arrange their liquidation or some form of purchase and assumption. These examples have been designated in the literature as financial crises. They are pseudo-financial crises.

Bailing out banks because of a pseudo-financial crisis, even if equity-holders are losers and management suffers job loss, encourages imprudent behavior by banks and by depositors. It misallocates resources. Political decisions substitute for market decisions. Institutions that have failed the market test of viability should not be supported by the authorities. Policy makers are led to take actions that harm economic efficiency in pursuit of the mirage of preventing domestic systemic risk.

How then should one view international relationships as a possible source of systemic risk? Three kinds of events have been pictured: a foreign bank with an office or subsidiary in another country collapses; the equity market in one country crashes and equity markets elsewhere crash; the payments system is disrupted in the process of transmittal of funds from a bank abroad to a domestic bank (Benston, 1994).

In each case central banks can offset by appropriate open market operations a reduction in bank reserves and preserve stability of the money supply. Dealing with the failure of a major bank in one country that is indebted to a bank in another country is no different than dealing with the failure of a major bank that holds domestic interbank deposits. If there are links between stock market crashes in different countries—the generalized case has not been established—central bank provision of liquidity to banks in each country to keep credit lines open to brokers is a well-understood measure in those circumstances.

Finally, individual private and central banks can protect themselves against the costs of payments system disruption that the failure of a participating bank may precipitate. The domestic central bank can require bank participants in the payments system to maintain adequate capital. Should a failure occur, legal obligations of the parties should be known in advance. A government-operated payments system can charge for or prohibit overdrafts. A private-operated payments system can refuse to deal with undercapitalized banks and require adequate collateral to minimize loss (Benston, 1994).

The validity of systemic risk has been established as a legitimate concern, I conclude, neither for the domestic nor for the international economy.

IV. CONCLUSION

In my view what has driven the attention recently focused on systemic risk is a belief in financial market failure. Market participants, according to the systemic risk literature, are either ignorant, investing in nonviable projects that fail, or dishonest, misleading lenders about the merit of the projects for which they borrow. Financial intermediaries in this approach exist at the mercy of their clients.

The main problem with the play based on systemic risk is that the role of the monetary authorities, the Prince of Denmark, is omitted from the first act of Hamlet. However, one cannot account for financial instability in the behavior of either borrowers or lenders without introducing the monetary authorities and their conduct of monetary policy and, secondarily, bank supervisors and regulatory policies.

The systemic risk play introduces the monetary authorities in the final act as the deus ex machina that comes to the rescue of the beleaguered market. The evidence, however, supports only a limited role for a lender of last resort, as in the case of a flight to currency, or in instances of obsessive fears that money will be unavailable, exemplified by the stock market crashes of October 1987 and October 1989. The Federal Reserve then provided liquidity to the market and urged banks to lend to imperiled securities firms. Otherwise the recent promotion of the exercise of the lender of last resort role is based on gratuitous inferences that panic would result if a large industrial firm or a bank or a municipality were permitted to declare bankruptcy. The potential for contagion and systemic risk in these instances is grossly exaggerated.

REFERENCES

Benston, George J. "International Harmonization of Banking Regulations and Cooperation Among National Regulators: An Assessment." *Journal of Financial Services Research*, September 1994, pp. 205-25.

Blanchard, Olivier J., and Mark W. Watson. "Bubbles, Rational Expectations, and Financial Markets." In *Crises in the Economic and Financial Structure*. Edited by Paul Wachtel. Lexington, MA: Lexington Books, 1982, pp. 295-315.

Brimmer, Adrew F. "Distinguished Lecture on Economics and Government: Central Banking and Systemic Risks in Capital Markets." *Journal of Economic Perspectives*, Spring 1989, Volume 3, pp. 3-16.

Calomiris, Charles W. "Is the Discount Window Necessary? A Penn-Central Perspective." Working paper, University of Illinois, September 1993.

Corrigan, Gerald. "Challenges Facing the International Community of Bank Supervisors." *Quarterly Review* (Federal Reserve Bank of New York). Autumn 1992, pp. 1-9.

Davis, E. P. *Debt, Financial Fragility, and Systemic Risk*. Oxford: Clarendon Press, 1992.

Diamond, David, and Phillip Dybvig. "Bank Runs, Deposit Insurance, and Liquidity." *Journal of Political Economy*, June 1983, 401-419.

Feldstein, Martin, ed. *The Risk of Economic Crisis*. Chicago: University of Chicago Press, 1991.

Feldstein, Martin, ed. *American Economic Policy in the 1980s*. Chicago: University of Chicago Press, 1994.

Flood, Robert P., and Peter M. Garber. "Bubbles, Runs, and Gold Monetization." In *Crisis in the Economic and Financial Structure*. Edited by Paul Wacht. Lexignton, MA: Lexington Books, 1982, pp. 275-93.

Friedman, Benjamin M. "The Risks of Financial Crises." In *The Risk of Economic Crisis*. Edited by Martin Feldstein. Chicago: University of Chicago Press, 1991, pp. 19-42.

Friedman, Milton, and Anna J. Schwartz. *A Monetary History of the United States, 1867-1960*. Princeton: Princeton University Press, 1963.

Glosten, Lawrence R., and Paul R. Milgrom. "Bid, Ask, and Transactions Prices in a Specialist Market with Heterogenously Informed Traders." *Journal of Financial Economics*, March 1985, pp. 71-100.

Guttentag, Jack M., and Richard J. Herring. "Credit Rationing and Financial Disorder," *Journal of Finance*, December 1984, 1359-1382.

Hubbard, R. Glen, ed. *Financial Markets and Financial Crises*. Chicago: University of Chicago Press, 1991.

Kaufman, George G. "Bank Contagion: A Review of the Theory and Evidence." *Journal of Financial Services Research,* April 1994, pp. 123-150.

Kaufman, George G. "Bank Runs: Causes, Benefits, and Costs." *Cato Journal,* Winter pp. 539-587, 1988.

Kaufman, Henry. "Debt: The Threat to Financial Stability." In *Debt, Financial Stability, and Public Policy.* Kansas City: Federal Reserve Bank of Kansas City. 1986.

Krugman, Paul. "International Aspects of Financial Crises." In *The Risk of Economic Crisis.* Edited by Martin Feldstein Chicago: University of Chicago Press, 1991, pp. 85-108.

Meltzer, Allan H. "Rational Expectations, Risk, Uncertainty, and Market Responses." In *Crises in the Economic and Financial Structure.* Edited by Paul Wachtel. Lexington Books, 1982, pp. 3-22.

Mishkin, Frederic S. "Asymmetric Information and Financial Crises: A Historical Perspective." In *Financial Markets and Financial Crises.* Edited by Martin Feldstein. Chicago: University of Chicago Press, 1991, pp. 69-108.

Schwartz, Anna J. "Real and Pseudo-Financial Crises." In *Financial Crises and the World Banking System.* Edited by Forrest Capic and Geoffrey Wood. London: Macmillan, 1986, pp. 11-31.

COMMENT ON SYSTEMIC RISK

Frederic S. Mishkin

I. DEFINING SYSTEMIC RISK

The papers by Anna Schwartz and Phillip Bartholomew and Gary Whalen present two very different views of systemic risk. Bartholomew and Whalen define systemic risk as the "Likelihood of a sudden, usually unexpected, collapse of confidence in a significant portion of the banking or financial system with potentially large real economic effects." Schwartz, on the other hand, doesn't even like the term systemic risk and feels that it could be dispensed with entirely because it adds nothing to our understanding of a financial crisis.

My views of systemic risk fall somewhat in between these two positions. I find the Bartholomew-Whalen definition to not be sufficiently precise, allowing it to be used as a justification for interventions by the government that are unnecessary and might be harmful to the economy. Schwartz's view of systemic risk, on the other hand, is far too narrow, and is far too restrictive on what might be appropriate interventions to prevent a financial crisis.

Because systemic risk is a justification for government intervention, to define it we must identify a market failure when a systemic event occurs in financial markets. The key market failure when a systemic event occurs is a breakdown

Research in Financial Services Private and Public Policy, Volume 7, pages 31-45.

ISBN: 1-55938-244-9

of information: that is, when a disruption in financial markets leads to an increase in information problems (adverse selection and moral hazard), so that financial markets are unable to channel funds effectively to those who have the most productive investment opportunities. Thus, I would modify the Bartholomew-Whalen definition of systemic risk to the following:

> **Systemic risk is the likelihood of a sudden, usually unexpected, event that disrupts information in financial markets, making them unable to effectively channel funds to those parties with the most productive investment opportunities.**

My reading of the Bartholomew-Whalen paper is that this is a definition they might feel comfortable with because they often mention the importance of information in discussing systemic risk.

Why is this modification of the Bartholomew-Whalen definition important? The reason is that focusing on disruptions in information flows in defining systemic risk helps rule out inappropriate government interventions that might otherwise be justified under the Bartholomew-Whalen definition. As pointed out in Mishkin (1994), analysis based on an information-based view rules out many "crisis" episodes as true financial crises. These financial market disturbances, although very dramatic, are not damaging to the economy in themselves. For example, sharp changes in asset prices, such as those occurring during a stock market crash or in a foreign exchange crisis often are viewed as financial crises. However, an information view suggests that such financial disturbances may not qualify for the financial crisis label because they do not necessarily lead to disruptions of information flows in financial markets. These financial disturbances which do not lead to increases in information problems in the financial markets will not seriously damage the economy and thus quality for Schwartz's designation as "pseudo-financial crises."

For example, there are many instances of stock market crashes, which show no manifestation of an increase in information problems in financial markets. One of the most severe stock market crashes in U.S. history occurred in May of 1940 in the aftermath of Dunkirk. Indeed, the monthly decline in May 1940 was the third largest negative monthly return in the 1834-1988 period examined by Wilson, Sylla and Jones (1990). However, this crash occurred at a time when the U.S. economy was booming and interest rates were low, so that other conditions were very unfavorable to worsening of adverse selection and moral hazard problems in financial markets. Not surprisingly, as pointed out in Mishkin (1991), there was no manifestation of a disruption of information flows in financial markets because the spread between interest rates on low and high quality bonds rose hardly at all and the U.S. economy kept on booming.

Armored with the information definition of systemic risk, it also should be clear that foreign exchange crises, which are often labeled as international financial crises, are likely to fit into the category of a "pseudo-financial crisis." Foreign exchange crises like the one that almost brought down the European Monetary System in September 1992 involve a speculative attack on currencies in a fixed exchange rate system, a key feature of which is that, in effect, central banks have established a one-sided bet for speculators by standing ready to intervene to prop up weak currencies. In this situation, private firms and banks in the aggregate are not exposed to large losses of wealth because a change in the exchange rate leads both to winners and losers. Furthermore, private firms and banks actually tend to benefit during these "crises" because the one-sided intervention on the part of central banks results in huge profits for the speculators at the expense of the central banks. During the September 1992 exchange rate crisis, reports in the press indicated that intervention by the central banks resulted in their losing from 4 to 6 billion dollars:

Indeed, the only danger of financial crisis might come from central bank attempts to prop up their domestic currency by raising interest rates to extremely high levels, as occurred in Sweden when the interbank rate went to 500 percent. If such tight money policies are continued for very long, then there is a potential for the high interest rates to lead to increased information problems in the financial markets. One of the reasons that central banks often are forced to give up on pegging the value of their currency during a speculative attack is that they sensibly have concluded that attempts to keep the exchange rate fixed will have inordinately high costs for the economy.

The information-based definition of systemic risk does support Schwartz's view that a flight to currency can lead to a financial crisis. However, the definition suggests that other disruptions to financial markets may lead to a financial crisis, and are thus appropriately classified as systemic risks which require a policy response. Included in this category is the Penn-Central bankruptcy episode, which is discussed more extensively in Brimmer (1989), Mishkin (1991), and Calomiris (1993), but which is ruled out as a systemic risk by Schwartz.

Prior to 1970, commercial paper was considered one of the safest money market instruments because only corporations with very high credit ratings issued it. It was common practice for corporations to continually roll over their commercial paper, that is, issue new commercial paper to pay off the old. Penn Central Railroad was a major issuer of commercial paper, with more than $200 million outstanding, but they May 1970 it was on the verge of bankruptcy and it requested federal government assistance from the Nixon administration.[1] Despite administration support for a bailout of Penn Central, after six weeks of debate Congress decided not to pass bailout legislation. According to Brimmer (1989), the Nixon administration then asked the Board of Governors to authorize a direct loan from the Federal Reserve Bank of New York to Penn

Central. However, on Thursday, June 18, the New York Fed informed the Board of Governors that its staff studies indicated that Penn Central would not be able to repay the loan, and as a result the Board decided not to authorize the loan. Without this loan, Penn Central was forced to declare bankruptcy on Sunday, June 21.

Once the Federal Reserve made the decision not to provide assistance to Penn Central, it was concerned that Penn Central's default on its commercial paper would, as Brimmer (1989) puts it, have had a "chilling effect on the commercial paper market", making it impossible for other corporations to roll over their commercial paper. The Penn Central bankruptcy, then, had the potential for sending other companies into bankruptcy which, in turn, might have triggered further bankruptcies—leading to a full-scale financial panic. As Brimmer (1989) notes, to avoid this scenario, the New York Fed got in touch with a number of large money center banks on Saturday and Sunday, June 20 and 21, alerted them to the impending Penn Central bankruptcy on June 22, encouraged them to lend to their customers who were unable to roll over their commercial paper, and indicated that the discount window would be make available to the banks so that they could make these loans.[2] Indeed, the banks proceeded accordingly and made these loans, receiving as much as $575 million through the discount window for this purpose. In addition, on June 22 the Fed decided to suspend Regulation Q ceilings on deposits of $100,000 and over in order to keep short-term interest rates from rising, and the formal vote was taken the next day to allow the FDIC and the FHLBB to take parallel action. The net result was that the Federal Reserve provided liquidity so that the commercial paper market would keep functioning.

A rationale for the Fed's action was that lenders would not be able to screen out good borrowers in this market from bad borrowers. Was this rationale plausible? Data from this period suggest that it was. As pointed out in Mishkin (1991), data on interest rates, stock prices, and most importantly, the spread between interest rates for high and low quality borrowers all fit the pattern found in earlier episodes of financial crises in U.S. economic history which support a disruption of information flows during these episodes. A major disturbance to the credit markets as a result of increased information problems seem to have been avoided by the Fed's willingness to perform its lender-of-last resort function.[3]

The information view of systemic risk and financial crises also explains why the stock market crash of 1987 was a systemic event that required intervention by the Federal Reserve. The causes of the stock market crash of 1987 are still being hotly debated, but the biggest danger to the economy appears not to have come from the decline in wealth resulting from the crash itself, but rather from the threat to the clearing and settlement system in the stock and futures markets. From the peak on August 25, 1987 until October 16, just prior to the crash, the Dow Jones Industrial Average had declined 17.5 percent. On

Monday, October 19, the market fell by 22.6 percent (as measured by the DJIA) on record volume of 604 million shares. Although October 19, 1987, dubbed "Black Monday," will go down in history as the largest one-day decline in stock prices to date, it was on Tuesday, October 20, 1987 that financial markets received their worst threat. In order to keep the stock market and the related index futures market functioning in an orderly fashion, brokers needed to extend massive amount of credit on behalf of their customers for their margin calls. The magnitude of the problem is illustrated by the fact that just two brokerage firms, Kidder, Peabody and Goldman, Sachs, had advanced $1.5 billion in response to margin calls on their customers by noon of October 20.[4] Clearly, brokerage firms as well as specialists were severely in need of additional funds to finance their activities. However, understandably enough, banks were growing very nervous about the financial health of securities firms and so were reluctant to lend to the securities industry at a time when it was most needed.

As reported in Brimmer (1989), upon learning of the plight of the securities industry, Alan Greenspan and E. Gerald Corrigan, the president of the New York Federal Reserve Bank and the Fed official most closely in touch with Wall Street, were concerned about a breakdown in the clearing and settlement systems and the collapse of securities firms. To prevent this from occurring, Alan Greenspan announced before the market opened on Tuesday, October 20, the Federal Reserve System's "Readiness to serve as a source of liquidity to support the economic and financial system." In addition to this extraordinary announcement, the Fed encouraged key money center banks to lend freely to their brokerage firm customers, and make it clear that it would provide discount loans to banks so that they could make these loans. The banks did make these loans, and by October 21 had increased by $7.7 billion their loans to brokers and to individuals to purchase or hold securities. As a result, the markets kept functioning on Tuesday, October 20 and a market rally ensued that day, raising the DJIA by over 100 points (over 5%). This action by the Fed is reminiscent of the actions taken by the Fed during the September 1929 panic period in which it provided liquidity to enable money center banks to take over call loans which had been called by others.

As in the case of the Penn-Central episode, the potential for a serious financial crisis resulting from the stock market crash is evident in the data on stock prices, interest rates and interest rate spreads described in Mishkin (1991). Again, we see that the pattern during the stock market crash episode is very similar to that found in earlier financial crisis episodes in the United States during the nineteenth and early twentieth century where financial markets were hit by a severe disruption of information flows. The fact that these variables seem to fit a classic pattern for financial crises suggests that the October 1987 stock market crash did have the potential to create major information problems in the credit markets. However, the prompt action by the Fed kept the asymmetric information problem from getting out of hand, as is indicated by the moderate increase in the Baa-Treasury spread relative to earlier financial panics. The failure of the U.S. economy to enter a recession after the stock market crash, despite many forecasters predictions along these lines, is consistent with the view that the Fed's actions prevented the development of serious asymmetric information problems in the credit markets. Furthermore, the fact that the stock market crash in the United States occurred simultaneously with stock market crashes in the rest of the world, suggests that a financial crisis, if it had been allowed to develop, would have been a world-wide phenomenon and would not have been restricted to the United States.

Anna Schwartz concedes that there can be systemic risk as a result of a stock market crash to which a response by the monetary authorities is appropriate. She states that the monetary authorities might need to "assure that deposits can be converted at will into currency and the *demands of all sound debtors for loans will be met* [italics added]." This statement seems to support an information view of financial crises more than Schwartz realizes. After all, the reason that the demands of sound debtors for loans may not be met in the aftermath is because the disruption of information flows during a financial crisis prevents this from occurring. Indeed, the description of the information disruption during the October 1987 crash I have provided here is entirely consistent with Schwartz's statement.

II. POLICY IMPLICATIONS OF THE DEFINITION OF SYSTEMIC RISK

Why should we care so much about the definition of systemic risk? The answer is that the definition of systemic risk has enormous implications for how regulatory and monetary policy should respond. The information-based definition of systemic risk I have provided here has important policy implications for the lender of last resort role of central banks, discount lending operations and regulation.

Lender of Last Resort

The traditional recommendation for prevention of financial crises goes back to Thornton (1802) and Bagehot (1873) who recommend that the central bank be a lender of last resort who will lend freely during a panic at a penalty rate. What does the asymmetric information framework outlined here say about his traditional recommendation? Does it provide further guidance on when the central bank needs to be ready to be a lender of last resort and how it should conduct this role? How would be policy prescription differ from that provided by the earlier literature on financial crises?

Schwartz's view of financial disturbances sees them as important only if they produce banking panics which lead to a decline in the money supply. With this view, the lender of last resort role should be very narrow one: the central bank should only lend freely to banks when there is a sudden desire on the part of depositors to withdraw their funds from banks. To lend freely at other times, during what Schwartz calls "pseudo-financial crises," will only lead to inefficiency because firms that deserve to fail are bailed out, or because such lending results in excessive money growth that stimulates inflation. Indeed, her position suggests that if the central bank is able to achieve the goal of price stability, it is unlikely that a lender of last resort role is even needed to promote the health of the economy.

An information view of systemic risk and financial crises, although it sees an important role for bank panics, does not see them as the only financial disturbances that can have serious adverse effects on the aggregate economy. Financial crises have effects over the above those resulting from banking panics, and analysis of such episodes as the Penn Central Bankruptcy and the stock market crash in October 1987 suggests that a financial crisis which has serious adverse consequences for the economy can develop even if there is no direct threat to the banking system.

Mishkin (1991) provides evidence that although there was no banking panic in 1937 or 1938, a financial crisis seems to have occurred in the 1937-1938 period. From its peak in February 1937 until its trough in March 1938, the stock market declined by 50%, with the stock market return of -23.9 percent in March 1938 ranking as the second worst monthly return in the 1834-1988 period. (Only the return of -29.3 percent in September 1931 is worse.) Coming at a time when the economy was already in trouble, adverse selection and moral hazard problems in financial markets appeared to worsen substantially, wi the spread between interest rates on low in high quality bonds rising back to the extremely high levels found in 1934. This episode thus also suggests that a financial crisis situation can develop even if a banking panic is not present.

The asymmetric information analysis thus suggests that a lender of last resort role may be necessary to provide liquidity to nonbanking sector of the financial system in which asymmetric information problems have developed. Furthermore, it suggests that financial disturbances outside the banking system in the postwar period have had the potential to have serious adverse effects on the aggregate economy and that these adverse consequences have in fact been prevented only by quick actions of the Federal Reserve to pursue an expanded role as a lender of last resort. However, it also supports Schwartz's position that a central bank should operate as the lender of last resort to prevent banking panics as well.

Although a central bank's role as a lender of last resort has the benefit of preventing financial crises, it does have a cost. If a bank's depositors expect that the central bank will provide a bank with discount loans when it gets into trouble and come to its rescue, then they have less incentive to monitor the bank and withdraw their deposits if the bank takes on two much risk. Thus the lender of last resort role in itself can produce a moral hazard problem because it can lead to expectations which encourage banks to take on too much risk. This moral hazard problem is most severe for large banks if they are the beneficiaries of a somewhat misnamed "too big to fail" policy in which depositors at a large bank in trouble are protected from any losses by a lender of last resort policy, such as that used when Continental Illinois failed in 1984 in the United States. (The "too big to fail" policy is somewhat misnamed because although depositors are completely protected from losses, the bank is in fact allowed to fail with losses to the equity holders.) Evidence in Boyd and Gertler (1993) suggests that the cost of the "too big to fail" policy has indeed been quite high in the United States after it was put into force with the failure of Continental Illinois in 1984.

Similarly, the lender of last resort role to prevent a financial crisis arising outside the banking sector may encourage other financial institutions and borrowers from them to take on too much risk. Knowing that the central bank will prevent a financial crisis if its appears imminent will encourage them to protect themselves less against systemic risk, that is, those that occur system-wide which will trigger a lender of last resort response. There is thus tradeoff between the moral hazard cost of the lender of last resort role and its benefits in preventing financial crises.

The information definition of systemic risk thus, like Schwartz's view, does see a danger in too liberal a use of the lender of last resort activities on the part of central banks. Although the information view has a broader definition of what constitutes a financial crisis than Schwartz's view, it also does not recommend that a central bank be a lender of last resort during a pseudo-crisis. It is important that central banks not perform the role of lender of last resort too frequently. As we have seen, a stock market crash by itself, as in May 1940 in the United States does not imply that a financial crisis is imminent, nor does a foreign exchange crisis or a collapse in other asset values, such as real estate. Thus, the need to use the lender of last resort role sparingly in order to keep moral hazard from getting out of hand argues against such intervention unless it is absolutely necessary. The lender of last resort role should therefore occur very infrequently.

One problem with deciding to engage in the lender of last resort role is that for it to be effective it has to be implemented quickly. Less intervention is required the faster the lender of last resort role is implemented because once market participants know that liquidity is being injected into the system, uncertainly in the financial markets will decrease. Thus, the Federal Reserve's actions during the stock market crash of 1987 are a textbook case of how a lender of last resort role should be performed. The Fed's action was immediate, with an announcement that operated to decrease uncertainty in the marketplace.

Reserves were injected into the system, but once the crisis was over, they were withdrawn. Not only was a financial crisis averted, but also the inflationary consequences of this exercise of the lender of last resort role were quite small.

However, the need for the lender of last resort action to be quick does mean that central banks may not be able to wait until all the information is in that tells them a financial crisis is about to occur or is occurring. To wait too long to implement a lender of last resort policy could be disastrous. Thus, even though the asymmetric information view of financial crises provides some guidance as to when a lender of last resort role should be implemented, deciding on when to do so will necessarily be an art rather than a science. Central bank "feel" for conditions in financial markets that comes from informal as well as formal signals about developments in these markets is necessary to make the appropriate decision on when a lender of last resort tole is necessary.

Discount Lending

A corollary of Schwartz's view is that the operation of central bank discount facilities may be unnecessary. Open market operations are sufficient to keep the money supply on its target path and this is all that is needed to keep the economy functioning well. Using the reasoning, Friedman (1958) advocated abolishment of the Federal Reserve's discounting operation and more recently Goodfriend and King (1988) seem to come to a similar conclusion. Goodfriend and King (1988) dichotomize the activities of the central bank into "monetary policy," that is, changes in the total volume of high powered money which can be entirely carried out with open market operations, and "banking policy," which involves regular lending and emergency financial assistance to individual banks and financial institutions along with regulatory and supervisory actions. Because they see financial crises as been essentially monetary in nature, they do not see the need for "banking policy" and discount lending. Since they consider the regulatory and supervisory activities that become necessary when there is discount lending by the central bank to be costly, they lean to elimination of Federal Reserve discount lending.[5]

The asymmetric information interpretation of financial crises, on the other hand, provides a strong rationale for the operation of the central bank's discount facilities. As the analysis of the response to the Stock Market 1929 and 1987 indicates, a central bank can only provide liquidity to a specific sector by providing it to the overall economy using open market operations. Because this provision of liquidity might be very indirect, a larger infusion of liquidity may be needed to prevent the financial disturbance from creating severe information problems. Consequently, in order for a central bank to achieve its objectives, it may have to put so much liquidity into the economy that it would produce substantial inflationary pressure. Having discounting at its disposal provides the central bank with a delicate tool that enables it to cope with financial disturbances without promoting inflationary tendencies.

The operation of discount facilities also provides a central bank with another major advantage in dealing with potential financial crises. Government bailouts of individual firms have the significant disadvantage that they are likely to keep inefficient firms in operation and also encourage excessive risk taking on the part of firms that expect to be bailed out. In essence, the problem is again one of asymmetric information because the government is unlikely to be able to separate out insolvent from temporarily illiquid firms. In addition, political pressures may influence bailout decisions to the detriment of economic efficiency.[6]

On the other hand, discount lending enables the central bank to encourage lending to a sector of the financial system in which asymmetric information has become a serious problem and yet minimizes some of the efficiency losses from this lending. Using discounting enables the central bank to take advantage of the monitoring and information collection expertise inherent in individual banks so that lending is likely to be made only to solvent business enterprises. In other worlds, the central bank is making use of the banks as delegated monitors on its behalf. In order to properly use banks as delegated monitors, the central bank must give banks the appropriate incentives to engage in monitoring and information collection: in other words, the banks must be responsible for the credit risk involved in lending. The central bank needs to indicate that it will provide liquidity to prevent systemic risk, but would not be responsible for idiosyncratic risk. This is exactly what the Federal Reserve did when it made discount loans to banks during the Penn Central bankruptcy crisis to that banks could in turn lend to borrowers in the commercial paper market and also when it lent to banks during the stock market crash of 1987 so that the banks would extend additional loans to their brokerage firm customers. It was made clear that these customers would have to be considered creditworthy by the banks. The burden of screening out good from bad borrowers was thus left to individual banks, who have the expertise to do this properly.

The use of banks as delegated monitors for the central bank during a financial crisis suggests that the traditional recommendation that the central bank should lend at a penalty rate when it performs its lender of last resort role might be problematic. In order to provide banks with the incentives to act as the central bank's delegated monitor, banks must be able to profit from this activity. Thus, there is a case for subsidizing banks by setting the discount rate below the interest rate they earn on their loans during a financial crisis. Without this subsidy, the banks might not be willing to make the necessary loans. The need for delegated monitors during a financial crisis might thus explain why central banks typically set their discount rate below market interest rates, which requires them to ration discount lending. Although monetary economists have typically criticized central banks for setting the discount rate too low and engaging in rationing of discount loans, there is a partial rationale for this policy. However, it is not clear why central banks would not obtain the full benefits from banks acting as delegated monitors by setting the discount rate below market rates only during a financial crisis and not in more normal times.

The information-based definition of systemic risk also provides a rationale for discount lending to banks in order to prevent banking panics. Clearly, during a financial crisis central banks should lend to illiquid but solvent banks. Lending to insolvent banks, however, creates the moral hazard problem that arises with the "too big to fail" policy: it creates incentives for banks to take on too much risk. The problem facing central banks is that they are unable to use delegated monitors to channel funds to illiquid but solvent banks. Rather they have to make the decision themselves as to whether a bank in trouble deserves to receive an infusion of liquidity. This raises two problems in turn. First, central banks must have sufficient information about banks they may need to lend to in order for them to be able to tell whether a bank needing liquidity is solvent or insolvent. Second, central banks may not have the right incentives to lend to illiquid but solvent banks rather than insolvent banks. In contrast to private banks, who are subject to a profit motive and thus have the appropriate incentive to lend only to solvent firms, central banks may be influenced by other considerations. They may be too anxious to protect the banks that they are close to and also may be put under intense political pressure to bail out insolvent banks. Indeed, there has been concern that discount lending may have allowed insolvent banks to continue in operation which then resulted in higher losses to the FDIC. As a result, there are provisions in the Federal Deposit Insurance Corporation Improvement Act of 1991 to limit Federal Reserve discounting to insolvent banks.

The information-based definition of systemic risk does provide a rationale for a "too big to fail" policy in which a central bank lends to a big, insolvent bank because a failure of a big bank can create uncertainly in the financial markets that make a financial crisis more likely. However, research such as Boyd and Gertler (1993) suggests that the "too big to fail" policy may have high costs. Analysis of the Penn Central and the stock market crash of 1987 episodes suggests an alternatively way for a central bank to keep a financial crisis from developing when a large bank becomes insolvent. As in the Penn Central case, the insolvent institution can be allowed to fail with consequent losses to both the equity holders and the debt holders, which in the case of a bank, would include the depositors uninsured by government deposit insurance. However, once the central bank make the decision to let the insolvent bank go under, it would need to make an announcement of its "readiness to serve as a source of liquidity to support the economic and financial system," as on October 20, 1987, and would make it clear that the discount window would be open to banks that needed liquidity. The result is that the large bank would be allowed to fail and produce losses for equityholders and debtholders, such as uninsured depositors, thus creating incentives for these parties to keep large banks from taking on too much risk. However, the lender of last resort role of the central bank would then keep a bank panic from spreading to the rest of the banking system, thereby preventing a financial crisis.

Regulation

The discussion of discount lending above indicates that central bank lending to financial institutions can create moral hazard incentives for them to take no too much risk. To prevent this, the central bank needs to restrict its lending to solvent institutions that are not taking on too much risk. Just as private financial institutions must have access to information about borrowers so that they can screen and monitor them to reduce adverse selection and moral hazard problems, a central bank must have similar access to information about the financial institutions it lends to. One way for central banks to have this information is for them to have a direct regulatory oversight over these financial institutions, as occurs in the United States where the Federal Reserve conducts periodic examinations of banks. This is one reason why the U.S. Treasury's recommendation in 1991 to take away the Federal Reserve's supervisory role over large national banks that it has through supervision of their bank holding companies was ill founded.[7] Some central banks, such as the Bundesbank, strenuously object to having a direct regulatory role because they believe that it will subject them to political pressures which may interfere with their ability to use monetary policy to combat inflation. Nonetheless, if a central bank is to run its discount operations to minimize moral hazard problems it needs to make sure that it has mechanisms in place that provide it with the required amount of information about its borrowers. Thus, even if a central bank does not have a direct regulatory role over the institutions it lends to, it must be a de factor regulator in that it examines the state of these institutions and can deny them discount loans if it believes they are taking on too much risk.

An additional implication to the analysis here is that once a financial institution is given access to the discount facilities of a central bank, the central bank must have access to information on the institution's risk-taking activities. This implication is important because central banks are often required to open their discount facilities to financial institutions other than banks. If these institutions are to receive discount privileges, they must bear the cost of being subjected to some regulatory oversight by the central bank.

Our earlier discussion of the decline of the banking industry suggests that regulation has another important role in preventing financial crises: it needs to promote the orderly decline of the industry if fundamental forces are causing this to happen. Edwards and Mishkin (1994) point out that fundamental economic forces are causing a decline in the profitability of the traditional business of banking, that is, borrowing short and lending long. This decline in profitability of traditional banking can increase the moral hazard incentives for banking institutions to take on more risk in order to keep their profits high given their loss of profitability. One of the reasons that the decline of the banking industry was so precipitous in the 1980s in the United States is that the regulatory system helped encourage risk-taking on the part of banks. Federal deposit insurance, especially combined with the "too big to fail" policy, protected depositors, even large ones, from losses when banks failed and so there was little incentive for depositors to monitor banks and withdraw funds if the bank was taking on too much risk. This lack of monitoring by depositors combined with lax regulation meant that, when faced with declining profitability, the banks took on even more risk to shore up their profits. For a while, the subsidy to risk-taking created by deposit insurance kept the banking industry from shrinking, but when many of the banks risky bets did not pay off, bank failures resulted. The outcome was then a much sharper drop in the size of the industry than would have occurred otherwise. Although a financial crisis was avoided in the United States through actions of the Federal Reserve and the deposit insurance agencies, the cost to the American taxpayer has been high, with losses to the deposit insurance agencies exceeding $100 billion. The Federal Deposit Insurance Corporation Improvement Act of 1991 has reduced some of the moral hazard incentives in U.S. bank regulation, although more needs to be done.[8]

The discussion here also leads to a very important point. Even if there were no deposit insurance, there still is an important rationale for regulation to prevent banking institutions from taking on excessive risk. Deposit insurance encourages banks to take on too much risk because it helps insulate them from monitoring by depositors who do not suffer losses if the bank takes on excessive risks and then fails. The lender of last resort role also encourages too much risk-taking, although probably not as much as does deposit insurance, because banking institutions know that they are more likely to obtain lender of last resort help during a crisis and so do not have to protect themselves as much as they would in the absence of a lender of last resort tole for the central bank. Furthermore, we have seen that even in countries that have a much less extensive deposit insurance system than exists in the United States, government bailouts of financial institutions are likely to occur during a financial crisis. For example, Scandanavian countries, such as Norway, Sweden and Finland, did not have an extensive deposit insurance system like ours, yet depositors and banks knew that if the largest institutions got into trouble, the government was likely to bail them out. As a result, these institutions took on excessive risk and when their bets went wrong, there was a massive bailout. Indeed the magnitude of the bailouts in these countries relative to GDP was very similar to that of the S&L bailout in the United States.

III. CONCLUSION

What I have tried to demonstrate here is that the definition of systemic risk does matter. An information-based view of systemic risk which I have provided here suggests that government intervention in financial markets is necessary to deal with systemic risk. However this view suggests that many interventions called for by market participants at great regularity may be both unnecessary and harmful to the economy. Anna Schwartz is quite right that interventions during pseudo-financial crises must be avoided. However, too narrowly defining what systemic risk and financial crises are might keep policymakers from intervening during a real financial crisis, which could lead to enormous costs to our economy.

ACKNOWLEDGMENT

Any opinions expressed are those of the author, not those of the Federal Reserve Bank of New York or the Federal Reserve System, Columbia University or the National Bureau of Economic Research.

NOTES

1. See Maisel (1973) and Brimmer (1989) for further discussion of the Penn Central bankruptcy episode.
2. It is noteworthy that when the Fed advanced discount loans to banks lending to customers who needed to roll over their commercial paper, the banks were told that they would be responsible for the credit risk involved in this lending. See Brimmer (1989), page 6.
3. Further evidence for this view is provided by Calomiris (1994).
4. See the *Wall Street Journal* (1987) and Brimmer (1989). These articles provide an excellent description of the events surrounding the stock market crash.
5. They do hedge their position, however, for they "wonder whether discount lending could be rationalized under a different criterion: to prevent the disruption costs of widespread insolvencies associated with temporary interest rate spikes." (Goodfriend and King (1988) p. 18.) The argument in this paper that disruption costs may indeed be high from widespread insolvencies provides a rationale for "banking policy" even in their framework.
6. The cost of politically motivated propping up of insolvent firms is amply demonstrated by what occurred during the 1980s when political forces led to the government to allow insolvent Savings and Loans to stay in business, which resulted in losses to the American taxpayer in excess of $100 billion.
7. See Mishkin (1992)
8. Mishkin (1995) contains a discussion of this legislation and what additional measures can help reduce the moral hazard incentives for too much risk taking.

REFERENCES

Bagehot, W. *Lombard Street: A Description of the Money Market.* London: HS King, 1873.

Boyd, J. and Gertler, M. "U.S. Commercial Banking: Trends, Cycles and Policy", 1993. *NBER Macroeconomics Annual.*

Brimmer, A.F. "Distringuished Lecture on Economics in Government: Central Banking and systemic Risks in Capital Markets", *Journal of Economic Perspectives, 3*, 3-16, 1989.

Calomiris, C.W., "Is the Discount Window Necessary? A Penn Central Perspective," *Economic Review*, Federal Reserve Bank of St. Louis, May/June 1994.

Edwards, F. and Mishkin, F.S. "The Decline of Traditional Banking: Implications for Financial Stability and Regulatory Policy," Federal Reserve Bank of New York, *Economic Policy Review*, July 1995.

Friedman, M. *A Program for Monetary Stability*, New York: Fordham University Press.

Friedman, M., and Schwartz A.J. A Monetary History of the United States, 1867-1960. Princeton: Princeton University Press. 1963.

Goodfriend, M. and King, R.G. "Financial Deregulation, Monetary Policy, and Central Banking", Federal Reserve Bank of Richmond *Review* 74, 3-22, 1988.

Maisel, S.J. *Managing the Dollar,* New York: Norton 1973.

Mishkin, F.S. "Asymmetric Information and Financial Crises: A Historical Perspective." In *Financial Markets and Financial Crises*, Edited by R.G. Hubbard. Chicago: University of Chicago Press. pp. 69-108, 1991.

Mishkin, F.S. "An Evaluation of the Treasury Plan for Banking Reform," *Journal of Economic Perspectives*, 6, No. 1, (Winter), pp. 133-53, 1992.

Mishkin, F.S. "Preventing Financial Crises: An International Perspective," *The Manchester School Supplement 1994*, pp. 1-40.

Mishkin. F.S. *The Economics of Money, Banking, and Financial Markets*, Fourth Edition. New York: HarperCollings. 1995.

Thorton, H. *An Enquiry into the Nature and Effects of the Paper Credit of Great Britain.* New York: Rhinehart and Company, 1938, 1802.

Wall Street Journal "Terrible Tuesday: How the Stock Market Almost Disintegrated a Day After the Crash," *Wall Street Journal* (November 20, 1987).

Wilson, J., R. Sylla and C.P. Jones "Financial Market Volatility, Panics Under the National Banking System Before 1914, and Volatility in the Long Run, 1830-1988." In *Crashes and Panics: A Historical Perspective.* Edited by Eugene N. White. Homewood, IL: Dow Jones/ Irwin, 1990.

COMMENT ON SYSTEMIC RISK

George G. Kaufman

Adelle Davis, the famous nutritionist of the 1960s, reportedly one said that "it is a shame that so much health food is sold, but so little is grown." The same may be said about systemic risk. It is a shame that so much is said about systemic risk, but so little appears. One major reason for this dichotomy is that, as both papers note, the concept of systemic risk is fuzzy, so that different analysts frequently talk about different phenomena. As a result, we have a tendency to talk past each other. The two papers in this session attempt to develop a definition that would serve as the basis for the rest of the conference.[1] Although I like both papers, I am not quite sure that they have succeeded in this difficult task.

To me, systemic or contagion risk is the probability that cumulative losses will occur from an event that sets in motion a series of successive losses along a chain of institutions or markets comprising a system. The key word is successive. A loss to player"A" causes a loss to player "B", which, in turn, causes a loss to player "C" and so on down the chain. That is, systemic risk is the risk of a chain reaction of falling interconnected dominos. This definition is consistent with the Bank for International Settlements (BIS) definition that systemic risk is "the risk that the failure of a participant to meet its contractual obligations may in turn cause other participants to default, with a chain

Research in Financial Services Private and Public Policy, Volume 7, pages 47-52.

ISBN: 1-55938-244-9

reaction leading to broader financial difficulties."[2] The importance of systemic risk depends not only on the probability of its occurring but also on the magnitude of any associated losses. Thus, even if the probabilities are small, systemic risk may still be important if the expected losses are large, particularly if they exceed the capital of the players and drive them into insolvency. Likewise, systemic risk would be relatively unimportant, even if the probability of it occurring were high, if the expected losses to the affected parties were relatively small and did not drive many or any into insolvency.

Note that this definition excludes instances where the dominos either fall simultaneously because of an independent event, say, an economic recession that causes banks and other firms to fail, or where the fall of one domino reveals new information about the weak foundation underlying other dominos, say, where losses at one bank provide new information about the possibility of losses at other banks with similar balance sheets but do not cause these losses, unless the losses at these banks cause later losses at other banks. As Anna Schwartz notes, most episodes of bank failures do not meet this definition of systemic risk.

Fears of systemic risk generally arise from doubts about the ability to contain liquidity problems and focus on banks as the prime transmitter of these problems.[3] Banks are viewed as "fragile," and fragility is equated with inherent instability. Banks are considered fragile because of their low cash to asset ratios (fractional reserve banking) and low capital to asset ratios (high leverage ratios), given their high short-term and even demand debt to total debt ratios. The former may cause large fire-sale losses if deposit outflows force hurried asset sales (and multiple contraction of deposits and credit for the banking system as a whole) and the latter provides little cushion for absorbing such losses before insolvency. Ironically, the fragility of banks is increased by government policies, such as deposit insurance, restrictions on product and geographic powers, and inaccurate accounting requirements, that encourage even lower capital ratios and greater portfolio risk.

But fragility does not imply excessive breakage for banks any more than it does for fragile chinaware, art works, or even egos. Rather, it implies "handle with care." As a result, fragile items often have a lower breakage rate than nonfragile items, which we handle with disdain. (An exception, of course, are items labelled "fragile" and sent throught the U.S. mails).

Banking has been known to be fragile since its earliest days and has been handled with care by owners, managers, and creditors. As a result, the average failure rate for banks has not been greatly different from that for other firms, even in the United States, where restrictions have prevented banks from minimizing their risk exposures through geographical and product diversification. Indeed, from the end of the Civil War to 1913, before the establishment of either the Federal Reserve or the FDIC, the average bank failure rate was substantially lower than that for nonbanks.[4] Thus, bank fragility *per se* has not resulted in bank instability.

Moreover, nearly all the available evidence suggests that, at least in the United States, both shareholders and depositor creditors as well as other banks have been able to successfully differentiate financially strong from financially weak banks. Insolvencies at one bank have rarely, if ever, caused insolvencies at other banks for reasons other than revealing new adverse information common to these banks. Bank failures have ignited neither regional nor national economic downturns, although they have undoubtedly exacerbated them.[5] That is, bank failure almost always result from economic downturns but do not start them. Banks tend to fail in bunches for the same reason that other firms fail in bunches—because the local, regional, or national economies have turned down, decreasing income and employment and increasing defaults in their market areas.

Indeed, the evidence suggests that, even during the Great Depression of the 1930s—when the high rate of bank failures suggested contagion and which is frequently used, even by Schwartz, as an example of contagion—systemic risk may not have been the major culprit. Large scale bank failures occurred in different geographic regions at different times and depositors appeared to be able to differentiate strong from weak banks, even at the height of a panic. Stronger and larger, more diversified banks rarely failed.[6]

But why, if there is so little evidence of systemic risk, is there so much shouting about it, even by supposedly knowledgeable persons? One reason may be that the perception of what is systemic is affected by where one stands. It is well known that markets do not always clear instantaneously and that sudden imbalances between buyers and sellers may cause prices to cascade for a while in one direction. Disorderly markets in a down direction are likely to cause large fire-sale losses. To participants in the trenches or pits, the first place where disruptions appear, such losses and the temporary absence of buyers at current prices are a serious cause for alarm. The losses may threaten a chain of defaults and the participants may feel that the world is collapsing around them.[7]

But all evidence suggests that in time markets stabilize at the old or new equilibrium prices. The question is how long is "in time"? The extend of the disorder and the length of time for markets to become orderly again depend on both the magnitude of the initial shock and the state of trading and information technology in the market. If the correction is quick, the disorder stays in the pits. Economic agents outside the pits will not be greatly affected, and see little or no threat of systemic risk. The longer the disorder and the larger the fire-sale losses, the more likely are the effects to spill over beyond the pits and affect financial institutions that provide credit to pit participants and even the macroeconomy. In such a scenario, the perception of systemic risk becomes more widespread and, as in the 1930s, may be accepted by the majority of all participants, It follows that shouts of systemic risk arise far more frequently and more loudly from participants than from those further removed from immediate liquidity stresses.

Where do the bank regulators stand? Their public policy concern should focus primarily on risks to the macroeconomy that may produce increases in unemployment and decreases in real income. Liquidity problems in the trenches should be of little concern to them unless they appear to seriously threaten the macroeconomy. Indeed, it is well documented that policies to alleviate any and all liquidity stresses will introduce moral hazard behavior that will only cause more serious problems later.

Unfortunately, because at least the central bank frequently deals directly with pit participants, bank regulators often associate themselves with pit participants. Moreover, they tend to be risk averse and apply excessively high discount rates to crisis costs, which skew their actions to preventing any and all disorders today even at the cost of creating the grounds for larger disorders in the future. In the words of Charles Kindleberger, "Actuality inevitably dominates contingency. Today wins over tomorrow.."[8] In addition, many regulators find crisis fighting exciting.[9] By doing so, they play into the deep rooted fears of the general public of major breakdowns in the financial system.[10] Systemic risk becomes a handy strawman.[11] Thus, there is a tendency for policy makers to perceive systemic risk more through the eyes of pit participants than through the calmer eyes of those further removed from the trenches. As a result, suboptimal and potentially costly financial policies, such as "too-big-to-fail," have often been adopted in the name of preventing systemic risk.

Bartholomew and Whalen correctly conclude that fears of systemic risk may be reduced greatly if credible regulators publicly promise to resolve all troubled institutions before their economic capital turns negative so that losses would be borne only by their shareholders, losses to whom are unlikely to spill over to other markets, and not by depositors, losses to whom are more likely to spill over to others. Moreover, in her very comprehensive analysis, Schwartz hits the nail on the head when she argues that concern over systemic risk "has shifted economists' focus from the behavior of monetary authorities ... to the behavior of market participants." A central bank that prevents abrupt declines in the money supply or abrupt increases in interest rates resulting from increased liquidity fears of market participants, primarily through open market operations, such as in 1987, and requires insured financial institutions to maintain capital ratios equivalent to those that the private market demands of competing noninsured institutions is the best protection against systemic risk.[12] These actions should reduce the probability of experiencing systemic risk in the future to near zero, which is not much different than history suggest has been the probability in the past when central banks did not err. That is, systemic risk is a central bank phenomenon. It reflects primarily government (regulatory) failure rather than market failure.

NOTES

1. Anna J. Schwartz, "Systemic Risk and the Macroeconomy," this volume and Phillip F. Bartholomew and Gary Whalen, "Fundamentals of Systemic Risk," this volume.

2. Bank for International Settlements, *Annual Report, 1994*, Basel, Switzerland, p. 177.

3. Such a potential systemic risk process was recently postulated by Governor John La Ware of the Federal Reserve Board in describing his belief of what would have occurred had the Continental Illinois Bank been "closed" in 1984.

> It might have been possible to close the Illinois bank and liquidate it in an orderly fashion. That would mean paying off insured depositors and then selling or collecting the remaining assets of the bank with the uninsured depositors and other creditors sharing whatever losses were realized on liquidation. But another serious problem arose. The bank was one of the nation's leading correspondent banks with deposit accounts from hundreds of banks all over the country, particularly from banks in the states in the Middle Western United States near Chicago. Many of these were small banks that maintained large accounts at the Illinois bank to facilitate check settlements, securities transactions, wire transfers, and other routine business transactions. For several hundred of these correspondent banks the amount of their deposits with the Illinois bank exceeded their capital. If the Illinois bank was closed, they would have been insolvent. The prospect of the failure of so many banks at one time was alarming. The result would have been serious losses to the depositors and stockholders of the smaller banks and disruption of commerce in the communities they served. Furthermore, if the banks had been closed by the authorities, many large companies and banks both in the United States and in foreign countries would have lost large amounts as their certificates of deposit, federal funds loans, Eurodollar contracts, and other claims were not honored. This might well have created a crisis of confidence that would have caused them to close out claims on other U.S. banks linked to the Oklahoma bank. That would have seriously destabilized the entire banking system. (La Ware, 1993, p. 96).

Like many believers in systemic risk, La Ware fails to recognize that liquidation is not the only alternative to a bailout of an insolvent institution. As in common practice today in resolutions by the FDIC, uninsured depositors may be given *pro rata* haircuts and the institution sold to another bank or other buyers. Moreover, an analysis of the Continental's 2,300 creditor banks indicated that, had the Continental suffered losses of 10 percent of its assets, twice as large as its actual losses, no creditor bank would have failed and only two banks would have experienced losses greater than 50 percent of their capital. Banks restricted their interbank exposures (Kaufman, 1994, pp. 130-131).

4. Kaufman, 1994, p. 134.

5. The evidence is reviewed in Benston and Kaufman (forthcoming).

6. Calomiris and Mason, 1994; Wicker, 1980, pp. 571-583 and Benston, 1973.

7. The participants are also unlikely to differentiate immediately between losses due to temporary disorders and losses due to new, lower equilibrium prices.

8. Kindleberger, 1978, p. 163.

9. Syron, 1994, pp. 3-8.

10. Devastating damage from bank failures, contagion, and systemic risk are also popular themes in works of fiction and likely have contributed to frightening the general public and intensifying their fears. A recent example of a fictional description of the human blight caused by bank failures is the best selling novel by Ken Follet, *A Dangerous Fortune*.

11. Indeed, when provided with an opportunity to reduce the probabilities of systemic risk, the regulators do not necessarily do so. For example, primarily at the urging of the regulators themselves, who argued in Congressionals hearings that interbank credit exposures increase the

probability of systemic risk, Section 308 of FDICIA required the regulators to establish restrictions on such exposures. But, instead of imposing meaningful restrictions that would encourage large banks to increase their capital ratios, the regulators backed away and restricted exposures only to undercapitalized institutions.

12. In the United States, lender of last resort assistance should be provided through open market operations rather than through the discount window because the Federal Reserve in the past has flagrantly failed to abide by the central bank maximum of lending only to illiquid but solvent banks. A Congressional study reported that 90 percent of the 418 banks that had received extended credit from the Fed in the 1980s subsequently failed. Either the Fed had insufficient information to distinguish economically solvent from economically insolvent banks or it knowingly preferred to lend to economically, although possibly book value, insolvent banks in the hope that they would recover or to provent systemic risk by directing credit directly to the source of the problem. The latter explanation is also consistent with the strong preference by the Fed for discretionary policy actions (Kaufman, 1991, pp. 95-110).

REFERENCES

Bank for International Settlements, *Annual Report, 1994*, Basel, Switzerland.

Bartholomew, Phillip F. and Gary Whalen, "Fundamentals of Systemic Risk," this volume.

Beston, George J. "Bank Examination," *The Bulletin* (88-90). New York Institute of Finance, May 1973.

Benston George J. and George G. Kaufman, "Is the Banking and Payments System Fragile?" *Journal of Financial Services Research* (forthcoming).

Calomiris, Charles W. and Joseph R. Mason, "Contagion and Bank Failures During the Great Depression: The June 1932 Chicago Banking Panic." Working Paper, National Bureau of Economic Research, November 1994.

Follet, Ken, *A Dangerous Fortune*, New York: Island Books, 1994.

Kaufman, George G., "Bank Contagion: A Review of the Theory and Evidence." *Journal of Financial Services Research*, April 1994, pp. 123-150.

Kaufman, George G., "Lender of Last Resort. A Contemporary Perspective." *Journal of Financial Services Research*, October 1991, pp. 95-110.

Kindleberger, Charles P., *Manias, Panics and Crashes*. New York: Basic Books, 1978.

La Ware, John P., "Bank Failures in a Sound Economy." In *The Basic Elements of Bank Supervision*. Edited by Frederick C. Schadrack and Leon Korobow. New York: Federal Reserve Bank of New York, July 1993, pp. 93-100.

Schwartz, Anna J., "Systemic Risk and the Macroeconomy." this volume.

Syron, Richard F., "The Fed Must Continue to Supervise Banks." *New England Economic Review* (Federal Reserve Bank of Boston), January/Febrary 1994, pp. 3-8.

Wicker, Elmus, "A Reconsideration of the Causes of the Banking Panic of 1930." *Journal of Economic History*, September 1980, pp. 571-583.

PART II

SOURCES AND CONSEQUENCES OF SYSTEMIC RISK

SYSTEMIC RISK:

BANK DEPOSITS AND CREDIT

Robert A. Eisenbeis

I. INTRODUCTION

The term financial crises clearly means different things to different people. Indeed, the literature is filled with terms like panic, financial crisis, runs, systemic crisis, contagion, and so forth. These terms are often used interchangeably and with a remarkable degree of imprecision. To some, a financial crisis is a disruption in the operation of some financial market like the collapse of the stock market or an interruption in the commercial paper market. To others, a financial crisis means a rash of bank or thrift institution failures with the associated disruptions to real estate, other credit markets, or the payments system. To others it means bank runs or panic withdrawals that are transmitted from weaker to stronger institutions—so called systemic risk.[1] Indeed, some researchers have even required that several of these events occur together to qualify as a financial crisis.

Clearly, all three types of financial distress noted above have occurred in the US economy, both together and separately. Often, these events have been associated with a recession or depression.[2] Because of the linkage to real

Research in Financial Services Private and Public Policy, Volume 7, pages 55-86.

ISBN: 1-55938-244-9

economic activity, a there are several general types of questions that need investigation. What is the catalyst for a financial crisis, and what are the mechanisms by which a crisis, however defined, unfolds? What is the direction of causation? That is, does a financial crisis cause declines and disruptions in real economic activity? Or is a crisis caused by, or precipitated by, declines in real economic activity? As a subset of this latter question, even if a crisis is caused by a disruption in the real sector, are there feedback effects from the financial sector which can exacerbate declines in real output?

Review of the literature reveals remarkably little agreement about or systematic investigation of these issues. Furthermore, the debate is heightened by the belief that governmental policies, such as pursuit of inflationary or deflationary policies, may have played a major role in creating a climate within which financial crises are more likely to occur. In the 1800s and early 1990s, adherence to the gold standard, as a matter of public policy, was alleged to be intimately intertwined with implicit or explicit governmental pursuit of deflationary policies. At the same time, it is also the case that there can be an important role for government in dampening financial crises.

The lack of clear understanding of either the specific causes of financial crises or the behavioral mechanisms by which they are carried out, however, has not deterred policy-makers from implementing policies to protect against their occurrence. For example, the need to protect the money supply and payments system have long shaped the structure of banking regulatory policy in the United States. It provided the rationale for imposition of branching and entry restrictions, convenience and advantage requirements, activity restrictions, and federal banking supervision.

Despite an elaborate regulatory structure designed to ensure a sound financial system, the perception is that the U.S. financial system has become increasingly vulnerable to shocks and disruptions. Witness the thrift crisis, the collapse of Penn Central, the New York City funding crisis, the Drexel-Burnham collapse, the demise of the junk bond market, and the failure of Continental Illinois Bank. While none of these events resulted in banking panics, in almost every instance, some form of ad hoc government intervention (usually by the Federal Reserve System) resulted. This intervention was usually rationalized by the need to protect against the threat of a problem in one institution from spreading so as to ensure the smooth functioning of financial markets. Indeed, given that few crisis occurred following such interventions, it becomes difficult to assess ex post whether in fact that intervention was either unnecessary or ineffective.

As the result of the large losses in derivative transactions by Metallgesellschaft, Proctor and Gamble and others, concerns about potential financial system vulnerability to shocks have reached new heights. The popular press and numerous regulatory bodies have identified a potential new threat and possible source of systemic risk. Yet, there are remarkably few examples in the checkered history of policies designed to protect the system against financial crises of clear articulation of the mechanisms and processes by which a financial crisis plays itself out in ways that allow one to develop testable hypotheses to determine the validity of the various concerns about crises.

This paper attempts to highlight the various views concerning financial crises which have historically been at the center of the debate over financial fragility. The task has been narrowed by the assignment to focus on what we know about the possible links between credit and deposits in a financial crisis. The remainder of this paper summarizes the competing interpretations of the underlying behavioral mechanisms linking deposits and credit so as to create systemic risk—where systemic risk is defined to be a transmission of problems at weak institutions to health institutions in ways that threaten the viability of many institutions or the system as a whole.[3] Finally, some questions are raised, given recent changes that have taken place in the financial system, of whether this past debate and the evidence that has been brought to bear on it are especially relevant in our current financial system.

II. HYPOTHESES TO EXPLAIN FINANCIAL FRAGILITY AND BANKING PANICS

Even a casual reading of the literature on financial fragility revels total lack of agreement on even the rudimentary definitions of fragility, the sequence of events constituting a financial crisis, or the causes of these events. Generally, the discussion divides itself into two broad categories. Macro economists typically are concerned with explaining business cycle fluctuations and determining when a recession will degenerate into a depression. They are equally concerned with the financial system's role in this process, since most depressions have been accompanied by serious disruptions in the financial system, including banking failures and panics. Eichengreen and Portes (1991), for example, define a financial crisis as:

> ... a disturbance to financial markets, associated typically with falling asset prices and insolvency among debtors and intermediaries, which ramifies through the financial system, disrupting the market's capacity to allocate capital within the economy.
>
> Our definition implies a distinction between generalized financial crisis on the one hand and bank failures, debt defaults and foreign-exchange market disturbances on the other.

Financial economists have examined the micro behavior of market participants to explain disruptions in financial markets. They have tended to focus on banking panics and runs, and the mechanisms by which depositors are induced to withdraw funds rather than on the subsequent macro consequences for the real economy *per se*.

Cutting across both the micro and macro approaches to analyzing financial stability have been several different themes. The first concerns alternative explanations for the occurrence of a crisis. Proponents of the random shock/ inherent instability hypothesis argue that for various reasons, the financial system is inherently unstable and is vulnerable to random shocks. These shocks, for whatever reason, cause market participants to lose confidence in the system and run to currency like lemmings leaping into the sea. Those who believe that the herd behavior can't solely be explained by animal spirits which randomly induce depositors to run from bank deposits offer more behaviorally oriented explanations and models to explain runs and financial panics. Most prevalent are the models based on information asymmetries between borrowers and lenders. Proponents attempt to show that rational depositors will indeed attempt to run on the banking system at times.

Most of the analysis in the random shock and information asymmetries models focuses on aggregate behavior, and don't admit that there may be differences among depositors and institutions or even more than one institution in the financial system. When the realistic features of market and financial structure are recognized, some researchers have examined the process by which a shock or problem in one part of the country or sector of the economy gets transmitted to other sectors and/or the system as a whole. These transmission models, which represent the second main theme in the literature, tend to be relatively undeveloped, and also have not been the focus of much empirical work. The third area concerns the causal direction of financial crises and their impact on the real economy. Do financial crises cause declines in real economic output, or are they a manifestation of deep problems in the real economy? The final area of analysis examines the role that government policies—both macro and micro—have had on the generation of financial crises and potential lessening of their severity.

The remainder of this section explores these issues in more depth, with particular emphasis on the linkages between deposits and credit availability. Empirically, attempts to test various hypotheses about financial crises and panics have focused on the National Banking Era and the period of the Great Depression. The reason for studying these periods is that no broad-based panics have occurred since. This is in part because of actions followed by the Federal Reserve. A legitimate question exists whether, given the changes in financial structure and markets, the rise of technology, the proliferation of information, and the globalization of markets, this work provides any insights or has relevance to today. These issues will be explored in the next section.

Random Shocks and Inherent Financial Instability

At the macro economic level, the claim that the banking system is inherently unstable is typically identified with models, such as those proposed by Minsky

(1982) and Kindleberger (1978). Minsky argues that a capitalist economy, and especially its banking system, is inherently unstable, and this instability is endogenous to the system. Simply stated, Minsky assumes that during relatively stable times, firms, engage in balanced financing—by which he apparently means that cash flows are sufficient to cover principal and interest payments. However, firms soon begin to reach for profits as an economy begins to grow and enter into the expansion phase of the business cycle, presumably because of a preference for short term gains. Firms start to leverage up and banks, in particular, begin to shorten the maturity structure of their liabilities relative to their assets. The desire to expand returns by funding long term investments with short term borrowing is driven by the desire to take advantage of an upward sloping term structure. This period of leveraging, which Minsky labels a period of speculative finance, is still one of relative stability, in that cash flows from investments are still sufficient to cover principal payments on debts. Finally, this speculation degenerates into a period of Ponzi finance, in which cash flows cover neither principal nor interest payments. Debt funding during this period, requires new debt issues, the proceeds of which are used to cover required interest and principal debt payments. During this period, an exogenous shock will result in a collapse of the financial and real economies. This shock can come from many different sources, and serves as the trigger for a collapse. He is silent on the exact mechanisms by which this happens. He defines instability as "a process in which rapid and accelerating changes in the prices of assets (both financial and capital) take place relative to the prices of current output (Minsky, 1982)."

Schwartz (1994) summarizes this view in a similar, but slightly different way. "Those who regard banks as inherently unstable assume no connection between monetary policy and the price conditions under which economic agents make decisions. Proponents of inherent instability see a recurring historical pattern in which many bankers abandon conservative standards of asset management during business expansions only to be caught short when booms collapse. For them instability resides in economic agents. Benevolent government then comes to the rescue. This is the central thesis offered by Charles P. Kindleberger in his 1978 book, *Manias, Panics, and Crashes: A History of Financial Crises.*"

Minsky does posit certain stylized facts that would be observed, although they are not the outcome from any model that is specified.[4] During an expansion, credit expands at rates which exceed the growth of income or the capital stock. Second, interest rates and asset prices must be increasing at a rapid rate. Third, debit maturities must become shorter, and fourth, some exogenous shock must occur to cause a change in expectations. Finally, governments must fail to intervene in ways to provide a soft landing to any asset revaluations accompanying any changes in expectations.[5]

A different view of the causal relationship is suggested by Bernanke and James (1991). For them, a precipitating force that could lead to a financial collapse is deflation. Deflation adversely affects credit quality as borrower equity cushions are reduced, and finally intermediaries become owners of real assets as companies default. To reliquify their balance sheets, banks are induced to reduce lending and call in loans. Those institutions that are unable to reliquify fail, and by implication, deposits will be destroyed, and the money supply will be reduced. The chief distinction between this scenario and that put forth by Minsky and Kindleberger is that banks are passive by bystanders in the process. They are not required to reach for risk, nor do they have to misprice risk or adjust their balance sheets to take on more interest rate or maturity risk. The model also suggests that crises only occur during and after a deflation (which is an exogenous event) has begun. Implicitly, they argue that deflations are largely the result of misguided public policies, since their empirical investigations are derived from periods when government held to the gold standard, such as in the early 1930s. They are careful to argue, however, that while deflation is a necessary condition for a crisis to occur, it is not sufficient. They highlight several aspects of banking structure which, if present, were also important contributors to increasing the likelihood that financial institutions would experience a crisis including: (a) lack of branch banking; (b) universal banking and the commingling of banking and commerce; (c) funding though short term, foreign deposits; and (d) the relative overall health of the real sector. Thus, banking and financial institution market structure can either mitigate or accentuate the likelihood that a financial crisis will result during a deflationary period.

Unlike the macro economists, the random shocks models of the financial economists, most closely associated with Dianomd and Dybvig (1983), look more deeply at the structure of the deposit contract and the process by which it is redeemed.[6] Because deposits are payable upon demand at par, they offer depositors with nearly costlessly liquidity, provided not all depositors wish to withdraw their funds at the same time. With sequential servicing, depositors, especially if they are geographically disbursed, rationally know that not everyone can withdraw at the same time. If bank loans are inherently not marketable or easily liquefiable, then at the first hint of potential trouble, it becomes less costly for depositors to step to the head of the line, rather than incur costs to determine whether and exactly when deposits will be paid.

In these micro random shock models, no particular attention is paid to the cause of the random shock which causes depositors to line up. Depositors just decide to run, and once this happens, all depositors run. These models also pay no particular attention to the credit side of the balance sheet as a factor in crises, other than the fact that loans are less liquid than deposits, preventing banks from paying all claims for redemption in currency. The Diamond and Dybvig model most closely approximates the situation that prevailed in the early history of the United States. Individual banks issued their own bank notes to the public, promising to redeem these notes at par for specie.[7,8] Since note issues typically were not backed 100 percent by specie, periodic liquidity problems arose whenever note holders became concerned that a bank might not be able to honor its redemption commitment. Runs on individual banks and the system sometimes occurred, and these resulted, albeit infrequently, in cumulative contractions in the money stock.[9] Suspension of convertibility was a common way for early banks to deal with temporary liquidity problems. It often resulted, however, in a decline in purchasing power and shifted the cost of nonconvertibility, at least temporarily, to the creditors (depositors) of the bank, giving all liability holders an important incentive to worry about bank solvency.

Diamond and Dybvig (1983) investigate the suspension of convertibility as one equilibrium solution to the problem of runs, but they do not consider the price level effects or how the costs of suspension of convertibility are distributed, because their model has no currency. A weakness of the Diamond and Dybvig model is that there is only one bank in their system, and hence the runs they are concerned with are runs on the banking system as a whole, involving flights to the currency.[10]

For these early banks, avoidance of runs meant maintenance of public "confidence" that the situation could convert notes into specie in sufficient amounts to avoid the need to suspend convertibility.[11] Indeed, the first forms of public regulation to deal with the problems of suspension of convertibility were the imposition of reserve requirements specifying permissible ratios of notes to specie. Maintenance of public confidence was assured by engaging in minimal maturity intermediation, by maintaining sufficient specie reserves, and having adequate capital and liquidity.[12,13]

The Information Asymmetries Model

Economists have been dissatisfied with the random stock models because they appear generally inconsistent with economic events, and also it is hard to believe that people randomly decide to run without some just cause rooted in economics. Recent modeling efforts have applied concepts of information asymmetries to derive conditions where it may be rational for depositors to engage in runs on banks. Under the information asymmetries model, banks are viewed as being opaque to depositors and thus costly for depositors to monitor. With imperfect and costly information, a type of lemon's model is applied in which depositors have a great deal of difficulty distinguishing between healthy and unhealthy banks.[14] Any shock or news even that might induce depositors to revise their assessments of bank risk—in combination with the sequential servicing constraint—will cause depositors to assume that all banks are more risky than previously believed. Under these circumstances, it costs relatively little for depositors to withdraw funds as compared with the alternative of seeking out and evaluating costly information and/or risk not getting their funds by not withdrawing. Again, the source of the shock is not specified, in that no cause is suggested for a particular failure. But usually it is hypothesized that the shock originated in credit markets, and releases relevant news about bank asset quality. The model's predictions are consistent with the view that shocks are more likely to result from disturbances in the real sector than from the default of a single borrower.

Macro economists have articulated a form of this same asymmetric information hypothesis in attempting to counter the inherent instability arguments. Anna Schwartz (1986) recently summarized in generic form one of the competing hypotheses concerning the macro view of financial crises.[15]

> A widely held belief in the United States and the world financial community is that the default of major debtors—whether companies or municipalities or sovereign countries—could lead to bank failures that would precipitate a financial crisis....
>
> A financial crisis is fuelled by fears that means of payment will be unobtainable at any price and, in a fractional-reserve banking system, leads to a scramble for high-powered money. It is precipitated by actions of the public that suddenly squeeze the reserves of the banking system. In a futile attempt to restore reserves, the banks may call loans, refuse to roll over existing loans, or resort to selling assets....
>
> The essence of a financial crisis is that it is short lived, ending with a slackening of the public's demand for additional currency.

Under this scenario, a banking crisis is precipitated by a major failure of a debtor which induces a sudden shift in the public's demand for currency. This in turn leads banks to scramble for reserve assets by curtail lending and selling assets. By implication, the decline in lending and refusal to roll over existing credits leads to a decline in economic output. The systemic nature of this process is that problems in one or several major creditors, raise questions about the quality of bank assets in general, and induces the public to switch to holding currency. The hypothesis implies that there is a direct linkage between increased demand for high powered money and the availability of credit, and hence the ability to finance and maintain the real economy. The information released is also not assumed to be bank specific. Instead it is information on the quality of banking assets in the aggregate which increases the private sector's relative demand for currency relative to deposits. The channel envisioned results in the calling in of loans and a build up of bank liquidity in response to a shift in the public's desire to hold currency relative to deposits.

Empirically, three elements are necessary for this view to hold. First, there must be a credit related shock which affects the public's desired holdings of currency relative to deposits. Second, this shock must induce a withdrawal of currency by the public. Third, bank credit must contract.

There are several important differences between the various random shock models and information asymmetric information models. First, under the random shock model of Minsky, for example, the leveraging up of balance sheets—both bank and corporate—is across the board, and furthermore, does not require an inflationary environment. Second, the collapse that results is not dependent upon runs nor rushes to liquify balance sheets to meet deposit withdrawals. Third, financial institutions accommodate the leveraging up of balance sheets by not appropriately pricing credit risk. They also take on more interest rate and maturity risk by shortening the maturity structure of liabilities relative to assets. Fourth, no interdependence among either borrowers or lenders is necessary for a collapse to take place. Finally, the direction of causation, in terms of propagators of the crisis, appears to run through the credit channels by eroding depository institution real equity values, and only if institutions fail is the money supply affected.

In the random shock model of Diamond and Dybvig (1983), the crisis does not result from any asset mispricing or from rational economic behavior, but from an exogenous event. Since there is only one bank, runs take the form of flights to currency and not to other healthy banks. The panic is due solely to the existence of the sequential servicing requirement and the fact that bank assets are not perfectly liquefiable.

Like the micro random stock models, the asymmetric information models also do not rest upon systematic *ex ante* asset mispricing or other problems of bank behavior. Changes in expectations and market assessment of bank asset quality, combined with opaqueness of bank balance sheets and sequential servicing make runs a rational customer response.

Empirical Evidence on Financial Fragility and Systemic Risk

When examined carefully, many of these alternative explanations of panics and financial crises appear to overlap, differing only slightly in their details. This can make separating them empirically very difficult. In this section, the empirical evidence is examined to determine which of the models appear to be more consistent with the data.

Random Shock and Financial Fragility Hypothesis

It seems reasonable to ask, given the lack of precision in specifying the models, whether whatever evidence there is, suggests that one or more of the models may be correct. With respect to the macro models, critics of the Minsky financial fragility hypotheses argue that it does not yield testable hypotheses and furthermore, it is inconsistent with the data.[16] Remember that for the "financial fragility hypothesis" to hold there must be a run-up debt burdens at rates exceeding the growth of income or capital stock. Interest rates and asset prices must be increasing at a rapid rate. Debit maturities at depository institutions must become shorter. Some exogenous shock must occur to cause a change in expectations. Finally, governments must fail to intervene in ways to provide a soft landing to any asset revaluation that must accompany any change in expectations.

Unfortunately, data don't readily exist to examine a number of the conditions that Minsky sets forward. However, in Table 1 the periods of economic recessions are listed together with information on when panics took place, and where possible, what possible shocks may have existed. Looking first at the timing of the panics relative to the peaks and troughs of the business cycles, in only one instance was there a panic before the peak of the business cycle. In most cases, the panic occurred anywhere from 3 to 6 months after the peak of the business cycle had been reached. Such long lags would seem to be logically inconsistent with the view that Minsky has put forth. Miskin (1991) devotes considerable attention to the pattern of rates and to risk premia and their relationship to the onslaught of panics. In general, he observes that the exception of the panic of 1873, the spread between rates on high and low quality bonds rose prior to the beginning of the panic, but these spreads generally widened after the onset of the recession rather than before as would be required by the Minsky hypothesis. In general, interest rate movements are inconsistent with the hypothesis. He also notes that with the exception of the panic of 1873, panics were preceded by the beginning of a recession rather than leading recessions, suggesting that declines in output had already begun before the effects were experienced by banks. To the extent this is true, panics were more likely the result, rather than the cause of a recession. This analysis suggests that panic may be predicted, which would be inconsistent with the random shock hypothesis as well.

The Asymmetric Information Hypothesis v. Micro Random Shock Models

Three papers by Gorton (1988), Miskin (1991), and Donaldson (1992) specifically investigate the information asymmetric hypothesis in detail. Gorton models depositor behavior in terms of the currency/deposit ratio looking at the National Banking Era and the post Federal Reserve Era through 1933, and he attempts to answer three questions. First, if panics are random events, then is the model predicting the deposit/currency ratio different during panic periods than in non panic periods? Second, are panics predictable in terms of movements of perceived risk? From these two questions Gorton (1988) suggests the following testable hypothesis:

> movements in variables predicting deposit riskiness cause panics just as such movements would be used to price such risk at all other times. This hypothesis links panics to occurrences of a threshold value of some variable predicting the riskiness of bank deposits.

Table 1. Panic Dates and Causes

NBER Cycle Peak-Trough	*Panic Date*	*% and # of Bank Failures*	*Approximate month interest rates began to rise before the onsought of the recession*	*% change in Currency to Deposits Ratio from previous year's average*	*Potential Exogeneous Shock*[1,2]
Trough July 1857	October 1857		Rates fell until the recession began Spread on bonds did not widen until after the onset of the recession.		With failure of Ohio Life and Trust, reserves were pulled from NY City banks. First bank failures occurred in September. Several railroads went bankrups in September and major runs on NY banks occured in October culminating in Specie suspensions in mid October.
Oct. 1873-Mar. 1879	Sept. 1873	2.8% (56)	Rates rose about 5 percentage points in August which was 5 months before the beginning of the recession Spread on bonds did not rise until the month of the panic, and did not rise prior to that	14.53	Began on Sept. 8 when NY Warehouse and Security Company Failed. These failures were followed by failures and suspensions of Kenyon, Cox & Co., Jay Cooke & Co., and Fish & Hatch. Panic selling on the NY Stock Exchange led to closing of the market for 10 days. The initial failures appeared to be related to debt problems and problems with railroad bonds. Sprague (1910) notes that all the failures were due to criminal mismanagement or to neglect or violation of the National Banking Act, and not to questions about bank solvency.
Mar. 1882-May 1885	June 1884	.9% (19)	There was no obvious pattern to rates preceeding the panic With the exception of a three month period, spreads on bonds declined steadly for two years prior to the panic	8.8	On May 6 Marine National Bank failed, and the Wall Street brokerage firm, Grant and Ward, linked to a bank failed on May 8th was followed by a run on Metropolitan National Bank and suspension of several other banks. However, there was an inflow of foreign capital and clearing house notes were issued which moderated the panic. It appeared the clearing house notes provided a signal to the market of bank solvency.
Mar. 1887-Apr. 1888	No panic	.4% (12)		3.0	

(continued)

Table 1. (Continued)

NBER Cycle Peak-Trough	*Panic Date*	*% and # of Bank Failures*	*Approximate month interest rates began to rise before the onsought of the recession*	*% change in Currency to Deposits Ratio from previous year's average*	*Potential Exogeneous Shock*[1,2]
Jul. 1890- May 1891	Nov. 1890	.4% (14)	Rates did not rise appreciable until after the recession had begun Spread on bonds was essentially flat for year preceeding the panic	9.0	NYSE proices had been falling in Nov. on Nov. 11, Decker, Howell & Co. involving the Bank of North America. On Nov. 12 a stock broker failed, and on Nov. 15, Baring Br failed in London.
Jan. 1983- June. 1894	May 1893	1.9 (74)	Rates rose approximately 2.5 percentage points in the seven months preceeding the recession beginning in Jan. 1892. Spread was essentially flat for more than one year preceeding the recession.	16.0	On Feb. 26th the Philadelphi & Reading RR went into receivership, and on May 4th National Cordage Co. failed and a stock market crash followed. NY banks faired all right but banks in the west and south experienced runs, which was transmitted to NYC as reserves were withdrawn to meet country bank liquidity needs. In August there was a general suspension of specie payments. national banks were reopened after esamination and certification by the Comptroller of the Currency.
Dec. 1895- June 1897	Oct. 1896	1.6 (6)0	Rates rose about 75 basis points in the three months preceeding the peak of the expansion, but rose substantially in the 3 months preceeding the panic, but about 6 months after the recession began. Spread on bonds did not widen until after the beginning of the recession and peaked just prior to the panic.		
June 1899- Dec. 1900	No Panic	.3 (12)		2.78	
Sept. 1902- Aug. 1904	No Panic	.6 (28)		-4.13	

May 1907-June 1908	Oct. 1907	.3 (20)	Rates were flat preceeding the recession and only rose slightly thereafter. Spread on bonds was essentially flat prior to the beginning of the recession	11.45	Stock Market declines in October. During week of Oct. 14, 5 NY members of the NYCH and 3 outside banks required assistance. These banks were used to finance speculation in stocks of copper mining stocks. On Oct. 12 the Knickerbocker Trust Co. (3rd largest in NYC) began to experience clearing problems and it suspended operations on Oct. 22.
Jan. 1910-Jan. 1912	No Panic	.1 (10)		-2.64	
Jan. 1913-Dec. 1914	Aug. 1914	.4 (28)		10.39	This crisis was linked to problems in London and disruptions to payments and discount bills by foreign (European borrowers). London accepting houses stopped the dscounting of foreign bills, and this disrupted the NY banks who were in a net debt position during the summer, as apparently was usual. NY banks were forced to remit gold, draining reserves. Both London and NY Stock Exchanges closed on July 31 and a panic threatened.

Notes: [1]Source Schwartz (1986).
[2]Source for Panic of 1857, 1893-Mishkin idge University Press, 1982).

Source: (Gorton, 1988).

Such variables might be extreme seasonal fluctuations, unexpected failure of a large corporation (usually a financial corporation) or a major recession.

The third question Gorton asks is which predictors of risk stand out as important predictors of panics? He concludes from examining panics that there is strong support for the asymmetric information hypothesis in that he finds no evidence that panics are random events. Furthermore, panics appear to be predictable, *ex ante*. Evidence, also suggests that recession, and not a triggering failure event, is the critical factor in determining whether a panic will occur. That is, "the recession hypothesis best explains what prior information is used by agents in forming conditional expectations. Banks hold claims on firms and when firms begin to fail (a leading indicator of recession), depositors will reassess the riskiness of deposits." Finally, he notes that after the introduction of the Fed, depositor behavior changed. In short, the direction of causation seems to run from the real sector to the financial sector, rather than the other way around.

Donaldson (1992) extends the Gorton analysis using a somewhat different specification of the model and weekly data between 1867 and 1907 to determine whether panics are systematic and predictable events. Unlike Gorton, Donaldson rejects the conclusion that panics are systematic events, and argues that the data are more consistent with the random shock model than the asymmetric information model.[17] However, for the panics of 1914 and 1933 following the creation of the Federal Reserve in 1913 and passage of the Aldrich-Vreeland Act of 1912 (which required expansion of the money supply during crisis periods), he finds that the earlier behavioral patterns had been dampened, suggesting that government involvement to increase liquidity can truncate panic situations. Thus, he concludes that panics are special events. But he also finds evidence that the likelihood of panics occurring increased when seasonal and cyclical factors are favorable.

Miskin (1991) in a somewhat different formulation of the asymmetric information hypothesis, argues that key variables help to capture differences in depositor assessment of bank risk. In particular, during periods of financial distress, high quality firms should be less affected and lenders should have less uncertainty about the risk assessments of such firms than for low quality firms. To the extent that these risks are priced, then an important index of asymmetric information uncertainty should be captured by the spread between the rates on high and low quality bonds, by stock prices (as a measure of net worth and collateral value) and interest rates (as a measure of agency costs and adverse selection). His analysis, like that of Gorton (1988) supports the information asymmetries hypothesis, to the extent that the proxy variables are in fact good proxies. He concludes that most financial crises periods began with an increase in interest rates and a widening of the spread between high and low quality bonds, and a decline in stock prices, rather than with a panic. "Furthermore, a financial panic was frequently immediately preceded by a major failure of a financial firm, which increase uncertainty in the marketplace" (Miskin, 1991). He also asserts that the information hypothesis explains better than the macro theories of financial fragility, the pattern of rate spreads and stock market movements, both before and after a panic, as well as its likely occurrence.

Finally, Park (1991) argues that information asymmetries, which played a role in runs on banks, were overcome by the provision of bank specific information that signaled the market concerning bank solvency. In particular, by analyzing the panics of 1873, 1884, 1893, 1907 and 1933, he concludes that the intervention of clearing houses and governments were effective devices in settling panics, but only when they provided bank specific information on institution solvency.[18] In the panic of 1884, a run was abated following certification of solvency by the Comptroller of the Currency and by subsequent extensions of clearing house certificates to Metropolitan National Bank, which was the bank suffering the greatest withdrawals. The panic of 1893 followed a long period of depression. Banks suffered prolonged periods of withdrawals of gold and uncertainty about U.S. adherence to the gold standard. Gold hording culminated in suspension of convertibility, and repeal of the Sherman Silver Act was promised by the president. The suspension of convertibility was lifted, and the runs stopped. Because no systematic attempt was made to release information on individual banks, public confidence in all banks remained low until the source of uncertainty—lack of confidence in U.S. maintenance of the gold standard—was removed.

In the panic of 1907, the problem began with runs on individual New York banks and trust companies that had been directly or indirectly associated with a failed attempt to corner the market in copper stocks. It was resolved only after intervention by the NYCHA which attested to the solvency of banks experiencing runs and provided financial assistance. Again, release of firm-specific information appeared to resolve the information asymmetries. Unlike other cases, runs did not affect all banks, and indeed, it was reported that some New York Clearing House member banks experienced reverse inflows. Certification by the Comptroller of the Currency of individual bank solvency before their reopening following the widespread suspension during the panic of 1893 is interpreted by Park (1991) as the major information factor which quelled depositor uncertainty. This same policy was followed by the Roosevelt Administration following the declaration of the bank holiday on March 6, 1933.

Transmission Models

Neither the basic random shock models or the information asymmetry models specifically addressed the issue of exactly what the mechanisms are by which panics or financial crises are transmitted through the economy. In fact, there have been no models that admit more than one institution so as to model the differential effects and circumstance under which customers will simply transfer funds from an unhealthy to healthy institution as distinct from the decision to retreat to currency.[19] We do not know what, if any, real impacts such funds transfers will have. Nor do we know when depositors will run on one bank and when they will run on the entire system. Researchers have addressed the transmission mechanism more indirectly by attempting to generalize from the basic models. For example, Calomiris and Gorton (1991), and others, maintain that it is the sequential servicing constraint imposed in the Diamond and Dybvig type models that can induce banks to "run" on other banks. This is especially the case when banks are geographically disbursed, but are permitted to count interbank deposits as legal reserves, as under the National Banking system.[20] Two other regulatory constraints—restrictions on branching and various restrictions on the payment of interest on interbank deposits—have also been regarded as important.

Although creation of the National Banking System resulted in the elimination of state bank notes, state banks remained viable and prospered because demand deposits, and not currency, had become the principal bank financial liability that was traded and used in making transactions.[21] Not all checks cleared at par, yet these liabilities were accepted and were readily used as a means of payment.[22] With the advent of demand deposits as the principal component in the money supply, liquidity concerns changed from converting state bank notes to specie to the ability to meet demands for withdrawals of specie, currency or payments of checks to other banks. This ability was assured when banks maintained sufficient volumes of reserve balances, demand notes, government securities or other marketable assets in their portfolios. For National banks prior to creation of the Federal Reserve in 1913, legal reserves included not only cash-in-vault but also deposits at Reserve City and Central Reserve City banks. This reserve requirement structure proved to be a crucial flaw in the National Banking System and a source of financial instability. In a fractional reserve banking system with pyramiding of reserves, it was easier for a run on an individual bank potentially to have systemic, system wide effects. That is, shocks originating in the countryside could induce country banks to improve their liquidity positions by recalling interbank deposits from Reserve City and Central Reserve City Banks. Hence, panics were also endemic to the structure of the system as a whole, and it becomes clear how a panic or run in a rural region could blossom into a systemic crisis for healthy banks in Reserve City and Central Reserve Cities. Chari (1989) addressed this issue directly in considering a model of spatially separated banks. He argued that the most likely sources of the shock causing this need to withdraw reserve funds were seasonally related shocks due to differences in currency demands which rose significantly during planting and harvest times.

Calomiris and Gorton (1991) specifically attempted to determine whether panics were transmitted from rural areas through the National Banking system, as the analysis suggested, and whether the patterns were more consistent with the random shock model or the information asymmetries models. They identify three important differences between the models that have empirical implications.

First, as just noted, the random shock model suggests that shocks would originate in rural areas due to seasonal demands for currency. In contrast, the information asymmetric model implies that adverse news would be related to asset quality problems and related adverse economic news prior to a panic.

Second, the two theories would seem to predict different patterns of failures during a crisis. The asymmetric information model would suggest that banks whose asset portfolios were closely linked to the specific shock would be more prone to failure where as the random shock model would predict that failures would be linked to areas experiencing the currency withdrawals.

Finally, the models differ in the conditions it would take to resolve a crisis. In the random shock model, the key to resolving a panic is liquefaction of assets, whereas in the information asymmetric information model, the key is the effectiveness of mechanisms initiated to resolve depositor uncertainty concerning bank solvency.

Calomiris and Gorton's exhaustive investigation of the sources of panics between 1873 and 1907 lead them to reject the concision that seasonal money-demand shocks were the cause of banking panics. Rather, the analysis suggests that the origins of panics were bad economic news and bank vulnerability to that news which accounted for panics. Moreover, their inspection of failure patterns show virtually no support for the random shock model, and instead suggest that region specific shocks were important in explaining the incidence of failures. Finally, they conclude that in terms of resolving crisis, the mere availability of currency—which would provide the ability to liquify assets—was not sufficient to stop panics, during the periods studied. Again, this suggests that the information asymmetric model was more consistent with the data than the random shock model.

Smith (1991) provides some specific evidence on the behavior of country banks vis-à-vis their holdings of reserves in the form of cash as compared with reserves held in the form of interbank deposits when panics occurred. He provides some anecdotal and other evidence, derived mostly from Sprague (1968), about the behavior of Reserve City Banks during the crises of 1873, 1893, 1907 and 1930-1933.

The situation leading up to the panic of 1873 suggests that interbank deposits were concentrated in 7 of the New York City banks. These interbank deposits constituted about 45 percent of their sources of funds and were the base upon which their bond holdings and loans were built. These banks were clearly vulnerable to demands for withdrawals for reserves from country banks, and funds were especially tight in the few months leading up to the crisis. When the key events triggering the crisis occurred (See Table 1), a combination of circumstances made the crisis severe. In addition to having virtually no excess reserves, several of the banks were in weak financial condition. As subsequent events would prove, several of the banks were also the victims of fraud and defalcations, which probably accounted in part for their weakened financial condition. Clearly, however, the problems for the institutions went from reserve withdrawals and inability to call in loans rather than from major credit problems in the New York Central Reserve City Banks. Similar problems for the reserve city banks were caused by currency outflows during the panics of 1893 and 1907. Thus, it seems clear reserve outflows, when coupled with no excess currency reserves at the New York City and Chicago Central Reserve City banks, forced contractions in loans and finally resulted in suspensions of payments of currency that was the prime transmission mechanism of panics, once a triggering mechanism occurred. Smith (1991) also concludes that the origins of the problems during the 1930-1933 period were in the rural agricultural areas and were intimately intertwined with the correspondent banking system.

Despite a fairly clear pattern in terms of the transmission mechanism of panics which emanate from large withdrawals of reserve deposits rather than from uncertainties about credit quality in reserve city banks (as the Minsky hypothesis would imply), a number of unsettled questions clearly remain. For example, Tallman (1988) indicates that longer looks at the data do not suggest a clear an unambiguous linkage between either increases in currency demand relative to deposits or to contractions in loans and to the incident of panics. Evidence is presented that loan contractions did occur at several intervals during the period between 1893 and 1907, for example, that exceeded the declines during periods when panics occurred. Similarly, there were periods of time between 1783 and 1930 where bank failures were far in excess of those that were observed during panic periods. Finally, Tallman provides some aggregate data on the growth in loans relative to high powered money and growth of manufacturing output between 1837 and 1914. Two observations seem relevant. First, loans do increase in the years prior to panic periods, but the panics occur after loan growth had fallen significantly. Second, there are numerous periods during the interval where the same patterns in loan and output growth and decline are observed which are also not accompanied by a panic. What we do not know from these aggregate data is if there are any differences in the loan contraction periods in terms of their concentration in particular parts of the country for the panic as compared with non panic episodes.

Causal Direction

The research evidence seems to be fairly consistent that the relationship between financial panics and changes in real economic output runs from the real sector to the financial sector rather than from the financial sector to the real sector. There are no examples in the history of the United States where the economy was running along at high levels of output, when a financial crisis occurred which resulted in a contraction in the real economy. As the discussion of the previous sections suggests, however, when banks were under pressure and forced to call in loans, it seems reasonable to assume that problems in the financial sector, once they become severe, could have feedback effects to the real sector. Indeed, this is just the point that Ben Bernanke (1983) attempts to make. He argues that financial crises can have real effects outside the normal reserve/loan transmission mechanism. This comes about because of the disruptions to the intermediation process. Bank failures disrupt borrower/lender relationships and make the attainment of financing more difficult and costly. But this observation should not obscure the fact that financial crises are better viewed as creatures of recession and economic downturns rather than primary causal agents precipitating economic downturns.

The Role of Government

There is now a substantial body of evidence that governmental actions have played significant roles in both contributing to crises and to mitigating them as well (see Calomiris and Schweikart, 1991). For example, Sprague (1910) notes that lack of access to a reliable lender-of-last resort to provide short term liquidity can result in the escalation of a period of financial tightness into one of crisis. Friedman and Schwartz (1963) have argued, for example, that several actions by the Fed during the Great Depression contributed to both its duration and magnitude. Its failure to liquify the assets of many small non-member institutions (the Fed was not obligated to lend to non-member banks) together with its insistence that it would only lend upon sound collateral clearly contributed to the number of bank failures that occurred. This policy in conjunction with the attempt by the Fed to adhere to the rules of the Gold Standard contributed to a 33 percent decline in the money supply during the period and clearly exacerbated the severity of the recession.

While it has become fashionable to criticize the Fed for its policy failures during the Great Depression, it is also the case that governmental interference impacted financial soundness long before the Fed was created. For example, the monetary base during the National Banking Era was tied, except for a period of suspension, to gold and silver specie monies through the Treasury.[23] When the United States adhered to the gold standard, fluctuations in the gold supply expanded and contracted the monetary base, and directly affected bank lending behavior. The decisions as to how much in the way of international gold flows would be permitted before suspension of conversion would be allowed was a matter of Treasury and governmental policy. Tallman and Moen (1994) note that each panic after 1897 was preceded by "unusual gold flows."

European central banks, and to a lesser extent the U.S. Treasury, often intervened to prevent loss of gold reserves by raising short term interest rates. Governmental policies often exacerbated gold flows, and by implication, induced fluctuations in the monetary base. For example, following passage of the Sherman Silver Purchase Act in 1890, foreigners became concerned that the United States would remain on the standard, and this precipitated gold outflows and contributed to the panic of 1890.[24] They conclude that political uncertainties concerning the U.S. commitment to the gold standard were important influences on gold flows and, hence, the U.S. monetary base. Political conditions outside the United States also affected gold flows. For example, in 1907 the Bank of England responded to problems in the money markets by raising its discount rate to stem potential speculative outflows of gold to the United States. At that time, the London markets were the most important market for discounting of U.S. trade bills. The increase in the discount rate not only disrupted the flow of gold to the United States but also discouraged the discounting of trade bills and caused a liquidity crisis in the United States.

Since the debacle of the Great Depression, U.S. intervention in markets has often been rationalized as providing liquidity to avoid a crisis. Numerous examples exist where emergency liquidity has been provided either directly or indirectly, such as in the Penn Central scare, the Chrysler problem, during the collapse of Drexel-Burnham, and the failure of Continental Illinois Bank, just to name a few. These episodes of Fed intervention have become broader and broader. The Fed has on occasion attempted to not only to provide liquidity to cushing problems in interbank markets but also to providing liquidity to prevent disruptions in other markets as well. Some have argued that this intervention has been, at times, unwarranted given the evidence that panics are not very frequent events and are unlikely to precipitate significant shocks to the real sector.[25]

III. RELEVANCE IN TODAY'S WORLD

It can be argued that inferences about financial crises and systemic risk drawn from study of the banking situation during the National Banking and early 1900s are not particularly meaningful or relevant in today's economic environment. Pyramiding of legal reserves in private banks is no longer a structural feature of the present reserve requirement regime. Markets are no longer isolated, and information availability problems that might have given rise in the past to information asymmetries have been reduced significantly. Communications technology and access to markets have increased the liquidity of all banking assets and given rise to new markets that make the kinds of liquidity crises that occurred in the National Banking Era unlikely today.

Furthermore, the United States has gone off the gold standard, and thus the domestic money supply is not subject to the random fluctuations and shocks that it was under strict adherence to the gold standard rules. Deposit rate ceilings have been phased out and branching restrictions which essentially prevented institutions from achieving geographical diversification are a thing of the past.

Certainly the focus on protecting the money supply from sudden shocks is no longer of prime policy concern for three reasons. First, it is unlikely that significant runs to currency will occur.[26] Runs on individual banks would simply transfer reserves from one institution to another. Second, Federal Reserve policy is likely to be more enlightened in terms of providing emergency liquidity to prevent such runs from disrupting other institutions. Finally, while still accounting for the bulk of payments, checks and currency are no longer the dominant form in terms of dollar volume of transactions in the economy. The concerns and risks have shifted to other sectors of the payments system that never existed during the National Banking Era.

Today, the payments system is larger, has many more components (both private and public), and is subject to different risks than in the past.[27] The check/demand deposit system, which accounts for the bulk of individual payments (except for currency), and the one that the present regulatory structure was primarily designed to protect, is small in terms of the dollar volume of payments. While about 40 billion checks, amounting to about $ 36 trillion, are written on average each year, checks account for only about 12 percent of the nation's payments in terms of value. The rest are made in the form of computerized transfers of reserve balances on the Federal Reserve's Fedwire system and the privately owned CHIPs (Clearing House Interbank Payments System) system, and in the form of Automated Clearing House Transactions. Payments on the former two systems account for about 85 percent of the transactions. Closely related to these systems are the automated transfers of book entry Treasury securities which also take place on Fedwire and which involve substantial volumes of transactions.

Transfers on the Federal Reserve's Fedwire system may be initiated by bank on behalf of customers, but actually involve bank to bank transfers of balances held at Federal Reserve Banks. These transactions are always very large, averaging $2.4 million per transaction. Average daily volume amounts to over 181,000 transactions totaling $ 435 billion. About 90 percent of these transactions are computerized, originating on terminals or through computers at over 7,500 depository institutions, directly connected to Federal Reserve computers.

Parallel to Fedwire is CHIPS (Clearing House Interbank Payments System). CHIPS is owned by the New York Clearing House and connects some 140 institutions, including 11 of the 12 members of the New York Clearing House, other U.S. commercial banks, about 80 branches and agencies of foreign banks, and numerous Edge Act Companies.[28] CHIPS handles both domestic and foreign payments and is the major clearing system for dollar denominated international payments. Over 90 percent of the dollar payments between countries throughout the world take place on CHIPs. The volume of transactions on CHIPS is nearly as large as those on Fedwire. Average daily volume is $ 425 billion for about 114,000 transactions; the average transaction size of more than $ 3.75 million is even larger than on Fedwire. Similar to Fedwire, all CHIPS transfers are on-line, electronic payments initiated by settling banks, sent directly to the CHIPS computer.

The third giant element in the current payments system is the book-entry system for transferring government securities, which also takes place over Fedwire. The electronic transfer of ownership of paperless book entry treasury obligations are initiated by the seller of securities through the seller's bank. Securities are transferred from the seller's bank's account to the account of the buyer's bank, and payment involves a debit of the buyer's bank reserve account and a credit to the seller's bank's reserve account. About 300,000 such transfers took place per day during 1986, amounting to a daily average volume of $ 260 billion. The average transaction size was $ 8.7 million.

In the case of all of these payments systems, they consist of two components. The first is a notification and accounting element in which messages of orders to debit and credit certain accounts are routed electronically to the appropriate institutions. The second is the actual transfer of funds among institutions. For reasons of economy, funds are not transferred with each transaction. Rather the electronic system keeps track of the net position each institution has with the other participants, and only the net differences are "settled" at the end of the day by transferring ownership of reserve balances held at the Federal Reserve.

The structure of these payments systems determine the risks they are subject to, who bears that risk, and how vulnerable the systems are to certain kinds of shocks. For example, in the case of Fedwire, once a payment is initiated and in the system, the receiving bank is guaranteed by the Federal Reserve that it will be delivered funds. That is, failure of the sending institution will not affect the receiving bank. Another convention of the system is that transactions result in immediately available funds for the receiving bank, but settlement by the sending bank with the Federal Reserve is at the end of the business day on a net basis, rather than on a transaction by transaction. In effect, the Federal Reserve interposes itself between the sending and receiving bank to guarantee the transaction. The Federal Reserve absorbs the credit risk (for a zero return) during the day that a sending institution will not be able to settle its net debit position at the end of the day.

Because of its structure, risks on Fedwire are mainly credit risks borne by the Federal Reserve and the participating banks.[29] These credit risks arise because of the way the settlement and clearing of transactions are structured, and it is unlikely that they could lead to systemic failures as the result of a major institution failing to settle its obligations, unless there is a policy failure by the Federal Reserve.

For the sending institution, there is the risk that the customer (which may be a corporate customer on a financial institution with an account at a clearing bank) requesting a payment to be made over Fedwire may not be able to cover the transaction. This risk is presently controlled through the establishment of customer overdraft limits which the clearing banks monitor on a real time basis. The Federal Reserve has significant risk exposure due to the convention of providing immediately available funds to the receiving bank, but not requiring settlement by the sending institution until the end of the business day. This policy encourages sending banks to make payments early, creating large daylight overdrafts to obtain free credit from the Fed. These banks then borrow Fed funds or otherwise cover net debit positions just before the close of business.[30] Daylight overdrafts grew significantly during the 1980s, and in many cases amounted to several times the invested capital of clearing banks. Daylight overdrafts averaged about $ 40 billion per day on the system.

For a long while the Federal Reserve did little to control its exposure to daylight overdrafts. Now, however, two methods of risk control are used: ex post monitoring and the establishment of bilateral ceilings, or caps, to set maximum overdraft exposure for institutions. The Fed established its caps in March of 1986. Unlike the normal situation where a lender does the credit evaluation and establishes limits for lines of credit, the Fed lets the borrower set the limits. For example, in the case of sender net debit caps, the Fed permits the caps (established as multiples of the institution's capital) to be based on a yearly self evaluation by the borrowing institution's board of directors. Factors to be considered in establishing the caps are the institution's ability to control, monitor and evaluate its daylight overdraft exposure, and an evaluation of its credit worthiness. As the result of continued concerns about the volume of daylight overdrafts, the Fed reduced the caps by 25 percent in July 1987. Today, the Twelve Federal Reserve banks have not yet put in place automated capabilities to monitor exposure to daylight overdrafts on a real time basis, except for financially distressed institutions which are monitored on a real time basis.[31]

The Federal Reserve's risks on the book entry securities system are similar those on Fedwire. In particular, if the receiving bank has insufficient funds at the end of the day to cover the securities purchased, the Federal Reserve is in the position of having to extend credit to the bank. One difference between book entry securities transfers and Fedwire payments is that in the former, when the Fed did transfer securities to the receiving bank, it should have a security interest in the treasury securities that had been purchased and transferred. However, perfecting that interest may not be straightforward, since the party for whose account the securities may have been purchased also has an interest in the securities.[32] In addition, since it may not be clear what securities in the bank's own account the bank actually has a perfected security interest in, eligible collateral may not be readily available to use as security for a discount window loan.

Risks in the payments system are presently greatest in the private systems which have net settlement, but do not have finality of payment. Not all payments systems have finality, and some of those that do, do not necessarily have absolute credible finality.[33] Again, a useful example can be taken from CHIPS. Until recently, CHIPS did not provide finality. Failure to settle on the part of a system member, meant that transactions involving the defaulting party would have to be unwound, and in the extreme, potentially all transactions would have to be unwound. Because of the extreme number and volume of transactions which flow through CHIPS everyday, unwinding the failure of a participant to settle could put other institutions in extreme deficit positions which might not easily or quickly be settled. The result would unwittingly transmit a problem in one institution to others in the system resulting in a systemic risk problem. The only resource to affected institutions would be to seek emergency loans or to discount assets with the Federal Reserve. This made the Federal Reserve the backup source of liquidity and lender of last resort to CHIPS, even though it did not run or was not directly involved with CHIPS, except to allow settlement through a reserve account at the Federal Reserve Bank of New York.

Concern for the systemic risks inherent in the structure of CHIPS lead participants to institute payments finality. To provide the necesary resources to attempt to make the promise of finality credible, loss sharing arrangements among members have been instituted in the form of posting of collateral to cover the largest net debit position to which a bank is exposed. On the one hand, the result is to use finality to avoid the need to unwind transactions in the event of a settlement failure, but it also ties the fate of all member institutions to the overall health of the system, and increases member institutions' exposure to catastrophic systemic risk. The effects of this change on member incentives to limit risk or to engage in moral hazard behavior to shift even greater burdens to the Federal Reserve remain to be seen.

Whether CHIPS finality is credible, is open to question. What would happen if losses exceed the value of posted collateral is not clear. It is certainly inconceivable that the member institutions would, in the extreme, all go out of business to meet their commitments. Rather, the more likely scenario is institutions facing default would turn to the Federal Reserve as lender of last resort. It is this problem that makes central banks the lenders of last resort to all payments systems, and raises the issue of whether and to what degree they are subject to moral hazard and adverse selection behavior during times of crisis and fragility.

As markets have become increasingly global, timing differences and differences in clearing and settlement conventions can add temporal and other dimensions to credit risks not always found in domestic markets. This was clearly demonstrated in 1974 when Herstatt bank failed and was closed by German authorities. The bank had entered into agreements to exchange marks for dollars. The Mark leg of the transactions was settled, but the dollar portion was not settled in New York at the time Herstatt was closed, because the deadline on CHIPS for final settlement was about 4:30 PM Eastern Standard time. This left the counter-parties to the foreign exchange transaction thinking that they had more funds than they did. When the dollar transactions failed to settle, large losses were imposed on the U.S. counter-parties. This temporal dimension to credit/systemic risk has come to be known as "Herstatt risk" and can be very large.

A more recent example is provided when BCCI (Bank of Credit and Commerce International) was closed in 1991. The Industrial Bank of Japan had paid 44 billion yen into BCCI's branch in Tokyo for which payment was to be received in New York from BCCI's New York Branch. When BCCI was closed, the dollar portion of the transaction was never completed, and Industrial Bank of Japan became a creditor for $ 30 million. Settlement of foreign exchange transactions originating in the Far East may be delayed in settlement through CHIPS by as much as 14 hours and amount to as much as $ 425 billion dollars.

The losses to counter parties in the Herstatt case were the consequence of the German authorities' timing of the closure of the institution rather than to the realization of estimable default risk. Had the authorities waited until the U.S. dollar markets had settled, then the losses to those expecting dollar transfers would not have occurred.[34] Such exposure is better characterized as settlement uncertainty rather than settlement risk since it is not possible to reliably estimate and cost out the implications of regulatory actions and policies. It also provides another example of how governmental policies can constitute a major source of risk to financial institutions.

Herstatt type risk can also be involved in solely dollar clearing systems. In Asia through its Tokyo branch, the Chase Manhattan Bank operates a dollar clearing and settlement service which offers finality and limited overdrafts and is guaranteed by Chase. Participants are permitted to settle these overdrafts in New York across the Tokyo/New York business day. Furthermore, Tokyo-balances at the end of the day may be transferred to New York, either through the New York offices of Chase or Tokyo banks, or through CHIPS. In this case, problems in this satellite settlement and clearing system quickly have the potential to transmit liquidity and credit risk from Asia to New York, and ultimately to the Federal Reserve, if it affects either CHIPS, Chase or significant New York correspondents. A failure to settle in New York on payments guaranteed in Japan by Chase would create a form of Herstatt risk that would end up having to be resolved in New York. How problems in this system might be handled are uncertain.

Many other significant sources of uncertainty can also be identified in the clearing and settlement process in modern financial markets. For example, when clearing and settlement of financial assets are separated, a given country's rules usually establish the exact point in time that a transaction has been completed. The issues center around transaction finality, the legal criteria for when debts are discharged, and who bears the losses in the event of default. Finality usually occurs when the party selling the asset actually has "good funds," and may or may not correspond to the time that the sender has actually settled. For example, because Fedwire provides finality, acceptance of a payment order "guarantees" the receiver "good funds." Acceptance also discharges the debt, since the sender's reserve account is debited and the receiver's bank's account is credited. The debt is regarded as discharged even though the sender's bank may default on the settlement of its reserve account with the Fed at the end of the day.[35] When the institutions are located in two separate countries, transactions can sometimes be governed by the laws of two separate countries, and if transactions involve clearing houses, the laws where they are located.

The large dollar volumes of transactions approach an average volume of a trillion dollars daily, far exceeding the capital of the banking system or its ability potentially to deal with systemic problems in the payments system. These potential systemic problems, as described, would not appear to be affected significantly by the governmental support structure put in place to protect the check clearing system. Deposit insurance, for example, is essentially irrelevant, since the accounts transferred are not federally insured; moreover, most demand deposit accounts are evolving into zero balance accounts. The systemic problems in the large dollar payments systems relate to possible disruptions to the flows of funds through the payments system and not the stock of funds in the payments system or in clearing institutions.

Maintaining the integrity of payment flows is a substantially more complicated and difficult problem today than protecting the stock of demand deposits for a number of reasons. First, given the large size of the transactions in the system and the size of the system itself, the resources required to support an unwinding of even a short run problem may be very large, and could exceed the capacity of the private participants to self insure themselves. The overnight extension of loans of $ 22.6 billion to the Bank of New York to cover a temporary computer program glitch is an example of the sums that could be involved. Second, because the transactions are electronic and occur instantaneously, monitoring the transactions and the net position of each participant is critical to controlling credit risk exposure by participants and the Federal Reserve who presently is the ultimate creditor in both the private and public systems. Third, many of the risks which the Federal Reserve faces in its payments system activities are derivative risks which flow into the system because bank customers may be initiating transactions for which they suddenly may not be able to pay, which would only become obvious when then clearing banks would be unable to settle. These derivative risks might be domestic or international in their origin, and in the case of foreign risks, are beyond the jurisdiction or control of U.S. authorities. Fourth, because of the international character of CHIPS, a settlement failure of non U.S. banks could cause the collapse of CHIPS, which in the process of unwinding transactions could also affect the domestic payments system as well. In such circumstances, the inability for the ultimate creditor to control or monitor the risks posed by foreign institutions, except by limiting net exposure to the system at anyone time, puts the Federal Reserve in a difficult position as lender of last resort. Fifth, when the international activities of U.S. banks and the links between our domestic payments system and foreign banking organizations are recognized, it becomes difficult to conceive of ensuring domestic financial stability without also ensuring international financial stability. Sixth, many of the present risks that are part of the large dollar payments system are in large part of functions of system structure and design. Putting the system on a real time basis and eliminating net settlement policies, which is becoming feasible with current technology, would eliminate the large overdraft and credit risk problems that are the core of the payments system risks today. Eliminating the credit features of the payments system would make it function similar to futures markets, where the operator of the system has virtually no risk exposure.[36]

Aside from the payments system issues, with their international dimensions, and the speed with which transactions may be accomplished today, there are other reasons to be concerned about potential systemic problems in the financial system. For example, the growth of derivative transactions, while certainly not as great in terms of their credit exposure risks to depository institutions as their notional amounts might suggest, nevertheless result in exposures that introduce new monitoring and measurement problems, which have not been fully explored to date. In particular, the contingent nature of the risks of derivatives and how they might be affected by indirect counterparty exposure have not been fully worked out.

Clearly different types of uncertainties exist with respect to systemic risk exposures today than existed in the past. There are also reasons to believe, however, that the informational asymmetric problems that seemed to be most consistent with the data on panics in the past may also be significantly different and less of a problem today. For example, with more and more assets being securitized, there is less chance that assets will be systematically mispriced or that investors will be as uncertain about the values of assets on bank balance sheets than in the past. Not only are asset markets deeper, but also because of securitization, more scrutiny of assets values take place at arms length. Credit quality of securitized assets are not only assessed by the originators of the assets, but also the rating agencies which now separately verify and evaluate credit risks. Moreover, these same rating agencies also provide independent assessments of various bank liabilities and other financial instruments traded in the market place.

There is also reason to believe that liquidity problems for borrowers may be significantly different than they were for borrowers in the 1800s. The growth of new mortgage lending instruments and particularly, the development of home equity lines of credit, provide ways for borrowers instantaneously to liquify previously illiquid assets during tight times. While this may enable borrowers to maintain payments on outstanding debts and lessen the severity of the credit component of a recession, it also suggests that a new discontinuity may have been introduced into market which might systematically transfer risks to the banking system at a critical trigger point. If borrowers, during times of financial distress, draw down lines on home equity and similar lines of credit, and then are forced into default, the burdens of these defaults will be shifted to the providers of the home equity lines. Should these losses be large, capital might be wiped out with few options available to lenders to avoid the costs of those defaults.

The analysis of this section attempts to refocus some of the conclusions about the importance or the lack thereof of concerns about contagion and systemic risk away from the past and towards attempting to evaluate the implications of new market developments for the safety and soundness of the financial system going forward. Few answers are suggested, but hopefully they may point to new directions of analysis and public policy concern.

IV. SUMMARY AND CONCLUSIONS

This paper has attempted to investigate the various theories of financial panics and crises with particular emphasis on the links between credit and deposits. The survey suggests that panics are not random events, as some of the theories suggest, but neither are they perfectly predictable either. Nevertheless, it does appear that information asymmetries about the ability to liquify deposits were a major contributing factor to banking panics in the past. Moreover, while panics do appear to be associated with recessions and deflationary periods, the direction of causation seems to run from the real sector to the financial sector rather than the other way around. This is not to say that financial crises can't exacerbate economic deadlines, rather it only suggests that they are not primary causal agents of recessions. The analysis also suggests that governmental policies have and can play a major role in affecting whether a not a financial crisis is likely. Intervention policies, can also affect whether the crisis will materialize. Finally, the paper also raises questions about the relevance of analysis of past crises for future risks, given the changes that have taken place in the U.S. and world financial system.

NOTES

1. See Benston and Kaufman (1994) for a review of the evidence on fragility.

2. Eichengreen and Portes would seem to require that declines in real output are necessary for a true financial crisis to have occurred.

3. The term systemic risk is used here to mean that a problem in a weak institution spills over to healthy institutions.

4. It is generally argued that the theory as put forth by Minsky is not a unified theory that yields testable hypotheses. See for example, Sinai (1977), Lintner (1977), Miskin (1991), Schwartz (1986).

5. Minsky argues that the ability to intervene is directly correlated with the size of government; and big government with its revenue capacity, has the resources to support, though fiscal and monetary policies, a longer run up of leverage. Also, through its lender of last resort capabilities, it can soften the landing during an exogenous shock period by supporting a gradual rather than precipitous liquidation of assets. It thereby avoids the corresponding collapse of credit, bank failures and destruction of the money supply.

6. For examples of models in this mode see Diamond and Dybvig (1983). Haubrich and King (1984), Cone (1983), Jacklin (1987), Wallace (1988), Bhattacharya and Gale (1987), Smith (1987), and Chari (1989).

7. In the Diamond and Dybvig (1983) model there is really no nonbank money in circulation. Individuals deposit a real consumption good in the bank in exchange for a deposit or warehouse receipt. This consumption good is close to specie.

8. It was not uncommon for notes issued by out-of-area banks to trade at discounts, which reflected several factors including transportation and transaction costs, lack of information on the issuing bank, and uncertainties about the credit worthiness of the issuing bank. This lack of par clearance in no way affected the ability of state bank notes to function as money.

9. For discussion of the evidence on runs see Kaufman (1988) and Gorton (1987).

10. Given the restrictions in this model, runs almost by definition, must have an adverse affect on the real economy.

11. For a discussion of bank runs see Kaufman (1986) or Bryant (1980).

12. Clearing houses and other banks in the region often provided temporary credit to institutions experiencing liquidity problems (see Kaufman, 1986).

13. Kaufman (1994) also notes that bank capital ratios were substantially higher during this period than they were subsequent to the introduction of deposit insurance.

14. Akerlof (1979).

15. While Anna Schwartz articulates this view, she clearly does not believe it is correct, or that the policies designed to protect against the events are appropriate.

16. See Sinai (1977), Lintner (1977), Miskin (1991), Schwartz (1986).

17. As a robustness test, he also reruns the analysis using monthly data like Gorton does and gets similar results to those found by Gorton. He concludes that monthly data are too spaced out to provide a sharp test of the hypothesis.

18. A more complete test of the Gorton-Miskin-Parke hypothesis about information asymmetries would be provided by examination of fund flows from individual solvent and insolvent institutions. Relying upon aggregate statistic can only be circumstantial, but not conclusive.

19. Smith (1991) does provide a model in which banks are permitted to hold funds at a reserve city bank. Bhattacharya and Gale (1985) provide a model with geographically disbursed depositors

and banks. Again, however, these models only look at the interdependance among banks through the interbank deposit markets.

20. See also the discussions in Haubrich (1990), Bordo (1986), and Williamson (1989). All emphasize the advantages that banks in Canada and other countries which permitted branching had in weathering panics when compared with the United States. Calomiris and Schweikart (1991) have explored in detail for the United States the effects that structure had on failure rates in different states with different branching statutes. They show that branch banks had both lower failure rates and in general paid lower premiums on their notes during the crisis of 1857 than banks in other parts of the country.

21. Strictly speaking, it was the tax imposed on state bank notes imposed in 1864 which ultimately drove state bank notes out of circulation.

22. This experience with both state bank notes and nonpar clearance suggests that par clearance was never a necessity as far as the public was concerned for bank liabilities to serve as money. Rather, the key attributes related to value determination and acceptability—attributes that are becoming increasingly important today for wide range of financial assets and liabilities of other financial intermediaries besides just commercial banks, such as money market mutual funds.

23. Specifically, the monetary base included gold coin, gold certificated backed 100 percent by gold, silver dollars, silver certificates, other small silver coins, U.S. notes, and other Treasury fiat, and national bank notes. See Tallman and Moen (1993).

24. Tallman and Moen (1993) indicate that this uncertainty was greatly reduced with the discovery of large gold supplies in the late 1890s.

25. See Benston and Kaufman (1994).

26. See Kaufman (1988).

27. Portions of this section are based on Eisenbeis (1994).

28. Although it is not a U.S. bank, American Express is a bank abroad, and it does participate in CHIPS.

29. There is always the operations risks that would be associated with technical problems with the system.

30. Customers have recently complained about delays on Fedwire.

31. Ireland (1986).

32. When perfecting a security interest is possible, price risk on the securities remains.

33. Because only central banks can create riskless money assets in unlimited amounts, only central bank lending can provide truly riskless guarantees of finality.

34. If CHIPS had finality, then the losses would have been born by CHIPS (and distributed across the membership according to agreed upon loss sharing arrangements) rather than by the counter parties to the transactions. This did not change the size of the losses, but only who would bear the losses.

35. In effect the Fed interposes itself between the parties of the transaction similar to the way that futures exchanges do.

36. If this were to be done for the payments system, then the question arises whether operating the switching and accounting mechanism is a proper governmental function.

REFERENCES

Akerlof, G. "The Market for Lemons: Qualitative Uncertainty and the Market Mechanism." *Quarterly Journal of Economics* 84(1979): 488-500.

Benston, G.J. and G.G. Kaufman. "Is the Banking and Payments System Fragile." Presented at the Conference on Coping with Financial Fragility: A Global Perspective, Maastricht, The Netherlands, September 7-9, 1994.

Barnanke, B. and H. James. "The Gold Standard, Deflation, and Financial Crisis in the Great Depression: An International Comparison, Pp. 109-173 in *Financial Markets and Financial Crises*, edited by R.G. Hubbard. Chicago: University of Chicago Press, 1991.

Bhattacharya, S. and D. Gale. "Preference Shocks, Liquidity, and Central Bank Policy." In *New Approaches in Monetary Economics*, edited by William Barnett and Kenneth Singleton. New York: Cambridge University Press, 1987.

Bernanke, B.S. "Non-Monetary Effects of the Financial Crisis in the Propagation of the Great Depression, *American Economic Review* 73(June 1983): 14-31.

Bruant, J. "A Model of Reserves, Bank Runs and Deposit Insurance." *Journal of Banking and Finance* 4(1980): 335-344.

Calomiris, C.W. and G. Gorton. "The Origins of Banking Panics: Models, Facts, and Bank Regulation." Pp. 109-173 in *Financial Markets and Financial Crises*, edited by R. Glenn Hubbard Chicago: University of Chicago Press, 1991.

Calomiris, C.W. and L. Schweikart, "The Panic of 1857: Origins, Transmission and Containment." *Journal of Economic History* 51(1991): 34-52.

Chari, V.V. "Banking Without Deposit Insurance or Bank Panics: Lessons from a Model of the U.S. National Banking System." *Quarterly Review*, Federal Reserve Bank of Minneapolis, Summer, 1989.

Cone, K. "Regulation of Depository Institutions." Ph.D. Dissertation, Stanford University, 1983.

Diamond, D. and P. Dybvig, "Bank Runs, Liquidity and Deposit Insurance." *Journal of Political Economy* 91(1983).

Donaldson, R.G. "Sources of Panics: Evidence from Weekly Data" *Journal of Monetary Economics*, 1992.

Eichengreen, B. and R. Portes. "The Anatomy of Financial Crises." In *Financial Markets and Financial Crises*, edited by R. Glenn Hubbard. Chicago: University of Chicago Press, 1991.

Eisenbeis, R.A. "Private Sector Solutions to Payments System Problems." Presented at the Conference on Coping with Financial Fragility: A Global Perspective. Maastricht, The Netherlands, September 7-9, 1994.

Flemming, J.S. "Comment." *Financial Crises: Theory, History, and Policy*." Cambridge, London: Cambridge University Press, 1982.

Friedman, M. and An Schwartz, *A Monetary History of the United States*, 1867-1960. (Princeton, NJ: Princeton University Press, 1963.

Goldsmith, R.W. "Comment." *Financial Crises: Theory, History, and Policy*. Cambridge, London: Cambridge University Press, 1982.

Gorton, G. "Banking Panics and Business Cycles: Data Sources, Data Construction and Further Results." The Wharton School, University of Pennsylvania, Mimeo, 1987.

Gorton, G. "Banking Panics and Business Cycles." *Oxford Economic Papers* 40(1988): 751-81.

Haubrich, J. "Non-Monetary Effects of Financial Crises: Lessons from the Great Depression in Canada." *Journal of Monetary Economics* 25(2), (March 1990): 223-252.

Haubrich, J. and R. King. "Banking and Insurance." NBER Research Working paper No. 1312, 1984.

Jacklin, C. "Demand Deposits, Trading Restrictions and Risk Sharing." In *Contractual Arrangements for Intertemporal Trade*, edited by Edward D. Prescott and Neil Wallace, Minneapolis, MN: University of Minnesota Press, 1987.

Kaufman, G.G., "Bank Runs: Causes, Benefits and Costs." *Cato Journal* (Winter, 1988): 539-587.

Kaufman, G.G. "Bank Contagion: A Review of the Theory and Evidence. *Journal of Financial Services Research* 8(1994): 123-150.

Kindleberger, C.P. *Manias, Panics, and Crashes*: A History of Financial Crisis. New York: Basic Books, 1978.

Lintner, J. "Discussion" In *Financial Crises: Institutions and Markets in a Fragile Environment*, edited by Edward I. Altman and Arnold W. Sametz. New York: John Wiley and Sons, 1977.

Melitz, J. "Comment." *Financial Crises: Theory, History, and Policy.*" Cambridge, London: Cambridge University Press, 1982.

Minsky, H.P. "The Financial-Instability Hypothesis: Capitalist Processes and the Behavior of the Economy." In *Financial Crises: Theory, History and Policy*, edited by Charles P. Kindleberger and Jean-Pierre Laffargue. Cambridge, UK: Cambridge University Press, 1982.

Miskin, F.S. "Asymmetric Information and Financial Crises: A Historical Perspective." Pp. 69-108 in *Financial Markets and Financial Crises*, edited by R. Glenn Hubbard. Chicago: University of Chicago Press, 1991.

Park, S. "Bank Failure Contagion in Historical Perspective." *Journal of Monetary Economics* 28(1991): 271-286.

Sinai, A. "Discussion." In *Financial Crises: Institutions and Markets in a Fragile Environment*, edited by Edward I. Altman and Arnold W. Sametz. New York: John Wiley and Sons, 1977.

Schwartz, A. "Real and Pseudo Financial Crises." Pg. 11-31 in *Financial Crises and the World Banking System*, edited by Forrest Copie and Geoffrey E. Wood. London: Macmillian, 1986.

Smith, D. "Bank Panics, Suspensions, and Geography: Some Notes on the 'Contagion of Fear' in Banking." *Economic Inquiry* XXIX (April, 1991): 230-248.

Sprague, O.M.W. *History of Crises Under the National Banking System* National Monetary Commission, (1910). New York: Augustus M. Kelley, 1968.

Tallman, E.W. and J. Moen. "Liquidity Shocks and Financial Crises During the National Banking Era." Federal Reserve Bank of Atlanta, Mimeo, April 1994.

Wallace, N. "Another Attempt to Explain and Illiquid Banking System: The Diamond and Dibvig Model With Sequential Service Taken Seriously." Federal Reserve Bank of Minneapolis, *Quarterly Review* (Fall 1988): 3-16.

Williamson, S. "Bank Failures, Financial Restrictions, and Aggregate Fluctuations: Canada and the United States, 1870-1913." Federal Reserve Bank of Minneapolis, *Quarterly Review* (Summer 1989): 20-40.

PAYMENT AND SETTLEMENT SYSTEMS: TRENDS AND RISK MANAGEMENT

Claudio Borio

I. HIGHLIGHTS

Payment and settlement systems are to economic activity what roads are to traffic: necessary but typically taken for granted unless they cause an accident or bottlenecks develop. Economic transactions give rise to settlement obligations to be discharged through the transfer of money between the contracting parties. The organization and mechanics of this process attracted no particular attention on the part of policy-makers or market participants until about a decade ago. Since then, the unprecedented surge in financial activity, both within and across national borders, and the emergence of episodes of financial distress have generated considerable interest in payment and settlement systems.

The spectacular growth in the value of transactions has put pressure on existing systems; against a background of heightened competition in the financial industry, it has also radically altered the scale of the liquidity and credit risks involved. A number of episodes of financial strain, such as the stock

Research in Financial Services Private and Public Policy, Volume 7, pages 87-110.

ISBN: 1-55938-244-9

market crash of 1987, have highlighted their potential for propagating and amplifying financial shocks. The management of payment system risks, at both firm and system-wide level, is now high on the agenda of public authorities and private agents. In recent years a broad range of initiatives have been taken with a view to ensuring the efficiency and soundness of the arrangements. As the institutions generally responsible for safeguarding the integrity of the payment system, central banks have played a key role.

It now seems appropriate to take stock of these developments from a longer-term perspective. This chapter first outlines the main changes that have taken place in the structure and workings of payment and settlement systems over the last decade or so. It then turns to the nature of payment system risks and reviews the steps taken to contain them. The main focus is on systemic risk, that is, the risk which arises from the linkages between institutions or markets. Finally, the chapter considers the common ground between the oversight of payment and settlement systems, on the one hand, and the prudential regulation and supervision of banks and securities firms, on the other.

II. THE TRANSFORMATION OF PAYMENT AND SETTLEMENT ARRANGEMENTS

The profound changes that have occurred in the structure and workings of payment and settlement arrangements since the early 1980s have mirrored the transformation of the financial industry more generally. Some of these developments are readily visible to retail customers. Examples include a wider spectrum of instruments available for executing payments; the application of information technology, for instance in the form of automated teller machines; a greater ability to economize on cash balances, such as through credit cards; a better remuneration of transactions deposits; and the introduction of explicit charges on hitherto free services. However, highly visible though they are, these developments have been less significant than those in the "wholesale" segment, which involves large-value transactions between banks, other financial institutions and non-financial companies.

Reflecting a surge in the number and average size of economic transactions, the period under consideration has witnessed an unprecedented increase in the value of payments. Since commercial transactions grow in line with economic activity, it is the expansion in financial activity that has been responsible for this trend. While figures on the overall value of payments are difficult to obtain, the trend is captured by the sharp rise in the ratio of interbank funds transfers to GNP in the Group of Ten countries (Graph 1). The rise has been especially pronounced in Japan, where the ratio jumped from around 20 in 1980 to 120 in 1990, before falling somewhat subsequently. Moreover, historical statistics for Japan confirm the unprecedented nature of the increase: estimates suggest

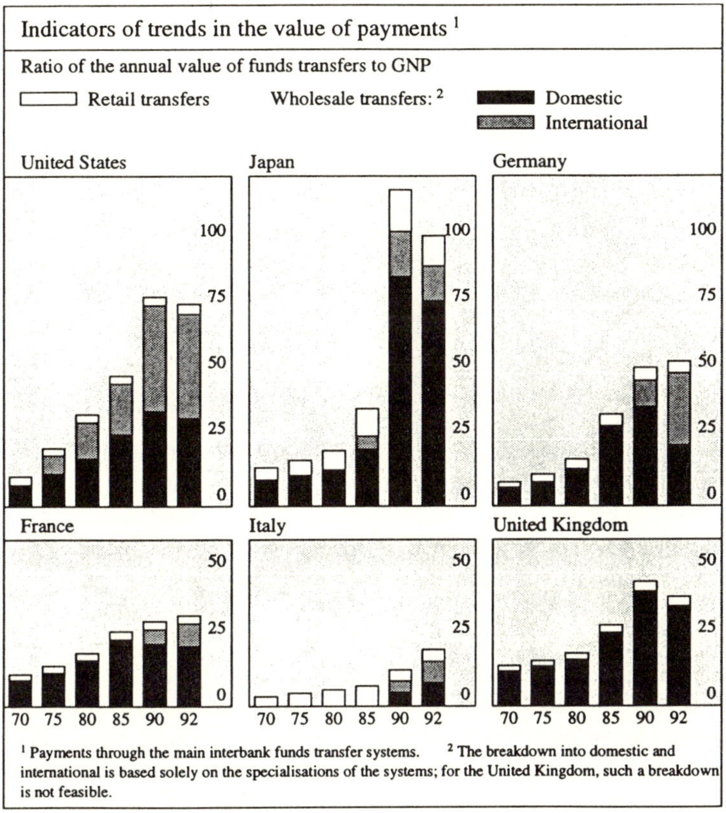

Graph 1. Indicators of trends in the value of payments[1]

that the ratio in the mid-1970s was still of the same order of magnitude as it had been in the early part of the century.

The overall value of payments is now very large in all countries. The figures indicate, for instance, that it takes only about two and a half business days for the interbank funds transfer systems in Japan to generate a turnover equivalent to the country's annual GNP. In the case of the United States and Germany, it takes a little over three and four days respectively. Moreover, albeit to an extent that differs across countries, these numbers underestimate the value of payment flows: they exclude payments that take place between accounts held at the same bank and the rapidly growing funds transfers in respect of securities and derivatives transactions carried out in separate sub-systems.

A large part of the increase in interbank funds transfers relates to domestic money market transactions, reflecting the introduction of new short-term instruments and the greater breadth and depth of existing markets. However, a typically larger share is associated with foreign exchange transactions, which have mushroomed as a result of the dismantling of foreign exchange controls and the internationalization of finance. Independent evidence is provided by the Group of Ten central banks' survey of foreign exchange market activity, according to which daily net turnover was close to US$900 billion in April 1992, almost three times its value in 1986, and around twelve times the combined GDP of OECD countries on an annualized basis. In some countries the settlement of foreign exchange transactions makes up the lion's share of activity in the interbank funds transfer systems. An extreme case is that of Switzerland: the value of the traffic handled falls to as little as 10 percent of its normal level on US bank holidays.

An additional factor behind the rise in the overall value of payments has been the rapid growth of turnover in securities markets, especially government securities (Graph 2). In line with the evidence on foreign exchange transactions, a significant part of this growth has taken place in international markets and has represented cross-border investments. Indeed, the increase in international capital flows, which has attracted so much attention in recent years, pales in comparison with that in the value of the underlying transactions, that is, all sales and purchases by residents and non-residents (Table 1).

Indicators of trends in turnover on securities markets[1]

As a percentage of GNP

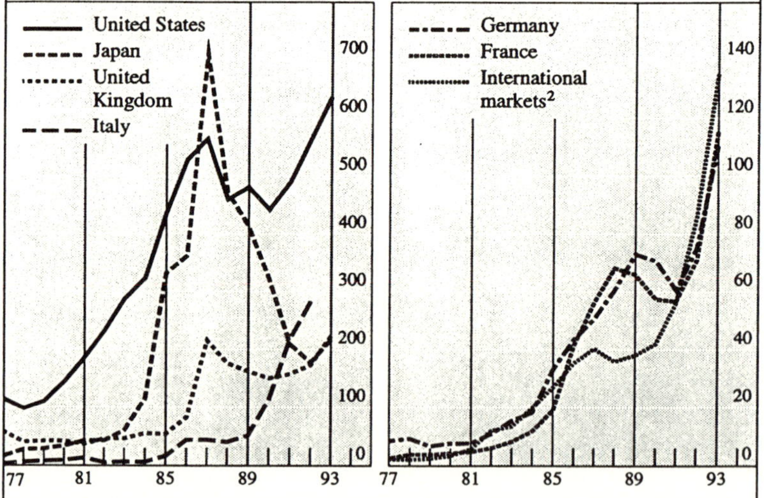

[1] Estimates of the annual value of secondary market transactions in equities and bonds, including in some cases those carried out over the counter. A purchase and corresponding sale are counted as a single transaction. [2] Total transactions settled through Euroclear and Cedel as a percentage of total GNP (in US dollars) in the Group of Ten countries.

Graph 2. Indicators of trends in turnover on securities markets[1]

Table 1. International portfolio capital flows and underlying transactions[1]

Countries		1975	1980	1985	1990	1993
		as a percentage of GDP				
United States	CF	0.9	0.7	2.1	0.9	3.8
	T	4.2	9.3	36.4	92.1	134.9
Japan	CF	0.6	1.6	5.7	2.5	1.5
	T	1.8	7.7	62.5	121.0	78.7
Germany	CF	0.4	0.6	3.8	1.6	8.9
	T	5.1	7.5	33.9	54.9	169.6
France	CF	0.7	0.7	2.2	4.3	5.2
	T	3.3	6.7	29.1	58.7	196.0
Italy	CF	0.1	0.2	0.4	3.5	7.1
	T	0.9	1.1	4.0	26.6	274.6
United Kingdom	CF	0.2	2.0	7.4	4.4	21.7
	T	n.a.	n.a.	366.0	689.0	1,015.8[2]
Canada	CF	0.2	0.7	1.1	0.5	3.1
	T	3.3	9.6	26.7	64.2	152.7

Note: CF capital flows; T underlying transactions.
[1]Capital flows are defined as the absolute value of the sum of gross portfolio inflows and outflows; underlying transactions include all purchases and sales by residents and non-residents.
[2]1991; the series has since been discontinued.

Source: National balance-of-payments data.

Payment and settlement systems have been extensively modified in order to accommodate the sharp rise in the number and average size of funds transfers and the growing complexity of financial activity. In particular, in all countries there has been a tendency towards greater specialization of settlement systems and a shortening of settlement lags.

Greater specialization has taken a variety of forms. Special arrangements have been developed to handle different types of financial transactions, including the clearing and settlement of trading in securities and derivatives. Automated clearing houses now generally process bulk small-value payments related to commercial and retail transactions. In each Group of Ten country there is currently at least one wholesale (large-value) electronic interbank funds transfer system. While some of these systems may also handle the payment leg of small transactions, there architecture has been conceived to deal with large, time-critical and hence mainly financial operations, which account for most of the traffic. An increasing number of these systems have been designed specifically to support the domestic counterpart of foreign exchange and Euro-market dealings. Settlement takes place on the books of the central bank.

Large-value funds transfer systems were established or substantially modified with the introduction of information technology during the 1980s (Table 2). Virtually all of them now provide at least same-day settlement. Most of the systems settle on a multilateral net basis at the end of the day: transfer

Table 2. Salient features of selected large-value interbank funds transfer systems[1]

Countries and systems		*Type*	*Launch date*	*Turnover (1992)*	
				in billions of US dollars	*as a ratio of GDP*
Belgium	(ELLIPS)	RTGS	planned	—	—
Canada	IIPS	Net	1976	8,359	14.7
	(LVTS)	Net	planned	—	—
France	SAGITTAIRE	Net	1984	10,981	8.5
	(TBF)	RTGS	(1994)	—	—
Germany	EIL-ZV	RTGS	1987	8,728	4.9
	EAF (EAF2)	Net	1990/planned	53,237	29.7
Italy	BISS (BISS2)	RTGS	1989 (1995)	80	0.1
	ME	Net	1989	8,480	6.9
	SIPS	Net	1989	9.733	8.0
Japan	BOJ-NET	Net + RTGS	1988	283,462	77.2
	FEYCS	Net	1989	49,029	13.4
Netherlands	FA (FA2)	RTGS	1985 (1995)	7,860	13.9
	BCH-8007	Net	1982	8,055	14.3
Sweden	RIX	RTGS	1986	7,660	31.0
Switzerland	SIC (SIC2)	RTGS	1987 (1994)	23,774	98.6
United Kingdom	CHAPS	Net	1984	36,969	35.2
	(CHAPS)	RTGS	(1995)	—	—
United States	CHIPS	Net	1970	238,255	39.5
	Fedwire	RTGS	1982	199,175	33.0
EU countries					
Private	ECU clearing	Net	1986	15,235	2.2[2]

Notes: [1]Planned systems in brackets.
[2]GDP of the European Union.

orders are accumulated in the course of the settlement cycle and only the net balance of each participant vis-à-vis all other participants is finally transferred. A growing number of them now also offer intraday settlement: in so-called real-time gross settlement systems (RTGSs) funds transfers are settled individually as soon as the corresponding orders are sent. As will be discussed below, the introduction of RTGSs has to a large extent reflected concerns about the risk management characteristics of systems which settle on a multilateral basis only at fixed intervals.

The structural trends described above have gone hand in hand with far-reaching changes in the nature of the risks involved in the settlement process. First, the surge in financial transactions has substantially increased the scale of the credit and liquidity risks faced by participants. The failure by a counterparty to fulfill its delivery or payment obligations can result in sizable losses to the agent on the other side of the trade. Secondly, heightened competition in the financial industry, coupled with the use of more sophisticated cash management techniques by customers, has tended to lead to a higher concentration of credit and liquidity risks among payment intermediaries, mainly banks. For instance, banks have increasingly offered overdrafts as part of their payment services and large customers have routinely come to expect funds to be available within the course of the day regardless of whether interbank settlement has taken place. Thirdly, the rapid growth in cross-border and foreign exchange transactions has meant that a greater proportion of the exposures are across national boundaries. This has highlighted the problems arising from the coexistence of separate domestic settlement systems, each governed by its own rules and legal framework.

III. THE NATURE AND MANAGEMENT OF PAYMENT SYSTEM RISKS

Systemic Risk

The fundamental policy concern in the context of payment and settlement systems is not so much the risks run by individual institutions or confined to particular market segments. Rather, it is systemic risk, namely the risk that the failure of a participant to meet its contractual obligations may in turn cause other participants to default, with the chain reaction leading to broader financial difficulties.

Payment and settlement systems are potentially a key institutional channel for the propagation of systemic crises. The failure of one or more institutions to settle or the fear that they might be unable to do so can trigger and spread a financial disturbance. And disruptions to the payment system can have repercussions throughout the economy: all economic activity is predicated on the ability to settle transactions and confidence that counterparties will do likewise.

Several characteristics of the risks incurred through payment and settlement systems suggest that their potential for exacerbating any particular disturbance is especially high. Since the value of transactions to be settled is so large at any given point in time and there is generally imperfect synchronization between payments and receipts or between the cash and delivery leg of trades, credit and liquidity exposures, albeit short-lived, can be very large in relation to the capital of participants. This is especially true in the case of those providers of payment services, such as banks, whose task is precisely that of absorbing liquidity risks which could otherwise have fallen on their customers. In addition, owing to the pace of financial activity, notably trading, it is extremely difficult for agents to form a view of the indirect exposures they face through the settlement position of their counterparties vis-à-vis others.

Large and unpredictable exposures, together with limited information about their true size and distribution, make up the mixture which could spread and intensify financial shocks. The concern is that, unable to distinguish short-run liquidity problems from underlying solvency difficulties, participants would naturally tend to curtail the availability of funds and withdraw from transactions. This could in turn force distress sales of assets, leading to general price declines and undermining the solvency of institutions. In a worst-case scenario, a vicious circle of induced defaults on settlement obligations, falling prices and insolvencies could ensue. Temporary failures to settle can thus lead to insolvencies as agents act on the limited information available.

That these risks should be taken seriously has been confirmed by the unfolding of events during several episodes of financial distress. As is described below, signs of self-reinforcing spiralling pressures were evident following the failure of Bankhaus Herstatt in 1974: even though typical exposures were much smaller than they are today, the bankruptcy of this medium-sized bank, quite active in foreign exchange trading, caused serious disruptions to CHIPS, the main settlement system for the dollar leg of the trades in the United States. At the time of the stock market crash of 1987, the tendency for money center banks to limit the provision of credit to securities firms threatened to force some of them into default and to exacerbate the crisis. Even in the case of the failure of Drexel Burnham Lambert, a medium-sized non-bank financial firm, it was only through major efforts by the authorities and market participants that systemic problems were contained. Counterparties refused to deal with subsidiaries of the firm despite public assurances regarding their solvency and there was an incipient generalized decline in confidence in counterparties. This pattern of behavior threatened to produce a wider liquidity squeeze and settlement "gridlocks" in a range of markets, including those for government securities, derivatives and foreign exchange.

The foregoing analysis points to several dimensions in which action may be taken to reduce the risks inherent in the settlement process, quite apart from safeguarding the operational integrity of the arrangements in place. One is improvements in the ability of participants to monitor and control their direct exposures to counterparties, possibly complemented by more centralized monitoring facilities. A second is a shortening of settlement lags commensurate with technical possibilities. A third is the reduction of "involuntary" credits arising from asynchronous payments and receipts or from lags between the execution of the delivery and payment legs of trades. A fourth, crucial one is the implementation of arrangements to limit the impact of a failure to settle by one participant on the ability of others to do likewise, commonly achieved through some form of risk-sharing. A fifth is ensuring that participants have the necessary incentives to control the risks they incur; limiting the reliance on central bank support to resolve a settlement failure is especially important in this context. A final dimension is the reduction of legal uncertainties which may impinge on the settlement process, such as those surrounding netting schemes and bankruptcy laws; this is a source of risk in its own right to the extent that it generates doubts about, or incorrect perceptions of, exposures and hence potential losses.

Action along all these lines has been taken in recent years. The complexity of payment and settlement arrangements in modern economies has contributed to a selective approach to risk reduction. Attention has centered on areas of risk concentration and where the potential systemic implications of disruptions have become forcefully apparent. The analysis that follows addresses four such areas: large-value interbank funds transfer systems and the settlement of three different types of transaction, namely securities, foreign exchange and derivatives. In the case of large-value transfer systems, only the payment leg of transactions is considered. Particular attention is paid to the risks incurred by banks as payment intermediaries. In the other three cases, the focus is primarily on the relationship between the delivery and payment legs and hence on the risks incurred by the counterparties.

Large-value Interbank Funds Transfer Systems

Interbank funds transfer systems have traditionally settled on a multilateral net basis at fixed intervals, at present generally at the end of the day. This procedure permits a reduction in settlement flows which is typically of the order of 90 percent or more of the underlying gross transfers, with substantial gains in terms of lower settlement balances and operating costs (Table 3). It does imply, however, that transfer orders are allowed to accumulate over time and that any settlement failure necessarily affects the backlog of instructions. A settlement failure gives rise to a liquidity shortfall for banks participating in the system. Moreover, it entails a direct credit exposure to the extent that banks have already advanced funds to their customers ahead of interbank settlement or that the funds transfers represent one leg of transactions entered into for their own account.

At least until recently, risk management in multilateral net settlement systems has relied almost exclusively on membership criteria and, indirectly, on the prudential regulation and supervision of the individual participants. Banks have generally not monitored their intraday positions and settlement has been open-ended: there has been no inbuilt mechanism designed to ensure that the *original* set of funds transfers could be settled in the event of the inability to settle by one or more of the participants. Most of the systems have allowed transfer orders to be made conditional on successful settlement. Such "unwinding" clauses were originally intended to give individual participants protection. However, they fail to address the basic problem, namely the system-wide liquidity shortfall implied by the settlement failure.

Table 3. Reduction of settlement flows through netting in selected interbank funds transfer systems[1]

Systems	*Gross transactions*	*Net settlement flows*	*Reduction through netting (in %)*
CHIPS	1,040.7	6.9	99
CHAPS[2]	94.8	1.7	98
SAGITTAIRE[3]	236.9	57.4	76
Clearing systems (Italy)[3]	116,212.0	9,645.6	92
Private ECU clearing	47.4	3.0	94
FEYCS	24,200.0	2,600.0	89
EAF	511.1	17.4	97

Notes: [1]1993 daily averages, in billions of local currency units.
[2]October.
[3]1992.

Comparatively informal arrangements of this kind were acceptable in a financial system generating limited interbank settlement traffic among a few institutions which could disregard the risk of unexpected defaults. They are less well-suited to the landscape that has been taking shape in recent years. This is best illustrated by CHIPS, in which the value of intraday multilateral net balances has been rising rapidly since the early 1970s (Graph 3). Simulations carried out in the mid-1980s revealed that the unexpected settlement failure of a major participant could result in close to half of all participants being unable to settle, with as much as one-third of the total value of transfers remaining unsettled. Moreover, it was not possible to predict which institutions would be affected and, because of the knock-on effects, even participants without direct dealings or in a net debit position vis-à-vis the failing institution might be unable to meet their obligations. Admittedly, owing to the large volumes handled in relation to the participants' size, CHIPS is probably an extreme case. Nevertheless, the example makes clear that as intraday exposures rise, so does the reliance of participants on emergency liquidity support from the central bank. In other words, the central bank faces something akin to a contingent liability, difficult to control and of uncertain magnitude.

There are several ways in which risk management can be improved in multilateral net settlement systems. These include a shortening of the settlement lag, the introduction of real-time monitoring facilities and the setting of caps on the bilateral and multilateral net debit positions of participants. The most important safeguard, however, consists in liquidity-pooling and loss-sharing arrangements among participants aimed at ensuring settlement despite the failure of individual institutions. Such mechanisms attempt to decouple illiquidity from insolvency problems, that is, to eliminate the cash-flow shortfall and to allow the losses on the underlying contracts to be dealt with separately

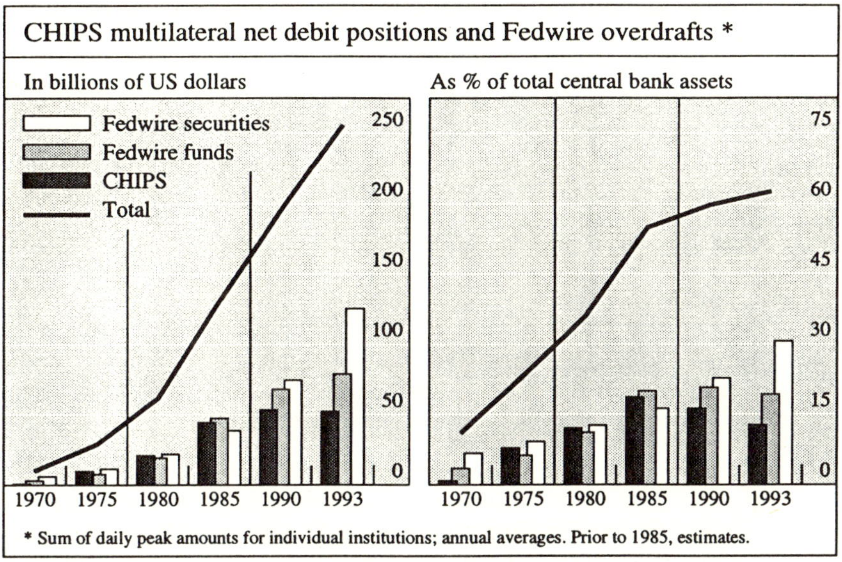

Graph 3. CHIPS multilateral net debit positions and Fedwire overdrafts*

through the courts. The risk management measures adopted or in prospect cover the whole range just outlined. The pace of the initiatives, while uneven across countries, has quickened in recent years (Table 4).

An alternative way of mitigating the problems entailed by delayed settlement is to introduce systems that settle on a real-time gross basis. In this case, funds transfer orders are settled as soon as they have been sent provided that the sending bank has sufficient cover in its account with the central bank. The individual transfers are thus unconditional and irrevocable ("final"); intraday finality is then possible and the uncertainty surrounding unwinding provisions is eliminated. Exposures become more transparent: participants should technically be in a position continuously to monitor their settlement accounts and credit limits, if any. The obvious gains in terms of risk management come at the cost of higher intraday liquid balances and operating outlays for participants.

The residual risks associated with RTGSs depend crucially on the mechanisms in place to deal with the tighter liquidity constraint implied by the arrangements in comparison with multilateral net settlement systems. At one end of the spectrum, if the central bank provides unlimited uncollateralized intraday credit at zero cost, settlement risk is entirely eliminated; the central bank, however, absorbs all the credit risk. This situation, which applied to Fedwire in the United States until 1986, is hardly conducive to prudent risk management on the part of participants. At the other end, if settlement balances

Table 4. Risk control measures in selected interbank net settlement systems

Measures	*US CHIPS*	*UK CHAPS*	*Japan FEYCS*	*Germany EAF/EAF2*	*Canada LVTS*	*ECU clearing*
			year of implementation			
Same-day settlement	1981	1984[1]	1989[1]	1990[1,2]	planned	1988
Real-time monitoring	1970[1]	1984	1989[1]	planned	planned	planned
Bilateral debit caps[3]	1984	1992	1989[1]	planned	planned	—
Multilateral debit caps	1986	1993	—	—	planned	1993
Loss-sharing rule	1990	—[4]	1989[1]	—	planned	1993
Collateral requirement	1990	—	—	planned	planned	—

Note: — = not envisaged.
[1]Year in which the system was launched.
[2]The planned EAF2 procedure envisages bilateral net settlement at the end of twenty-minute cycles and multilateral net settlement of residual balalnces at the end of the day.
[3]Sometimes called net sender or credit limits.
[4]Since 1992 losses have been explicitly related to bilateral exposures.

are inadequate and intraday borrowing facilities and procedures to manage the traffic of funds transfers not well-developed, there is a risk that orders may not be executed. Knock-on effects can lead to a generalized gridlock with potential systemic consequences. Incipient gridlocks were not infrequent in the early days of SIC, the Swiss system, in which the central bank does not provide an intraday overdraft facility: at times banks did not have enough funds to complete their transfer orders and the system risked grinding to a halt. Partly encouraged by an appropriate fee structure, participants have adjusted by spreading transfers more evenly during the day and breaking up large orders.

The fundamental issue underlying the operation of RTGSs is the need to strike a balance between the availability of central bank lending to supply liquidity to the system and the preservation of participants' incentives to prudently manage risks. Among the Group of Ten countries, intraday central bank overdrafts in support of RTGSs are available everywhere except in Switzerland, where a few banks account for the bulk of the interbank transfers, and Japan, where only a very small fraction of transfers are channelled through the gross system and an intraday interbank credit market has emerged. Elsewhere, overdrafts are generally granted at a zero interest rate but are limited by ceilings and/or by eligible collateral. Concern about the comparatively lax terms on which the rapidly increasing volume of daylight credit was granted through Fedwire (Graph 3) has prompted a series of risk reduction measures. The program, launched in 1986, has introduced self-imposed caps and, since April 1994, the pricing of overdrafts.

There is a growing consensus on the benefits that RTGSs can yield in terms of risk management provided that the systems are properly designed. Several RTGSs have been introduced recently and more are planned to begin operating in the near future or are in the process of being upgraded, notably through the introduction of more sophisticated queuing facilities for the regulation of order traffic (Table 2). Moreover, RTGSs have been endorsed in a report by the Ad Hoc Working Group on EC Payment Systems to the Committee of EC central bank Governors, published in 1992. The report addresses the main issues raised in the field of payments by the single market and economic and monetary union. It calls, inter alia, for "minimum common features" for domestic payment systems. A follow-up document published in late 1993 recommends more specifically that "as soon as possible, every member state should have a real-time gross settlement system into which as many large-value payments as possible should be channelled".

The Settlement of Securities Transactions

The two main sources of risk for counterparties in securities transactions are the time-lags between trading and settlement ("settlement lags") and the non-simultaneous execution of the delivery and payment legs of the trades. The settlement lag not only makes the assessment of indirect exposures more difficult, it also exposes counterparties to the risk that the trade may fail to be settled. In that event, one of the two parties would suffer a loss if the price of the security had moved against it ("forward replacement cost risk"). This risk can be especially large at times of turbulence in the markets, when price volatility is high. A shortening of the settlement lag can considerably reduce

Forward replacement cost risk [1] for alternative settlement lags

In percentages

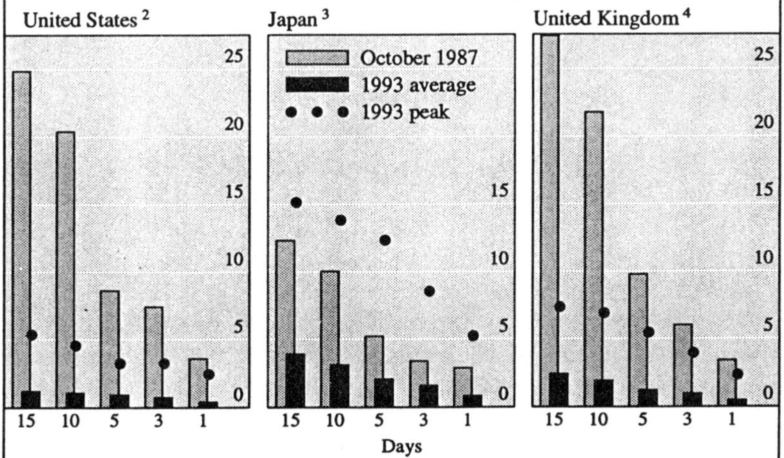

[1] Absolute percentage change in the equity price indices calculated over different rolling horizons. The actual settlement lags for equities in the United States, Japan and the United Kingdom are currently five, three and between six and fifteen days respectively. [2] S & P 500. [3] TOPIX. [4] FT-SE 100.

Graph 4. Forward replacement cost risk[1] for alternative settlement lags this form of risk (Graph 4). In addition, unless the settlement of the two legs of the transaction is simultaneous ("delivery versus payment," or DVP), the party performing its obligation first runs the risk that the counterparty may fail to perform its own obligation. This is by far the more serious concern because the potential loss is equal to the full value of the transaction ("principal risk").

Market participants and public authorities had been aware of the risks involved in the settlement of securities transactions for some while, but the severe settlement problems experienced at the time of the global stock market crash prompted a series of policy initiatives. Several reports have been published since then by domestic and international bodies with a view to improving risk management procedures, including the Group of Thirty (1989), the Fédération Internationale des Bourses de Valeurs (1989), the International Organization of Securities Commissions (1992) and the Committee on Payment and Settlement Systems of the central banks of the Group of Ten (1992). In all of these reports, the shortening of the settlement lag and the introduction of DVP mechanisms are given high priority.

Settlement lags have traditionally been rather long in securities markets, primarily reflecting the need to process, confirm and match trades as well as to transfer the securities and legal title to them. In recent years considerable progress has been made towards reducing such lags. A vital step facilitating this process has been the progressive introduction of central securities depositories (CSDs). This has made it possible to immobilize physical securities or to transform them into pure book entries, thereby avoiding the need for physical transfers. However, the three-day target recommended in the Group of Thirty report, to be achieved by the end of 1992, has proved too ambitious in many cases, especially for equities.

The development of CSDs has also paved the way for the achievement of DVP. As late as the mid-1980s very few systems included DVP mechanisms; the Fedwire book-entry securities system in the United States was one of the exceptions. By now, however, a majority of Group of Ten countries have at least one system which meets this standard. There are a number of ways in which DVP may be attained. One is to settle irrevocably and simultaneously both legs of the transaction on a gross basis, as in the Fedwire securities system or Cedel and Euroclear, the two international CSDs. A more common procedure is to net all the payments of each participant and, possibly, some of its trades. The payment leg is then generally settled via a large-value funds transfer system. An alternative arrangement achieves quasi-DVP through the issuance of a third-party (bank) guarantee for the payment leg of the transaction ("assured payment", as in the Central Gilts Office system (CGO) in the United Kingdom).

As the last example makes clear, the introduction of DVP is not just a matter of technical possibilities; more fundamentally, it may require substantial extensions of credit, typically collateralized by the underlying securities, as well as the active use of securities lending facilities. The need for this form of liquidity is especially acute in the case of cross-border transactions, because of time gaps between the processing cycles of both delivery and payment legs in national systems. Its main suppliers are central banks, participating banks and CSDs. The risks involved in its provision need to be adequately managed if the benefits of DVP are not to be undermined.

Certain risks also arise from the methods of aggregation of transactions and the arrangements for the resolution of settlement failures. Just as in large-value interbank funds transfer systems, a common way of resolving a settlement failure is through partial unwinds of trades. Moreover, the unwind may in principle result from settlement difficulties in the large-value funds transfer systems which channel the payment leg of the transactions, not from defaults on the securities trades as such. An increasingly favored way of limiting these risks is to settle the payment leg through an RTGS, which guarantees irrevocability and finality. A complementary approach is to put in place system guarantees through loss-sharing arrangements, possibly backed by collateral. Very few systems at present have such facilities.

The Settlement of Foreign Exchange Transactions

Most foreign exchange transactions are settled two days after the trade date. Since the exchange rates between the major currencies can easily move by a significant amount in that interval, the potential forward replacement cost is not inconsiderable. However, by far the most important risk again stems from the non-simultaneous settlement of the two legs of the transaction ("cross-currency settlement risk" or "Herstatt risk"). This risk has been a source of greater concern than that associated with the settlement of securities for several reasons: the amounts involved are much larger; the risk necessarily has an international dimension; it is more difficult to manage; and the trades giving rise to it are mainly between banks. According to the April 1992 survey of foreign exchange market activity by the Group of Ten central banks, around 80 percent of total net foreign exchange market turnover can be estimated to be interbank.

A key constraint at the origin of Herstatt risk is that there is no effective overlap between the operating hours of the large-value interbank funds transfer systems of the countries of the three most actively traded currencies, namely the US dollar, the Deutsche Mark and the yen (Graph 5). Since settlement typically takes place in the country of issue of each currency, one of the parties to the trade is exposed to credit risk. In the case of a yen/dollar transaction, for instance, the party delivering the yen would have to wait between five and a half and seventeen hours before receiving the corresponding dollar amount.

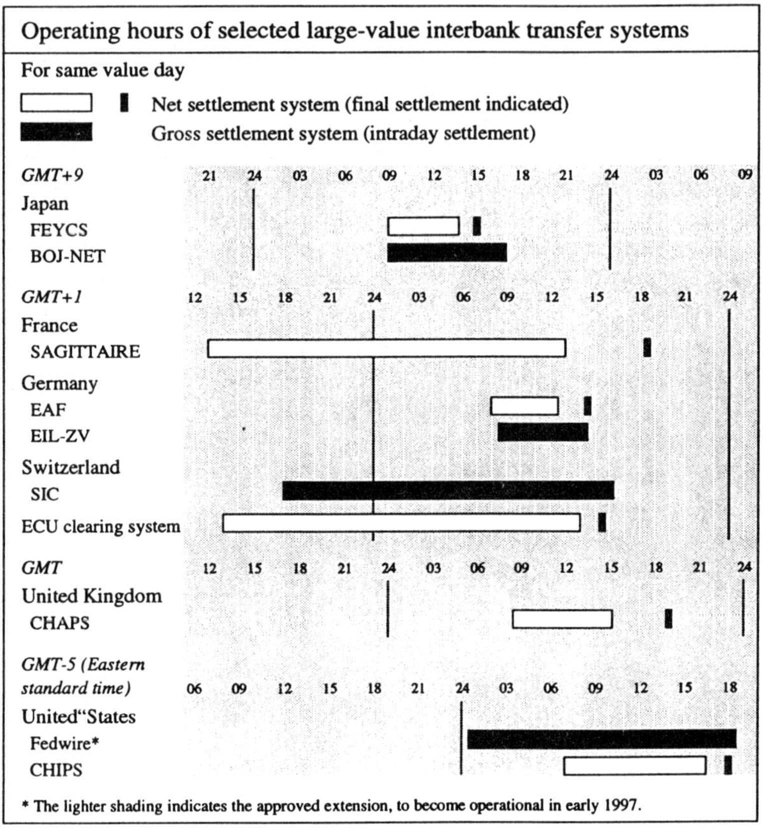

Graph 5. Operating hours of selected large-value interbank transfer systems

Herstatt risk derives its name from the risk vividly illustrated by the failure of Bankhaus Herstatt in 1974. The closure took place after the irrevocable settlement of the Deutsche Mark leg of foreign exchange transactions but before settlement of the dollar leg. This left Herstatt counterparties expecting the dollars facing non-payment and caused major disruption to the operations of CHIPS. General confidence in counterparties was badly shaken. Banks in New York refused to make payments on their own account or for their customers, triggering a chain reaction across the system. It was only with great difficulty that normal operations could be resumed. Estimates indicate that the value of daily gross funds transfers declined from the usual $60 billion to around $36 billion during the three days following the failure.

There are several ways in which the management of Herstatt risk can be improved. First, the safety of the settlement mechanisms of each of the two legs can be enhanced. The Herstatt episode, for instance, was a powerful motivation for the risk control measures subsequently adopted in CHIPS (Table 4). Secondly, the settlement flows between counterparties associated with the original trades can be reduced. Although partly aimed also at limiting traditional credit exposures, several private schemes for the netting of foreign exchange contracts, either recently introduced or planned, also imply a significant reduction in the amounts to be settled (Table 5). Thirdly, payment arrangements outside the country of issue of a currency can be used to limit interbank settlement flows across borders. One such scheme is based on correspondent bank relationships and clears the dollar leg of yen/dollar transactions in the books of a private bank in Tokyo; any related overdrafts granted by the bank are subsequently repaid and settled in New York during the US business day. Finally, full DVP mechanisms can be introduced. This would generally call for the upgrading of central bank services as a complement to private initiatives.

Although cross-border netting and settlement schemes can make a significant contribution to the management of risks, their potential benefits will remain beyond reach if they are poorly designed. In 1990 a report on interbank netting schemes by the central banks of the Group of Ten countries (the "Lamfalussy Report") addressed these issues. The report recommends a set of minimum standards for the operation of cross-border multi-currency netting schemes and sets out the principles for cooperative central bank oversight. It stresses the importance of a well-founded legal basis and well-structured mechanisms for the management of credit and liquidity risk. In particular, the arrangements "should, at a minimum, be capable of ensuring the timely completion of daily settlements in the event of an inability to settle by the participant with the largest

Table 5. Salient features of selected cross-border netting arrangements

Features	*FXNET*	*ISDA master agreement*	*ICSI*	*Multinet*	*ECHO*
Netting	bilateral	bilateral	bilateral	multilateral	multilateral
Contracts	forex	swaps	forex	forex	forex and other
Participants					
Type	banks	all market participants	banks	banks	banks
Number	±40	±200	15	15	15
Location	—	—	Chicago	Chicago/New York	London
Area of operation	global	global	North America/ London	OECD	OECD
Year of introduction	1987	1987	1992	planned	planned

Note: ISDA: International Swaps and Derivatives Association; ICSI: International Clearing Systems Inc.; ECHO: Exchange Clearing House Organization.

single net debit position". The standards have served as the blueprint against which all recent schemes have been assessed; given their compass, they have also been applied to a variety of purely domestic settlement systems.

The central banks of the Group of Ten countries are also studying ways of upgrading their services to support DVP mechanisms. The range of possibilities was described in a report published in September 1993. An important, through limited, step is the introduction of procedures permitting intraday final settlement in the domestic interbank funds transfer systems, most notably through RTGSs. A second step could be the extension of their operating hours so as to narrow or eliminate time zone gaps. In February 1994, for instance, the Federal Reserve announced that it would bring forward the daily opening of Fedwire by six hours as from early 1997 (Graph 5). Taken together, such measures would facilitate the achievement of DVP by private agents. They would not, however, guarantee that participants would make the necessary investments to take advantage of the new opportunities. Securing DVP on central bank accounts requires operational linkages between them. The central banks could conceivably provide such multi-currency settlement services directly, either individually or through a specialized international institution which would settle irrevocably and simultaneously both legs of the cross-currency trades on its books (a "common agent"). These services, however, would represent a major departure from existing arrangements, call for much closer cooperation and raise a host of difficult issues, ranging from the monetary policy implications to the need for agreement on the appropriate balance between public involvement and market discipline.

The Settlement of Derivatives Transactions

The settlement lag in spot transactions arises from technological and operational frictions; by contrast, the relationship between the buyer and the seller of a derivative instrument is by definition longer-lived. Derivative contracts involve commitments to transfer cash or perform exchanges at future dates. Just as in the case of the extension of a loan, credit risk between the two counterparties is inherent in the nature of the transaction. It is the result of frictions only to the extent that the mandated future *spot* exchanges of cash for financial or real assets are themselves subject to settlement lags or are not on a DVP basis.

The expansion of derivatives markets in recent years has been truly remarkable in terms of both turnover and notional amounts outstanding; nevertheless, the impact on settlement flows has been much smaller than those figures might suggest. By design, the settlement techniques for many types of derivatives limit settlement flows. Some transactions, for instance currency futures and interest rate swaps, involve no exchange of principal. In addition, netting mechanisms are extensively used and positions may be closed simply by reversing trades, as in the case of exchange-traded derivatives. For example, the average daily payments made by members to the Chicago-based Options Clearing Corporation in 1993 amounted to $71 million, or only some 0.4 percent of estimated turnover.

This does not mean, however, that settlement risk is unimportant; rather, its management is more difficult to disentangle from procedures aimed at limiting the forward replacement cost risk implied by the contracts. Indeed, the related settlement flows may be highly variable and unpredictable: not only are the exposures longer-lived than those in spot transactions, the market values of some types of derivatives, such as options, are more volatile than those of the underlying instruments. The management of the forward replacement cost risk and the associated settlement risk differs substantially depending on whether the derivatives are traded on exchanges or over the counter.

Risk management for exchange-traded instruments is centralized. A clearing house acts as counterparty to all the trades between its members, which enter into transactions for their own account and on behalf of their customers. The underlying credit exposures are thereby effectively netted on a multilateral basis. In order to protect itself from the risk of default, the clearing house requires the posting of collateral ("margin") and, as in the case of futures, daily settlement of the amounts due ("variation margin"). When price volatility is especially high, intraday margin calls are also possible. The actual settlement of these obligations generally takes place the following day. In many respects, the additional risk management mechanisms resemble those found in some large-value funds transfer systems: limits on members' positions (multilateral caps), the power to assess members (loss-sharing agreements) and backup credit lines (interbank and central bank standing credit facilities).

By contrast, the credit risk in over-the-counter (OTC) markets is managed on a bilateral basis. Participants typically rely on credit limits on their mutual exposures and netting, as in the case of the ISDA master agreement for swaps. They have also made increasing, though still limited, use of collateral requirements, adjustable in relation to the size of the exposures or the creditworthiness of the counterparty. Daily settlement is rare.

A major current policy issue is the desirability and feasibility of extending clearing house arrangements to OTC products. By their very nature, such arrangements tend to concentrate risk on the clearing house, whose soundness underpins the whole market. They also imply greater short-run liquidity pressures because of the daily margining of contracts. Both factors were evident during the 1987 stock market crash in the United States: a liquidity squeeze developed as margin calls and settlements jumped from less than $1 billion to around $4 billion in certain key derivatives markets and the severe financial difficulties of a large clearing member of the Options Clearing Corporation threatened to force the closure of the market. In the wake of that episode a number of large institutions have begun to treat clearing houses like other counterparties, setting exposure limits and diversifying their trades across exchanges. Similarly, several steps have been taken to avoid unnecessary pressures on liquidity, notably through greater reliance on the netting of margins across contracts ("cross-margining"). Nevertheless, as the Lamfalussy Report concludes, provided clearing house arrangements are properly designed they can yield considerable benefits in terms of risk management.

At the same time, a number of practical obstacles stand in the way of their extension to OTC markets. A large proportion of OTC products are highly customized; prices are not observable and there are considerable difficulties in agreeing on valuations. The instruments are often traded across borders, which raises serious legal and regulatory problems. In addition, the introduction of multilateral netting may not be in the individual interest of all participants. The most creditworthy players, which now dominate the market, may find their comparative advantage being undermined. The scheme would only be attractive to them to the extent that it resulted in a compensating increase in activity in a broader, more efficient and liquid market.

Overall Assessment

The foregoing analysis indicates that much has been set in motion in recent years to improve risk management in payment and settlement systems. The risks involved are now better understood and concrete steps have been taken or are planned to contain them. At the same time, progress has been neither easy nor uniform; the agenda for the future is still a full one.

Several purely economic factors have contributed to slowing down progress. The necessary changes are costly. They typically call for heavy investment in new technology, which may in turn undermine the profitability of past investment decisions. They may also involve the posting of considerable amounts of collateral. While the costs are easily quantifiable, the benefits are not. The costs are generally private, the benefits a common good. The distribution of the costs is clear, that of the benefits less so. For example, while the merits of RTGSs have been acknowledged by banks, there has sometimes been resistance to their introduction or active use. Similarly, cost considerations largely explain the limited progress made in the implementation of mechanisms aimed at avoiding unwinds in systems for the settlement of securities and in setting up multilateral netting schemes for cross-border transactions.

A second factor hindering progress is the difficulty of adapting the legal framework to the new market realities. The framework has failed to keep pace with the rapid changes that have taken place in payment and settlement arrangements. As a result, considerable legal uncertainty surrounds the rights and obligations of participants. For example, present laws regarding the ownership, transfer and pledging of securities often date back to the period when securities were held only in physical form. Similarly, in some countries "zero-hour" rules may render void all transactions entered into by the failing institution on the day of bankruptcy, hindering the achievement of intraday final settlement.

It is perhaps not surprising that progress has been slowest in the area of international transactions. It is there that competitive forces are strongest and voluntary cooperation indispensable. It is there, too, that the tension between the borderless nature of finance and essentially national, not necessarily consistent legal frameworks is most apparent. The complex choice-of-law and conflict-of-law questions that beset cross-border netting and settlement schemes are a vivid illustration of these difficulties.

IV. PRUDENTIAL REGULATION AND SUPERVISION

The oversight of payment and settlement systems and the prudential regulation and supervision of banks and securities firms have much in common. In particular, they share a fundamental concern for the solvency of financial institutions and, ultimately, for the stability of the financial system. As already discussed, it is the insolvency of participants, or the threat thereof, that typically lies at the origin of disruptions to payment and settlement arrangements. Conversely, the propagation of distress through these arrangements can lead to multiple insolvencies. Pure liquidity problems, *provided they are correctly and unambiguously identified as such*, represent less of a concern. For example, owing to a technical failure affecting its transfers of securities, in November 1985 a New York bank accumulated a daylight overdraft of almost $30 billion with the central bank and borrowed over $20 billion through the discount window at the end of the day, almost double its balance sheet and over twenty times its capital. The episode highlighted the speed and ease with which credit exposures vis-à-vis the central bank could be incurred under existing arrangements and the potential knock-on effects that would otherwise be involved. It also made clear, however, that when the solvency of an institution is secure problems are manageable.

While the concerns overlap considerably, there are major differences in approach between the two areas of oversight. Prudential regulation and supervision focuses on individual institutions; to an extent that depends on the institutions' business, it tends to give higher priority to the risks outstanding after settlement; it pays limited regard to intraday risks. By contrast, the focus of risk management in payment and settlement systems is the inter-relationship between institutions; particular attention is paid to settlement risks; intraday risks play a dominant role.

That being said, the profound changes in the nature of financial activity over the last decade or so have tended to erode some of these distinctions. Although prudential regulation and supervision has maintained its emphasis on the financial strength of individual institutions, it has come to attach greater weight to some of the risks arising in the process of settling transactions and to the mechanisms partly aimed at reducing them. Mention need only be made here of two examples, both in the context of capital standards: the treatment of unsettled trades and the recognition of contract netting.

Historically, the capital standards for banks have largely ignored the credit risk associated with unsettled trades, just as they have made no allowance for market risk; by contrast, similar requirements for securities firms have given high priority to both forms of risk. As banks have become increasingly active in trading, pressures for a greater harmonization of capital standards have grown. In the EC Capital Adequacy Directive of March 1993, which applies to both credit institutions and securities firms, certain unsettled obligations are explicitly taken into account. The Directive is due to be implemented by January 1996 at the latest.

The issue of the recognition of contract netting in formulating the standards has gained greatly in importance with the spread of the use of netting procedures. In April 1993 the Basle Committee on Banking Supervision issued proposals for amendments to its 1988 Capital Accord, partly in the light of the publication of the Lamfalussy Report. The amendments put forward extend the recognition of bilateral netting schemes to all those deemed to be effective under the relevant laws and in compliance with the minimum standards set forth in that Report. The document also provides an analysis of the considerations that might guide the Committee's future assessment of multilateral schemes.

Given the similarity in the concerns of the oversight of payment and settlement systems, on the one hand, and prudential regulation and supervision, on the other, it is not surprising that in many cases both functions are at least in part performed by the same institution, namely the central bank. Although to different degrees, central banks in all Group of Ten countries play an active role *de jure* or *de facto* in the oversight of the payment system. In a majority of them they are also involved in the supervision of individual banks. Historically, both functions have their origin in the role of the central bank as ultimate supplier of a risk-free settlement medium to the financial system: the provision of liquidity is the last line of defence in the containment of systemic crises.

Regardless of whether the central bank has specific responsibility for prudential regulation and supervision, access to information about the financial soundness of participants in the payment system is crucial for the performance of its oversight function and crisis management. Distinguishing solvency from mere liquidity problems is a difficult task; it becomes practically impossible without the necessary advance knowledge of the financial condition of participants. Lack of information narrows considerably the range of options open to the central bank. These problems have become more acute as a result of the profound changes that have taken place in the nature of financial activity: the rapidly changing size and often greater opaqueness of market and settlement exposures; the greater range of markets and market participants, some of which are further removed than the central bank's "privileged interlocutors" (the banks); and the increased speed with which disturbances can be transmitted across market segments, institutions and national borders.

The information needs of the central bank are an important dimension of the problem of the organization of the lines of defence to deal with systemic risk. This issue is in the forefront of current policy discussions in the United States, where there are plans to reallocate the responsibility for banking supervision, at present divided among several bodies, including the central bank. It is also topical in Europe. The creation of the single market for financial services in the European Union implies a shift from host to home-country supervision and the possibility of cross-border ("remote") direct participation in domestic large-value funds transfer systems; the existence of appropriate channels for the exchange of information between national authorities becomes all the more essential. Looking ahead, the precise contours of central bank involvement in the oversight of payment systems and prudential regulation and supervision in the future European monetary union are still to be decided.

As the nature of financial activity continues to evolve, the years ahead are likely to see an intensification of the cooperative efforts between the authorities in charge of prudential supervision and those responsible for the oversight of payment and settlement systems. The progressive expansion in the sphere of markets and hence in trading can be expected to further heighten the risks involved in the execution of financial transactions, whether these are incurred by the counterparties to the trades or by the intermediaries facilitating their completion. The challenge is to put in place a series of lines of defence capable of containing systemic risk without impairing, and indeed if possible improving, the efficiency of the arrangements. In the present financial landscape meeting that challenge will inevitably call for chose international cooperation.

ACKNOWLEDGMENT

Reprinting from Chapter 8 of the *1994 Annual Report* of the Bank for International Settlements. The chapter was drafted by Claudio Borio with assistance from Paul Van den Bergh. Claudio Borio presented the paper at the conference whose proceedings are published in this volume.

REFERENCES

Bank for International Settlements: *Report on netting schemes*, prepared by the Group of Experts on Payment Systems of the central banks of the G-10 countries, Basle, February 1989

Bank for International Settlements: *Payment systems in eleven developed countries*, prepared by the Group of Experts on Payment Systems of the central banks of the G-10 countries, Basle, April 1989.

Bank for International Settlements: *Survey of foreign exchange market activity*, Basle, February 1990.

Bank for International Settlements: *Large-value funds transfer systems in the G-10 countries*, prepared by the Group of Experts on Payment Systems of the central banks of the G-10 countries, Basle, May 1990.

Bank for International Settlements: *Report of the Committee on Interbank Netting Schemes of the central banks of the G-10 countries*, Basle, November 1990.

Bank for International Settlements: *Delivery versus payment in securities settlement systems,* report prepared by the Committee on Payment and Settlement Systems of the central banks of the G-10 countries, Basle, September 1992.

Bank for International Settlements: *Recent developments in international interbank relations*, prepared by a Working Group established by the central banks of the G-10 countries, Basle, October 1992.

Bank for International Settlements: *Central bank survey of foreign exchange market activity in April 1992*, Basle, March 1993.

Bank for International Settlements: *Central bank payment and settlement services with respect to cross-border and multi-currency transactions,* report prepared by the Committe on Payment and Settlement Systems of the central banks of the G-10 countries, Basle, September 1993.

Bank for International Settlements: *Payment systems in the Group of Ten countries*, prepared by the Committee on Payment and Settlement Systems of the central banks of the G-10 countries, Basle, December 1993.

Bank for International Settlements: *64th Annual Report 1993/1994*, Basle, June 1994.

Bank for International Settlements: *Cross-border Securities Settlements*, report prepared by the Committee on Payment and Settlement Systems of the central banks of the Group of Ten countries, Basle, March 1995.

Borio, C.E.V. and P. Van den Bergh: *The nature and management of payment system risks: an international perspective*, BIS Economic Paper No. 36, Basle, February 1993.

Committe of Governors of the Central Banks of the Member States of the European Economic Community: *Issues of common concern to EC central banks in the field of payment systems*, prepared by the Ad Hoc Working Group on EC Payment Systems, Basle, 1992.

Committee of Governors of the Central Banks of the Member States of the European Economic Community: *Minimum common features for domestic payment systems*, prepared by the Ad Hoc Working Group on EC Payment Systems, Basle, November 1993.

DERIVATIVES AND SYSTEMIC RISK:

ISSUES, VIEWS, AND ANALYSIS

Robert J. Mackay

There is far less risk today than in the past of something happening. All major financial intermediaries have dramatically increased their internal-control and risk-management systems.

E. Gerald Corrigan, Former President
The Federal Reserve Bank of New York, (May 10, 1994)

The dramatic growth of activity in over-the-counter (OTC) derivatives transactions in the last decade has led some observers—legislators, regulators, members of the financial press, and even some industry participants—to question whether this now global activity might pose a systemic risk to the financial markets. These concerns have been expressed despite the now widely recognized benefits of derivatives to end users. The initial response to these concerns was the commissioning of numerous studies of derivatives activities. In the past two years, over ten major studies of derivatives activities have been completed, including two private sector studies by the Group of Thirty, numerous public sector studies by banking, securities, and commodities regulators around the world, and the General Accounting Office. These studies

Research in Financial Services Private and Public Policy, Volume 7, pages 111-169.

ISBN: 1-55938-244-9

have not been purely academic exercises. They have been supplemented by concrete actions from both the private and public sectors aimed at specific improvements in risk management practices for derivatives.

Nevertheless, calls for legislation continue to come from several quarters, designed in each case according to the authors to address the alleged potential for derivatives activities to increase systemic risk. The proffered legislative solutions range from statutory endorsements of existing regulatory actions at one extreme, to tinkering reforms in the middle, on to radical expansions of the scope and scale of federal regulation at the other extreme. Despite confident assertions from some quarters that the financial system is at risk and that a legislative overhaul of financial markets regulation is essential, a wide divergence of views on the basic public policy issues surrounding derivatives remains. This is especially so with respect to the question of whether or not derivatives add to systemic risk. While two years of intensive study have deepened our understanding of the benefits and risks of derivatives and improved risk management practices and supervision, they have not resolved this important public policy issue.

The purpose of this paper, therefore, is to provide a balanced assessment of the risks of derivatives activities, especially the potential for derivatives to increase systemic risk. To do so, systemic risk must first be defined. With this definition in hand, the risks of derivatives to dealers and end-users are identified, assessed, and, wherever possible, quantified. The various channels through which derivatives activities might possibly increase systemic risk are then described in terms similar to those used by concerned observers so as to avoid fighting strawmen. The range of possible risk factors underlying systemic concerns are identified and analyzed in light of the new information base provided by the recent studies of derivatives. As difficult as it may be to achieve, the ultimate goal is a balanced assessment of how much the systemic anxieties surrounding derivatives activities are warranted. Towards this end, this paper presents a sampling of the range of views on the key issues at stake in this important debate and provides an extensive bibliography of the relevant literature.

I. HOW MIGHT DERIVATIVES POSE SYSTEMIC RISK?

Defining Systemic Risk

Some legislators, regulators, members of the financial press, and others have expressed concern that derivatives activities might lead to an increase in the level of "systemic risk" in financial markets. While widely used, the phrase "systemic risk" is seldom defined. This raises the question then of how derivatives might pose a risk to the financial system as a whole? In answering this question, an engineering analogy might be helpful. Engineers operating a system, such as a power grid, might speak of a particular activity as posing a risk to the system—systemic risk—if that activity could either:

- Cause a failure in a major component of the system exceeding the planned backup supports for that component, or cause a failure in a major component that spills over to other components, leading to a serious malfunction or, in the extreme, to a complete breakdown of the system; or,
- Impair the efficient working of the system, causing system performance to be degraded on an on-going basis so that it falls significantly below potential.

While the metaphor of the financial system as a power grid is not completely apt—there is, of course, no engineer pushing buttons and pulling levers to control the workings of an economy that follows mechanical laws of operation—it nevertheless provides some useful insight into the issue of systemic risk. It suggests, for example, that an activity—such as the use of derivatives—can pose a systemic risk if that activity:

- Poses a risk of directly causing or exacerbating a disruption at a major firm, in a significant market segment, or an entire market that could cause widespread and substantial difficulties at other firms, in other market segments, or—in the limit—in the financial system as a whole; or,
- Poses a risk of significantly impairing, on an on-going basis, the efficient working of the financial system—degrading the system's ability to efficiently allocate credit, distribute risks, settle payments, and discover prices.

This concept of systemic risk appears to be consistent with that articulated in the more thoughtful discussions of the issue, such as the Promisel Report.

From this perspective, the potential for derivatives activity to increase systemic risk can be assessed in terms of the following four questions:

- Does derivatives activity increase the likelihood of default of a major derivatives dealer or end user?
- Does derivatives activity increase the likelihood of contagion of default—the likelihood that a major default will spill over and cause defaults at other institutions or cause disruptions to broader markets or the financial system as a whole?
- Does derivatives activity cause or exacerbate major market moves, threatening to override the natural abilities of the economy to withstand such shocks?

- Does derivatives activity have a negative impact on the on-going workings of underlying cash and related derivatives markets, degrading their ability to efficiently perform fundamental economic functions?

General concerns and anxieties about derivatives—both those expressed by casual observers of derivatives activities as well as more informed participants—are reframed below in terms of these four questions. The purpose is to identify the potential sources of systemic risk resulting from derivatives activities.

Likelihood of a Major Default

The growth, size, and complexity of derivatives operations at major dealers and end users have led some observers to question the ability of senior management and boards of directors to understand and control the risks posed by derivatives to the safety and soundness of their institutions. Risk management failures, it is feared, could result in financial distress due to inappropriate or excessively risky positions being taken on, without the understanding or control of management. The result, of course, would be a risk management failure leading to a derivatives induced default at a major dealer or end user.

Concern has also been expressed that the rapid growth of derivatives activities has outpaced the technological capabilities of existing internal control and audit systems at various institutions so that even with an informed senior management, these institutions cannot adequately identify, measure, and manage the credit, market, and liquidity risks in their complex derivatives portfolios. If true, this could increase the likelihood of a major default as a result of an internal control failure leading to poor credit decisions, excessive market risk taking, or inadequate operational controls.

The extremely large size and continued rapid growth of derivatives activity has led some observers to worry that further growth is unsustainable without bringing in less informed and less sophisticated participants (e.g., smaller municipalities, savings and loan associations, and corporations with inadequate treasury operations) who supposedly are more likely to misuse derivatives, whether knowingly or not. The size and growth of derivatives activities has also raised concerns that dealers increasingly will be doing business with lower credit quality firms, reducing the average credit quality of dealers' derivatives portfolios. While it may take time for this greater risk to appear in actual default rates (as, some would argue, it did in the junk bond market), the fear is that with further seasoning and maturing of derivatives portfolios these losses will show up and, in the process, the natural result will be the default of a major dealer.

Some regulators, in particular, have expressed concern about what they perceive as a growing lack of transparency of derivatives' risk. They fear that counterparty risk has become more difficult to assess—due to the growth and complexity of derivatives and the intricate linkages between institutions created by derivatives—leading to a situation where, when financial distress occurs in a dealer with a large derivatives portfolio, other firms are more likely to "step back" from their dealings with that firm. The result could be severe liquidity and cash flow problems, sufficient even to turn an illiquidity problem into an insolvency problem.

Likelihood of Contagion of Default

In addition to concerns about derivatives activity leading to increases in the likelihood of a major default, concern has also been expressed that derivatives activities may increase the likelihood of contagion in the event of a major default, exacerbating the initial distress. The fear appears to be that a disruption or default at one firm—whether derivatives induced or not—is now more likely as a result of derivatives created linkages to spread and infect other firms, leading to wider disruptions and further defaults with systemic implications. More specifically, some regulators and others have expressed the specific concern that the concentration of derivatives exposures, with large exposures supposedly accumulated within a small set of key institutions, could lead to a situation where the failure of a major dealer (through its own risk management failure or the failure of a counterparty) could easily infect other dealers leading to further failures of major dealers and end users.

A related concern, expressed by numerous banking regulators, is that derivatives have created a complex web of linkages between bank and non-bank dealers, increasing the number of potential trouble spots where financial problems can start and then spread into the banking system. To be specific, the fear is that a default of an "unregulated" derivatives affiliate of a securities firm or insurance company, subject to less stringent oversight and supervision than banks, could spill over into the banking system as a result of the linkages created by derivatives, increasing risk to the settlement system and exposing taxpayers to the risk of bailing out federally insured institutions.

While it is widely recognized that derivatives have increased the linkages between global money, capital, and currency markets with obvious benefits in terms of increased efficiency of financial flows and greater diversification of risks, some observers have worried that a volatility or liquidity problem in one market might now more quickly spread into these more closely linked markets. Without being buffered or dampened, these initial financial shocks, it is believed, could cause further financial disruptions in these related markets. Shocks to one market, which in the past might have been isolated to that market, it is feared will now be spread rapidly by derivatives activities to economically linked markets before policymakers have a chance to respond.

Some regulators, with responsibility for overseeing the payments systems, also have expressed concern that the sheer size, complexity, and increased linkages between OTC derivatives activities and other related markets, especially futures markets and underlying cash markets, may have increased the potential for and likely severity of settlement and payments problems during periods of volatile and illiquid markets.

Exacerbating Major Market Moves

While derivatives activities may not be the original source of a market disruption, some regulators (especially those who lived through the market crash of October 1987) have worried that derivatives activities may exacerbate major market moves, leading to more extreme swings in market volatility. These swings could ultimately threaten the stability of the financial system.

The particular concern is dynamic hedging related to the growth of activity in option-based derivatives. These positions may be difficult to hedge directly with offsetting option positions so that dynamic hedging, which relies heavily on the liquidity of underlying cash markets and related futures markets to adjust hedges as the market moves, may have increased proportionately. Dynamic hedging of these options positions requires positive feedback trading—buying into rising markets and selling into falling markets. Some regulators (most notably current and former securities regulators) fear that this type of trading exacerbates market moves, causing excessive volatility by compounding liquidity demands under already stressed market conditions.

A related concern is that the increased complexity of derivatives portfolios makes it more difficult for dealers to hedge adequately against market risk. The concern is that many dealers may be simultaneously exposed to positions that are difficult to hedge in the event of rapid and large changes (or gaps) in prices, sharp jumps in volatility, and serious deteriorations in basis relationships and correlations. The result could be an increase in systemic risk if several major dealers are simultaneously faced with large losses from these inadequate hedges. This concern is further magnified into a fear that these difficulties could in turn reduce market liquidity, exacerbating the initial market disruption.

Negative Impact on Underlying Markets

Concern has been expressed that the growth in OTC derivatives has negative consequences for underlying cash and related markets—increasing the volatility and reducing the liquidity and pricing precision of these markets on an on-going, rather than just episodic, basis. The concern is with an on-going degradation in the efficiency with which certain related markets perform their designated economic functions.

Some observers, including some securities and futures exchange officials, have expressed concern that OTC derivatives activities divert order flow from centralized and transparent exchange markets, reducing the flow of information to these markets, thereby impairing price discovery and market liquidity. The expressed fear, of course, is that market fragmentation results in less informative and more volatile prices for key exchange-traded instruments.

A few observers have even gone so far as to express concern that the concentration of derivatives dealing in a small number of firms might result in these institutions acting individually or collectively to set the prices of derivatives above competitive levels. If true, such an exercise of market power would harm end users and restrict the use of derivatives, impairing market efficiency on an on-going basis.

Identifying Possible Sources of Systemic Risks

In light of the above definition of systemic risk and summary of various concerns about derivatives activities, certain key risk factors can be identified that could possibly serve as sources of systemic risk. Some of the possible risk factors are the basic, firm-level risks that every derivatives dealer or end user faces.

- Credit Risk
- Settlement and Payments Risk
- Market Risk
- Liquidity Risk
- Operational Risk
- Legal Risk

These risks are widely recognized and are not unique to derivatives. Their likely magnitudes, both on an absolute scale and relative to the risks of other more traditional financial activities, must be assessed, however, in order to determine if derivatives activities somehow raise these traditional risks to systemic proportions.

Other potential risk factors that could possibly increase the risks of derivatives, raising them to the systemic level, can be identified from the litany of concerns summarized above. These concerns suggest that the following factors may play a contributing and, in some cases, interactive role in determining the extent of systemic risk resulting from derivatives activities:

- Size and Growth
- Concentration

- Complexity
- Transparency
- Management Understanding
- Unregulated Entities
- New Entrants
- Market Linkages
- Dynamic Hedging
- Regulatory Capacity

While certain of these risk factors can be dismissed rather quickly as serious sources of systemic risk, they are all nevertheless briefly described and their likely contribution to systemic risk, if any, assessed in the following sections.

II. WHAT ARE THE FUNDAMENTAL RISKS OF DERIVATIVES?

The fundamental risks facing dealers and end users of derivatives are neither new nor unique. They are the same types of risks—credit risk, settlement risk, market risk, liquidity risk, operational risk, and legal risk—that banks, securities firms, and many end users have faced in their traditional businesses. On this point there is widespread agreement. Each of these fundamental risks is assessed below. The risk is defined and systemic concerns regarding these risks are summarized. These risks are analyzed and where possible quantified, so as to put them into perspective relative to the risks of other more traditional financial activities. Only in this manner can their systemic relevance be assessed.

Credit Risk

Definition of Credit Risk

Credit risk is the risk that a loss will be incurred because a counterparty fails to make the payments due. In the event of the default, the loss is the cost of replacing the contract with a new counterparty. Counterparty default in a derivatives transaction, such as a forward or swap, does not necessarily result in a loss. For a loss to occur, two conditions must be met simultaneously—the counterparty must default and the replacement cost of the contract must be positive. This contrasts with the one-sided credit exposure of a loan, where the creditor faces default risk on interest payments and the unamortized principal of the loan throughout the life of the loan.

Credit risk on a derivatives transaction has two components: the credit exposure in the event of default and the probability of a counterparty's default.

The credit exposure in the event of default is the sum of "current" and "potential" exposure, both of which depend upon movements in the underlying market risk factors. Current exposure is the loss on a contract should default occur today and is usually referred to as the "replacement cost" of a contract, measured as today's mark-to-market value of the contract. The second ingredient of credit exposure is "potential exposure," or the exposure which could result if a counterparty defaults on a contract sometime in the future. Potential exposure depends upon the volatility of the underlying prices or interest rates which determine the value of the derivatives contract. Under conservative assumptions about volatility and the likelihood of default, expected exposure and a likely "worst case" exposure can be estimated.

Concerns About Derivatives and Credit Risk

Concern has been expressed that derivatives may have substantially increased the credit risk taken on by financial institutions (especially derivatives dealers) leading to an excessive level of credit risk that is not adequately managed, exposing these institutions, the financial system, and taxpayers to a greater likelihood of suffering the consequences of a major default.

Analysis of Derivatives and Credit Risk

The accumulation of credit risk that results from derivatives activities, instead of from traditional lending activities, can nevertheless be managed within the traditional credit risk management function, supplemented by the more precise identification and measurement of credit risk made possible by derivatives technology. The credit risk of derivatives, in other words, can be managed by the time-tested methods of evaluating the creditworthiness of counterparties, setting risk limits for each counterparty to avoid excessive concentrations of risk, regularly measuring current and potential exposures, and monitoring them against risk limits.

While credit risk is in all likelihood the largest risk derivatives dealers face, the size of their credit exposures due to derivatives is relatively small both in comparison to the notional principal of the dealers' outstanding derivatives positions and the credit risk taken on by these same dealers in their more traditional activities.

The current credit exposure of a derivatives transaction, it is essential to note, is not measured by the notional principal of the contract, but rather by the cost of replacing the transaction with a new one. On a gross basis—before bilateral close-out netting—current replacement cost is a small percentage (approximately 1 percent to 3 percent) of the total notional principal of the typical dealer's derivatives portfolio. For example, the GAO in its report surveyed 14 major U.S. dealers and found that the dealers' combined gross credit exposure was only $114 billion, or just 1.8 percent of their $6.5 trillion notional principal outstanding, as of year-end 1992.

The gross replacement costs of derivatives contracts held by the lead banks of the 50 largest U.S. bank holding companies, provides another point of comparison. According to Federal Reserve Board data, gross replacement costs ranged from $26.2 billion or 1.15 percent of notional principal in 1990 to $49.7 billion or 1.61 percent in 1992 for interest rate contracts and from $76.3 billion or 2.82 percent in 1990 to $94.3 billion or 2.98 percent in 1992 for currency contracts. The relatively larger exposure for currency contracts reported by the Federal Reserve Board results overwhelmingly from traditional forward foreign exchange contracts rather than currency swaps. The GAO survey—including commercial banks, securities firms, and two insurance companies—reveals similar findings for a much more diverse set of dealers. Gross credit exposure as a percent of notional principal ranged from 0.80 percent in 1990 to 1.05 percent in 1992 for interest rate derivatives and 2.57 percent in 1990 to 3.18 percent in 1992 for currency derivatives. The GAO survey numbers for currency derivatives focus on currency swaps by excluding traditional forward foreign exchange contracts.

Even these surprisingly small percentages greatly overstate the credit risk of derivatives since bilateral close-out netting reduces current and potential exposure significantly. Bilateral close-out netting covenants in Swap Master Agreements specify that in the event of default by one of the counterparties to the agreement, the portfolio of swaps will be marked to market and only the net obligation will be exchanged. The GAO survey empirically confirms that close-out netting significantly reduces aggregate credit exposure. For the 14 dealers surveyed, netting agreements reduced the combined credit exposure by $41.2 billion, or approximately 36 percent in 1992. The credit risk of derivatives is sometimes reduced even further through the use of collateral arrangements and other risk mitigation schemes, such as periodically resetting rates to market with a compensating cash payment. The GAO survey, for example, found that collateral reduced net credit exposure by $4.7 billion, or approximately 4 percent.

The upshot of these considerations is that the net credit exposure of derivatives (i.e., after adjusting for close-out netting, collateral, and other risk mitigation schemes) is significantly less than the frequently cited gross exposure numbers. In fact, the GAO survey shows that these adjustments reduced credit exposure by over 40 percent in 1992. The net credit exposure for all derivatives for the 14 dealers surveyed was only 1.06 percent, compared with a gross exposure of 1.78 percent.

Even these net credit exposure numbers for derivatives activities need to be put in proper perspective. In terms of potential systemic risk, an important perspective is the size of these derivatives related exposures relative to the overall credit risk in the banking system. The credit risk that banks take on from derivatives is a relatively small percentage of their overall credit exposure from loans and commitments and letters of credit. The GAO report, for example, found that "the derivatives-related credit exposure for seven U.S. bank dealers surveyed were, with one exception, much lower than the credit exposures arising from their loans." The GAO numbers, moreover, tend to overstate the relative credit exposure due to derivatives activities since, on the one hand, they used the gross credit exposure of derivatives rather than the net credit exposure and, on the other hand, they only accounted for the credit exposure due to loans, omitting other non-derivatives related sources of credit risk such as commitments and letters of credit. When properly measured it is clear that derivatives generate a relatively small fraction of the overall credit risk taken on by the banking system.

The risk that derivatives activities pose to the financial system through the creation of credit risk depends, moreover, not just on the size of the net credit exposures but also on the probabilities of default—the credit quality of the counterparties. Credit quality of derivatives participants generally is quite high. Because derivatives, especially swaps, are frequently entered into in connection with the issuance of securities in public markets, parties to these transactions tend to be more creditworthy than the typical bank borrowers. As a result, being involved in swap activity as a dealer tends to increase the average quality of a bank's credit exposure while diversifying the credit risks to which it is exposed. The high average credit quality of swap counterparties is confirmed by the GAO survey of 200 firms which found that 97.5 percent of the $5.5 trillion notional principal of swaps entered into by these firms were of investment grade (i.e., BBB or above). The GAO survey of seven U.S. bank dealers also revealed that the credit quality of the derivatives books at these institutions was uniformly higher than the credit quality of their loan books.

Despite the fact that credit risk is the largest risk dealers face, actual credit losses in derivatives have been surprisingly low, both on an absolute scale and compared with loss rates for traditional banking products. According to a 1992 ISDA default survey, the actual losses incurred on over 500 defaulted transactions reported by ISDA members over a 10-year period was $358 million. The GAO's survey of 14 U.S. derivatives dealers found that derivatives defaults accounted for losses of only $246 million, or about 0.2 percent of notional principal outstanding in 1992.

Settlement and Payments Risk

Definition of Settlement and Payments Risk

Some financial transactions exhibit a type of credit risk, known as settlement and payments risk. Broadly, this risk is present when the physical exchange of assets or the exchange of gross cash flows is required. Same-day settlement risk exists for transactions in which delivery of an asset or security is not synchronized with the payment for that asset or security; the security can be surrendered and payment never received for it. The same risk exists when gross payments are exchanged, rather than having the obligation settled by a single netted payment. In the extreme, the firm making the payment without receiving value in return could be driven to default on its own obligations.

Concerns About Derivatives and Settlement and Payments Risk

Concern has been expressed that the dramatic growth in derivatives activities over the past decade has greatly increased the volume, size, and complexity of financial transactions creating a significant expansion of settlement and payments activity. The fear is that these increased daily settlement requirements may overwhelm the payments system resulting in gridlock.

Analysis of Derivatives and Settlement and Payments Risk

Settlement and payments risk for many derivatives transactions, however, is significantly less than for traditional securities transactions, and foreign exchange transactions. Interest rate swaps, for example, are referred to as "notional" contracts precisely because the principal is not exchanged. Moreover, most notional derivatives contracts contain payment netting provisions, which also serve to limit settlement risk by ensuring that on any given settlement date only one party is making a payment.

Derivatives contracts, such as cross-currency contracts, which call for physical settlement, are subject to settlement risk. The magnitude of this risk, however, is limited relative to the settlement risk of traditional transactions such as spot and short-dated forward foreign exchange transactions. Indeed, settlement risk is often called "Herstatt risk," named after the 1974 failure of Bankhaus Herstatt in which a number of counterparties had remitted payments to Bankhaus Herstatt on currency spot and short-dated forward transactions but did not receive their promised settlements in return.

The *relative* size of the settlement and payments risk posed by derivatives activities is clearly revealed by the following comparison. According to the Group of Thirty's, the Bank for International Settlements (BIS) estimated daily net turnover in spot foreign exchange markets at roughly $880 billion as of April 1992. By comparison, ISDA has estimated that daily global cash flows averaged $0.65 billion from notional interest rate swaps and $1.9 billion from currency swaps. In total, then, the average daily cash flow for swaps was a mere $2.55 billion compared to $880 billion in net turnover for foreign exchange transactions. The dramatic growth in interest rates and currency swaps over the last decade has, therefore, only slightly increased daily settlement flows. These additional settlement flows can hardly be said to impose systemic risk, especially when compared to settlement and payment system demands resulting from traditional foreign exchange transactions. To the extent settlement risk is a systemic concern, the source of this concern is the same as it always has been—the spot and short-dated forward markets for currency.

Market Risk

Definition of Market Risk

Market risk is the risk that the value of a position in a contract, financial instrument, asset, or portfolio will decline when market conditions change. Interest rate risk is one of the most common forms of market risk. The holder of an outright position in a corporate bond or Treasury note obviously bears market risk. If the maturity mismatch between its assets and liabilities exposes a bank to losses when interest rate increases, then that bank also bears market risk. A fixed-for-floating interest rate swap, a fixed rate loan funded with floating rate deposits, and a long position in Treasury notes financed through overnight repos are all exposed to the same market risk of losses due to an increase in interest rates.

Like credit risk, market risk must be viewed from a portfolio or balance sheet perspective rather than as the market risk of individual transactions. For example, a bank's exposure to interest rate risk is determined by the combination of the bank's interest rate-sensitive balance sheet items with its off-balance sheet, interest rate-sensitive items, including derivatives. This portfolio perspective is essential when evaluating the contribution of derivatives to the overall level of market risk, given the availability of both cash instruments and derivatives to manage existing market risks.

Concerns About Derivatives and Market Risk

Some concern has been expressed that derivatives, such as swaps, expose financial institutions such as banks to new market risks, subjecting them not just to the risk of interest rate changes, but also to foreign exchange fluctuations, commodity price shifts, and volatility in equity prices. Concern also has been expressed that derivatives have increased the level of exposure to market risk for dealers and end users, because of the potential leverage inherent in derivatives, the ease of taking on new exposures, and the complexity of derivatives.

Analysis of Derivatives and Market Risk

Derivatives have not exposed institutions such as banks to new sources of market risk. The reality is that banks have been exposed to these same market risks for years. Interest rate exposure, of course, is inherent in the repricing mismatch between a bank's loans and its deposits. Foreign exchange exposure is inherent in a bank's foreign exchange trading and in its foreign currency denominated borrowing or lending. Commodity price exposure is inherent in a bank's oil field production payout loans. Equity exposure is inherent in a bank's margin loans. These types of risk exposures, therefore, are not new to banks and are not unique to derivatives.

A fundamental principle of finance is that the market risks of derivatives activities must be evaluated on the basis of the net exposure of overall portfolios. A dealer's derivatives portfolio, for example, contains many positions with offsetting market exposures as a result of the normal flow of customer orders. Some customers, for example, want to pay a fixed rate and receive a floating rate from the dealer, while others want to receive a fixed rate and pay a floating rate. These balanced or matching positions leave a much smaller residual market risk to be managed. The residual market risk of the derivatives portfolio, in turn, may offset in part the market risk of the dealer's other activities, such as a mismatch in the duration of its assets and liabilities.

In practice, dealers determine their net exposure to various market risk factors by looking beyond particular derivatives contracts and focusing instead on identifying the particular risk factors they contain. Overall portfolio risk then can be decomposed into these underlying risk factors and measured and managed on this basis. Residual exposures then can be hedged by buying or selling liquid securities (e.g., Treasury notes or bonds), by entering into exchange-traded futures contracts (e.g., Eurodollar futures or Treasury bond futures) or by entering into other offsetting OTC derivatives transactions. While these hedges may expose the dealer to basis or correlation risk, this occurs as a byproduct of reducing the more substantial overall market risk of the portfolio.

The first and most important step in effectively managing market risk for dealers (and active end users) is marking derivatives portfolios to market on a daily basis. Intraday (or even realtime) valuation is used by major dealers with significant option portfolios. Frequent and regular marking to market is essential because it provides vital information about current market risk, the past performance of hedges, and the need for additional hedging. In addition, it provides immediate feedback to traders, auditors, and senior managers, disciplining the risk management process and providing the information and incentives necessary for corrective action to be taken before derivatives related losses accumulate. The widespread practice of marking to market is the single most important factor that will keep derivatives dealing from becoming the next "S&L crisis" as some predict.

The Group of Thirty's Survey of Industry Practice (Survey) reveals that dealers overwhelmingly recognize the importance of marking to market for risk management purposes. Over 85 percent of the 80 dealers responding to the Survey used a mark-to-market valuation method while over 94 percent planned to do so. The larger and global full range dealers had a greater tendency to mark to market and did so with greater frequency than smaller or purely domestic dealers.

As revealed by the Group of Thirty's recent Follow-Up Survey of risk management practices, the evolving industry standard for measuring market risk is the "value at risk" approach. Value at risk measures, however calculated, attempt to account for all the risk factors in different instruments and underlyings in a consistent and coherent fashion so as to allow the market risks of all derivatives to be reduced to a single common dominator. The pace of innovation among dealers in developing, refining, and applying value at risk measures is currently quite rapid. Once identified and measured, market risk can be controlled through risk limits set by senior management, with regular monitoring of positions against limits, and reporting of limit exceptions to senior management.

Since the release of the Group of Thirty's report recommending twenty principles of good risk management practice, there has been significant improvement in the way in which firms, especially the medium and smaller sized dealers, manage market risk. For example, these dealers have moved to adopting a value at risk methodology for measuring market risk and to conducting more stress tests, on a more regular basis, over a wider range of stress scenarios. End users have also become more widely aware of the need for stress testing.

The same sound principles and practices that are now being used for managing the market risk of derivatives portfolio can be applied (and increasingly are being applied) by financial and other institutions to their more traditional risk management activities, whether it's managing asset/liability mismatches or position taking in proprietary trading accounts. For example, value at risk measurements and stress tests can be done in the same manner for a portfolio of mortgage loans or a currency trading book as for a portfolio of interest rate swaps entered by a dealer in response to customer demands.

Finally, to keep derivatives activities in proper perspective it is important to remember that most corporate end users of swaps use them as part of another activity of the firm, such as a debt issuance, and usually manage these positions as related activities. The market risk that results in these situations is quite minimal. Corporates, who are more active users of derivatives, tend to use many of the same techniques for managing market risk as the major dealers.

Liquidity Risk

Definition of Liquidity Risk

Institutions can face two types of liquidity risk. First, "market liquidity risk" is the risk that a transaction in a particular instrument could have an adverse impact on its market price. For example, if an equity fund sells a large number of shares of a particular stock in a short period of time, the sale could depress significantly the price of the stock. A closely related type of liquidity risk is the risk that sudden and sharp price moves or volatility changes may make it difficult for an institution to hedge or unwind a losing position. Institutions can face a distinct and second type of liquidity risk, often known as "funding risk." This type of liquidity risk is simply the risk that cash flow mismatches may give rise to contractual nonperformance.

Concerns About Derivatives and Liquidity Risk

Concern has been expressed that a sharp market move may force a derivatives dealer to enter new positions or replace existing contracts which have defaulted as a result of the price move, the execution of both transactions could be complicated by adverse liquidity shocks. The institution may find itself bearing more market risk than it intended for longer periods of time.

Analysis of Derivatives and Liquidity Risk

Liquidity risk is not unique to derivatives. Traditional financial products and on-balance sheet positions are subject to liquidity risk as well. As the Group of Thirty's original Survey and its Follow-Up Survey indicate, dealers are quite aware of these liquidity risks and increasingly incorporate them in their measurement and management of market risks, particularly for stress testing. Virtually all active financial institutions have liquidity or funding plans to avoid these types of cash flow mismatches for traditional financial products, and derivatives are increasingly being incorporated into these funding plans to avoid having a cash shortfall when a required payment on a derivatives contract is due.

Market liquidity risk of the first type, moreover, is less likely to be a major factor in interest rate and foreign exchange derivatives, because of the depth and liquidity of the underlying markets and the presence of numerous substitute products for trading the various risk factors. A "plain vanilla" interest rate swap transaction of significant size is unlikely, for example, to affect the going swap rate, since the transaction would have to be large relative not only to the LIBOR swap market itself, but also relative to the markets for other LIBOR instruments, including Eurodollar futures, Forward Rate Agreements, the cash market for Eurodollar deposits, LIBOR based caps, floors, and collars, and other interest rate derivatives based on rate indexes which are closely related to LIBOR.

As the Group of Thirty pointed out, the liquidity of derivatives transaction has been tested by several substantial, but non-derivatives induced, failures of major firms. The derivatives portfolios of these firms were transferred or unwound fairly quickly: in most cases, they were disposed of more rapidly than the portfolios of more traditional instruments.

Operational Risk

Definition of Operational Risk

Another risk that arises in all businesses is operational risk—the risk that losses will be incurred as a result of inadequate systems and control, inadequate disaster or contingency planning, human error, or management failure. The risk that a power outage could prevent an institution from monitoring securities positions, hence leading to accumulating losses, is a type of operational risk. Similarly, employing a professional staff with inadequate training in the risks of the activities they are supervising can result in unexpected losses.

Concerns About Derivatives and Operational Risk

Concern has been expressed that derivatives dealers lack adequate incentives to implement the costly systems and techniques that are necessary for effectively controlling the credit and market risks of their rapidly expanding derivatives portfolios. Entering into these complex derivatives positions without adequate systems for measuring and controlling credit, settlement, market, or liquidity risk is a classic example of operational risk.

Analysis of Derivatives and Operational Risk

No aspect of operational risk is unique to derivatives. Nevertheless, it is especially important for institutions actively engaged in derivatives activities to have adequate oversight of well-trained and knowledgeable staff by informed and involved senior management as it would be for any institution engaged in a similarly complex task.

As the Group of Thirty's original Survey and its Follow-Up Survey show, operational risk for derivatives is controlled in many ways, including: requiring approval by senior management and/or directors of any important policies and procedures pertaining to derivatives activities; using a risk management function independent of risk-taking areas, such as the trading desk, to evaluate, review, and report to senior management on the nature and size of risks taken by the institution and the effectiveness with which those risks are being managed; using a comprehensive internal audit and review process; establishing checks-and-balances throughout the transaction process; using up-to-date technology and management information systems; and developing adequate and well-known contingency and disaster planning.

Despite the concerns about dealers willingness to spend the time and money necessary to establish operational controls, it seems clear that the major dealers have made and continue to make great strides in improving their system. For example, the GAO survey of 14 major U.S. dealers reveals that they have made substantial and costly improvements to their risk management and control systems over the last three years. The costs of these improvements ranged from $7.4 million to $45 million, averaging $18 million for reporting dealers.

Legal Risk

Definition of Legal Risk

Legal risk is the risk of loss because a contract cannot be enforced or because the contract terms fail to achieve the intended goals of the contracting parties. As with other types of risk, legal risk has long been present in traditional lending and trading activities.

Concerns About Derivatives and Legal Risk

Because of the relative newness of derivatives transactions, however, their treatment under existing laws and regulations has been (and, to some extent, still is) ambiguous. This legal uncertainty can lead in particular cases to significant unexpected losses and, because of the potential for legal risk to be highly correlated across firms, it raises potential systemic concerns.

Derivatives contracts are susceptible to several types of legal risk. First, a contract may be unenforceable because one of the parties is legally incapable of entering into the agreement (i.e., ultra vires). For example, a 1991 ruling by the United Kingdom House of Lords found that a local government authority in the London Borough of Hammersmith and Fulham lacked the legal capacity to enter a number of swap contracts it had entered into in the mid-1980s. As a result, the borough was not liable to make payments on those contracts on which it would otherwise have suffered large losses. The decision, however, had more far reaching effects, rendering swap contracts involving other local governments void, affecting more than 600 counterparties.

Second, derivatives contracts are susceptible to the risk that they will be declared unenforceable for example, as conflicting with anti-gambling or bucketshop laws. In the United States, there has been widespread concern that swaps might be found to be illegal off-exchange futures contracts. The Commodities Futures Trading Commission (CFTC) issued an exemption for some swaps from regulation under the Commodity Exchange Act in early 1993, reducing to some extent the legal uncertainty. The authority to do so was granted to the CFTC by Congress in the Futures Trading Practices Act of 1992.

Third, particular provisions of derivatives contracts, such as the provision for netting of close-out payments, may be unenforceable in certain jurisdictions. Should close-out netting prove to be unenforceable, an institution may be "cherry-picked" by a counterparty in bankruptcy, with the defaulting counterparty demanding payment on contracts with positive value without remitting payments on other obligations with negative value.

Fourth, derivatives contracts often contain "early termination" provisions, allowing the termination of the contract prior to its maturity on the occurrence of certain events. Federal banking law, however, affords certain protections to the Federal Deposit Insurance Corporation (FDIC) which may inhibit the ability of an institution to terminate its derivatives contracts with a counterparty in a timely fashion if the FDIC is appointed as conservator. This restriction on timely termination can increase the dealer's market risk, since it no longer knows what contracts are in force and what its market risk is and, hence, cannot hedge this uncertain exposure.

Analysis of Derivatives and Legal Risk

Users of derivatives attempt to manage and, hence, minimize legal risks in several ways. One of the most important ways of minimizing legal risk is the use of standardized documentation. The industry, moreover, has worked to reduce legal risk through the development of standardized documentation such as the ISDA Master Agreement to cover a wider range of products and underlyings, such as commodity swaps and equity swaps.

The industry also has worked through the political process, both regulatory and legislative, to address legal uncertainty in many jurisdictions. For example, the U.S. Congress has acted on numerous occasions to legislatively reduce the legal risks of derivatives transactions. The most important examples include the passage of the Financial Institutions Reform, Recovery, and Enforcement Act (FIRREA) in 1989, amendments to the Bankruptcy Code, the enactment of the Federal Deposit Insurance Corporation Improvement Act (FDICIA) in 1991, all of which clarified the treatment of derivatives in bankruptcy. In addition, the Futures Trading Practices Act of 1992, which reauthorized the CFTC, reduced the legal threat of swaps being challenged as illegal off-exchange futures contracts.

Nevertheless, as the Group of Thirty pointed out, legal risks remain a significant factor, despite persistent efforts to reduce these risks, and have the potential to create systemic problems. While a risk management failure at a single firm is likely to be a containable event, a flaw in the legal framework can affect many participants simultaneously and adversely with possible systemic consequences.

III. AN ASSESSMENT OF FACTORS THAT POTENTIALLY MAY INCREASE SYSTEMIC RISK

While the previous section attempted to address the fundamental risks of derivatives—credit risk, settlement and payments risk, market risk, liquidity risk, operational risk, and legal risk—there are other risk factors that some commentators have suggested could raise the risks of derivatives activities to a systemic concern. An assessment of these remaining risk factors is the subject of this section.

Size and Growth

Concerns About Size and Growth

Public concerns over derivatives have been driven in large part by the rapid growth in the volume and the extraordinary size of derivatives activity measured in trillions of dollars of notional principal written or outstanding. Such rapid growth has raised concerns about the ability of both senior management and regulators to understand the risks of derivatives and ensure that these activities are properly managed and supervised. It also has raised concerns that new entrants, drawn into the business by the rapid growth, may be less sophisticated, less prudent, and of lower credit quality than existing participants, thereby exposing the major dealers to unexpected risks. These concerns are analyzed below, while this section addresses concerns related to the sheer size of the market. The large volume of derivatives transactions outstanding, with various estimates running well in excess of $10 trillion is taken as evidence by some that the capital base of U.S. financial institutions and the financial system itself are both exposed to significant risks from derivatives activities.

Analysis of Size and Growth

The first and most important point to note is that while notional principal (written or outstanding) is a common measure of derivatives activity, notional principal to quote the GAO "is not a meaningful measure of the actual risks involved" in derivatives activities. To briefly summarize the earlier discussion, the actual risk exposure of a derivatives portfolio is only a small fraction of the notional principal outstanding. For example, when the GAO surveyed major U.S. dealers it found that the net credit exposure (i.e., after adjusting for close-out netting, collateral, and other risk mitigating arrangements) was a mere 1.06 percent of the $6.5 trillion notional principal outstanding for these dealers. The GAO also found that the derivatives-related credit exposure for all but one of the bank dealers surveyed were much lower than their credit exposures arising from loan activity.

Because of payment netting and close out netting the notional principal outstanding for derivatives is also not a meaningful proxy for the size of cash flows resulting from derivatives. As mentioned above, ISDA estimated the average daily global cash flows for swaps was only $2.55 billion in 1992 as compared to $880 billion for daily net turnover in foreign exchange transactions as estimated by the BIS.

While the wide variation in estimates of "derivatives activity" reported in various surveys adds to the "mystery" of derivatives, these differences result from rather mundane sources—they result from different definitions of derivatives, different institutional and geographic bases for the survey, and different degrees of double counting. The GAO estimate of derivatives activity of $12.1 trillion for 1992, which greatly exceeds ISDA's estimate, results from including $4.8 trillion in exchange-traded futures and options. The difference of $7.3 trillion measures OTC derivatives activity and is made up of $4.7 trillion in interest rate and currency swaps, $.6 trillion in OTC interest rate options, and $2.0 trillion in forward rate agreement.

Despite its apparent size, OTC derivatives activity is small compared to the level of activity in the underlying markets. At year-end 1991, for example, notional principal outstanding for swaps amounted to $4.5 trillion as compared with $14.4 trillion for global bonds and $10.1 trillion for global equities.

Concentration

Concerns About Concentration

Concern has been expressed that the concentration of derivatives activities within a small set of major dealers, linked by a complex web of transactions, could lead to a situation where the failure of a major dealer could easily threaten other dealers either directly or indirectly through induced liquidity problems. Some also have worried that the concentration of dealing activities could lead to non-competitive pricing.

Analysis of Concentration

Concerns about excessive concentration generally arise from focusing on only one segment of global derivatives activity. The GAO, for example, notes that as of year-end 1992 the top seven domestic bank derivatives dealers accounted for more than 90 percent of total U.S. bank derivatives activity while the top five U.S. securities firms dealing in derivatives accounted for 87 percent of the derivatives activity of all U.S. securities firms. These figures, however, are misleading. U.S. banks and U.S. securities firms compete with one another and both of these in turn compete with foreign banks and securities firms. This broader market definition greatly reduces the level of concentration. Surveys by *Swaps Monitor*, based on the annual reports of dealers, indicate that the top eight dealers accounted for only 58 percent of interest rate and currency swap activity at year-ends 1991 and 1992. No dealer in either survey had over a 10 percent share of the activity. The share of the eighth largest dealer was only 4.4 percent in 1991 and 5.1 percent in 1992.

Concentration of credit risk also does not appear to be excessive nor to warrant the concerns that have been expressed about systemic risk. According to the Group of Thirty Survey more than 60 percent of the responding dealers indicated that their top 10 counterparties accounted for less than 30 percent of their derivatives related credit exposure. The GAO survey of 14 major U.S. dealers found similar results. For the U.S. dealers surveyed, less than 11 percent of their total net credit exposure was with other U.S. dealers in 1992. The U.S. dealers' exposure to non-U.S. dealers was slightly more than 27 percent in 1992.

Leading banking and securities regulators, moreover, do not appear to believe that concentration is a serious systemic issue. The SEC, for example, has stated that "derivatives dealers tend to be well-diversified, highly capitalized firms that are, arguably, well suited to weather adverse market conditions." The Federal Reserve Board, for its part, views the concentration of derivatives activities that does exist among the major dealers as a positive element. It restricts dealing to well capitalized and better managed institutions and facilitates the supervisory process.

Non-competitive pricing of derivatives due to excessive concentration is "unlikely" in the words of the OCC. Given the truly global nature of derivatives activity—the large number of both domestic and foreign banks and non-bank financial institutions competing for derivatives customers and the ability of large customers to reverse engineer and produce transactions in-house—it is unlikely that collusive or non-competitive pricing of derivatives could persist for any significant period of time.

Complexity

Concerns About Complexity

Concern has been expressed that the increasing variety and complexity of derivatives transactions is making it more difficult for dealers and end users to properly value and adequately hedge individual transactions and portfolios, exposing these dealers and end users to greater market risks. Given the relationship between market movements and credit risk for derivatives, similar concerns have been expressed about the ability of firms to measure and manage credit risk for complex derivatives.

Analysis of Complexity

Part of the complexity of derivatives is more apparent than real. Many of the seemingly endless new varieties of derivatives simply represent the application of established structures to new underlyings. For example, the development of commodity swaps in the mid-1980s and equity swaps in the late-1980s followed from applying the well established structures and techniques developed with currency and interest rate swaps to these new underlyings. Interest rate caps, floors, and collars, as another example, developed as bundles of simpler interest rate options.

It is also important to keep in mind that the vast bulk of the activity in OTC derivatives is in these simpler structures. According to the GAO, interest rate and currency swaps plus forward rate agreements made up 92 percent of the notional principal outstanding for OTC derivatives at year-end 1992. These, of course, are the simplest derivatives to value and hedge so that the measurement and management of market risk and credit risk is quite straightforward.

To the extent derivatives are complex, that complexity generally reflects (as the GAO has recognized) the underlying complexity of the risks end users are attempting to manage. The holder of a portfolio of fixed-rate mortgages with prepayment options, a U.S. company submitting a committed bid on an airport construction project in the United Kingdom payable in British pounds, a U.S. pension fund with U.S. dollar liabilities holding Japanese equity, a bank making a floating-rate oil field production payout loan, and a homeowner preparing to refinance his mortgage all face inherently complex risk exposures. Derivatives created to manage these risks will be as complex as the underlying risk themselves.

The complexity of derivatives would merit concern if it outstripped the ability of dealers and end users to manage the resulting risks. This does not appear to be the case. As has been noted, "a revolution in risk management practices" is being driven by the involvement of dealers in derivatives as they develop the systems needed to identify, measure, and manage the risks of derivatives. The progress of this revolution is well documented in the recent studies of derivatives, especially the GAO report, the Group of Thirty's original Survey, and its Follow-Up Survey of industry practice.

Transparency

Concerns About Transparency

Concerns about a lack of transparency in OTC derivatives activities come from three sources, the lack of consistent and comprehensive accounting standards for derivatives, inadequate disclosure of the risks of derivatives, and a lack of publicly available real time price and volume data for derivatives transactions. Inconsistent accounting and inadequate disclosure make it more difficult for dealers and end users to determine their credit exposures to their counterparties increasing the likelihood of unexpected credit losses. The lack of real time publicly available pricing data makes it more difficult for some dealers and end users to mark to market their portfolios and manage market risk.

Analysis of Transparency

There is widespread recognition of the need for improved accounting and disclosure for derivatives. The Group of Thirty, for example, recognized the need for improved accounting and disclosure practices for all financial instruments and put forward specific recommendations pending the adoption of internationally harmonized standards. The derivatives industry, through individual and voluntary improvements in disclosures in 1993 Annual Reports and through ISDA's Subcommittee on Disclosure, is working to improve transparency. Standard setting bodies such as FASB and the IASC are working to promulgate new accounting and disclosure rules for derivatives. In addition, the regulators, both domestic and international, are also working to improve required disclosures and coordinate regulatory reporting requirements to obtain more useful information on risk exposures. This is one important area in which all the relevant parties are working hard to resolve the difficult issues and develop means of improving the transparency of not just derivatives activities but all financial activities.

The privately negotiated and customized nature of OTC derivatives transactions makes it infeasible to have exchange-style reporting of price and transaction data for standardized products. This does not mean, however, that there are not good indicators of market value readily available from brokers' screens for the vast bulk of OTC derivatives transactions. In fact, for internal risk management purposes, the risks of derivatives are becoming more and more transparent as a result of the nearly universal adoption of daily mark-to-market measures for valuation and risk management purposes.

Management Understanding

Concerns About Management Understanding

Concerns have been expressed that the rapid growth and increasing complexity of derivatives may have led to a situation where the risks of derivatives are not well understood by boards of directors and senior management at some major dealers and active end users. This lack of understanding could lead to risk management failures exposing these particular firms to excessive risks and a possibility of a derivatives-induced failure. Other firms may be endangered if the initial default spreads through contagion causing additional disruptions and defaults.

Analysis of Management Understanding

Since the now famous "warning" by former President of the Federal Reserve Bank of New York, Gerald Corrigan, senior management and boards of directors at the major derivatives dealers have devoted substantial time to improving their understanding of their derivatives operations. The time devoted to this effort is most clearly indicated by the Group of Thirty's Global Derivatives Study Group which had direct ongoing involvement from senior management at many of the major dealers. Moreover, according to the Group of Thirty's Follow-Up Survey senior management at all major dealers and many of the leading end users have benchmarked their institution's risk management systems against the Group of Thirty's recommendations for good risk management practices.

The importance of senior management understanding the risks of derivatives and ensuring that they are used in a manner consistent with the overall risk management and capital policies approved by the boards of directors is widely understood and recognized by both the private and public sectors. The Group of Thirty considered this issue of such importance that it focused its first recommendation on the role of senior management. The banking supervisors in their recent releases providing guidance to examiners have also emphasized the importance of active and knowledgeable involvement by senior management and boards in the risk management process.

The success of these educational efforts, both private and public, is indicated by Corrigan's recent comments about the "significant progress that has been made in learning about derivatives" and about the "truly great progress [that] has been, and is being made, in developing risk management, information, and control systems."

Unregulated Entities

Concerns About Unregulated Entities

Concern has been expressed, most recently by the GAO, about the largely unregulated activities of U.S. derivatives dealers that are affiliates of securities firms and insurance companies. A particular concern is that the derivatives activities of these affiliates are not subject to capital standards or regulatory examinations. The GAO was also concerned that FDICIA type mandates—independent audit committees, public reporting on assessments of internal control systems, and an annual external audit of risk management systems—did not apply to these derivatives' affiliates or to major end users of complex derivatives. Apparently, the fear is that a failure of one of these firms, whether a dealer or large end user, could pose risks to other firms, including federally insured depository institutions.

Analysis of Unregulated Entities

While the GAO recognizes a direct federal interest in the safety and soundness of major bank derivatives dealers because of payment system concerns and the federal Bank Insurance Fund guarantee, they go on to assert that derivatives transactions carry the same risks to the financial system whether the major dealer is a bank, securities firm, or an insurance company. The apparent logic is that because of the concentration of credit exposures among the major dealers and the linkages created by derivatives, the failure of any dealer threatens the banking system and the deposit insurance fund. Unfortunately, the GAO does not provide empirical evidence to support this conclusion.

In fact, the evidence actually presented in the report runs counter to this contention. While no evidence is presented that the derivatives affiliates of securities firms and insurance companies are undercapitalized, the GAO actually points out that the market's "demand for a top credit rating" has driven securities firms to set up separately capitalized, credit-enhanced AAA affiliates. While no evidence is presented that the so-called "unregulated" derivatives affiliates are less well managed than the regulated major bank dealers, the GAO actually points out that all 15 major dealers they visited—including the affiliates of securities firms and insurance companies—described risk management systems that conformed to the Group of Thirty's recommendations. (Moreover, the AAA credit ratings that the special purpose vehicles receive come only after rigorous examinations of their risk management systems by rating agencies such as S&P or Moodys.) As mentioned above in the discussion of concentration, the GAO survey of major U.S. dealers does not indicate that credit exposures are excessively concentrated among the major dealers. This implies that there is less risk that the failure of, say, a derivatives affiliate of a securities firm would be likely to spread and bring down a major bank dealer with systemic repercussions.

Finally, the derivatives affiliates of securities firms are not without federal oversight. The holding company provisions of the Market Reform Act can be effectively used by the SEC to monitor the financial condition of affiliates of securities firms, acting as an early warning system, allowing the SEC to minimize the social cost and spill-over effects of periodic failures.

New Entrants

Concerns About New Entrants

Concern has been expressed that new entrants into derivatives activities will tend to be less knowledgeable about the risks of derivatives, less sophisticated in their management of these risks, less prudent in the use of derivatives, and of generally lower credit quality than existing participants. The fear is that a failure at one of these firms from the misuse of derivatives or simply as a result of low credit quality will lead to the default of a major dealer with consequences for the overall financial system.

Analysis of New Entrants

The industry and regulators alike are concerned about the entry of unsophisticated participants. The industry responded to this concern, in part, through its participation in the Group of Thirty's Global Derivatives Study Group. The resulting recommendations for good risk management practice represent a massive transfer of state-of-the-art risk management know how and expertise to potential entrants, both dealers and end users alike. In addition to providing detailed guidance on safe and sound risk management practices, the banking regulators have also required that dealers understand the risks of derivatives and have good systems in place before they undertake new dealing activities such as in commodity or equity derivatives.

On the purely empirical issue that is raised by these concerns, no evidence has been presented supporting the concern that the credit quality of derivatives participants has declined because of the entry of new, higher risk participants. To the contrary, the survey of credit quality reported by the GAO reveals that derivatives participants overwhelmingly have been, and remain, of high credit quality. Marginal credit risks are either excluded from doing business or can only do so on a collateralized basis.

In light of the lack of empirical support for these concerns about new entrants, it is important to ensure that these concerns are not misused as an excuse for anticompetitive restrictions on entry into profitable lines of derivatives activity.

Market Linkages

Concerns About Market Linkages

It is widely recognized and applauded that global markets for trade and finance have become increasingly integrated, accessible, and competitive. Derivatives have both benefitted from and contributed to this development.

In these circumstances, however, derivatives are considered by some to be a source of concern because with more closely linked markets the fear is that derivatives make it possible for shocks in one part of the global financial system to be transmitted farther and faster than before, being reinforced rather than dampened as they are transmitted from one market to another.

Analysis of Market Linkages

Increased market linkages should be seen in a positive light as increased diversification of risks rather than as a negative development. An equity portfolio that is "linked" to markets for stocks, say, other than IBM—including foreign equities—is a better diversified and less risky portfolio. The same is true of the U.S. financial institutions that have diversified their credit exposure through derivatives transactions that create new linkages to other U.S. banks, U.S. securities firms, foreign banks, non-financial firms, foreign securities firms, and U.S. insurance companies. As long as undue concentrations of credit exposures are avoided, these additional linkages create greater diversification and should reduce risks rather than creating new systemic problems. As a general proposition, the greater diversification and wider sharing of risks made possible by derivatives should serve to diffuse and dampen market shocks, reducing systemic consequences of any disruptions.

There is voluminous academic research on the effects of derivatives and market linkages. This literature has examined the effects of the introduction of derivatives trading—generally exchange-traded futures and options—on the underlying cash markets. Various derivatives trading strategies, especially arbitrage strategies, assure that these markets are closely linked. The academic research (summarized in Tables 1 and 2) strongly indicates that derivatives trading either has no effect on, or reduces, volatility in the underlying and linked market. Shocks to one market, apparently, are not amplified as they spread to linked markets. There is little in these studies, in short, to support the concern that derivatives trading either increases market volatility on an on-going or episodic basis, or poses any significant threat of systemic disruption.

Dynamic Hedging

Concerns About Dynamic Hedging

Concern has been expressed that derivatives activities may exacerbate market moves through dynamic hedging strategies that rely upon positive feedback trading. Particular concern has focused on the possibility that attempts to dynamically hedge large, complex OTC option positions by adjusting hedge positions in the more liquid, underlying cash markets and

Table 1. Summary of Studies Estimating the Effect of Index Futures on Spot Volatility

Style	*Index*	*Period*	*Increase in Volatility*	*No Change in Volatility*	*Decrease in Volatility*
Before and After Study					
Santoni (1987)	S&P500	1975-1986	—	√	—
Edwards (1988a), (1988b)	S&P500/VLCI	1973-1978	—	√	—
Becketti & Roberts (1990)	S&P500	1962-1990	—	√	—
Lockwood & Linn (1990)	DJIA	1964-1989	√	√	—
Freris (1990)	Hang Seng	1984-1987	—	√	—
Chan and Karolyi (1991)	Nikkei (Simex)	1985-1987	—	√	—
Hodgson & Nicholls (1991)	All Ordinaries	1981-1987	—	√	—
Baldauf & Santoni (1991)	SP&500	1975-1989	—	√	—
Brorsen (1991)	S&P500	1962-1986	√	√	—
Maberly, et al (1989)	S&P500	1963-1988	√	√	√
Cross Section Study					
Aggarwal (1988)	S&P500/DJIA	1981-1987	—	√	—
Harris (1989)	S&P500	1975-1987	√	—	—
Laatch (1991)	MMI	1982-1986	—	√	—
Gerety & Mulherin (1991)	DJIA	1974-1989	—	√	—

Source: J. Board, C. Goodhart and C. Sutcliffe, "Intermarket Volatility Linkages: The London Stock Exchange and London International Financial Futures Exchange," Securities and Investments Board, June 1992, pg. 50.

Table 2. Summary of Studies Estimating the Effect of the Introduction of Futures Trading on Spot Price Volatility

Study	*Decrease in Volatility*	*No Change in Volatility*	*Increase in Volatility*
Working (1960 & 1963)	Onions	—	—
Gray (1963)	Onions	—	
Powers (1970)	Live cattle/Pork bellies	—	—
Tomek (1971)	Wheat	—	—
Johnson (1973)	—	Onions	—
Taylor and Leuthold (1974)	Live cattle	—	—
Labys and Thomas (1975)	—	—	Cocoa, Sugar, Zinc, Rubber, Lead, Tin
Froewiss (1978)	GNMA	—	—
Tomek (1979-80)	—	Cattle, Hogs	—
Dale and Workman (1981)	—	T-bills	—
Figlewski (1981)	—	—	GNMA
Simpson and Ireland (1982)	—	GNMA	—
Corgel and Gay (1984)	GNMA	—	—
Bortz (1984)	Treasure bonds	—	—
Simpson and Ireland (1985)	—	T-bills	—
Moriarty and Tosini (1985)	—	GNMA	—
Edwards (1988)	T-bills/Eurodollars	—	—
Brorsen, Oellermann & Farris (1989)	—	—	Live cattle
Ely (1991)	T-bills/Time deposits	—	—
Antoniou and Foster (1991)	—	Crude Oil	—

Source: J. Board, C. Goodhart and C. Sutcliffe, "Intermarket Volatility Linkages: The London Stock Exchange and London International Financial Futures Exchange," Securities and Investments Board, June 1992, pg. 51.

exchange-traded derivatives markets could exhaust the liquidity of these markets. As dynamic hedgers buy into rising markets or sell into falling markets, the fear is that price fluctuations may be greatly amplified, threatening various market participants with insolvency.

For most regulators their fear of dynamic hedging was forged in the heat of experiences surrounding the October 1987 stock market crash. The lessons learned during this period, reinforced apparently by recurring flashbacks and nightmares about the next meltdown, continue to guide public policy with respect to derivatives. Is there an evidentiary basis for this fear of dynamic hedging and derivatives? Is this fear, in other words, warranted on the basis of the best available scientific evidence? Or, is it a costly (although understandable) anxiety induced by a misreading of a uniquely painful experience?

Analysis of Dynamic Hedging

At the most general level, there is little empirical support for the concern that the introduction of derivatives trading adversely affects the underlying cash market by increasing volatility. The most direct empirical evidence derives from numerous academic studies of the impact of the introduction of trading in individual stock options on the underlying stocks. These studies (summarized in Table 3) provide powerful tests of the hypothesis that dynamic hedging of option positions increases volatility. Market makers in these options have regularly relied on dynamic hedging to protect their inventories. Moreover, the empirical studies examine hundreds of option introductions, not just one event such as with the S&P 500 futures contract. This greatly increases the power of these results. Uniformly, these studies find no impact on, or a reduction in, volatility as a result of options listing.

Despite widespread opinion to the contrary, moreover, there is little empirical support for the allegation that dynamic hedging in the form of portfolio insurance either caused or accentuated the October 1987 market crash. Not only is there little empirical support for the general concern that dynamic hedging might increase market volatility, direct tests of this hypothesis based on both October 1987 and periods other than October 1987 find little or no market impact from positive feedback trading.

Because of the lessons learned in the October 1987 market crash regarding the possibility of discontinuous markets and breakdown in particular trading mechanisms, dynamic strategies now are executed using a mixture of trading in the underlying and related assets, in futures, and in options. This greatly reduces execution risk. Moreover, there is less reliance today on dynamic hedging with major dealers instead attempting to hedge directly the risks of options written with purchased options. That is, dealers tend to run balanced portfolios, hedging options with options, while only dynamically hedging the

Table 3. Summary of Studies Estimating the Effects of Option Listing on the Variance of the Price of the Underlying Stock

Study	*Firms*	*Sample Period*	*Results*
Effect of Listing on Variance			
Hayes & Tennenbaum (1979)	43	1972-77	Volatility Decreases
Whiteside, Duke & Dunne (1983)	71	1973-81	No Change
Ma & Rao (1986, 1988)	251	1972-83	Volatility Decreases
Bansal, Pruitt & Wei (1989)	175	1973-86	Volatility Decreases
Skinner (1989)	304	1973-86	Volatility Decreases
Conrad (1989)	78	1973-80	Volatility Decreases
Nabar & Park (1988)	494	1973-85	Volatility Decreases
Damodaran & Lim (1991)	200	1973-86	Volatility Decreases
Effect of Listing on Beta			
Trennepohl & Dukes (1979)	32	1970-76	Lower Betas
Klemkosky & Maness (1980)	40	1972-79	Lower Betas
Skinner (1988)	304	1973-86	No Change
Demodaran & Lim (1991)	200	1973-86	No Change

Source: A. Damodaran and M. Subrahmanyam, "The Effects of Derivative Securities on the Markets for Underlying Assets in the United States: A Survey," *Financial Markets, Institutions and Instruments*, V.1, N.5, December 1992, p. 9.

smaller residual risk arising from any remaining mismatches in the options portfolio.

Any large transaction is likely to move prices in the direction of that transaction. But this is simply a small transaction cost—a market impact cost—paid by any transactor. Furthermore, to the extent these market impact costs, or liquidity costs, are significant and known to be so they will limit the extent of dynamic hedging. Hedge ratios will be adjusted less frequently resulting in less active trading.

Regulatory Capacity

Concerns About Regulatory Capacity

In an industry as fast growing and innovative as the derivatives industry, it is inevitable that regulators will find themselves having to work hard to keep up with the latest developments in the private sector. Concern has been expressed that this regulatory lag could pose risks if regulators and examiners are inadequately equipped to assess the products, strategies, models, and internal controls used by derivatives dealers. Inadequate training of regulators, moreover, can penalize innovative institutions when risk-averse regulators naturally oppose what they do not understand. The downside to this risk aversion, however, is the potential for regulatory overreaction during a market disturbance.

Analysis of Regulatory Capacity

Regulatory and supervisory agencies, for the most part, have responded well to the challenges posed by derivatives. For example, the Federal Reserve Board's recent supervisory letter to examiners and its more detailed trading manual provide detailed guidelines for examiners evaluating the derivatives activities of banks. The OCC's recent circulars and its financial derivatives handbook provide similar guidance to their examiners. While extensive educational efforts directed at training examiners have been undertaken by the banking agencies, these agencies also acknowledge the need for continued staff training in the derivatives area. Continued training is essential since inadequately trained examiners are more likely to question sophisticated and complex risk management systems and models they do not understand. In the extreme, this overreaction could deter institutions from developing the more sophisticated systems often required for responsible risk management.

Most importantly, a fundamental lack of understanding at the regulatory or legislative level about the nature and management of derivatives risks could result in a significant potential for "regulatory risk"—the risk that inappropriate regulations or ill-conceived and ill-timed regulatory actions, such as unexpected trading halts and capital controls, could exacerbate normal market disruptions, reducing liquidity and heightening volatility. Indeed, Nobel laureate Merton Miller has argued that the major source of systemic risk from derivatives owes to this source—regulatory overreaction. This overreaction, can result from both the initiative of regulators and the insistence of legislators.

On a positive note, the proper training of regulators and examination staff in the "derivatives way of thinking" is essential if the derivatives driven "revolution in risk management" is to flow into the more traditional activities of financial institutions and, thereby, enhance the safety and soundness of these institutions and the overall economy.

IV. ARE SYSTEMIC CONCERNS WARRANTED: A SUMMING UP?

Having identified, defined, and separately assessed the various factors that commentators have described as having the potential for creating systemic risk, it is time for a summing up. Have derivatives activities increased systemic risk? After weighing the available evidence and accounting for the private and public sector actions that have addressed the real risks of derivatives, it seems reasonable to conclude with confidence that the answer is no. The alarmist rhetoric about the systemic risks of derivatives is simply unsupported by the evidence. The basis for this conclusion warrants summarizing.

The risks of derivatives are not new or unique. They are the same risks—credit, settlement, market, liquidity, operational, and legal—that dealers have long experience in managing in their traditional businesses. Moreover, senior management and boards of directors at major U.S. dealers are fully aware of their responsibilities for overseeing the derivatives activities of their firm.

Significant progress has been made in understanding the risks of derivatives in both the private and public sectors. All major U.S. dealers—including banks, securities firms, and insurance companies—and many major end users have dramatically enhanced their systems for identifying, measuring, managing, and controlling the risks of derivatives. These improvements in internal-control and risk-management systems are spilling over to improve the management of all aspects of the operations of these institutions, enhancing their overall safety and soundness. The regulatory agencies with responsibility for supervising the derivatives activities of bank dealers have improved their understanding of the risks of derivatives and enhanced their examination procedures. Further improvements in supervision are underway.

The risks of derivatives have tended to be grossly overstated in popular discussions. For example, this paper has shown that:

- The net credit risk of the major U.S. dealers' derivatives portfolio is just 1.0 percent of the notional principal of their derivatives transactions outstanding.
- The net credit exposure taken on by bank dealers through derivatives is a small fraction of the overall credit exposure taken on in their traditional activities.
- The credit quality of derivatives participants—dealers and end users alike—has been, and remains, quite high.
- Credit exposures among the major U.S. dealers are not excessively concentrated.
- The market risk of derivatives portfolios at the major U.S. dealers is relatively small and is well managed and supervised.

Once the actual risks of derivatives are seen in proper perspective, it is clear that the capital base of the financial institutions involved in derivatives is more than adequate to absorb the incremental risk exposures resulting from derivatives activities.

Finally, the market linkages created by derivatives have increased diversification and broadened the sharing of risk, making the financial system more (rather than less) robust in the face of financial shocks. This economically intuitive conclusion is supported by substantial empirical evidence that overwhelmingly finds that increases in market linkages created by derivatives do not increase market volatility or exacerbate market moves. There is little or no empirical support, in short, for the view that derivatives increase systemic risk.

APPENDIX

VIEWS ON THE RISKS OF DERIVATIVES

"The risks to end-users and dealers involved in derivatives can be broadly categorized as market, credit, operational and legal. These risks are the same types that banks and securities firms have faced in their traditional lines of business–taking deposits and making loans, or purchasing and financing securities positions. The risks of derivatives, in other words, are not new."

The Group of Thirty, (July 1993)

"While derivatives are relatively new, their risks are not. They reflect essentially the same risks that banks have always faced: credit risk, settlement risk, operating risk, market risk and so forth. They will surely also help us create important new products."

Alan Greenspan, Chairman
The Federal Reserve Board, (November 7, 1993)

"The types of risk-management practices described in the guidance issued by the OCC and the Federal Reserve could be used by regulators not only as a basis for assessing risk-management of derivatives activities, but also for assessing the overall risk-management activities of the institution."

The General Accounting Office, (May 17, 1994)

"In looking at regulatory issues relating to these products, one must ask whether these products are inherently more risky than traditional products. Is an interest rate swap entered into by a bank inherently more dangerous than a loan to a real estate developer, or holding a portfolio of long term fixed rate government bonds? Is a currency swap inherently more dangerous to a broker dealer than the underwriting of a major securities offering or a bridge loan to finance a client's proposed acquisition? Is it inherently more difficult for management to operate risk management controls for trading in swaps than in mortgage backed securities or spot foreign currency? Is the legal risk of a repeat of Hammersmith and Fulham worse than the risks to bondholders in Washington Public Power System?"

Richard Breeden, Chairman
The Securities and Exchange Commission, (March 11, 1993)

"The risks associated with derivatives–counterparty credit risks, market risks, and operational risks–are the same types of risks that banks are accustomed to managing in their traditional activities. But derivatives combine these risks in especially complex ways. Thus, banks that are highly active in the derivatives markets must develop new risk management methodologies, stronger risk controls, and better management systems."

Susan Phillips, Governor
The Federal Reserve Board, (March 3, 1993)

"[T]here is little that can be clearly said to be unique about derivatives in so far as supervisory interest is concerned."

The Bank of England, (April 1993)

VIEWS ON CREDIT RISK

"[T]he notional value of a derivative contract is not a useful measure of credit exposure. That exposure generally amounts to only a small fraction, say two to three percent, of notional value."

Joint Study by Banking Supervisors, (January 27, 1993)

"Gross credit risk for 14 major U.S. financial institutions that responded to a GAO survey was $114 billion, or 1.8 percent of their $6.5 trillion notional amount, as of year-end 1992."

The General Accounting Office, (May 17, 1994)

"[W]hile we are all understandably preoccupied with the daunting task of trying to keep pace with the latest developments in this world of "high-tech" banking and finance, we should remember that, almost without exception, the most serious banking problems which have been encountered in recent years have grown out of old-fashioned difficulties with bad loans and excessive concentrations."

E. Gerald Corrigan, President
The Federal Reserve Bank of New York, (October 8, 1992)

"[T]he derivatives related credit exposures for the seven U.S. bank dealers were, with one exception, much lower than the credit exposure arising from their loans."

The General Accounting Office, (May 17, 1994)

"To date, there have not been any spectacular failures where derivatives books have led to a firm's collapse. In fact, the record in this area so far has been far more enviable than the record of traditional credit intermediaries. The problems in the derivative market will have to be enormous to ever rival the recent loan loss and bank failure experience."

J. Carter Beese, Jr., Commissioner
The Securities and Exchange Commission, (December 1, 1992)

"[V]ery few banks they rate have been materially affected by their derivative activities except in a positive way. Moody's does not think derivatives are a ticking time bomb for the banking industry as a whole. Standard & Poor's indicates that banks benefit from derivative profits in that they are a stable source of income, and should be viewed as good-quality earnings for banks."

House Banking Committee Minority Staff, (November 1993)

"In 1992, ISDA commissioned an independent survey of swap credit losses. Dealers responding to the survey held 113,000 transactions aggregating $3.1 trillion in notional amount with an average life of 3.3 years. The survey asked for all defaults and losses over the entire history of a dealer's involvement in swaps. Respondents reported 513 defaulted transactions over a 10-year period with a notional amount of $12.8 billion. The notional amount of transactions giving rise to a claim totalled $9.8 billion and the actual losses incurred were $358 million."

The Group of Thirty, (July 1993)

VIEWS ON SETTLEMENT AND PAYMENTS RISK

"[Y]ou had all better take a very, very hard look at off-balance sheet activities, including the payments, clearance and settlement risks associated with many of those activities. The growth and complexity of off-balance sheet activities and the nature of the credit, price and settlement risk they entail should give us all cause for concern, especially when it seems so easy to accept the view that what counts is net, not gross, exposure. ... [I]n the event of a major market disruption, I assure you that it will be gross, not the net, that will really matter in most segments of the marketplace both nationally and internationally."

E. Gerald Corrigan, President
The Federal Reserve Bank of New York, (January 30, 1992)

"Of the various risks faced in interbank markets, the greatest concern attaches to credit risk. However, the increase in the volume and average size of transactions in recent years, the strengthening of linkages among market segments and players, and the increased level of concentration in many market segments have also led to heightened awareness and concern about settlement risk and market liquidity risk."

The Bank for International Settlements, (October 1992)

"The growth of derivative instruments has created complex chains of counterparty exposures and, in the case of exchange rate contracts, a significant expansion of payments and settlements activity. Consequently, the Federal Reserve, in particular, closely monitors the payment and settlement mechanisms and has taken steps designed to reduce risks and guard against payments gridlock."

Joint Study by Banking Supervisors, (January 27, 1993)

"[T]he daily cash flow requirements in derivative markets are far less than those resulting from spot foreign exchange transactions, settlements in government securities, mortgage backed securities and many other investments. In all of these markets, there are higher daily settlement requirements."

Richard C. Breeden, Former Chairman
The Securities and Exchange Commission, (May 10, 1994)

"The largest source of settlement risk in payment systems is the settlement exposure created by foreign exchange transactions. ... While OTC derivatives would benefit from a reduction of [settlement] risk, it must be noted that the amounts involved are very small relative to the amounts involved in traditional foreign exchange activities. ISDA has estimated that daily global cash flows from interest rate swaps and currency swaps average $2.5 billion. In contrast, the BIS estimates daily global net turnover in the foreign exchange markets at $880 billion. The payments netting provisions that are standard in derivatives contracts are an important way in which participants reduce the settlement risk of payments made in the same currency."

The Group of Thirty, (July 1993)

VIEWS ON MARKET RISK

"One aspect of derivatives that makes measuring and, therefore, managing market risk difficult is that their values are influenced by many different factors. For example, the value of a portfolio of foreign exchange options is affected by changes in exchange rates, interest rates, and the length of time remaining before the options expire."

The General Accounting Office, (May 17, 1994)

"Dealers now typically manage the market risks of their derivatives activity on the basis of the net or residual exposure of the overall portfolio. A dealer's portfolio generally will contain many offsetting positions, which substantially reduce the overall risk of the portfolio, leaving a much smaller residual risk to be hedged. ... Dealers look beyond the particular contracts and focus instead on identifying the fundamental risks they contain so the overall portfolio can be decomposed into underlying risk factors that can be quantified and managed."

The Group of Thirty, (July 1993)

"Market risk, by contrast, is said to be more manageable now than in the past, owing to the efforts firms have made in recent years to control these risks through the use of derivative instruments and other techniques. Market risks are also more easily priced than other risks."

. . .

"Participants consider market risk to cover the risk of price changes in explicit positions, as well as spread and basis risk in imperfectly hedged positions. Despite continued volatility in asset prices and exchange rates, the richer menu of instruments available for hedging and position-taking, and the greater expertise in using them, both appear to have made market risk much less of a concern than in the past. By contrast, basis or spread risk can be substantial across a firm's derivatives business because it may not be possible [in the short run], desirable [because exposure is intentional] or cost-effective to hedge transactions exactly."

The Bank for International Settlements, (October 1992)

"Risk management of derivatives was admitted to be highly complex and costly, but complex products could be broken down into their constituent parts and revaluation rates [for marking-to- market] were on the whole readily available. Perfect hedges were not always obtainable [certainly not always immediately obtainable], but effective risk management, we were told, should not be confused with risk elimination. Derivatives players were in some sense felt to be better placed than banks trading only in cash markets, in that there were a variety of ways they could lay off risk."

The Bank of England, (April 1993)

"Regulators and the 15 major OTC dealers GAO visited said that improvements in risk-management systems have been made in response to both the Group of Thirty recommendations and bank guidance."

The General Accounting Office, (May 17, 1994)

VIEWS ON LIQUIDITY RISK

"Banks face two types of liquidity risk in their trading activities: those related to specific products or markets and those related to the general funding of the bank's trading activities. ... Since neither type of liquidity risk is unique to trading activities, management should evaluate these risks in the broader context of the institution's overall liquidity. ... In developing guidelines for controlling the liquidity risks in trading activities, banks should consider the possibility that they could lose access to one or more markets, either because of concerns about the bank's own creditworthiness, the creditworthiness of a major counterparty, or because of generally stressful market conditions."

The Federal Reserve Board, (December 20, 1993)

"Therefore, it is fair to conclude, as a general matter, that the U.S. securities industry is well capitalized, highly liquid, and adequately managed. In addition, it would appear that the U.S. securities industry is on a footing comparable to that of U.S. depository institutions with respect to the liquidity necessary to conduct derivatives activities."

The Securities and Exchange Commission, (October 27, 1993)

"The use of such dynamic hedging methods can generate liquidity problems [since they] can trigger an avalanche of sales into a relatively illiquid market for the underlying security, thereby collapsing the price or causing a breakdown in trading."

International Monetary Fund, (August 1993)

"The liquidity of derivatives transactions has been tested in several situations of failure by important participants. When insolvent financial institutions have been wound up in the last few years, including DFC New Zealand, Bank of New England, British &

Commonwealth Bank, and Drexel Burnham, the derivatives activities were transferred or closed out reasonably quickly.

The magnitude of illiquidity risk varies greatly depending upon the extent to which market participants have similar positions to manage, and the extent to which they use dynamic hedging. ... [M]ost derivatives portfolios require only limited amounts of hedging relative to their overall size because, to a large extent, positions are well matched. Derivatives dealers attempt to hedge directly the ... risks of options written with purchased options, while dynamically hedging only the smaller residual risk arising from any remaining mismatches in the options portfolio. It is these dealers who need, and typically have, the most sophisticated risk management systems."

The Group of Thirty, (July 1993)

VIEWS ON OPERATIONAL RISK

"Operational risk is the risk of losses occurring as a result of inadequate systems and control, human error, or management failure."

The Group of Thirty, (July 1993)

"[S]trong internal control systems; independent, knowledgeable audit committees; and public reporting on internal controls are critical to firms engaged in complex derivatives activities and should play an important role in ensuring sound financial operations and protecting shareholder interests of these firms."

The General Accounting Office, (May 17, 1994)

"Many, including most of the key firms active across the range of wholesale markets, accept the need to make very considerable resources available for evaluating, monitoring and managing the risks incurred across offices, product and the range of counterparties with which they deal. ... However, the current state of risk management among the key players in the wholesale markets covers a wide range of levels and styles, and significant gaps remain between the desired risk management systems and the systems actually in operation."

The Bank for International Settlements, (October 1992)

"Because these instruments are new, rapidly changing and somewhat more complex than traditional products, risk management controls are relatively speaking even more important than normal. This is a prime area of inquiry for the SEC in evaluating broker-dealers under our risk assessment program. We expect firms to know who is responsible for decision-making, and to have in place systems to manage risk-taking activities."

Richard Breeden, Chairman
The Securities and Exchange Commission, (March 11, 1993)

"[T]he increasing scope and complexity of derivatives–coupled with the urging of supervisors–has induced financial institutions to upgrade significantly their risk management capabilities. This enhancement of risk management systems has been an evolutionary process as banks themselves have identified important new risk measurement methodologies and management techniques. ... The evolution of risk management systems is expected to continue at a rapid pace. Indeed, the recent Group of Thirty study on derivatives marks an important step in this process by contributing importantly to a better understanding of sound risk management and operating practices. As pointed out in the study itself, not all institutions currently follow all of the study's recommended practices. However, many are well underway toward effective implementation of these sound practices."

The Federal Reserve Board, (October 26, 1993)

"All 15 major U.S. derivatives dealers we visited told us they had controls over their derivatives activities. Examples they cited included the separation of duties between trading and administrative staff, independent transaction confirmations, and independent pricing of their OTC portfolios."

The General Accounting Office, (May 17, 1994)

VIEWS ON LEGAL RISK

"Legal risk is the risk of loss because a contract cannot be enforced. This includes risks arising from insufficient documentation, insufficient capacity or authority of a counterparty [ultra vires], uncertain legality, and unenforceability in bankruptcy or insolvency."

The Group of Thirty, (July 1993)

"One immediate goal that can reduce systemic risk is to ensure that netting agreements are enforceable in all major markets."

Alan Greenspan, Chairman
The Federal Reserve Board, (November 7, 1993)

"[A]ny and all actions to strengthen legal certainty as to the enforceability of obligations, including netting agreements, will powerfully contribute to systemic stability by significantly reducing potential liquidity demands."

Richard Breeden, Former Chairman
The Securities and Exchange Commission, (May 10, 1994)

"The [S.E.C.] staff supports efforts to remove the uncertainty surrounding bilateral close-out netting, multi-branch netting, and collateral arrangements in bankruptcy. Experience ... suggests that there is a need for greater certainty and coordination in this area."

The Securities and Exchange Commission, (October 27, 1993)

"The Federal Reserve also has supported efforts to reduce legal uncertainty by clarifying the Commodity Futures Trading Commission's authority to exempt classes of OTC derivative instruments from regulation under the Commodity Exchange Act, including the Act's prohibition on off-exchange trading of futures. The Futures Trading Practices Act of 1992 indicated explicitly that the Commission has this authority, and the Commission has acted promptly to exercise it, ..."

Susan M. Phillips, Governor
The Federal Reserve Board, (February 25, 1994)

"Enforceability presents the greatest risk participants face in derivatives transactions. The International Swaps and Derivatives Association [ISDA] recently sponsored a survey of default experiences among a diverse group of its members. At those institutions, cumulative losses over the 10-year history of their involvement in swaps totaled $358 million. Almost half of these losses was attributable to English local authorities–the result of the decision of the U.K. House of Lords in the Hammersmith and Fulham case ... which held that English local authorities did not have the capacity to enter swap and other derivatives transactions."

The Group of Thirty, (July 1993)

VIEWS ON SIZE AND GROWTH

"Many observers, both inside and outside Washington, are questioning whether the increased volume of trading activities and the rapid growth of new and complex derivatives products are healthy for commercial banks and for the U.S. financial system. They ask whether these activities have introduced risks that may be difficult to understand, manage, and supervise and whether trading and derivatives profits can be sustained."

Alan Greenspan, Chairman
The Federal Reserve Board, (November 7, 1993)

"The rapidly expanding activities of banking organizations in the derivatives markets clearly has been a source of interest and even concern to some banking regulators. Regulators are understandably concerned that rapid growth may be a sign of trouble ahead. At the level of individual institutions, rapid asset growth in the 1980s very often was followed by credit quality problems that burdened not only shareholders but also taxpayers. Too often, rapid growth at an individual institution has been a sign that internal risk controls were inadequate or that intermediation services were being provided at unprofitable margins. At the industry level, every banking regulator is aware of how industry-wide deterioration of credit standards produced huge losses in the LDC, HLT, and commercial real estate sectors."

Susan M. Phillips, Governor
The Federal Reserve Board, (December 3, 1992)

"In reality, however, while the $1 trillion in contracts that U.S. broker-dealers are booking annually seems large, the amounts actually at risk in these markets do not appear to be unusually large compared with the size of exposures that banks, broker-dealers and insurance companies maintain for their traditional businesses."

Richard Breeden, Chairman
The Securities and Exchange Commission, (March 11, 1993)

"The notional amount is one way that derivatives activity is measured. However, it is not a meaningful measure of the actual risks involved."

The General Accounting Office, (May 17, 1994)

"It does not help matters that discussions of the size of this market have focused on notional amounts, and that estimates include numbers as different as $4 trillion and $7 ½ trillion. These numbers, of course, are based on different definitions of derivatives and do not tell us anything about the amount at risk. Short-term derivatives and long-term derivatives are equally weighted in the calculation, and nothing is indicated by these numbers about the credit quality of the counterparties or the volatility of the underlying cash markets."

Frank N. Newman, Undersecretary
The Department of the Treasury, (October 27, 1993)

VIEWS ON CONCENTRATION

"A greater degree of concentration in the wholesale markets has meant that larger exposures are incurred vis-a-vis a smaller set of key players. ... Since the failure of one such key player would entail larger losses to other participants in the markets than if exposures were more dispersed, increased concentration implies that financial market stability could be affected more heavily than in the past by the sudden decline of any such firm. ... [The] increased concentration of funds has increased the ability of some large players individually and collectively to affect market prices."

The Bank for International Settlements, (October 1992)

"[A]mong U.S. firms, eight banks and a small number of securities firms presently account for the great majority of over-the-counter derivative transactions, and it appears that there is similar concentration on an international scale. Given this concentration, we should be concerned that a crisis involving any one major dealer could quickly and substantially affect the others."

Mary L. Schapiro, Commissioner
The Securities and Exchange Commission, (October 14, 1993)

"With regard to concentration, the staff does not believe that derivatives activities are concentrated in too few institutions. While concentration is a concern, OTC derivatives dealers tend to be well-diversified, highly capitalized firms that are, arguably, well-suited to weather adverse market developments."

The Securities and Exchange Commission, (October 27, 1993)

"[S]ome have argued that ... those banks would be able to extract extra-normal profits from derivatives transactions, to the detriment of their customers. However, such arguments neglect to account for the large number of foreign bank and non-bank financial institutions that also participate in derivatives markets. As a consequence, it is unlikely derivatives market participants are disadvantaged by the aforementioned concentration of derivatives activities."

The Office of the Comptroller of the Currency, (October 14, 1993)

"With respect to concentration in derivatives markets, the fact that market-making is feasible only for firms in a strong financial condition and with long experience in dealing with similar risks in foreign exchange markets [because only such firms have the resources needed to manage these risks properly and are the most attractive counterparties] is a positive element."

The Federal Reserve Board, (October 6, 1993)

VIEWS ON COMPLEXITY

"The rapid growth and increasing complexity of derivatives reflect both the increased demand from end users for better ways to manage their financial risks and the innovative capacity of the financial services industry to respond to market demands."

The General Accounting Office, (May 17, 1994)

"[T]he complexity of risks incurred in OTC derivatives markets means that firms that want to participate profitably and safely in them must have at their disposal advanced hardware and software systems and highly skilled individuals."

The Bank for International Settlements, (October 1992)

"[T]he complexity of some derivative instruments ... tends to make the problem of risk management more difficult. To assess the impact on their total portfolios of potential changes in market prices, financial institutions must monitor and value their positions in a wide range of markets, and must assess liquidity in each of those markets. ... At the same time, assessment of credit risk is especially important because of the credit exposures that can arise from derivatives transactions, but the complexity of derivatives books and the evolving but still disparate nature of disclosure in various countries make the assessment of counterparties somewhat opaque and difficult."

The Federal Reserve Board, (October 6, 1993)

"These general types of risk exist for many financial activities, but the specific risks in derivatives activities are relatively difficult to manage, in part, because of the complexity of some of these products and the difficulties in measuring these risks. For example, because derivatives might be used in conjunction with other assets and liabilities, measuring the extent of market risks of derivatives products alone is not sufficient to understand a firm's total market risk."

The General Accounting Office, (May 17, 1994)

"The complexity of derivatives activities, along with the intense scrutiny these activities have attracted, are forcing a revolution in risk management practices."

Susan M. Phillips, Governor
The Federal Reserve Board, (February 25, 1994)

"Its complexity, which is a reflection of the equally complex risks in the real economy, would merit concern if it out-stripped participants' ability to evaluate and manage the attendant risks. There is much evidence to the contrary, as the Survey of Industry Practice confirms. Most dealers have gone to great lengths to establish sophisticated techniques to manage their derivatives exposures with considerable precision; many are extending the benefits of these techniques."

The Group of Thirty, (July 1993)

VIEWS ON TRANSPARENCY

"The participation in wholesale markets by entities subject to few disclosure requirements, as well as the growth of off-balance-sheet activities, more generally [adequate details of which are rarely disclosed], has made the assessment of counterparty credit risks considerably more difficult.

...[T]he greater complexity of financial transactions has reduced the transparency of firms' balance sheets, and has made it more difficult to determine the distribution of risks in financial markets. In a crisis situation, a lack of transparency might cause firms to back away from troubled institutions and, perhaps, from other institutions perceived to be subject to similar stress. As a result of this behavior, which reflects incomplete information, disturbances can spread more quickly and more broadly across firms and markets."

The Bank for International Settlements, (October 1992)

"[T]he increased use of derivative instruments, combined with the inadequacy of current accounting concepts in this area, has reduced the transparency of a firm's exposures, and of the financial system more broadly."

William J. McDonough, President
The Federal Reserve Bank of New York, (September 27, 1993)

"The market is losing transparency, and we do not know who is dependent on whom anymore. Now we only know after the fact, and by then it could be too late."

Alexandre Lamfalussy, General Manager
The Bank for International Settlements, (October 1992)

"For the future, the best way to prevent the development of systemic risks is to maximize the transparency of financial reporting by both U.S. and foreign derivatives dealers and end users."

Richard C. Breeden, Former Chairman
The Securities and Exchange Commission, (May 10, 1994)

"Within the global securities community, market authorities have sought to analyze the determinants of market fairness and efficiency in secondary markets and the role of transparency in achieving these requirements. To date, market authorities have been unable to achieve consensus on the relative importance of the elements underlying transparency, or on the need for transparency in all markets."

The Commodity Futures Trading Commission, (October 1993)

"[*I*]*nternally the risks of derivatives are becoming increasingly transparent thanks to the growing and nearly universal reliance on daily mark-to-market measures for risk management. According to the Survey* [*of Industry Practice*], *80 percent of dealers and 100 percent of global full range dealers follow this practice. Doing so instills greater risk management discipline; problems are identified more quickly and management is driven to take steps to address them before they grow."*

The Group of Thirty, (July 1993)

VIEWS ON MANAGEMENT UNDERSTANDING

"I hope this sounds like a warning, because it is. Off-balance sheet activities have a role, but they must be managed and controlled carefully, and they must be understood by top management, as well as by traders and rocket scientists. They also must be understood by supervisors."

E. Gerald Corrigan, President
The Federal Reserve Bank of New York, (January 30, 1992)

"I do understand that people of my generation who are not astrophysicists have to strain to understand these products. But it simply not responsible to use that difficulty as an excuse for non-involvement. To put it simply and directly, if the bosses do not or cannot understand both the risks and rewards in their products, their firm should not be in the business."

William J. McDonough, President
The Federal Reserve Bank of New York, (September 27, 1993)

"[*I*]*t seems to me that the information gap that sometimes exists between the regulators and the market is probably similar to the information gap that also sometimes exists between trading desks and CEOs and boards of directors."*

J. Carter Beese, Jr., Commissioner
The Securities and Exchange Commission, (December 1, 1992)

"The banking agencies recognize that regulation cannot substitute for effective management. ... To date, those management processes have been generally successful. However, to keep pace with the rapidly changing financial environment, including expansion of derivatives activities, all market participants need to continue to enhance their procedures and infrastructures for managing and controlling risks. This effort will

require increased management awareness and understanding of the nature of the risks assumed."

Joint Study by Banking Supervisors, (January 27, 1993)

"[*T*]*here can be no doubt that each organization's conscious and disciplined attention to understanding, measuring, and controlling risk along the lines suggested* [*by the Global Derivatives Study Group*] *should help ensure that the risks to individual institutions and to markets as a whole are limited and manageable."*

Paul Volcker, Chairman
The Group of Thirty, (July 1993)

"With the passage of almost two and one-half years, I am pleased with the significant progress that has been made in learning more about derivatives in both private and official circles. For example, in the private sector truly great progress has been, and is being made, in developing the risk management, information and control systems that are so crucial for individual firms and the marketplace more generally,"

E. Gerald Corrigan, Former President
The Federal Reserve Bank of New York, (May 10, 1994)

VIEWS ON UNREGULATED ENTITIES

"The Board is aware that concerns have been expressed about unregulated dealers and unsophisticated end-users and is in the process of evaluating whether regulatory changes are needed to address these concerns. In addressing these issues, the Board and other policy makers need to balance carefully the need to contain systemic risk, protect unsophisticated investors and avoid moral hazard against the need to maintain efficient and internationally competitive markets."

The Federal Reserve Board, (October 6, 1993)

"[*T*]*he unsupervised status of, for example, large swap players does represent a supervisory hole at the very heart of the derivatives markets."*

The Bank of England, (April 1993)

"With the passage of the [*Market Reform Act*], *the completely "unregulated" status of U.S. broker-dealer affiliates was ended, at least where any such affiliate has a material level of financial market exposure. These entities are unquestionably less regulated than banks or broker-dealers, but a lesser degree of regulation is also appropriate because these entities are not engaged in a public client business and their liabilities are not backed by the federal government or the SIPC."*

Richard C. Breeden, Former Chairman
The Securities and Exchange Commission, (May 10, 1994)

"Whether we ultimately will need to move toward greater oversight of the activities of the affiliates themselves is an open question and subject to extensive and healthy debate. ... [I] am not convinced that consolidated regulatory supervision of securities firms and their affiliates is necessary or appropriate at this time. There may be other ways to restrict risks to regulated entities... that preserve the benefit to financial innovation that may result from a more flexible regulatory paradigm."

Mary Schapiro, Commissioner
The Securities and Exchange Commission, (October 14, 1993)

"[I]t would be a colossal mistake to expand regulation to corporate users of derivatives."

E. Gerald Corrigan, Former President
The Federal Reserve Bank of New York, (May 10, 1994)

"Unregulated entities-such as affiliates of U.S. broker-dealers or of insurance companies, and certain non-financial firms - have promoted competition and innovation without any evidence to date of increased risk to regulated dealers or increased systemic risk. Participants can evaluate for themselves the risks and benefits of trading with unregulated entities."

The Group of Thirty, (July 1993)

VIEWS ON NEW ENTRANTS

"In the derivatives arena there is also a problem of the new kids on the block. If problems develop in the derivatives marketplace, it is a good bet that they will be less likely to stem from the major firms operating in the mainstream, than from firms that are new entrants or operating at the fringes of this market. Any regulation in the derivatives area must be premised on the assumption that all market participants are not equal in sophistication or integrity and that distinctions must inevitably be made between prudential and less prudential actors."

James A. Leach, Member
U.S. House of Representatives, (September 27, 1993)

"We believe that the largest players–the ones with by far the most experience with derivatives–already have systems in place to perform such analyses. The newer players are where our deepest concerns focus."

Eugene A. Ludwig, Comptroller of the Currency
The Department of Treasury, (September 27, 1993)

"In contrast to the situation of the largest derivatives dealers, where overall risk management systems tend to be fairly high, new market entrants, second or third tier dealers, firms with limited scope and others may have failed to make the generally high level of investment in people, analytics and data systems that are required to manage risk effectively."

Richard C. Breeden, Former Chairman
The Securities and Exchange Commission, (May 10, 1994)

"We are concerned, for example, that as derivative products become more popular, small and less sophisticated institutions will turn increasingly to derivative products as tools to counter the effects of market volatility or to reallocate certain risks, particularly currency risks, associated with portfolio assets. Certain derivative products, such as detachable call options on municipal bonds or collateralized mortgage obligations, are available even to retail investors. Many derivative products, however, may not be suitable for less sophisticated institutional and retail customers."

The Securities and Exchange Commission, (October 27, 1993)

"We all recognize the benefits associated with derivative instruments. Participants in financial markets, and potential end users in all sectors of the economy, should not be discouraged from realizing some of those benefits. So long as participants understand the risks and manage those risks appropriately, their involvement can add to the liquidity and hasten the maturing of these still young markets."

Larry Promisel, Senior Associate Director
The Federal Reserve System, (December 2, 1993)

VIEWS ON MARKET LINKAGES

"[T]he speed, volume, value and complexity of international banking transactions have introduced new linkages and interdependencies between markets and institutions that have the potential to transmit problems and disruptions from place to place and institution to institution at almost breakneck speed.

E. Gerald Corrigan, President
The Federal Reserve Bank of New York, (October 8, 1992)

"[L]inkages between markets have been greatly strengthened by the more rapid dissemination of information, the increased use of derivative instruments and strategies that span many market segments. At the same time, the presence of the same small set of key players in most of the wholesale markets has deepened linkages among the participating institutions."

. . .

"[F]rom the perspective of the financial system's resilience to market disturbances, linked markets can act as a safety valve. By offering alternative sources of supply and demand, price changes may be transmitted from one market to others and can thereby help to diffuse disturbances. ... [T]here are some circumstances in which close linkages can be a source of concern. This would be the case if, as price movements or uncertainties are transmitted from one market to another, they are reinforced rather than dampened."

The Bank for International Settlements, (October 1992)

"Moreover, there are reasons to believe that capital market innovations have, in some important respects, increased structural stability. Derivatives should after all, allow banks to better manage risk and so should help to insulate the payments system from financial and real shocks. Similarly, the increased substitutability among instruments and intermediaries should buffer the economy from disruptions affecting specific markets or classes of intermediaries."

Alan Greenspan, Chairman
The Federal Reserve Board, (August 19, 1993)

"Derivatives have increased market linkages by intermediating markets efficiently and providing effective risk management tools to facilitate the operation of global businesses. At the same time there is concern that by fostering these linkages, derivatives make it possible for shocks to be transmitted faster and farther than was possible before. The academic research indicates that derivatives trading does not increase volatility in underlying markets."

The Group of Thirty, (July 1993)

VIEWS ON DYNAMIC HEDGING

"Undoubtedly, there is at least one big limitation on the effectiveness of any dynamic hedging strategy–liquidity may not be there when you need it most. The portfolio insurance debacle of 1987 showed that buyers in the listed markets may be reluctant to absorb the selling interest generated by non-transparent activities the size of which is unknown. This is an issue that is particularly relevant to the U.S. equity market. Of course, dealers with over-the-counter equity derivative positions may not all be lined up on the same side of the market, but there's a good chance that in a crisis, many of them will be trying to swim with the tide, and many may not make it to shore."

Mary L. Schapiro, Commissioner
The Securities and Exchange Commission, (October 14, 1993)

"One concern is the phenomenon frequently referred to as positive feedback, that is, those mechanisms that have the potential to exacerbate an already sharp price move. ... Positive feedback mechanisms always have existed in financial markets in one form or another, but the tremendous growth of options and option-like instruments creates an added source of positive feedback. This is because written options, as a matter of course, tend to be dynamically hedged and require selling into a falling market."

William J. McDonough, President
The Federal Reserve Bank of New York, (September 27, 1993)

"Most end-users use derivatives for hedging purposes and are provided with customized transactions that do not require ongoing hedge adjustments on their part. As for dealers, most derivatives portfolios require only limited amounts of hedging relative to their overall size because, to a large extent, positions are well matched. Exposure to this

risk is greatest for dealers whose portfolios have large short convexity and volatility positions. Derivatives dealers attempt to hedge directly the convexity and volatility risks of options written with purchased options - hedging options with options, while dynamically hedging only the smaller residual risk arising from any remaining mismatches in the options portfolio. It is these dealers who need, and typically have, the most sophisticated risk management systems."

. . .

"The close links between derivatives and underlying markets might result in an increase in market volatility, possibly because of dynamic hedging of option positions. The academic research on the effects of derivatives on market volatility is increasingly consistent in its findings, and particularly voluminous after the 1987 crash. The research strongly indicates that derivatives trading either has no effect on, or reduces, volatility in underlying markets."

The Group of Thirty, (July 1993)

VIEWS ON REGULATORY CAPACITY

"The federal banking agencies should establish coordinated training programs for examiners involved in monitoring derivatives activities at dealers banks and end users."

James A. Leach, Member
U.S. House of Representatives, (November 22, 1993)

"While the history of industry self-regulation has not been overly impressive, clearly to date, in the derivatives area, the private sector is leading the public, not only in the development of new market instruments, but with techniques to manage and constrain risk."

House Banking Committee Minority Staff, (November 1993)

"Before introducing any additional regulations, we need to identify clearly the public policy objectives that the regulations are intended to achieve. We should also consider whether official encouragement of private sector initiatives is a more effective means of meeting those objectives."

Susan M. Phillips, Governor
Federal Reserve Board, (December 3, 1992)

"Bank regulators have recently taken steps to improve their examinations of bank's derivatives activities. In February 1994, the Federal Reserve issued its new examination manual, which consolidates and expands examination procedures relating to trading and derivatives activities. ..."

. . .

"... The Federal Reserve and OCC have also conducted specialized training on derivatives for their staffs and designated certain staff to serve as advisors on derivatives issues to the heads of the agencies or to examination staff."

The General Accounting Office, (May 17, 1994)

VIEWS ON SYSTEMIC RISK

"I believe we would all be well served to operate on the assumption that systemic risk may be greater as we look ahead. ... [T]he speed, volume, value and complexity of international banking transactions have introduced new linkages and interdependencies between markets and institutions that have the potential to transmit problems and disruptions from place to place and institution to institution at almost breakneck speed. ... This is the fundamental reason why supervisors must be concerned about the astronomical growth of off-balance sheet and related activities and about the financial and operational integrity of national and international payment and settlement system."

E. Gerald Corrigan, President
The Federal Reserve Bank of New York, (October 8, 1992)

"There is far less risk today than in the past of something happening. All major financial intermediaries have dramatically increased their internal-control and risk-management systems."

E. Gerald Corrigan, Former President
The Federal Reserve Bank of New York, (May 10, 1994)

"Regulators have expressed concerns about the systemic risks that could result from the failure of a major dealer in the OTC derivatives markets. In part, they are concerned about the potential losses that a failure could impose on the dealer's counterparties. But concerns about systemic risk ... extend to the potential impacts on the liquidity of markets, not only the OTC derivatives markets but also the cash markets and the exchange markets to which the OTC derivatives markets are closely linked through the complex arbitrage strategies employed by major dealers. A loss of market liquidity would heighten both credit and market risks for all participants in the derivatives markets. Furthermore, the expansion of market linkages, which cut across national boundaries and embrace a wide range of financial and nonfinancial firms, raises concerns about the ability of central banks to contain systemic difficulties should they emerge."

Susan M. Phillips, Governor
The Federal Reserve Board, (December 3, 1992)

"[A]mong U.S. banks, only a few large institutions appear to have material exposures arising from activity in the derivative products markets. Most of them are perceived by the market to present little credit risk and, in practice, they all have sophisticated risk management procedures and capital bases large enough to absorb sizable derivative

products losses. Moreover, the concentration of derivative activities in only a few large institutions facilitates supervision of their activities. Therefore, the failure of one of these institutions as a result of derivative products appears unlikely in the current risk environment."

Joint Study by Banking Supervisors, (January 27, 1993)

"I wish to emphasize that I do not believe that derivatives are the sole, or perhaps even the principal, source of systemic risks in today's financial markets. At least equal risk of a sizable default or failure of a major financial firm, or group of firms, could result from losses on more traditional activities. Still, the increasingly widespread use of derivatives has altered firm-level exposures and market dynamics, and we must consider how these changes modify our thinking on possible sources of systemic disruptions and how they play out."

William J. McDonough, President
The Federal Reserve Bank of New York, (September 27, 1993)

"Considerable thought has been given ... to the question of whether–and in what ways–derivatives activities significantly change the level of systemic risk in financial markets. The Federal Reserve believes that the greater awareness and understanding of risk and the enhanced methods of managing risks probably have reduced the likelihood of systemic problems, and will continue to do so over time as industry and supervisory practices advance."

The Federal Reserve Board, (October 6, 1993)

"[D]erivatives transactions have not been responsible for the failure of any significant depository institution in the U.S., although thousands of banks and thrifts have failed due to poor lending practices or inside transactions. That is certainly not a guarantee for the future, but it should provide some helpful perspective."

Richard C. Breeden, Former Chairman
The Securities and Exchange Commission, (May 10, 1994)

"The first area of concern deals with the failure of market participants. This concern is not unique to derivative products and, indeed, it is possible that a securities firm or other financial institution could fail as a result of trading or other business activities, with such a failure having collateral effects throughout the marketplace. The staff believes, however, that the Commission and the SROs have in place sufficient regulatory controls to ensure that the failure of a registered broker-dealer, for whatever reason, could be handled without resulting in serious, system-wide problems."

The Securities and Exchange Commission, (October 27, 1993)

"[R]esearch suggests that no statistically significant evidence has been published to support the hypotheses that there is a relationship between spot market volatility and the existence of derivative markets."

Ontario Securities Commission, (January 1994)

"[B]ased on what we now know, I believe that concerns that derivatives could perpetrate a financial meltdown are overblown."

Frank N. Newman, Undersecretary
The Department of Treasury, (October 27, 1993)

REFERENCES

Aggarwal, R. "Stock Index Futures and Cash Market Volatility." *The Review of Futures Markets*, 7(2), 1988, pp. 290-299.

Antoniou, A. and A.F. Foster. "The Effect of Futures Trading on Spot Price Volatility: Evidence for Brent Crude Oil Using GARCH." Mimeo, 1991.

Baldauf, B. and G.J. Santoni. "Stock Price Volatility: Some Evidence from an ARCH Model." *Journal of Futures Markets*, 11(2), April 1991, pp. 191-200.

Bank of England. *Derivatives: Report of an Internal Working Group*. April 1993.

Bank for International Settlements. *Recent Developments in International Interbank Relations*, (the "Promisel Report"). Basle, October 1992.

Bank for International Settlements. *Report of the Committee on Interbank Netting Schemes of the Central Banks of the Group of 10 Countries*, (the "Lamfalussy Report"). November 1990.

Bansal, V.K, S.W. Pruitt and K.C. John Wei. "An Empirical Reexamination of the Impact of CBOE Option Initiation on the Volatility and Trading Volume of the Underlying Equities: 1973-1986." *The Financial Review*, 24, 1989, pp. 19-29.

Becketti, S. and Dan J. Roberts. "Will Increased Regulation of Stock Index Futures Reduce Stock Market Volatility?" *Economic Review*, Federal Reserve Bank of Kansas City, November/December 1990, pp. 33-46.

Beese, J. Carter, Jr. "Concerning the Regulation of Derivatives Activities." October 28, 1993.

________. "Remarks." Public Securities Association Panel Discussion on Derivatives, Orlando, Florida, March 4, 1994.

________. "The Regulatory Treatment of Derivatives." AIC Conference on Derivatives, January 13, 1994.

________. "The Great Derivatives Debate: Where Do We Go From Here?" *Risk Magazine* (*C*ATS*) Software Symposium, London, England, December 1, 1992.

________. "OTC Derivatives: Taking Risk Management to New Heights." London, England, April 20, 1993.

Board, John, Charles Goodhart and Charles Sutcliffe. "Inter-Market Volatility Linkages: The London Stock Exchange and London International Financial Futures Exchange." Securities and Investment Board, June 1992.

Bortz, G.A. "Does the Treasury Bond Futures Market Destabilize the Treasury Bond Cash Market?" *Journal of Futures Markets*, 4(1), Spring 1984, pp. 25-38.

Breeden, Richard C. "Directors, Control Your Derivatives." *The Wall Street Journal Europe*, March 8, 1994.

________. "Remarks." Annual Meeting of ISDA, Hong Kong, March 11, 1993.

Brorsen, W. "Futures Trading, Transaction Costs, and Stock Market Volatility." *Journal of Futures Markets*, 11(2), April 1991, pp. 153-163.

________. Charles Oellermann and Paul Farris. "The Live Cattle Futures Market and Daily Cash Price Movements." *Journal of Futures Markets*, 9(4), August 1989, pp. 273-282.

Chan, K.C. and G.A. Karolyi. "The Volatility of the Japanese Stock Market: Evidence from 1977 to 1990." In William Ziemba, Warren Bailey and Yasushi Hamao (Eds.), *Japanese Financial Market Research*. North Holland, 1991.

Commodity Futures Trading Commission. "Working Paper 4: Several Significant Defaults Affecting the Over-the Counter Derivatives Market." *OTC Derivative Markets and Their Regulation*, October 1993.

________. "Response to the Questions Posed By Congressman Leach." October 29, 1993.

Congressional Research Service. *Derivative Financial Markets*. Prepared for U.S. House of Representatives, August 1993.

Conrad, Jennifer. "The Price Effect of Option Introduction." *Journal of Finance*, 44(2) June 1989, pp. 487-498.

Corgel, J.B. and G.D. Gay. "The Impact of GNMA Futures Trading on Cash Market Volatility." *American Real Estate and Urban Economics Association [AREUEA] Journal*, 12(2), Summer 1984, pp. 176-190.

Corrigan, E. Gerald. "Remarks." 7th International Conference of Banking Supervisors, Cannes, France, October 8, 1992.

________. "Remarks." 64th Annual Mid-Winter Meeting of the New York State Bankers Association, New York, NY, January 30, 1992.

Dale, Charles and Rosemarie Workman. "Measuring Patterns of Price Movements in Treasury Bill Futures Market." *Journal of Economics and Business*, 33(2), Winter 1981, pp. 81-87.

Damodaran, Aswath and Marti G. Subrahmanyam. "The Effects of Derivative Securities on the Markets for Underlying Assets in the United States: A Survey." *Financial Markets, Institutions, and Instruments*, 1(5), December 1992, pp. 1-22.

________ and J. Lim. "The Effects of Option Listing on the Underlying Stock's Return Processes." *Journal of Banking and Finance*, 15, 1991, pp. 647-664.

Deutsche Bundesbank. *Off-Balance-Sheet Activities of German Banks*. Monthly Report, (English Translation), October 1993.

Edwards, Franklin R. "Futures Trading and Cash Market Volatility: Stock Index and Interest Rate Futures." *Journal of Futures Markets*, 8(4), August 1998b, pp. 421-439.

________. "Does Futures Trading Increase Stock Market Volatility." *Financial Analysts Journal*, 44(1), January/February 1988a, pp. 63-69.

Ely, D.P. "Derivative Securities and Cash Market Stability." *Applied Economics*, 23(2), February 1991, pp. 391-402.

Federal Deposit Insurance Corporation. "Response to the Questions Posed By Congressman Leach." September 30, 1993.

Federal Reserve Board. "Response to the Questions Posed By Congressman Henry B. Gonzalez." October 26, 1993.

________. "Response to the Questions Posed By Congressman Henry B. Gonzalez." November 24, 1993.

________. "Response to the Questions Posed By Congressman Leach." October 6, 1993.

________. Supervisory Letter on "Examining Risk Management and Internal Controls for Trading Activities of Banking Organizations." December 20, 1993.

Figlewski, Stephen. "Futures Trading, and Volatility in the GNMA Market." *Journal of Finance*, 36(2), May 1981, pp. 445-456.

Freris, A.F. "The Effects of the Introduction of Stock Index Futures on Stock Prices: The Experience of Hong Kong 1984-1987." In S. Ghon Rhee and Rosita P. Chang (Eds.), *Pacific Basin Capital Markets Research*. North Holland, 1990, pp. 409-416.

Froewiss, Kenneth C. "GNMA Futures: Stabilizing or Destabilizing?" *Economic Review*, Federal Reserve Bank of San Francisco, (Spring) 1978, pp. 20-29.

Furbush, Dean. "Program Trading and Price Movement: Evidence from the October 1987 Market Crash." *Financial Management*, Autumn 1989, pp. 68-83.

Gerety, M.S. and J.H. Mulherin. "Patterns in Intraday Stock Market Volatility, Past and Present." *Financial Analysts Journal*, 47(5), September/October 1991, pp.71-79.

Global Derivatives Study Group. *Derivatives: Practices and Principles.* The Group of Thirty, July 1993.

________. "Working Paper of the Systemic Issues Subcommittee." *Derivatives: Practices and Principles*, The Group of Thirty, July 1993.

Gonzalez, Henry B. "Statement on Derivatives." Congressional Record-House of Representatives, June 10, 1993.

________. "Statement on Banks and Derivative Products." Congressional Record-House of Representatives, June 18, 1993.

Gramm, Wendy Lee. "In Defense of Derivatives." *The Wall Street Journal*, September 8, 1993.

Gray, R.W. "Onions Revisited." *Journal of Farm Economics*, 45, May 1963, pp. 273-276. Reprinted in Anne E. Peck (Ed.), *Selected Writings on Futures Markets: Basic Research in Commodity Markets*, Volume 2, Chicago Board of Trade, 1977.

Greenspan, Alan. "International Financial Integration." Federation of Bankers Associations of Japan, October 14, 1992.

________. "Remarks." Conference on Changing Capital Markets, August 19, 1993.

________. "Remarks." Annual Convention of the American Bankers Association, San Diego, California, November 7, 1993.

________. "Remarks." Bankers Club Banquet, London, United Kingdom, February 1, 1994.

________. "Remarks." International Symposium on Banking and Payment Services, Washington D.C., March 10, 1994.

Hansell, Saul and Kevin Muehring. "Why Derivatives Rattle the Regulators." *Institutional Investor*, International Edition, September 1992.

Harris, Lawrence. "S&P 500 Cash Stock Price Volatilities." *The Journal of Finance*, 44(5), December 1989, pp. 1155-1175.

Hayes, S. and Michael Tennenbaum. "The Impact of Listed Options on the Underlying Shares." *Financial Management*, 8, (Winter) 1979, pp. 72-76.

Hodgson, A. and D. Nicholls. "The Impact of Index Futures Markets on Australian Share Market Volatility." *Journal of Business and Accounting*, 18, No. 2, January 1991, pp. 267-280.

House Banking Committee Minority Staff. "Part One: Market Overview and Supervisory Concerns." *Financial Derivatives*, November 1993.

International Monetary Fund. "The Growing Involvement of Banks in Derivative Finance—A Challenge for Financial Policy." *International Capital Markets, Part II: Systemic Issues in International Finance*, August 1993.

Joint Study by Banking Supervisors. "Derivative Product Activities of Commercial Banks," *Joint Study Conducted in Response to Questions Posed by Senator Riegle on Derivative Products.* Board of Governors of the Federal Reserve System, the Federal Deposit Insurance Corporation, and the Office of the Comptroller of the Currency, January 27, 1993.

Johnson, Aaron C. *Effects of Futures Trading on Price Performance in the Cash Onion Market, 1930-1968.* Economic Research Service, U.S. Department of Agriculture, Technical Bulletin No. 1470, February 1973. Reprinted in Anne E. Peck (Ed.), *Selected Writings on Futures Markets: Basic Research in Commodity Markets*, Volume 2, Chicago Board of Trade, 1977.

Kaufman, Henry. "Financial Derivatives in a Rapidly Changing Financial World." City of London Conference on Derivatives, Skinners' Hall, London, England, October 14, 1993.

Klemkosky, Robert and T.S. Maness. "The Impact of Options on the Underlying Securities." *Journal of Portfolio Management*, 7, (Winter) 1980, pp. 12-18.

Kodres, Laura E. "Positive Feedback Traders in the S&P 500 Index Futures Market." University of Michigan, School of Business Administration, November 1990, Revised February 1992.

Laatsch, F.E. "A Note on the Effects of the Initiation of Major Market Index Futures on the Daily Returns of the Component Stocks." *Journal of Futures Markets*, 11(3), June 1991, pp. 313-317.

Labys, W.C. and H.C. Thomas. "Speculation, Hedging and Commodity Price Behavior: An International Comparison." *Applied Economics*, 7(4), December 1975, pp. 287-301.

Lamfalussy, Alexandre. "The Restructuring of the Financial Industry: A Central Banking Perspective." SUERF Lecture, City University, London, March 5, 1992.

Leach, James A. "A Legislative Perspective on Derivatives." September 27, 1993.

________. "Derivative Regulations." Congressional Record, January 26, 1994.

________. "Statement." Institute of International Bankers, December 6, 1993.

________. "Statement on Derivatives." The Group of Thirty Symposium, The Federal Reserve Board, September 27, 1993.

Lockwood, L.J. and S.C. Linn. "An Examination of Stock Market Return Volatility During Overnight and Intraday Periods, 1964-1989." *Journal of Finance*, 45(2), June 1990, pp. 591-601.

Loomis, Carol J. "The Risk That Won't Go Away." *Fortune*, March 7, 1994.

Ludwig, Eugene A. "Remarks." Institute of International Bankers, September 27, 1993.

Ma, C.K. "Information Asymmetry and Options Trading." *The Financial Review*, 23, 1988, pp. 39-51.

________ and R.P. Rao. "Market Characteristics, Option Trading and Volatility of the Underlying Stock," in *Advances in Futures and Options Research*, Vol. 1, Part A, 1986, pp. 193-200.

Maberly, E.D. and D.S. Allen and R.F. Gilbert. "Stock Index Futures and Cash Market Volatility." Financial Analysts Journal, 45(6), November/December 1989, pp. 75-77.

Mayer, Martin. "A Bad Swap for the World's Taxpayers." *The Wall Street Journal*, June 16, 1993.

McDonough, William J. "A Regulatory Perspective on Derivatives," in James A. Leach, et al. (Eds.), *Global Derivatives: Public Sector Responses*. Occasional Papers, No. 44, Group of Thirty, Washington, DC, 1993, pp. 11-19.

________. "A Regulatory Perspective on Derivatives." September 27, 1993.

________. "Remarks." Financial Markets Conference, Federal Reserve Bank of Atlanta, Coconut Grove, Florida, February 26, 1994.

Moriarty, Eugene and Paula Tosini. "Futures Trading and Price Volatility of GNMA Certificates—Further Evidence." *Journal of Futures Markets*, 5(4), Winter 1985, pp. 633-641.

Mullins, David W., Jr. "Remarks on the Global Derivatives Study Sponsored by the Group of Thirty." ISDA, Summer Conference, New York, NY, July 28, 1993.

Nabar, P. and S. Park. "Options Trading and Stock Price Volatility." Working Paper, Salomon Brothers Center, NYU, 1989.

Neal, Robert. "Is Program Trading Destabilizing?" *The Journal of Derivatives*, 1(2), Winter 1993, pp. 64-77.

Newman, Frank N. "Remarks." CFTC Conference on OTC Derivative Markets, October 27, 1993.

Office of the Comptroller of the Currency. *Banking Circular 277*. October 27, 1993.

________. "Response to the Questions Posed By Congressman Leach." October 14, 1993.

Office of Thrift Supervision. Derivative Product Activities of Savings Associations: A Study Conducted in Response to Questions Raised by Senator Riegle on Derivative Products. March 1993.

________. "Response to the Questions Posed By Congressman Leach." October 4, 1993.

Ontario Securities Commission. *Over-The-Counter Derivatives in Ontario: OSC Staff Report*. January 1994.

Phillips, S.M. "Challenges Posed by OTC Derivatives." Tenth Annual Meeting of the National Futures and Options Society, New York, NY, December 3, 1992.

________. "Derivatives and Risk Management: Challenges and Opportunities." Conference on Financial Markets, Federal Reserve Bank of Atlanta, Coconut Grove, Florida, February 25, 1994.

————. "Remarks." Institute of International Research Conference, New York, March 3, 1993.

Powers, Mark J. "Does Futures Trading Reduce Price Fluctuations in the Cash Market?" *American Economic Review*, 60(3), June 1970, pp. 460-464.

Promisel, Larry. "Remarks." International Association of Financial Engineers Conference, New York, December 2, 1993.

Roberts, Richard Y. "Derivatives: Regulatory Concern, Not Panic." Bank Derivatives Conference, Washington, D.C., February 28, 1994.

————. "Derivatives: Q and A." *The Bond Buyer*, February 16, 1994.

————. "Emphasis on the Watchdog Role and Responsibilities of Mutual Fund Directors." IDS Mutual Fund Conference, Scottsdale, Arizona, February 10, 1994.

Rubinstein, Mark. "Portfolio Insurance and the Market Crash." *Financial Analysts Journal*, January/February 1988.

Santoni, G.J. "Has Programmed Trading Made Stock Prices More Volatile?" *Review*, Federal Reserve Bank of St. Louis, May 1987, pp. 18-29.

Schapiro, Mary L. "The Derivatives Revolution and the World Financial System." U.S. Securities and Exchange Commission, Remarks made at the Eighth Annual Symposium for the Foundation for Research in International Banking and Finance, Lugano, Switzerland, October 14, 1993.

Securities and Exchange Commission, the Commodity Futures Trading Commission, and the Securities and Investments Board. "Joint Statement on OTC Derivatives Oversight." March 15, 1994.

Securities and Exchange Commission. "Response to the Questions Posed By Congressman Leach." October 27, 1993.

Simpson, W. Gary. "The Impact of Financial Futures on the Cash Market for Treasury Bills." Journal of Financial and Quantitative Analysis, Vol. 20, No. 3, September 1985, pp. 371-379.

———— and Timothy C. Ireland. "The Effect of Futures Trading on the Price Volatility of GNMA Securities." *Journal of Futures Markets*, 2(4), Winter 1982, pp. 357-366.

Skinner, Douglas J. "Options Markets and Stock Return Volatility." *Journal of Financial Economics*, June 1989, pp. 61-78.

Standard & Poor's Creditweek. "Banks Face Manageable Risks in Derivatives Businesses." November 1992.

Taylor, G.S. and R.M. Leuthold. "The Influence of Futures Trading on Cash Cattle Price Variations." *Food Research Institute Studies*, 13(1), 1974, pp. 29-35. Reprinted in Anne E. Peck (Ed.) *Selected Writings on Futures Markets: Basic Research in Commodity Markets*, Volume 2. Chicago Board of Trade, 1977.

Tomek, W.G. "A Note on Historical Wheat Prices and Futures Trading." *Food Research Institute Studies*, 10(1), 1971, pp. 109-113.

————. "Futures Trading and Market Information: Some New Evidence." *Food Research Institute Studies*, 17(3), 1979-80, pp. 351-359.

Trennepohl, Gary L. and William P. Dukes. "CBOE Options and Stock Volatility." *Review of Business and Economic Research*, 14, 1979, pp. 49-60.

U.S. General Accounting Office. *Financial Derivatives: Actions Needed to Protect the Financial System*. Washington D.C., May 1994.

————. *Securities Firms: Assessing the Need to Regulate Additional Financial Activities*. Washington D.C., April 1992.

Volcker, Paul. "Forward," in Global Derivatives Study Group, *Derivatives: Practices and Principles*. The Group of Thirty, July 1993.

Working, Holbrook. "Futures Markets Under Renewed Attack." *Food Research Institute Studies*, 4, February 1963, pp. 13-24.

________. "Price Effects of Futures Trading." *Food Research Institute Studies*, 1(1), February 1960, pp. 3-31. Reprinted in *Selected Writings of Holbrook Working*, Chicago Board of Trade, 1977.

COMMENT ON SOURCES OF RISK

James R. Barth

A problem with the title of this conference is so little is known about systemic risk. Indeed, there is disagreement about how to define the term, doubt about the usefulness of the term itself, and disagreement about when systemic risk has actually materialized in our economy. Despite this doubt and disagreement, there does appear to be a consensus that "systemic risk" is important from a public-policy perspective to the extent that, should it materialize, the real economy collapses.

There also appears, if I may be so bold, somewhat broad agreement that "systemic risk" materializes when in a world of incomplete and imperfect information difficulties (such as bank runs or a stock market collapse) in one part of the financial system spread in a domino-like fashion throughout the entire financial system because of the extensive inter-relationships between financial firms. The result of these events will be a breakdown in the payment and settlement systems as well as in the credit system, leading to the collapse of economic activity.

The obvious question for one to ask is: What is the likelihood that systemic risk, or alternatively, the risk of financial and economic crisis will occur? Stated differently, is the apparent stability in the real economy since the 1930s misleading, with such a crisis lurking in the background? Since crises are

Research in Financial Services Private and Public Policy, Volume 7, pages 171-174.

ISBN: 1-55938-244-9

relatively infrequent, quite complex, only temporary, and brutally turbulent events, they are extremely difficult to model formally. Indeed, they are not even included in standard economic models. It is therefore not surprising that the economic projections of the Congressional Budget Office and the Office of Management and Budget do not incorporate crisis scenarios. Instead, they only incorporate relatively small shocks to the real economy.

Despite the lack of formal economic models and their accompanying projections, there does appear to be a clear consensus that the likelihood of a financial and economic crisis depends importantly upon whether the Federal Reserve behaves as intended. More specifically, the risk of a crisis is substantially reduced, it not eliminated, so long as the Federal Reserve provides liquidity through open-market operations or the discount window to preclude firms and investors from having to sell assets at distressed prices. There is, however, an important disagreement about which firms should be able to obtain liquidity. Some individuals believe liquidity should be provided to insolvent, not just solvent, firms to prevent a financial crisis and economic collapse. It is argued, for example, that the seizure of all the insolvent savings and loans in the early 1980s would have precipitated just such a crisis. Excessive risk taking, in other words, may be necessary, according to some, if a crisis is to be prevented. In this regard, I urge everybody to read Ed Kane's most recent paper entitled "Ethical Conflicts in Managing the S&L Insurance Mess."

More generally, given the recent interest in systemic risk or the risk of financial and economic crisis, there is a danger that the mere admission that such a risk does exist may engender well-intended but nevertheless inappropriate policy actions, such as a rush to enact more regulations that will only impede innovation and retard risk-management improvements.

Now to focus specifically on the three papers I have been asked to discuss. Not unexpectedly, the three authors do not provide formal models of systemic risk or the risk of financial and economic crisis. They do, however, provide excellent discussion to better understand such a crisis, especially all the recent financial developments that may affect the likelihood of occurrence.

In particular, Claudio Borio in an informative and non-alarmist manner focuses on systemic risk in the context of payment and settlements systems. The concern, he states, that "Temporary failures to settle can [not will, I might add] ... lead to insolvencies as agents act on ... limited information" (p. 8). In this regard, Claudio points to the 1987 stock market crash and the Drexel Burnham Lambert failure as events that posed potential systemic problems. But the problems did not materialize because the Federal Reserve behaved as it was suppose to under such circumstances. Claudio recognizes this crucial role for the Federal Reserve in preventing a crisis when he states that "the provision of liquidity is the last line of defense in the containment of systemic crises" (p. 21). Furthermore, this use of the phrase "last line of defense" is essential because Claudio nicely discusses important actions that have been taken in recent years to reduce the risks inherent in the payment and settlement systems, while simultaneously limiting reliance upon central bank support to resolve such problems. (i.e., curtailing the moral hazard problem.).

Bob Eisenbeis provides a competent and useful survey of several views of theories of "systemic risk." Despite being a tedious and difficult task, he nicely compares and contrasts various theories, both in terms of assumptions and conclusions, and, to the extent possible, in terms of consistency with the data.

There are, however, a few specific areas in Bob's paper that merit further clarification. First, he importantly states that "the fact [is] that financial crises are better viewed as creatures of recession and economic downturns ...." Does this mean that a necessary condition for a financial crisis is a recession or economic downturn? If so, what are the sufficient conditions? It would be helpful if Bob would elaborate on this point.

Second, Bob states that with the thrift crisis, collapse of Penn Central, demise of the junk bond market, failure of Continental Illinois Bank, among other recent events, there was always "some form of ad hoc government intervention, usually by the Federal Reserve." He further states that "given that few crises occurred following such intervention was either unnecessary or ineffective." I'm not sure if Bob really believes there have been a "few crises." If so, it would be useful for him to identify them. But, more importantly, he also points out that Benston and Kaufman argue that "the Federal Reserves' intervention has been, at times, unwarranted given the evidence that panics are not very frequently events and are unlikely to precipitate significant shocks to the real sector." Has the Federal Reserves' behavior been "*ad hoc*," "unnecessary," "inefficient" or "unwarranted"? It would be useful if Bob would say more about the criteria one might use to judge the appropriateness of Federal Reserve policies, particularly when the market fails us. This is crucial, because Bob also says that since the Great Depression "no broad-based panics have occurred, in part because of actions followed by the Federal Reserve." What are these actions and did they resolve a market failure?

Finally, Bob states that "the payments system is large, has many more components (both private and public), and is subject to different risks than in the past." He adds that "the contingent nature of the risks of derivatives ... have not been fully worked out." And obvious question is: what are the policy implications of these statements? Since Bob believes these development do affect the likelihood of a financial crisis, it would be helpful if a discussion were provided of what he views as appropriate governmental policies to prevent a crisis.

This is a good point to turn to the last paper by Bob Mackay. He is quite blunt in concluding that "there is little or no empirical support ... for the view that derivatives increase systemic risk." Fine, but do they reduce it? The paper does not answer this question. Nor does the paper explain how one should empirically determine whether or not derivates increase systemic risk. Despite these omissions, I thoroughly enjoyed reading the paper and broadly agree with the conclusions.

More generally, Bob has delivered on his stated promise "to provide a balanced assessment of the risk of derivatives, especially the potential for derivatives to increase systemic risk." In a systematic and insightful manner, he lists and then assesses all the major concerns about the risk of derivatives. In this regard, it is worth repeating a point Bob emphasizes early in his paper, "The fundamental risks facing dealers and end users of derivatives are neither new nor unique." However, he does admit that "the legal risks [of derivatives] remain a significant factor, despite persistent efforts to reduce these risks, and have the potential to create systemic problems." It would therefore be nice if he would elaborate on this important point. More generally, is it possible that derivatives have reduced "systemic risk" because risk has been shifted to those most able to manage and bear it?

All in all, for all those concerned about the risk of derivates, this paper is must reading. Even for those not concerned, it is extremely well worth reading. And everyone should enjoy the incredibly delightful selection of quotes and appreciate the extensive bibliography.

In view of these three excellent papers, what do I conclude. There is little or no hard economic evidence to support any fear that a financial and economic crisis is lurking in the background.

PART III

TRANSNATIONAL ASPECTS

INTERNATIONAL ASPECTS OF SYSTEMIC RISK

Morris Goldstein

I. INTRODUCTION

The basic notion of systemic risk, namely, that difficulties in one part of the financial system might spread to otherwise healthy parts and generate either a costly disruption of the payments system, or adverse effects on the performance of the macroeconomy, or a large public-sector liability, clearly carries an international dimension as well as a domestic one. Financial strains can move across countries, just as they can across firms and industries within a country.

My task in this paper is to discuss international aspects of systemic risk. I will not attempt to be comprehensive. Instead, I will focus on four international systemic issues that have been much in the news over the past three to four years: (1) international transmission of asset price changes; (2) liquidity strains during bouts of market turbulence; (3) alleged holes in the international supervisory and regulatory framework; and (4) the infrastructure for international financial transactions. Finally, I will close with some summary remarks on how best to reduce international sources of systemic risk.

Research in Financial Services Private and Public Policy, Volume 7, pages 177-194.

ISBN: 1-55938-244-9

II. INTERNATIONAL TRANSMISSION OF ASSET PRICE CHANGES

One concern that has accompanied both the trend toward increased integration of national capital markets and the substantial volatility of asset prices in that market risk could be spread around the industrial world, with adverse consequences for systemic stability. Suppose, for example, that a major industrial country implemented a significant and somewhat unexpected change in monetary policy. Wouldn't increased integration then mean that the sharp change in interest rates in the initiating country would quickly be reflected elsewhere, possibly inflicting sizeable losses on those market participants at home and abroad who had wrong-footed positions or imperfect hedges?

Answering this question hinges in part on inferring the degree of substitutability among assets that might be thought of as close substitutes.[1] Michael Mussa and I have recently undertaken such an exercise (Mussa and Goldstein, 1994) within the broader context of reviewing alternative approaches to the measurement of international capital market integration. Suffice to say that our investigation suggests that the degree of international financial integration on the whole is indeed considerably higher today than it was a decade ago. Integration has proceeded farthest for those liquid, financial instruments traded in the major financial centers. For fixed-income securities, integration is higher for nominal returns than for real ones, for assets that are covered against currency risk than for those that are not, for assets traded in wholesale markets than for those traded in retail markets, and for capital markets in industrial countries than for those in developing ones. For equities, the evidence suggests, *inter alia*, that there has been no significant increase in correlations of stock price indices across industrial countries over the past twenty years or so, that cross-country linkages are much tighter during periods of extreme turbulence than during more tranquil times, and that cross-country spillovers are asymmetric—with spillover from the U.S. market to others stronger than the other way around.

We also conclude from our review that it is still premature to think in trerms of a single, world capital market where the bulk of global wealth is sold to the highest bidder by the Grand Walrasian Auctioneer. The largest component of wealth in almost all economies is human wealth—an asset that is not traded domestically or internationally. Retained earnings still occupy an important role in financing business investment. The lion's share of domestic investment in the great majority of countries is financed by domestic saving—and not by world saving. Net international capital flows as percentage of GNP are still considerably lower today than during the heyday of the international gold standard. While international diversification has been on the rise over the past decade, it is still relatively low and well below what studies suggest would be optimal. U.S. investors, for example, hold close to 95 percent of their equity holdings in U.S.

securities, and the 300 largest pension funds in the world still have only about 7 percent of their assets in foreign-currency denominated instruments. Fifty years after the Bretton Woods conference, less than one-fourth of the IMF's member countries have achieved full capital-account convertibility.

In short, integration of financial markets is considerably higher now than it used to be and is already high enough to place important constraints on the conduct of macroeconomic and regulatory policy in the industrial countries. This means that market participants and regulators alike will need to pay closer attention to market risks associated with the international transmission of asset price changes. But integration it is not yet so high for broad asset classes as to make the "law of one price" the dominant paradigm for thinking about market risk. The degree of international integration differs substantially across different financial instruments. Also, as the experience of the past two decades should remind us, the domestic financial sector is fully capable on its own of generating large losses from garden-variety mismatches.

Whatever the source of market risk—be it international or domestic, or be it foreign exchange, bonds, or equities—banks, security houses, and others need to hold adequate capital against it. In this regard, the recent proposal by the Basle Committee on Banking Supervision to amend the 1988 Accord to include market risk, is welcome. If we are going to have a common, risk-weighted capital standard for internationally active banks, and if trading books are becoming more important relative to loan books in banks, there is no point in leaving out of the framework a potentially significant source of bank failure. As is well known, there is currently a controversy about whether the capital requirements for market risk are best gauged by relying on a common formula or by allowing banks to use their own risk management models. So long as supervisors develop explicit criteria—preferably harmonized across the major countries—to determine whether the assumptions embedded in banks' own risk management models are reasonable, I see no problem in allowing those banks who wish to do so to use their own models for that purpose.[2]

III. LIQUIDITY STRAINS DURING BOUTS OF MARKET TURBULENCE

During he past three years, there have been two major international episodes of market turbulence that have underscored the role of liquidity considerations in systemic risk. One was the ERM crises of the fall of 1992 and the summer of 1993. The other was the sharp rise in long-term government bond yields across the industrial countries of 1994 during the first quarter.

In both cases, the turbulence was the result of a sudden shift in expectations by the majority of market participants, following upon a period when large open positions had been built up based on a specific interest rate and exchange rate scenario.

The ERM crisis was preceded by large, cumulative inflows of capital into higher-yielding ERM currencies during the 1987-1991 period. The assumption was that the EMS countries were on an irreversible convergence path toward Economic and Monetary Union (EMU).[3] This implied that interest rate differentials in favor of high-yielding ERM currencies would overestimate the actual risk of exchange rate depreciation. Why settle for the yield on a deutschemark bond when you could get the higher yield on a lira or paseta bond, absent the corresponding currency risk? In the recent bond market turbulence, the dominant bets were that European interest rates would display a fairly rapid and significant fall (as European monetary authorities utilized the greater room for maneuver, made possible by wider exchange rate bands, to spur economic recovery), and that the U.S. dollar would appreciate vis-à-vis then yen (because interest rates in the United States and Japan would increasingly favor dollar-denominated fixed-income assets).

In both cases, market participants got it wrong.[4] In the ERM episode of the fall of 1992, the negative outcome of the Danish referendum and the uncertainties associated with the outcome of the French referendum—in concert with deterioration in certain fundamentals—put into question the ratification of the Maastricht Treaty and the implementation of EMU. All at once, the markets rediscovered currency risk. In the 1994 bond market episode, unexpected events also forced a sudden revision of expectations.[5] European interest rates did come down—but at a much slower pace then expected. Prospects for interest rate reduction in Japan were dampened, *inter alia*, by better than expected performance of Japanese equity prices. And the intensification of the U.S. Japan trade dispute upset the long dollar currency play. As in the ERM case, market participants had to run for the exits.

But it is precisely when the crowd gets to the exit at the same time that the width of the doors matters. And here, those accustomed to the wide doors of the forex market for the three major currencies, or the wide door of the U.S. government securities market, found that liquidity was much more limited in many smaller markets.

In the ERM case, the liquidity situation was strongly aided by the fact that European central banks were standing on the other side of the market intervening in massive amounts to defend their parities. In the end, no major financial firms failed, nor did the crisis spread to national debt and equity markets. Even so, liquidity strains where evident in some areas.[6] Forex spreads for some ERM cross-rates widened at times to five to ten times the norm, and the size of trades sometimes declined sharply. Forward exchange quotations for certain currencies (including the lira, sterling, and the Swedish krona) were at times virtually impossible to get. OTC options markets suffered, as interest rate volatility many times the norm made quotation of prices difficult. In the

European currency unit (ECU) market, it was not possible to complete transactions for a period in September and October, and a significant spread developed between the official ECU and the private ECU.

In the recent bout of bond market turbulence, the authorities were of course not intervening as they had in the currency crises, with the result that the sharp revision in expectations showed up in prices—with yields on ten-year government bonds in the G-10 countries rising from anywhere between 50 and 170 basis points between the beginning of February and the end of March (1994). Again, on the whole, markets stood up to the increased pressure quite well, with no systemic fallout. But here too, there were strains, particularly in the smaller, European government bond markets. In some cases traffic had to be redirected to the futures exchanges. Even then, MATIF, for example, had to briefly suspend trading on the ten-year government bond futures on March three because the contract price dropped by more than the 250 basis points daily limit.

The lessons I take away from these episodes are two. First, when participants take very large, open positions in relatively small markets, liquidity factors can become a significant source of systemic concern. Even when firms are marking positions to market and operating under reasonable internal loss-limits, they can still suffer a large loss if liquidity in that market dries up during a period of turbulence. Firms therefore need to take these liquidity factors into account in their risk management programs (even though this admittedly presents formidable technical difficulties). Authorities can always step in to supply liquidity, but of course with the usual, adverse moral-hazard or public liability costs. Second, on-going efforts to increase liquidity in many smaller, global markets (for example, in government securities markets, by concentrating issues in several benchmark issues, by establishing primary dealer systems, by setting up futures trading in a few benchmark issues, etc.) are worthy of support.[7]

IV. HOLES IN THE INTERNATIONAL SUPERVISORY AND REGULATORY FRAMEWORK?

Concerns that the globalization of finance will lead to regulatory arbitrage, with adverse effects on systemic risk, are longstanding. As the size and influence of offshore markets and of unregulated (or less regulated) players has grown, so too have the questions raised by regulators. In this connection, it is relevant to consider: (1) hedge funds; (2) derivative dealers that are unregulated affiliates of U.S. security houses; and (3) international coordination among non-bank supervisors.

While they carry no formal definition in securities law and are quite diverse in practice, it is sufficient for our purposes to think of *hedge funds* as private investment vehicles for wealthy shareholders. It has been estimated that there are now 800-900 such firms, with aggregate capital somewhere on the order of $ 75-100 billion. Four factors distinguish hedge funds from other large players. First, because they are private companies with less than 100 partners and are frequently chartered offshore, they carry a relatively light regulatory burden—a factor that allows them to have great flexibility in their investment strategies. Second, their investors are wealthier and have a higher tolerance for risky investments than the public at large. Third, they are generally regarded as the most leveraged players in major financial markets. And fourth, they displayed, on average, superior investment performance over the 1987-1993 period.

Authorities might harbor concerns about the activities of hedge funds in three areas. One is simple credit risk. Because larger hedge funds obtain loans from banks and securities houses to help fund their positions, large losses by hedge funds could generate significant loan losses for their creditors. But this concern should be reduced by the fact that most lending to hedge funds is fully collateralized, with the lender holding the financial instrument.[8] The point to be careful about then is that margin requirements on loans to hedge funds are set at the right level, that margins are increased when the market price of the collateral falls, that lenders know the consolidated exposure of the hedge fund, and that the revenue (and market information) that hedge funds generate for their creditors in other areas (e.g., equity commissions) does not result in laxity by creditors in enforcing margin calls.

A second potential concern is that hedge funds, because of their market clout and high turnover of positions, could generate excessive volatility in asset prices. Quite apart from the thorny issue of defining what constitutes "excessive" volatility, it is by no means clear that hedge funds exacerbate volatility. In this connection, there have apparently been cases where hedge fund activities have worked to stabilize asset prices, because they could afford to take positions when other, more-regulated large players could not. Some observers have even labeled hedge funds the "buyer of last resort." Clearly, we need to know more before we can evaluate this issue.

Last but not least, when hedge funds are operating at large scale in smaller markets, there is a concern that they could engage in market manipulation. This is more a matter of protecting market integrity than of systemic risk and would apply to any large player. Concerns about market integrity presumably have motivated existing legislation that limits the share or the size of the position that any firm can take in futures markets or in government bond auctions. Because market integrity in fact and in perception is so important, there could well be merit in putting in place across the G-10 countries large-trader reporting requirements, along the lines of existing U.S. legislation, for government securities, and perhaps for publicly-traded equities and options as well.

I want to emphasize that I see no case for singling out hedge funds for special new regulations. Where there has been market turbulence, it is doubtful that it would have been lessened by restricting the activities of hedge funds. Also, the aim of public policy should not be to limit risks, for risk-taking in financial markets serves a useful social function. The aim instead should be to ensure that risk are undertaken by those who are aware of the risks and by those who are able to bear any losses without having those losses spillover onto others.

A second alleged hole in the supervisory and regulatory net is the regulation of derivative dealers who are *unregulated affiliates of U.S. securities houses*[9] They are unregulated in the sense that they are currently not subject to regulatory examinations and are not required to hold a specified amount of capital to cushion again potential derivates-related losses. In contract, banks who are OTC derivative dealers are subject to both these regulations. According to the GAO (1994), the five largest securities affiliate dealers, along with the three largest insurance affiliate dealer, accounted in 1992 for about 30 percent of the total over-the-counter (OTC) volume in derivatives; moreover, their derivatives business has been growing more rapidly than those of dealers that are banks.

The concerns is that failure or withdrawal from trading by one or more of these unregulated dealers could cause liquidity and credit problems that could be systemic, at least in the sense that the central bank might be forced to intervene as lender of last resort to avert a crisis. These problems are said to arise due to the relatively concentrated nature of the derivative dealing business[10] and due to the close linkages between this market and other markets.[11].

I believe this is an issue on which they jury is still out. On the one side, there are factors that reduce systemic concern. Many of these affiliates are highly capitalized and triple-A rated. The high capital not only serves as a cushion against losses but also reduces the incentives the owners have to take excessive risks (since more of their own money is at stake). Similarly, the fact that these affiliates have found it desirable to devote enough capital and expertise to the business to obtain a high credit rating suggests that counterparties value these attributes in selecting a derivatives dealer. This attention to credit risk is also apparently two-sided, as suggested by the statistic that 78 percent of the counterparties of these derivative dealers have a single A or better credit rating.[12] As regards market spillovers, the charters of these affiliates go to some lengths to specify how a failure is to be resolved and specifically, how financial claims on the parent are to be minimized or prohibited. Dealers are reported to generally run balanced portfolios and to lay off remaining net exposure using exchange traded options. No single derivatives dealer has more than a 10 percent share of the total (national) contract amounts of any particular derivative product. Also, not all market spillovers have negative implications for systemic risk. As noted in Section III, the existence of relatively deep futures markets sometimes acted as a safety valve to relieve liquidity strains in certain OTC markets, and occasionally, in markets for the underlying instruments themselves.

On the negative side of the ledger, a potential problem with counting exclusively on creditors and counterparties to do the monitoring is that they may not have adequate information to make good judgments. Unlike a loan book, the riskiness of a derivatives portfolio can be altered substantially overnight or even more frequently. Quarterly reports on notional amounts outstanding by product type, or on replacement cost, or on counterparty credit exposure above a threshold, would provide some useful information—but that information could become obsolete quickly. Even when the credit-rating agencies have an analyst on site all the time—as some do according to Darby (1994), it is not clear what real time access they have to true risk exposure. The poorer is the ability of private market participants to monitor risk, the more scope there is for rumors to initiate liquidity problems. An since these affiliates are not subject to regulatory examinations, the official sector presumably has relatively limited, current information on the quality of their internal risk management systems.[13]

None of this would be a problem if when a failure or withdrawal from trading occurred, there would be little fall-out on either market liquidity or the other firms. (including the parent). Here too, however, one cannot be completely confident of the outcome. The effect on market liquidity presumably differs by product type. In the thinner markets, mark-to-market values may be a poor guide to liquidation value during a periods of real stress. How market participants would react to alleged difficulties at a major derivatives dealer is also unknown. Would creditors withhold funding during the hours of a major price break until they have had time to investigate the dealer's perhaps weakened credit standing? Would alleged difficulties at one affiliate dealer raise questions about the health of other dealers? Notwithstanding covenants that limit calls on the parent for support, would creditors reckon that the reputation of the parent is damaged by potential large losses at its affiliate, and therefore restrict funding to the parent? After all, some temporary contagion after a major disturbance is not without precedent.

For example, after the Penn Central bankruptcy in 1970, issuance of commercial paper declined sharply and nonfinancial companies found borrowing in all markets more expensive. Similarly, after the failure of Bank Herstatt in 1974, there was significant tiering of interbank interest rates, many smaller banks were excluded from the market, and depositors moved funds from Eurocurrency markets to national markets. In the wake of the October 19878 equity crash, trading in futures and options markets for equity instruments was disrupted, issues of equity related Eurobonds dropped sharply, and there was a flight to quality (as reflected in a shift from equity to government bonds).

Likewise, the market for junk bonds was adversely affected by the U.S. saving and loan crisis. And in the 1994 episode of bond market turbulence, it was reported that large losses on long dollar currency plays led some hedge funds to liquidate long European bond positions. Granted, Drexel was allowed to fail without systemic effects, and Solomon was able to downsize its balance sheet fairly smoothly and without serious spillovers after public announcement of its illegal behavior in government securities auctions. But would the same result hold in the OTC derivatives market?

In view of these questions—many of which also apply to the more regulated portion of the OTC derivatives market, there could be merit in considering a self-regulating clearinghouse for OTC derivatives, along the lines recently suggested by Folkerts-Landau and Steinherr (1994). While custom-tailored products would have to remain off-exchange, the plain vanilla OTC products—which Folkerts-Landau and Steinherr estimate represent perhaps three quarters of the business—could be accommodated. The advantages of a clearinghouse arrangement are well known: strict, rule-based implementation of initial and maintenance margins, netting and marking-to-market of positions, and the clearinghouse as counterparty to all trades. In short, better management of credit risk. Liquidity too might be increased for the products traded on the exchange, and banks that lost some of their business to the clearinghouse would make some of it back by extending loans to finance margin requirements. In some sense, the OTC market is already mimicking some of these (clearinghouse) features by concentrating the dealing business in the most creditworthy institutions and by moving toward mark-to-market accounting and greater transparency and disclosure. But if systemic risk is the measuring rod, a clearinghouse would be safer.

At present, *international coordination* among supervisors is much more extensive for banking supervisors than for their nonbanking counterparts. Banking supervisors have an international agreed framework for risk-weighted capital standards (the Basle Accord), they have negotiated a series of concordats on the sharing of information and the division of responsibility as between host and home country supervisors, they have the authority to obtain at short notice any information on banking activities that they deem necessary to fulfill their responsibilities, and the G-10 supervisors meet monthly in Basle to discuss current developments of mutual interest, including the identification of any potential systemic threats. For *nonbanks*, both international sharing of information (through bilateral memoranda of understanding) and efforts toward international harmonization of capital standards (under the auspices of IOSCO), have progressed one less far. Moreover, there is no international group of nonbank supervisors that meets frequently to review market developments or to discuss potential sources of systemic risk.

These differences in arrangements for international coordination between banking and nonbanking supervisors are no accident. Instead, they reflect fundamental differences in the orientation to, and rationale for supervision, between the two kinds of institutions.[14] Specifically, the traditional assumption is that failure or difficulty at a nonbank is much less likely to provoke negative externalities or systemic threats (than would a banking failure) since the liquidity of a nonbank's assets facilitates the winding down of a troubled institution (during a run), since nonbanks are farther away from the payments mechanism, and since nonbanks are less important for the successful implementation of monetary policy. As such, bank supervisors focus on the safety and soundness of individual banks, banks receive government-supplied deposit insurance and have access to the (discount) "window and the (Fed) wire," and banks in most countries are required to hold reserves at the central bank. In contrast, nonbanking supervisor focus their efforts on investor protection (leaving it to the market to monitor safety and soundness of individual institutions), nonbanks are not eligible for officially managed deposit insurance, they do not have access to the discount window or the wholesale payments mechanism, and they have no reserve obligations.

In line with the assumptions underlying this differential approach to supervision, there has been one powerful empirical regularity over the past few decades: troubles at banks and at other government-insured depository institutions have has much more serious systemic consequences—mostly in the form of a large public-sector liability or a weakened performance of the macroeconomy—than troubles at nonbanks.[15] The $64,000 question, however, is whether this will necessarily continue to be so in the future.

Those who argue for greater attention to safety and soundness in nonbanking supervision—and for greater international coordination among nonbank supervisors—make at least three arguments. First, the muscle in international financial markets is shifting away from banks toward nonbanks (that is, mutual funds, pension funds, insurance companies, hedge funds, securities houses), while the lines of demarcation that once separated their activities have become increasingly blurred, particularly at the wholesale level where they are more and more offering similar products to the same customers.[16] In the United States, the share of credit assets intermediated by commercial banks has fallen from about 60 percent at the end of World War II to slightly over 20 percent today. Merrill Lynch, the world's largest broker-dealer, has approximately $500 billion in client assets, and Fidelity Investments, the largest mutual fund, has roughly $ 300 billion under management. U.S. and European fund managers now control over $ 8 trillion in assets.

Meanwhile, by looking at balance sheets, funding sources, and lists of activities, one would be hard pressed to tell which large traders are banks and which are nonbanks. All of this is taken to suggest that the "uniqueness" of banks relative to nonbanks is slipping away, and that, more important, a future systemic threat is just as likely to arise in capital markets as in the banking sector. Some would interpret recent legislation in the Unites States that makes it easier for the Federal Reserve to lend to nonbanks with liquidity needs in a crisis as but one indicator of the recognition of this trend.

A second related argument is that the internationalization of the financial services industry is now so far advance as to make monitoring of systemic risk—be it for banks or nonbanks—impractical on a national basis alone. Even for the United States, non-resident ownership of government securities is close to 20 percent,[17] and branches and agencies of foreign banks now account for about 18 percent of the assets of all banking offices in the United States.[18] Major U.S. derivatives dealers reported to the GAO (1994) that about one quarter of their OTC derivatives volume represented transactions with foreign dealers. For many financial instruments, it would no longer be effective for one or two countries to temporarily suspend trading in the wake of say, a major political disturbance because the same securities trade in several other financial centers.

Third, some have argued that the increasing importance of nonbanks to small depositors has increased the risk of government intervention if these institutions experience difficulties. In the United States, the ratio of mutual fund assets (excluding money market funds) to saving and small time deposits in banks has grown from 21 percent in 1986 to 65 percent at the end of 1993. As highlighted by Kaufman (1994), U.S. households now own directly about $ 1 trillion in mutual assets, representing almost 10 percent of household financial net worth; moreover, he notes that these mutual fund investors have yet to experience a prolonged bear markets in equities or bonds. It has often been argued that it is in the case of small depositors that official monitoring of risks may be more efficient than private monitoring. Also, the greater the risk of a government bailout, the greater the rationale, ceteris paribus, for stronger official monitoring and/or regulation of the risks undertaken by these institutions.

But there is another way to intepret the growing similarity between banks and nonbanks. It is to try to make regulation over banks more like that toward nonbanks (rather than the other way around), and in the process, attempt to shrink the size of the explicit and implicit, official safety net. This might involve: giving banks expanded powers (to deal in securities, insurance, etc.) so as to diversify their risk; placing greater reliance on private creditors and depositors to monitor the safety and soundness of banks (fewer regulatory examinations, greater public disclosure requirements, giving greater publicity to private credit ratings), and moving away from publicly-supplied to privately-supplied deposit insurance.[19] New Zealand has recently proposed adopting such a "market oriented" approach to bank regulation (although several features of New Zealand's banking system, including foreign ownership of most of the largest banks, make its situation special).

In this country, the focus of recent banking legislation—as best represented by the Federal Deposit Insurance Corporation improvement Act (FDICIA) of 1991—might be interpreted as an efforts to mimic the monitoring and disciplining function of private markets by dealing with some of the more egregious moral hazard features of earlier bank regulatory policy (Kaufman and Litan, 1993). The major elements in FDICIA (aside from the increase in the FDIC's borrowing authority) are: the introduction of risk-weighted deposit insurance premia, the creation of a new system of mandated, structured early intervention and resolution (SEIR) tied to bank capital, and the insertion of greater transparency into granting of "too big to fail" assistance.[20] The aim of these reforms is to ameliorate the incentives created by the official safety net for depositary institutions to take excessive risk, to reduce bank regulation and to grant expanded powers to good performers, to mandate corrective actions and/or prompt closure of poorly performing banks before that cost spills over to the public at large, and to make it more difficult for public officials to bail out troubled banks citing systemic concerns.

In my view, we will find it hard to make real progress on reducing systemic risk until we internalize much of the externalities associates with excessive risk taking by banks. Based on experience, banks are still the most likely habitat for systemic risk. In that sense, the reform elements included in FDICIA are a most welcome step forward, and one that has considerable export potential for other banking systems where moral hazard factors and slow resolution of failed banks loom large in costly public-sector bailouts. That being said, I find it hard to dismiss out of hand the notion that large nonbanks now too have some potential to create systemic difficulties. For that reason, prudence would suggest that nonbank supervisors give somewhat more attention to market developments, to international sharing of information, and to coordinated monitoring of potential systemic threats.

At this point, I see no convincing case for new international rule-making for nonbanks. But I see little that would be lost and perhaps much that could be gained by having nonbank supervisors meet more frequently with their counterparts in other countries to discuss developments of mutual concern. Focusing just on investor protection and fraud now longer seems appropriate.

V. STRENGTHENING THE INFRASTRUCTURE

Just as central banks and other regulatory authorities have over the past decade increased the priority accorded to reducing credit and systemic risk in domestic wholesale payments systems, so too have the design and functioning of arrangements for clearing and settling international transactions taken on increased attention. The reaons for that increased attention are not hard to decipher. First, the volume of payments for international financial transactions (and particularly for derivative transactions) has grown very rapidly over the past five years.[21] Second, because both domestic payments systems and existing private multilateral payments systems differ from each another in various ways (e.g., finality, operating hours, currency, supervision, payment techniques), the substantial existing and prospective traffic between them has increased the demands for harmonization and for more assured enforcement. Third, there has been increasing recognition that the rising volume of intraday credit and the moral hazard associates with end-of-day net settlement systems—along with the risk of disturbances in one payments system spreading to others—constitute a potentially serious systemic threat. Fourth, there were and are questions (Padoa-Schioppa and Saccomanni, 1994) about whether the externalities and incentive-compatibility issues associates with the operation of a safe and efficient multilateral payments system (e.g., provision of final funds to avert a systemic crisis, investment in improvements, etc.) can be handled by private banks (who compete with one another)—or instead, whether a public manager is indispensable. Fifth, central banks have realized that if stress does develop in an offshore, private multilateral netting arrangement, decisions would need to be taken both on if to intervene (to avert systemic difficulties) and, if answered in the affirmative, who should intervene. Finally, it is increasingly appreciated that the credibility of a pre-announced policy to allow some financial institutions to fail depends in part on being able to prevent such a failure from disrupting the payments system.

When it comes to dealing with systemic stress—domestic or international—payments systems are where the ruber meets the road. For this reason, several ongoing initiatives to reduce risk and moral hazard in payments systems merit explict mention.

First, there has been a move toward reducing the credit risk borne by central banks in their domestic payments systems. For the most part, this has taken the form of replacing end-of-day, net-settlement payments systems with real-time gross settlement (RTGS) systems. RGTS reduces settlement risk by providing immediate finality of payments it also provides a basis for achieving delivery versus payment in securities settlement. By 1996, all but two European Union member countries are expected to have RTGS systems in operation. In the United States, the Federal Reserve has set up a fee structure for daylight overdrafts, so as to increase the incentives for private market netting and to make participants pay a market price for borrowing from the authorities. Given the potential risks associated with both unwinding the chain of transactions following a default of a participant, and with an upward trend in the ratio of gross transactions value to participants' capital, these reforms to domestic payments systems merit strong support.

Admittedly, there are some concerns with respect to a move to RGTS. They mainly involve liquidity considerations. One concern is that RTGS will squeeze liquidity in certain activities, with adverse externalities for economic performance. The funds to collateralize gross settlements have to come from somewhere. Presumably, those activities that are very liquidity intensive and that previously had benefitted from an implicit sudsidy when there was no charge for intraday credit exposures, will be most affected (Folkerts-Landau and Garber, 1994). To the extend that there were externalities associated with such subsidies, there could be some cost to eliminating them. Second, some worry that an international linking of domestic RGTS systems could transmit liquidity disturbances across borders. This has to be weighed againts the lower propensity of RGTS to generate disturbance in the first place. In the end, I would regard these liquidity considerations as a reasonable price to pay for the greater safety of RGTS systems.

A second initiative is to encourage the use of interbank netting schemes and to reduce remaining uncertainties about the legal enforceability of such netting arrangements, especially when they involve international contracts. Netting is regarded as helpful in reducing systemic risk since it reduces credit exposures.[22] Legal enforceability is important since, without it, market participants will be wary about entering into such netting arrangements; moreover, the absence of legal inforceability can result in cherry-picking behavior at the time of bankruptcy. In the 1988 Basle Accord, only netting by novation was recognized for the purposes of calculating the capital requirement. The 1990 Lamfalussy Report recommended that any legally enforceable form of bilateral netting be recognized. The 1993 proposals of the Basle Committee essentially adopt that recommendation, subject to the requirement that the netting scheme meet the minimum standards laid out in the Lamfalussy Report.

Yet a third set of initiatives relates to the harmonization of domestic payment systems in terms of technical and operational features, access, risk, and so forth. As outline by Padoa-Schioppa and Saccomanni (1994), EU central banks have agreed on a set of principles to guide this harmonization (including the move to RTGS), and have agreed to restrict access to credit institutions subject to supervision. In Europe, of course, such harmonization efforts are motivated in part by the prospect of EMU and its single central bank and single currency. Even elsewhere however, efforts at greater international cooperation and coordination on payments system questions are in evidence. One example is the decision to extend the hours of operation of Fedwire, so as to increase the overlap of the Japanese and U.S. settlement periods. Another is the series of studies undertaken jointly by the G-10 central banks on payments and settlements issues and its formation of a permanent committee to guide policy recommendations in this area, including those that might involve engagement by central banks.

VI. CONCLUDING REMARKS

International capital markets, like their domestic counterparts, serve several important functions. They loosen the constraints imposed by self-finance and enable increases both in the overall productivity of investment and in the smoothing of consumption. They provide liquidity. They provide liquidity. They allocate and diversify risk. They can help to discipline errant borrowers—either by subjecting them initially to a rising default premium and ultimately, to the threat of credit rationing, or by forcing adjustments in exchange rates. For all of these reasons, there is a strong presumption that welfare will be increased by allowing trade in financial assets to take place without regard to either national boundaries or the nationality of market participants.

All that being said, there is a legitimate public interest in trying to ensure that increased international financial liberalization and intergration do not result in costly international financial crises. An underlying theme of the arguments presented in this paper is that the best strategy for reducing international sources of systemic risk is closely related to that for reducing the domestic sources of systemic risk. The aim of public policy should not be to reduce risk-taking in financial markets but rather to see that risks are taken by those who are aware of the risks and by those who are able to absorb losses without those losses spilling over onto others, be it in the form of a disruption in the payments system, or of a large public-sector liability, or of a deterioration in the performance of the macroeconomy.

Some more specific recommendation on supervisory and regulatory policy have already been outlined in the paper but a quick checklist might include the following. Try to reduce credit risk and legal risk in the payments system. Try to improve the ability and incentive of private markets to monitor and to price risk appropriately by increasing the quality of information that is publicly available, and by reducing, where feasible, moral hazard associated with the implicit and explicit official safety net. Where government monitoring and/or gurantees can be justified, obtain the information necessary to gauge risk, and charge those taking higher risk a higher premium for insurance. Beware of excessive concentration in the assets of financial institutions. Establish best practice guidelines for internal risk management, encourage market participants to implement those guidelines, and reward better managed institution for those efforts. Specify capital requirements for banks that provide an adequate cushion against credit and market risks, and that limit their incentives to take excessive risk at the expense of other parties. Check that banks are setting and enforcing appropriate collateral and margin requirements on their lending to aggressive, position-takers. Where derivatives products can be standardized, encourage self-regulating clearinghouse arrangements that reduce credit risk. Close-down promptly insolvent depository institutions before they have the chance to play fourth-quarter football (ultimately, with the public's funds). In designing supervision over nonbanks, try to make distinctions between institutions that, if they were to get into difficulties, could be wound down and closed without systemic repercussions from those that cannot. Watch the latter. Protect the integrity of markets, particularly in smaller markets where manipulation is a threat. Increase international cooperation and sharing of information among supervisors of banks and nonbanks, in order to help identify emerging sources of systemic risk at an early stage. Try to increase (at the margin) the liquidity of smaller markets where there is nevertheless significant international activity, so that concerted changes in market sentiment can be accommodated without large-scale markets disruption. Pray for good fortune.

NOTES

1. I say "in part" because market risk needs to be approached from a portfolio perspective in which less than perfect correlation across risk elements is taken into account. See Goldstein et al., (1993) for an explanation of how market risk and specific risk are to be defined for capital charge purposes under the 1993 proposals of the Basle Committee on Banking Supervision.

2. In this connection, it would be useful if supervisors could lay out *how* they go about evaluating the quality of firms' risk management programs.

3. For a full analysis of the ERM crisis, see Goldstein et al., (1992).

4. A full account of the revision of expectations, along with the role played by leverage and various institutional features of the market, is given in Goldstein et al., (1994).

5. The Fed's action on February 4, 1994, in tandem with the very strong fourth-quarter U.S. GNP figure, seems to have been interpreted by markets as a signal that the awaited "turn" is U.S. monetary policy was now.

6. See G-10 (1993) and Goldstein et al., (1993).

7. Another issue worth investigation is how differential trading-halt rules across makets affect liquidity.

8. See Ludwig (1994) and La Ware (1994).

9. There are similarly unregulated affiliates of insurance companies that act as derivative dealers. Like securities affiliates, they are not subject to regulatory examinations or capital requirements. Also, their reporting requirements (which are consoliated with those of the parent) appear to be less stringent than those for banks or for securities firm affiliates.

10. The GAO (1994) reports that 90 percent of all banks derivative activity as of December 1992 was accounted for by the top seven dealers; similarly, the top five dealers on the securities side accounted for 87 percent of the total derivatives activity of all U.S. securities firms. Moreover, the same firms are reported to hold large market shares in many derivative markets.

11. The market linkages are attributed to concentration across several derivative markets and to the close relations between various markets in same earlier episodes of turbulance, especially during the October 1987 stock market crash.

12. See Darby (1994).

13. Some useful information on the risk management practices of dealers is available from surveys conducted by the Group of Thirty (1993), the GAO (1994), and others. But it is not clear how close a substitute that survey information is for current, on-site examinations.

14. See Edwards (1994).

15. The public-sector tab for the recent banking crises in three Scandinavian countries, as well as the costs to the public of the U.S. saving and loan crisis, are key cases in point.

16. This is of course less true in those industrial countries where universal banging is the norm and many of the activities of nonbanks elsewhere are conducted by banks.

17. U.S. Treasury (1993).

18. See Terrell (1993).

19. In this connection, an analysis of the experience of U.S. states with privately-supplied deposit schemes would be useful.

20. Several other reforms proposed by the U.S. administration were did not make into the final bill, including interstate branching, broader permitted activities, and commercial ownership' see Glauber (1993). Interstate branching was enacted into law in later banking legislation.

21. Padoa-Schioppa and Saccomanni (1994) report that over the past five years, international paymens through SWIFT have increased by more than 60 percent, while transactions through Cedel and Euroclear (which handle the international settlement of security transactions) have more than tripled.

22. Netting also reduces transactions costs and can reduce liquidity risk as well.

23. More generally, legal risk can be an important element of systemic risk. In this connection, recall the large losses sustained in the derivative markets when certain U.K. local councils had to default on contracts that were ruled to have exceeded their legal authority.

REFERENCES

Darby, M. "Over the Counter Derivatives and Systemic Risk to the Global Financial System." National Bureau of Economic Research, Working Paper No. 4801, July 1994.

Edwards, F. "Financial Markets in Transition—Or the Decline of Commercial Banking?" In *Changing Capital Markets: Implications for Monetary Policy?*. Federal Reserve Bank of Kansas City, 1994.

Folkerts-Landau, D. and P. Garber. "What Role of the ECB in Europe's Financial Markets." In *Thirty Years of European Monetary inegration*, edited by Alfred Steinherr. London Longmans Group, 1994.

Folkerts-Landau, D. and A. Steinherr. "The Wild Beast of Derivatives: To be Chained Up, Fenced in, or Tamed?" In *In Finance and the International Economy: The Amex Bank Review*. Oxfford: Oxford University Press, 1994.

General Accounting Office. *Financial Derivatives: Actions Needed to Protect the Financial System*, Report to Congressional Requesters, GAO/GGD-94-133, Washington D.C., May 1994.

Glauber, R. "FDICIA: Where the Wheels Came Off on the Road to Congress." In *Assessing Bank Reform*. Washington DC: edited by George Kaufman and Robert Litan.

Goldstein, M. D. Folkerts-Landau, and other. *International Capital Markets, Part I: Exchange Rate Management and International Capital Flows*. IMF World Economic and Financial Surveys. Washington DC: IMF, April 1993.

________. *International Capital Markets, Part II: Systemic Issues in International Finance*. IMF World Economic and Financial Surveys. Washington DC: IMF, September 1994.

Group of Ten. *International Capital Movements and Foreign Exchange Exchange Markets*. A Report to the Ministers and Governors by the Group of Deputies, April 1993.

Group of Thirty. Global Derivatives Study Group. *Derivatives: Practices and Principles*, Washington DC, July 1993.

Kaufman, G. and R. Litan. "Introduction and Summary." In *Assessing Bank Reform*, edited by George Kaufmam and Robert Litan.

Kaufman, H. "Structural Changes in the Financial Markets: Economic and Policy Significance." Federal Reserve Bank of Kansas City *Economic Review*, Second Quarter, 1994.

LaWare, J. Governor of the Federal Reserve System, Statement to Congress, April 13, 1994.

Ludwig, E. Comptroller of the Currency, Statement to Congress, April 13, 1994.

Mussa, M. and M. Goldstein. "The Integration of World Capital Markets." In *Changing Capital Markets: Implications for Monetary Policy*. Federal Reserve Bank of Kansas City, 1994.

Padoa-Schioppa, T. and F. Saccomanni. "Managing a Market Led Global Financial System." In *Managing the World Economy*, edited y Peter Kenen. Washington DC: Institute for International Economics, 1994.

Terrell, H. "U.S. Branches and Agencies of Foreign Banks: A New Look." *Federal Reserve Bulletin*, October 1993.

SYSTEMIC RISK WHEN DEPOSITORS BEAR LOSSES

FIVE CASE STUDIES

Herbert Baer and Daniela Klingebiel

I. INTRODUCTION

Financial sector policymakers often favor the government-funded recapitalization of insolvent banks without losses to depositor over solutions which force depositors to bear some of the losses. Such recapitalizations are often costly. In Finland, costs amounted to 8 percent of GDP; in Norway, 4 percent of GDP; in Sweden 4.5 percent of GDP; in Mauritania 15 percent of GDP[2] in Ghana, 6 percent of GDP,[3] in Hungary, 10 percent of GDP,[4] and in Venezuela 16 percent of GDP.[5] This preference is particularly interesting given the incentive problems associated with such bailouts and the fiscal strain they create for the government. While the governments of rich countries may be able to incur these expenditures with relatively little macroeconomic disruption, bailouts of the same magnitude can prove a terrible burden for many developing countries.

Research in Financial Services Private and Public Policy, Volume 7, pages 195-302.

ISBN: 1-55938-244-9

Policymakers in government may choose to recapitalize banks for a number of reasons. First, they may place little faith in the theoretical arguments against government funded recapitalization.[6] Second, they may fear political backlash from a frustrated populace that believed that they had entrusted their monies to well-managed or fully guaranteed institutions.[7] Third, a failure to recapitalize the banking system may reduce the usefulness of the banking system as a vehicle for channeling wealth to themselves and their supporters.[8] Finally, policymakers may be concerned about the marcoeconomic consequences of imposing losses on depositors, so-called systemic risk. We define systemic risk as a sharp decline in macroeconomic activity resulting from shifts in the willingness of the public to hold banking system liabilities.

There is surprising little evidence concerning the macroeconomic impact of imposing losses on depositors.[9] This paper will focus on this last issue. The goal will be to present some empirical evidence on the links between treatment of depositors of insolvent institutions and subsequent macroeconomic performance. We develop this evidence using a case study approach. Five episodes are studied: Estonia, 1992; Argentina, 1989; Malaysia, 1986; Japan, 1946; and the United States, 1933.

Our analysis of these episodes lead us to three conclusions:

1. The imposition of losses on depositors had minimal negative impact on economic performance.
2. The nature of the restructuring plan seems to have been essential to this outcome. In each of these episodes, policymakers took a comprehensive approach to resolving financial system distress and sought to ensure that only well capitalized institutions will remain in operation.
3. Banks can be successfully restructured even if their depositors suffer losses in the process. This makes it possible to maintain appropriate incentives while at the same time avoiding the loss of nontransferable information about the banks' borrowers.

These findings suggest that in at least some cases the economic costs of imposing losses on depositors are lower than are generally believed. However, the final decision about whether or not to allow of insolvent institutions a second chance by bailing out depositors and injecting new capital depends on two other factors, the deadweight economic losses associated with providing this second chance and the political costs of failing to do so. This paper does not provide any analysis of the political costs of failing to revive insolvent banks. However, our findings do suggest that while concerns about systemic risk should play a big part in determining how losses are imposed on depositors, concerns about systemic risk should play a relatively minor role in determining whether losses should be imposed on depositors.

The Theory of Systemic Risk

The proponents of government funded recapitalizations cum depositor bailouts for the depositors of insolvent banks argue that the threat banking panics preclude loss-sharing by depositors. It is argued that the imposition of losses on depositors may in the end lead to runs on the banking system as a whole and result in a contraction of aggregate money and credit.

Although this fear of systemic risk is seldom well articulated by proponents of government funded depositors bailouts, it always dominates policy discussion on the appropriate bank insolvency resolution mechanism.[10] The limited academic literature on this subject is more helpful (see Bernanke, 1983; Calomiris and Gorton, 1991; Gorton 1985; and Kaufman, 1990 for instance) but suffers from limited degrees of freedom. Insights are also provided by the growing literature on debt renegotiation under financial distress (Myers, 1977 and Gertner and Scharfstein, 1991, among many others).

The academic literature identifies two factors which make the banking system sensitive to declines in depositor confidence. First, there is the bank's sequential service constraint "the first - come - first - serve rule" which prevents allocation of banks' resources on a *pro rata* basis. This constraint rewards those depositors who arrive first to withdraw their funds because their deposit contracts are honored in full.

If the bank is facing a bank run, depositors at the end of the line might suffer losses and might not be able to redeem their funds at par. While this structure appears to be an optimal response to information asymmetries (see for instance Calomiris and Kahn, 1991) it means that a bank closed as a consequence of a run must, at minimum, have its liabilities restructured before it is reopened. Second, because the information available to depositors about the value of banks' assets are incomplete and costly, depositors may perceive the failure of a single bank as a signal to revise their assessment of the risk of other banks. If they fail to differentiate between solvent and insolvent banks they will begin to withdraw their funds even from solvent institutions.

The academic literature provides a number of insights on how to deal with systemic risk. Bernanke monetary contractions. He argues that this occurs because banks have nontransferable informational capital regarding their borrowers.[11] This would suggest that bank liquidation rather than imposition of losses on depositors is the basic problem. Groton and Calomiris, and Kaufman emphasize the important role that interbank lending plays in protecting solvent banks against runs by imperfectly informed depositors. This suggests that after financial restructuring, the health of the remaining banks must at least be obvious to the interbank market. Gorton emphasizes the role of systemwide suspensions of convertibility of deposits for currency or specie. The suspension permits bank liabilities to continue providing their medium of exchange functions while eliminating the ability of borrowers to act on their imperfect information once it appears that redemption at par is no longer possible. This suggests that a financial restructuring plan needs to be preserve the usefulness of bank liabilities as a medium of exchange. Finally, corporate finance theory emphasizes the importance of restructuring existing debt in order to permit financially distressed firms to fund positive NPV projects. Restructuring existing debt is particularly important in banking, where most liabilities are very short term. Free-rider problems encourage individual creditors to hold back from restructuring existing debt (see Gertner and Scharfstein, 1991 for instance). In particular, when debt is widely dispersed it may be impossible to get depositors to voluntarily accept a write down of their deposits since this creates a wealth transfer from those accepting the write-down to those creditors that opt to retain their existing claim. This suggests that an effective restructuring of bank liabilities may have an element of coercion to it. In Gertner and Scharfstein, the coercion takes the form of an offer to exchange of existing debt for a smaller amount of more senior debt. These exchanges can be structured so that individual creditors are willing to accept this exchange, even if it creates a wealth transfer from creditors to shareholders, because failure to go along leads to even greater transfers of wealth. However, there may be other ways to overcome the free-rider problem. For instancc, rcstructuring could also be accomplished by having the government mandated writedowns or exchanges. Once the restructuring of existing debt is completed, it then becomes possible for the firm to attract funding for new loans (Myers, 1977).

Controlling Systemic Risk: Five Components

This literature clearly suggests that to limit systemic risk, a resolution scheme would need to accomplish the following objectives:

Comprehensive action. It is essential that policymakers simultaneously deal with all insolvent and marginal solvent institutions. Intermittent regulatory intervention in depository institutions increases depositors' nervousness and damages regulatory credibility, especially in cases where regulators had previously argued that the institutions were in fact solvent. For the plan to be comprehensive that regulators must possess a clear understanding of the scope of the problem at insolvent and solvent but poorly capitalized institutions. A comprehensive approach presents an additional advantage, of reducing the demand on supervisory resources. Under a piecemeal approach, insolvent and marginally solvent institutions would continue to exist at the same time that other insolvent institutions were being closed or restructured. These institutions would be subject to moral hazard and fraud and would be unable and unwilling to raise additional capital. This in turn creates a significant supervisory burden. Comprehensive restructuring reduces this burden by creating incentives for the owners of the restructured bank to act in a prudent fashion.

Restore public confidence. It is equally critical that regulatory forces restore public confidence in the system by demonstrating that the remaining institutions in operation are solvent and well-capitalized. Possible measures include injections of (preferably private) capital into marginally solvent banks and relicensing procedures for cases in which the banking solvency crisis affected a large proportion of total financial system assets and deposits.

Financial restructuring of insolvent institutions. Restructured institutions can only be viable if they can maintain existing deposits to fund their existing assets and attract new deposits if they have profitable investment opportunities. This can only happen if new depositors are protected from the risk of the old bank portfolio. At a minimum, this requires the write down of old deposits, and may require the creation of claims that are junior to new deposits, when it is difficult to accurately mark assets to market.

Correctly priced deposits. The public's widespread attempt to shift from deposits to currency is influenced by cost considerations.

Table 1. "Universe" of Banking Crises

Country:	*Crisis Episode:*
Venezuela	1994
Estonia	1992
Hungary	1990s
Poland	1990
Benin	1990
Kenya	1990
Congo	1980 & 1990
Central African Republic	1980s & 1990s
Chad	1980s & 1990s
Guinea	1985
Mauritania	1988/1993
New Zealand	1980s
Ghan	1982-89
Malaysia	1985-1988
Spain	1977-1985
Uruguay	1974-1987
Thaland	1983-1987
Phillippines	1981-1987
Chile	1980s
Argentina	1930s, 1980-1982, 1989
France	1930
Austria	1931
Germany	1931, 1945, 1989
Japan	1927, 1946
Hongkong	1965
The United States	1890s, 1907, 1929-1932, 1933, 1974, 1982-1989

In an inflationary environment the opportunity cost of holding currency are not confined to foregone interest. They also include losses in the real value of their deposits. Thus inflation imparts a natural stability to banking systems in crisis. Regulations which keep deposit rates well-below the inflation rate serve to destabilize the system. Artificially high exchange rates have a similar impact because they encourage currency substitution.

Liquify deposits. The time frame over which the deposits of insolvent banks are liquified is absolutely critical. A complete deposit freeze or a lengthy workout over an extended period of time imposes additional costs to depositors of insolvent banks in the form of illiquidity and foregone interest on their unimpaired deposits. The macroeconomic consequences of a deposit freeze are likely to be more serious than are the implications of loss sharing by depositor. Indeed, this seemed to be the principal concern in the United States prior to the creation of the Federal Reserve (Sprague, 1910).

Sample Selection

In our study we have sought to identify instances where countries adopted policies of more or less comprehensive bank restructuring while forcing depositors to bear some loss or risk of loss. The following five country examples are chosen from a larger sample of 39 banking crises involving 27 countries from 1880 onwards (see Table 1). Five episodes were selected for further study. We focused on those episodes where depositors of insolvent institutions were forced to bear some loss as part of a comprehensive plan. Key features of each episode are summarized in Table 2.

Although the sample of cases we focus on have similarities, they differ in the magnitude of the financial crisis and in the specifics of the resolution mechanism adopted. Furthermore, each case highlights different aspects of the problem in question. The Estonian case is of interest because the insolvent institutions accounted for a large segment of the banking system—46.9 percent of total system deposits—and therefore the systemic risk associated with imposing losses on depositors could be considered to be high. In contrast, the insolvency crisis was confined to a small segment of the financial system in Malaysia. However, the government decided to intervene and resole the crisis by exposing depositors to possible losses. This choice is particularly interesting when one considers that Malaysia is a country with a high level of intermediation and as such should be particularly concerned about the stability of its financial system. Argentina is of particular interest since by imposing losses on time deposit holders throughout the system, the Argentine government—according to the traditional view—risked a flight to currency and foreign exchange. The U.S. case study illustrates the importance of adopting a comprehensive approach for restoring public confidence in the banking

Table 2. Characteristics of Banking Crises Included in our Study

Feature	*Estonia*	*Argentina*	*Malaysia*	*Japan*	*US*
Time	1992	1989/90	1986-1988	1946	1933
Resolution Approach	Comprehensive	Quasi-Comprehensive	Comprehensive	Comprehensive	Comprehensive
% of deposits at insolvent institutions	46.9% of financial system deposits		3.4% of financial system deposits	10% of financial system deposits	5.6% of financial system deposits
Bailout of Depositors	No Bailout	Partial Bailout	Partial Bailout	Partial Bailout	Partial Bailout
Measures to Restore Public Confidence	- Relicensing of banks	- Measures to curb budget deficit	- Capital injextion	- Capital injection	- Relicensing of banks - Capital injection
Financial Restructuring of Insolvent Banks	Frozen assets and corresponding deposits moved from bank's balance sheet	Affected deposits replaced with government bonds	Merger with solvent institutions; old deposits were partly converted into equity or loan stock	Separation of banks' balance sheet into old and new account	New deposits senior to old deposits
Government Capital Injection Into Surviving Banks	yes	no	yes	yes	yes
Princing of Deposits	No interest regulation in place		No interest rate regulation in place	Interest rate regulation in place	No interest regulation in place; misrvaluation of dollar
Liquification of Deposits at Insolvent Banks	- General liquification procedure - Deposits converted into tradeble certificate of VEB fund	deposits were converted into tradeable claim	Different procedures: - extension of maturity of deposits - 50% cash repayment and 50% converted into equity or loan stock	Marking to market of assets and deposits in the old account took place two years after separation of accounts	RFC lent money to closed institutions to accelerate depositors repayments

system. In 1933, the measures implemented by the Roosevelt administration were successful in putting an end to increasing rates of bank failures which had plagued the system for the preceding three years. Finally, the Japanese case study offers insight in how to restructure an insolvent financial system on a going concern basis without further distorting market incentives.

Methodology

We begin by describing the nature of the crisis and the plan to resolve it. In a number of our cases there already exists a fairly detailed English-language summary of the plan to resolve the crisis.[12] With the exception of work on the United States, these works pay little attention to the links between the features of the resolution plan and the macroeconomic response. For each country, we present a systematic description of the plan, filling in the sometimes considerable gaps with information from other sources.

A Typology of Resolution Mechanisms

We begin by summarizing the resolution mechanism. Approaches to resolving financial crisis can vary in how losses are allocated, how depositor's claims are liquidified, and the fate of insolvent and undercapitalized banks.

Loss allocation. Loss allocation is an important part of the resolution mechanism. Potential bearers of losses include shareholders, healthy banks, depositors of the insolvent institution, and the government. Losses to depositors can be distributed through a write-down of their uninsured deposits, through the conversion of their deposits into bank equity, or both. But even if they regain their deposit principal, depositors might incur losses from illiquidity or from forgone interest payments. They also suffer losses if the government imposes interest rate controls that push interest rates on bank deposits below their "market" level. Losses can be allocated to the government through central bank assistance, guarantee of bank deposits, tax write-offs of bad loans, or direct intervention. Government bailouts are then passed on to the tax-payer or, if they lead to budget deficits which are financed through monetary expansions, to the currency holding public.

Liquification of deposits. The liquification of the deposits of insolvent institutions can be accomplished in various ways. For example, Argentine time deposit holders saw parts of their deposits converted into tradeable government bonds. In Malaysia, depositors saw a portion of their deposits converted to equity in the institutions being recapitalized. In the United States, a government agency extended loans to insolvent institutions in liquidation so that they could compensate depositors' claim before the liquidation was complete.

Disposition of insolvent banks. Insolvent banks may face one of three fates. Governments may choose to restructure an insolvent bank if it has important nontransferable lending information on borrowers. The restructuring may occur on a stand alone basis with the government or private investors injecting new capital with government removing the non-performing assets from the bank's balance sheet, or it may occur by converting deposits into equity. Alternatively, the bank may be merged with a healthy institution. Finally, the government may force the insolvent institution to undergo liquidation.

Treatment of undercapitalized but solvent banks. For marginally solvent institutions, the government may require existing bank shareholders to inject new equity (e.g., Japan 1946). Alternatively, it may inject capital inform of cash payments, new stock issues underwritten by government agencies, government or central bank securities yielding market rates. The government may also choose to purchase bad loans. This occurred in the United States when the Reconstruction Finance Corporation purchased preferred stock in marginally solvent institutions which was later retired out of bank profits at preferential prices.

Evaluating Outcomes

Our approach to interpreting the impact of the crisis resolution is similar in spirit to the approach employed by Friedman and Schwartz in *A Monetary History of the United States.* This work focuses on industrial production, the ratio of currency to deposits, the ratio of reserves to deposits, and broad money supply as indicators of the condition of the economy. However, in recognition of arguments made by Bernanke (1983), we also focus on growth in bank lending in order to capture impacts on the banking system's willingness to lend. We attach the following interpretations to each of these variables.

Industrial Production: Because it is available on a monthly basis, we use the industrial production index as our indicator of economic activity. This permits us to more accurately link policy actions to macroeconomic activity. At a minimum, an improvement in the index of industrial production would indicate that the resolution approach taken by the government did not derail economic growth. However, the positive correlation between the Industrial Production Index and a comprehensive approach can just be regarded as a weak test for positive spillover effects.

Credit Growth: The question which needs to be addressed here is whether the resolution mechanism impaired intermediation in the immediate aftermath of the restructuring. We employ two measures of credit availability, total lending and the loan to asset ratio. A credit crunch may arise with any combination of the following four actions. First, a crunch may be caused by a run on deposits which, if not offset by monetary policy, forces a contraction in total assets and total lending. Second, a crunch could be the consequence of a post-crisis tightening of regulatory capital requirements. Third, a crunch could occur because the resolution mechanism reduces the banking system's informational capital. Finally, a crunch could be a voluntary response to a reduction in the banking system's capital cushion or an increase in the risk of its current portfolio. The latter would be especially likely if banks view the issuance of new equity as relative expensive.[13]

The deposit to currency ratio: The deposit to currency ratio is an indicator of public confidence in the banking system before and after the restructuring efforts by the government. An increase in the deposit to currency ratio indicates a reduction in uncertainty and strengthened public confidence in the system.

The deposit to reserve ratio: The ratio of deposits to reserves indicates the banks' reaction to the crisis and the resolution procedure. A falling deposit to reserve ratio other things held equal (including reserve requirements) indicates that banks prefer to hold excess reserves in order to be prepared to meet increased depositors' withdrawals. Thus, a falling ratio of deposits to reserves indicates banks' uncertainty.

II. CASE STUDIES

The following case studies will suggest that governments can adopt crisis resolution mechanisms that include imposing losses on depositors while keeping systemic risk to a minimum if they successfully address the issues that were discussed earlier.

Estonia in 1992/1993

Estonia's experience is of particular interest for our study for three reasons. First, the bank insolvency crisis affected a large segment of the financial system; the commercial banks affected accounted for 40.9 percent of financial system assets and 46.9 percent of total system deposits. Therefore the danger of systemic risks associated with imposing losses on depositors could be considered to be high. Second, by marking assets to market, Estonia dealt with its banks' bad loan portfolio at a much earlier point than did other transitional economies. Finally, as a transitional economy, Estonia's experience is particularly relevant for other countries in Central Europe and the former Soviet Union.

The Scope of the Financial Crisis

In June 1992, 10 months after gaining independence, Estonia launched its own currency under a currency board.[14] The introduction of the currency board brought the growing bad debt problem of some Estonian banks to surface. Previously, banks with severe bad debt problems or mismatched terms of liabilities could remain liquid by using large profits earned from foreign exchange trading,[15] or by onlending cheap central bank credit as high spreads.[16] The banks' deteriorating loan portfolios were mainly caused by two factors: the banks' inappropriate lending policies and the severe adverse shocks experienced by Estonian enterprises. The generally tight stance of monetary policy was further exacerbated by a sharp endogenous decrease in the money multiplier resulting from a shift by the public from domestic currency into hard currency. This shift was driven in part by expectations that the Kroon would be devalued at the end of the year.[17]

Three large Estonian banks accounting for 40.9 percent of total banking system's assets and for 46.9 percent of total deposits[18] experienced growing illiquidity, forcing them to start delaying payments to other banks. These banks were primarily funded with corporate deposits. In October 1992, the illiquidity of the Northern Joint Stock Bank (NEJSB) which is 100 percent owned by the Central Bank of Estonia (BoE), the Union Baltic Bank (UBB) with public and private owners, and the Tartu Commercial Bank (Tartu) also public and private owners[19] reached a critical point when they became unable to meet further deposit withdrawals. When this point was reached, the three banks were subject to intervention by the Bank of Estonia.[20]

The Distress Resolution Plan at the Crisis Point of November 1992

Immediate Actions Following the Central Bank Interventions. The Bank of Estonia quickly announced a moratorium on payments by the three commercial banks. Assets and deposits were frozen and the CEOs of all three banks were fired. Whereas UBB and NEJSB's problems were mostly caused by the freezing of foreign exchange deposits at the Vneshekonombank[21], the Foreign Trade Bank in Moscow, Tartu Bank's problems stemmed from a combination of non-performing loans, loans contracted at low interest rates and losses on foreign exchange operations. According to BoE's examinations "based on common accounting principles," all three banks were insolvent. A few days later, the banks were allowed to reopen for transactions involving sums deposited after the start of the moratorium. At the same time, depositors were granted access to up to 10 percent of their frozen deposits at NEJSB and UBB, and 5 percent at TCB. The banks were given several weeks to present a restructuring plan to the BoE.[22]

On December 15, 1992, the BoE board rejected the rescue package presented by the TCB management and decided to liquidate the bank by immediately revoking its license and auctioning of its physical and financial assets.[23] The restructuring solution for NEJSB and UBB which the BoE board agreed upon at the same meeting did not receive the approval of the government.[24] Eventually the government announced the following solution.[25] NEJSB and UBB were to be merged and the new entity was recapitalized with EEK 300 million in long-term low interest government bonds issued by the Ministry of

Finance. At the same time, the frozen assets and corresponding deposits were moved to BoE and placed in a fund known as the VEB Fund managed by the BoE.[26] The new entity, the North Estonia Bank (NEB), reopened in March 1993.[27]

The depositors[28] of the three commercial banks are going to face heavy losses.[29] It is estimated that the liquidation of Tartu will allow its depositors to recover 75 percent of their deposits.[30] By April 1993, depositors had received 50 percent of their deposits.[31] In the case of NEJSB and UBB, according to preliminary estimates, depositors will recover at most 20-25 percent of their deposits.[32] Depositors of UBB and NEJSB whose claims were placed into the VEB fund would receive, according to Hansson, "tradeable certificates of equal face value" which entitle the owner of any fixed share of any sums which might actually be recovered from VEB.[33]

Additional Policy Measures. In addition to restructuring the three large insolvent commercial banks, the central bank strengthened prudential regulation and the supervision of banks, and gradually moved accounting standards towards international standards, tightening the accounting rules for bad debts.[34] The central bank also tried to control the entry of new banks and the merging or closing of weak banks by sequential increases in minimum capital requirements and by refusing to issue new banking licenses.[35] The number of Estonian banks decreased from 42 at the onset of the banking crisis to 23 at the end of 1993. Furthermore, the BoE continued to show its willingness to close and liquidate insolvent banks without bailing out depositors.[36]

The BoE took a number of steps to increase public confidence in the banking system. In the immediate aftermath of the crisis, wholesale banks of the banking sector were required to apply for a relicensing.[37] Eight bank licenses were not renewed. These banks were forced to discontinue operations immediately and enter liquidation.[38] Moreover, on April 13, 1993, the BoE specified more detailed reporting and stricter prudential requirements for banks becoming effective on January 1, 1994. Commercial banks have to adhere to a set of prudential requirements which include among other things a solvency ratio of 8 percent, a liquidity ratio of 30 percent, an 800 percent limit on risk concentration, and a limit on loan exposure to one client to 50 percent of the bank's own funds.[39] In December 1993, the BoE required banks to fully write down loans in arrears for over 150 days.[40]

The Economic Impact of the Financial Crisis Resolution Plan

Macroeconomic Indicators. Following the adoption of market reforms, Estonia experienced the sharp decline in industrial production that is the hallmark of an economy in transition. Although the government decided to impose losses on deposits accounting for 46.9 percent of total system deposits,

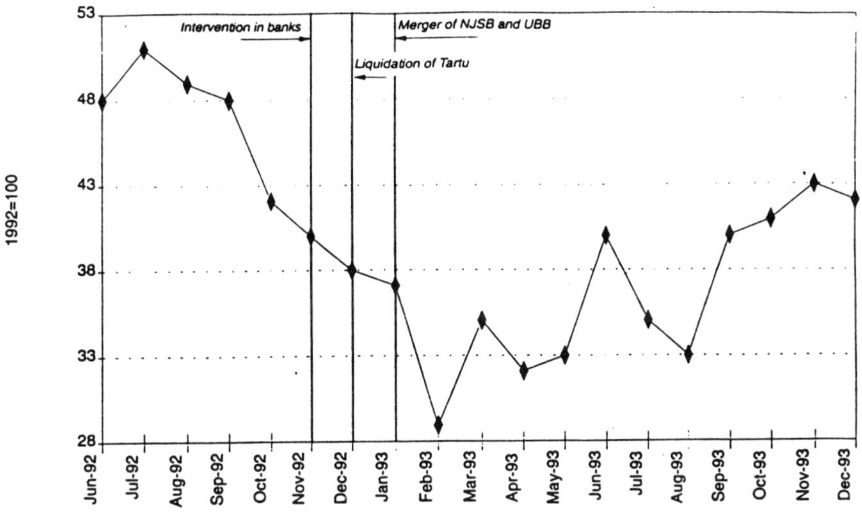

Note: Monthly data.
Source: Estonia Division, World Bank, June 1994.

Case 1. ***Chart 1.*** Estonia Index of Industrical Production from June 1992 to December 1993

this decision did not trigger a systemic crisis capable of derailing the economy's nascent recovery. Industrial output bottomed out in the first half of 1993 and preliminary estimates by the World Bank indicate that a recovery is under way: real GDP growth was recorded at 6 percent for the fourth quarter of 1993, the first growth in GDP since independence.[41,42] This trend is reflected in the Industrial Production figures: industrial Production bottomed out in February 1993 after having declined sharply from its level in January. Production began rising more or less steadily beginning in September of 1993 (See Chart 1).

The restructuring mechanism adopted did not derail lending. On the contrary, after having fallen steadily during the second half of 1992 (first month for which numbers are available) real lending bottomed out in January and started to rise steadily and at an accelerating path until November 1993 (see Chart 2). Lending to the private and public sector by deposit money banks developed differently in the aftermath of the financial restructuring. As apparent in Chart 2b, rather than causing a downturn in lending to the private sector, the restructuring seems to have put an end to the sharp decline of the previous months. Two months after the central bank actions to intervention at the three banks, real loans to the private sector started to increase again, growing steadily thereafter and reaching their pre-crisis level in January (see

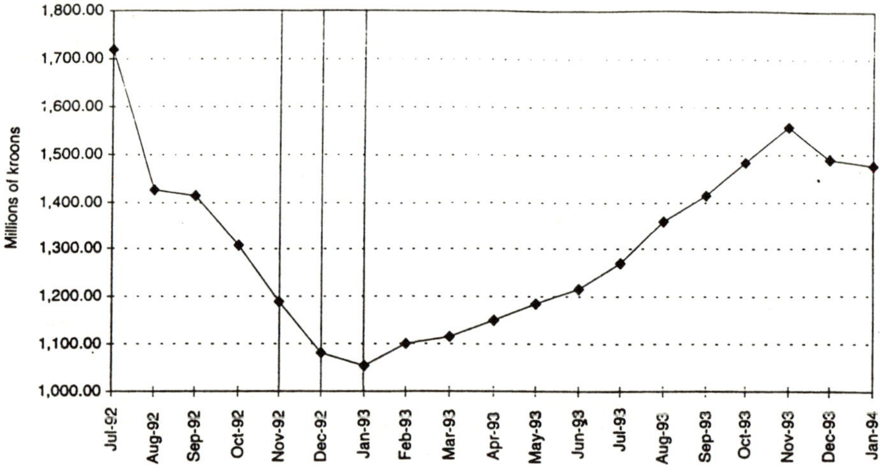

Note: Monthly data.
Source: Eesti Pank, several issues.

Case 1. ***Chart 2a.*** Estonia: Real Loans Outstanding of Deposit Money Banks from July 1992 to January 1994

Chart). In contrast, real loans to nonfinancial public enterprises decreased quite steeply in the immediate aftermath of the crisis and remained more or less stable in the following months. Finally, in the aftermath of the restructuring operation the loan to asset ratio increased steadily from 30 percent in November 1992 to 48 percent in January 1994 (see Chart 3a). This suggests that the resolution mechanism did not trigger a flight to quality by banks.

The continued decline in the deposit to currency ratio in the immediate aftermath of the crisis indicates that it took a few months for depositor confidence to be restored. The decline in the deposit to currency ratio following the bank restructuring was the result of falling foreign currency deposits and a steady increase in currency held by the public. The rapid growth in currency held by the public in the months after the implementation of the restructuring

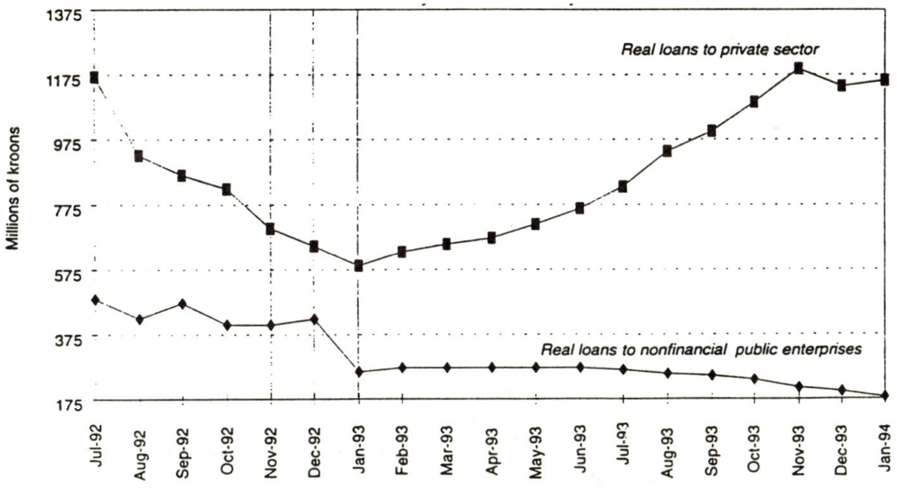

Note: Monthly data.
Source: Eesti Pank, several issues.

Case 1. ***Chart 2b.*** Estonia: Real Loans to Nonfinancial Public Enterprises and to the Private Sector of Deposit Money Banks from July 1992 to January 1994

measures must be seen against the backdrop of disinflation which sharply reduced the public's costs of holding currency. The monthly inflation rate fell from 17 percent in August 1992 to 3.22 percent in December 1992.[43] Despite the restructuring and the rapid decline in the rate of inflation, aggregate nominal holdings of demand, time, and savings deposits remained more or less stable during the period from October 1992 (first figures available) to April 1993. In real terms, deposits declined by 14 percent between January 1993 and April 1993. Total bank deposits, both nominal and real, began to rise in May 1993. This suggests that by May, public confidence in the banking system had stabilized. However, currency held by the public continued to grow more rapidly, resulting in a further decline of the deposit to currency ratio in June

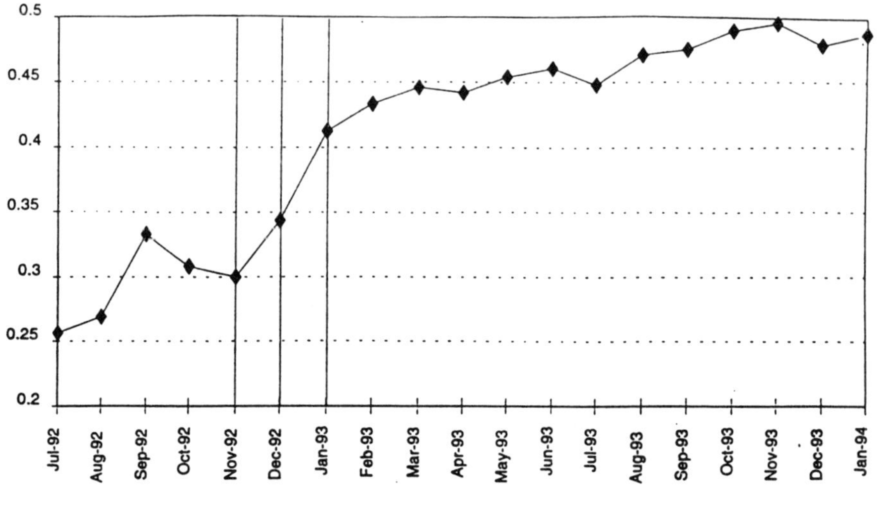

Note: Monthly data.
Source: Eesti Pank, several issues.

Case 1. ***Chart 3a.*** Estonia: Loan to Asset Ratio of Deposit Money Banks from July 1992 to January 1994

(see Chart 4a). By June 1993, only six months after the implementation of the resolution plan, the deposit to currency ratio had ceased to decline. It began to slowly increase in July 1993 which suggest a return of the public's confidence into the banking system. This is further supported by the fact that foreign currency deposits, which had fled the banking system in the beginning of the crisis, began returning to the Estonian banking system.[44]

Although the deposit to reserve ratio fell significantly in the immediate aftermath of the crisis, it bottomed out in February 1993 (see chart 4b) one month after the restructuring measures were implemented. The ratio starts to rise again in August 1993. These movements suggest that bank's expectations about their exposures to runs stabilized quickly. However, the high level of excess reserves suggests that banks took the threats of future runs very seriously.[45] While such fears might be expected to cripple the banking system's lending activities, it did not. As noted earlier, the recovery of banks' lending activities started to rise in February 1993 two months after the central bank interventions.

Complementary Monetary Policy Actions. The range of complementary monetary policy actions that the central bank could pursue was limited due to its operation of a currency board. Under a currency board, the central

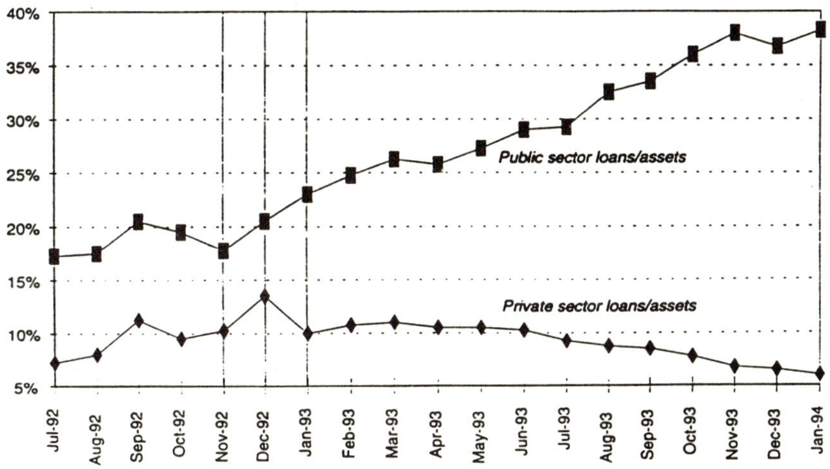

Note: Monthly data.
Source: Eesti Pank, several issues.

Case 1. ***Chart 3b.*** Ratio of Public Sector Loans to Total Assets and Ratio of Private Sector Loans to Total Assets of Deposit Money Banks from July 1992 to January 1994

bank has little scope to act as a lender of last resort and does not operate a discount window.[46] Furthermore, since the kroon must always be fully backed by gold and hard currency reserves,[47] and the central bank cannot devalue the kroon, the monetary base can only be expanded as a response to a rise in foreign currency reserves. As chart 4 shows, real high-powered money increased steadily during November 1992 to January 1994 except for the period from December to January during which it remained stable (see Chart 5). Due to a fall in the money multiplier which was not offset by a rise in high powered money, real M2 decreased significantly from December 1992 to January 1993. It bottomed out in April 1993 and started to rise in May 1993 when the reserve to deposit ratio recovered slightly (see Chart 6).

The Argentine Banking Crisis of 1989

The resolution approach adopted by the Argentine government in 1989 cannot be considered fully comprehensive since it did not address the bad loan problems of the government owned banks. Nevertheless, it is of interest. By imposing losses on time deposit holders throughout the system, the Argentine

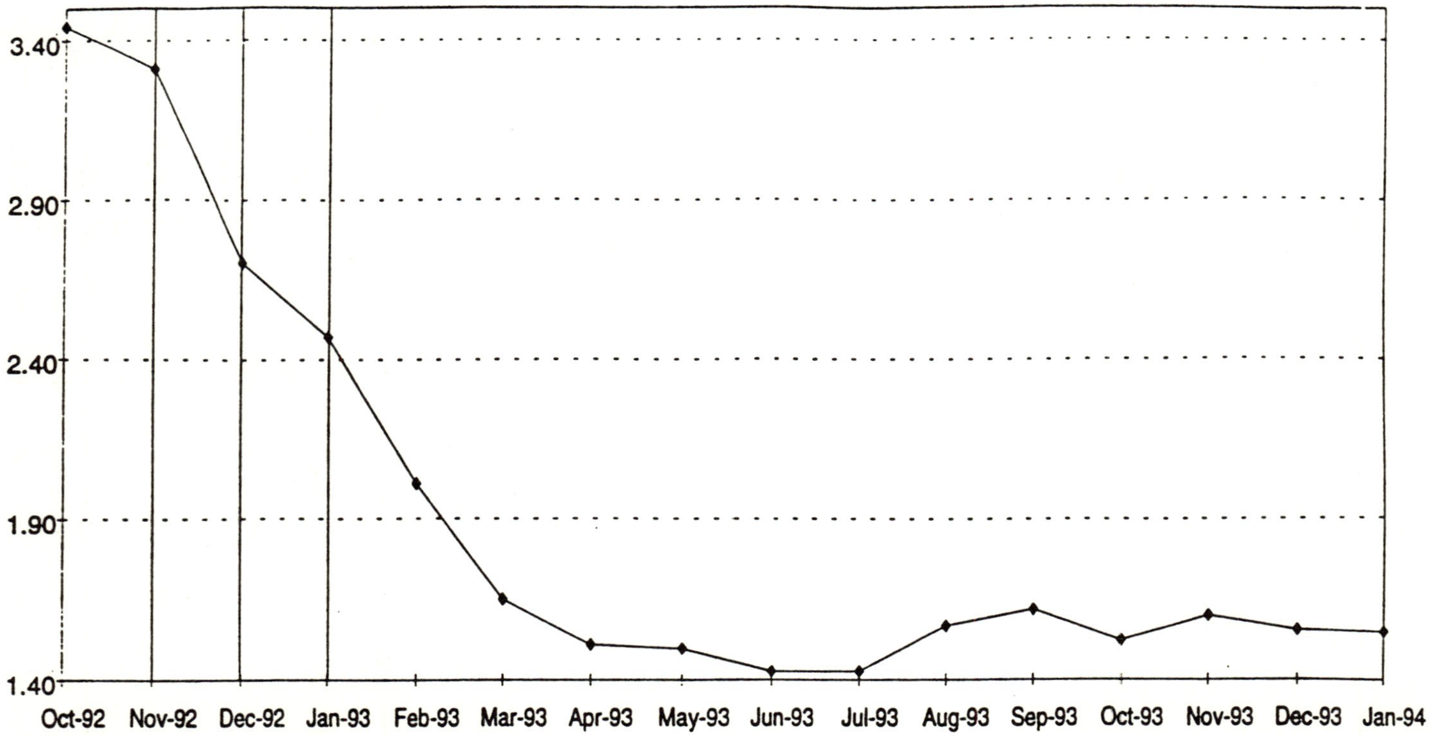

Note: Monthly data.
Source: Estonia, Key Economic Indicators, 1994; Eesti Pank, several issues.

Case 1. ***Chart 4a.*** Estonia: Deposit To Currency Ratio from Oct. 1992 to Jan. 1994

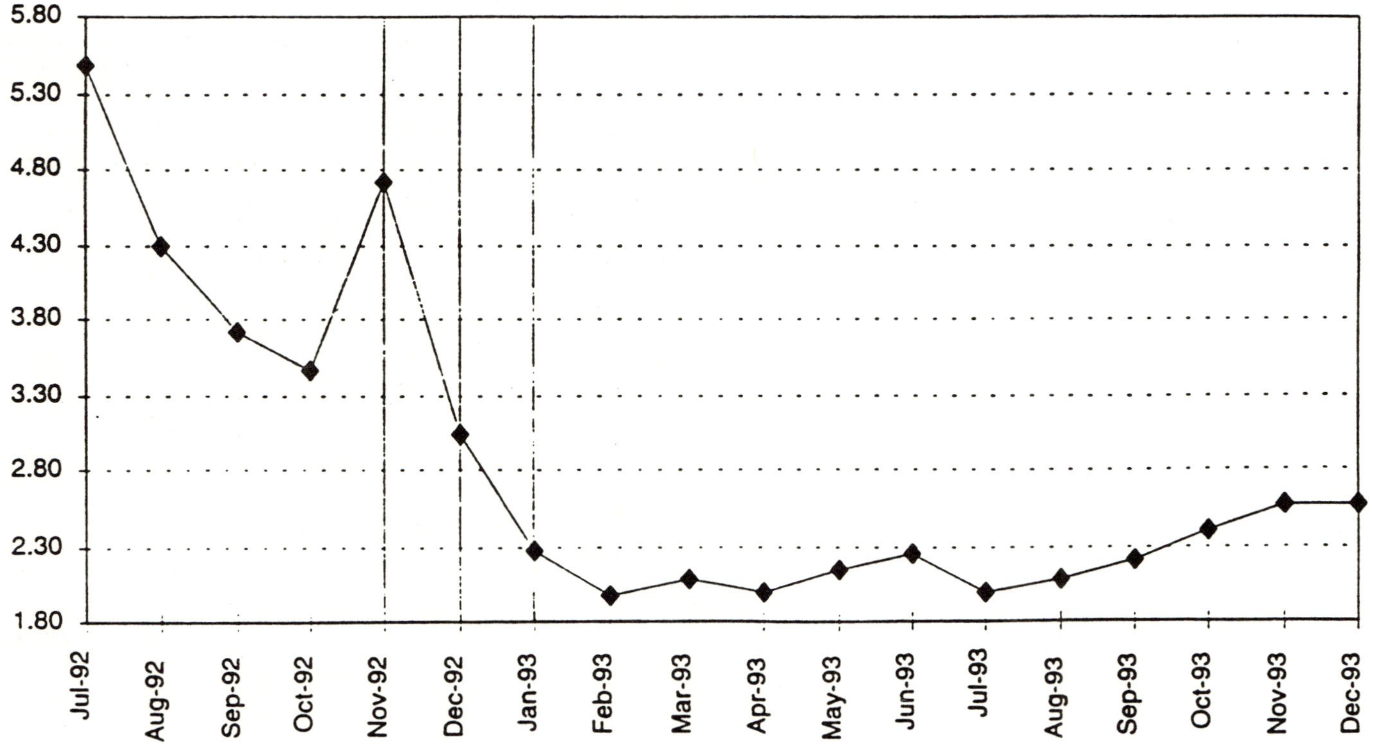

Note: Monthly data.
Source: Estonia, Key Economic Indicators, 1994; Eesti Pank, several issues.

Case 1. ***Chart 4b.*** Estonia: Deposit To Reserve Ratio from July 1992 to Dec. 1993

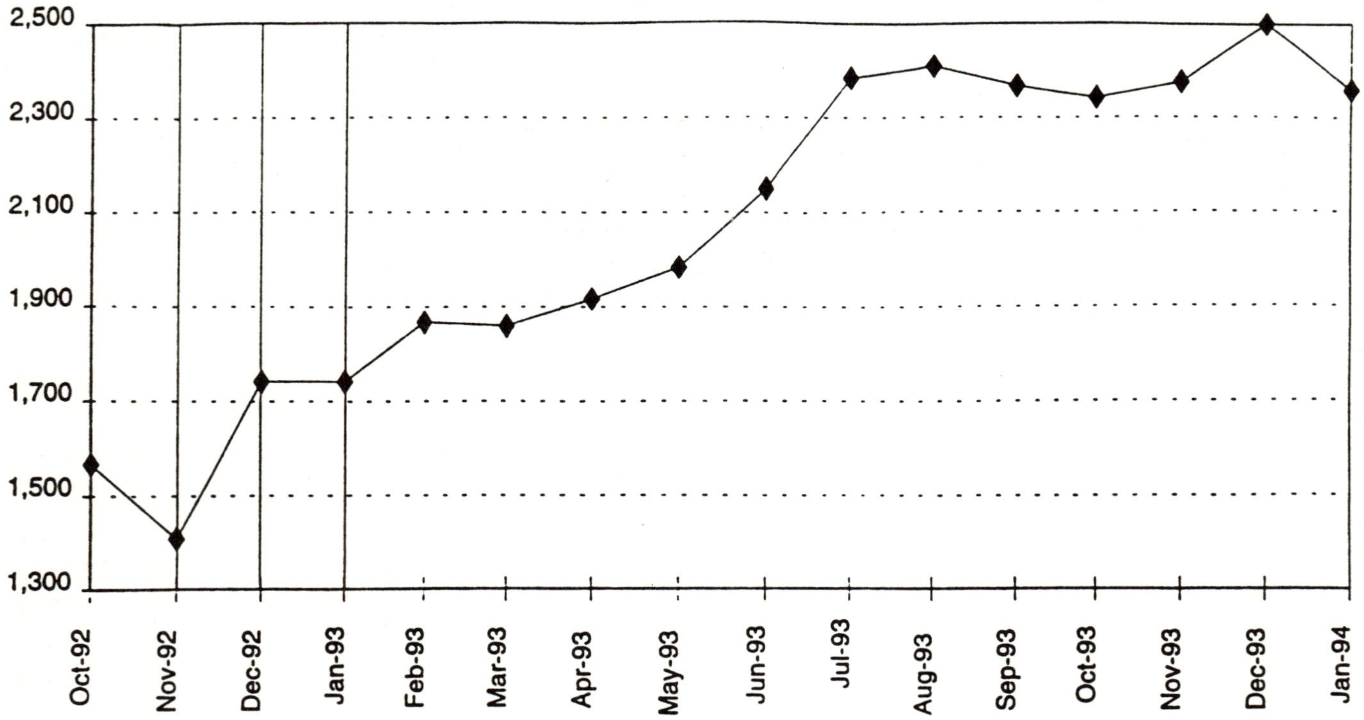

Note: Monthly data.
Source: Eesti Pank, several issues.

Case 1. ***Chart 5.*** Estonia: Real High Powered Money from October 1992 to January 1994

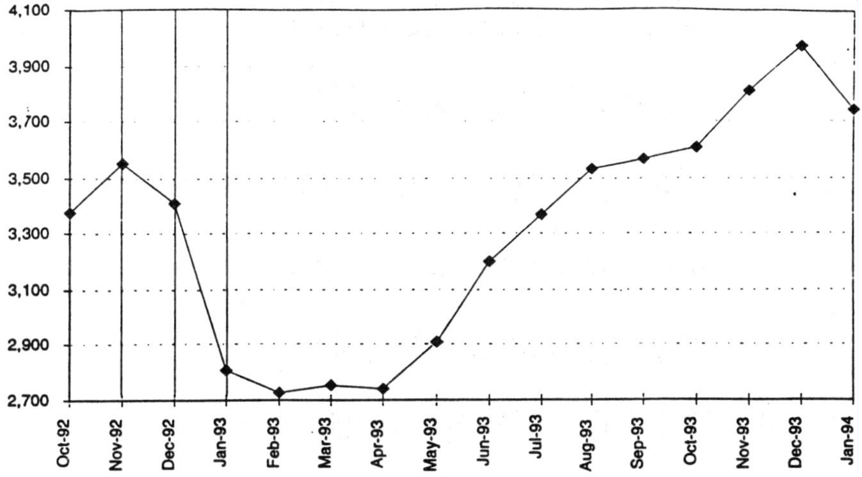

Note: Monthly data.
Source: Eesti Pank, several issues.

Case 1. ***Chart 6a.*** Estonia: Real M2 from October 1992 to January 1994

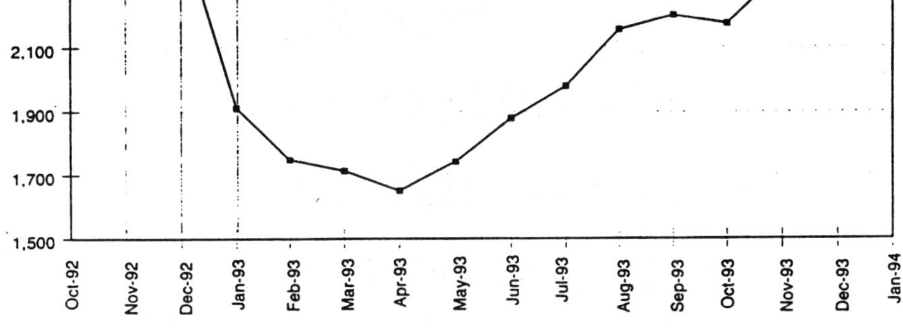

Case 1. ***Chart 6b.*** Estonia: Real Deposits

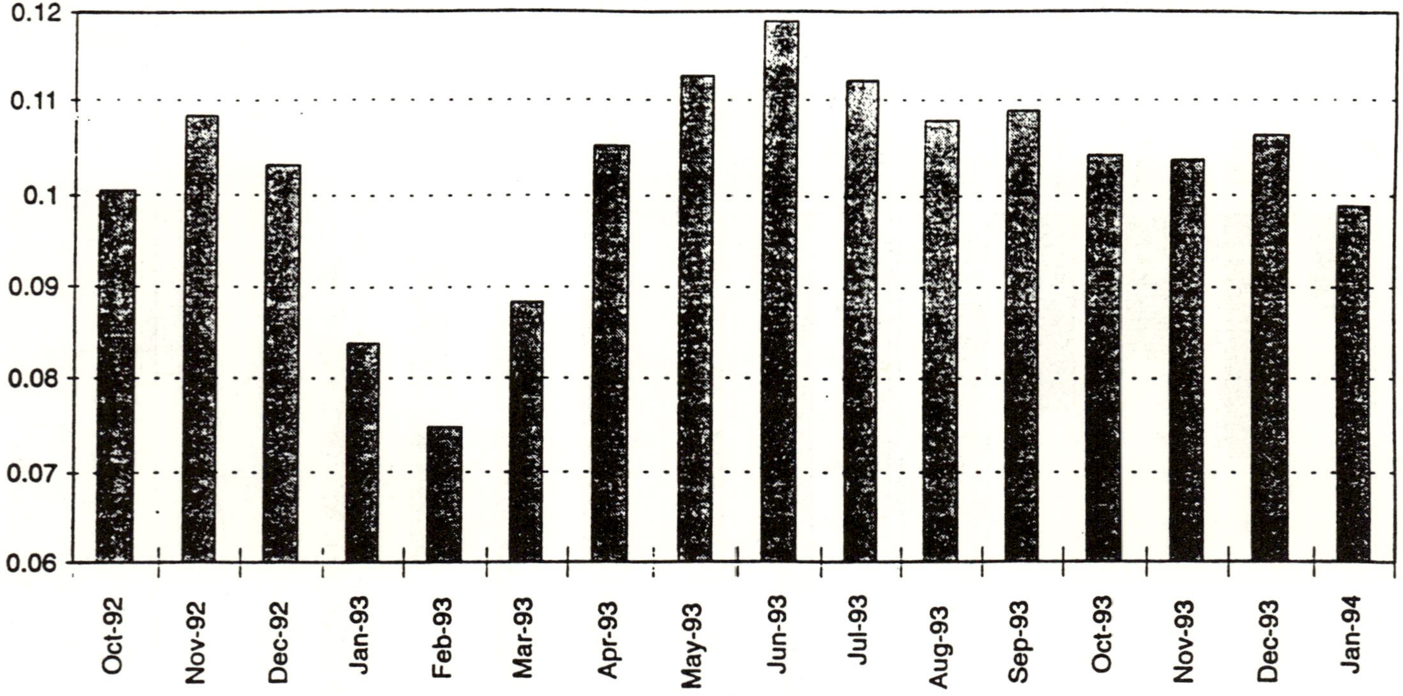

Note: Monthly data.
Source: Eesti Pank, several issues.

Case 1. ***Chart 7.*** Estonia: Capital to Asset Ratio Deposit Money Banks from Oct. 92 to January 1994

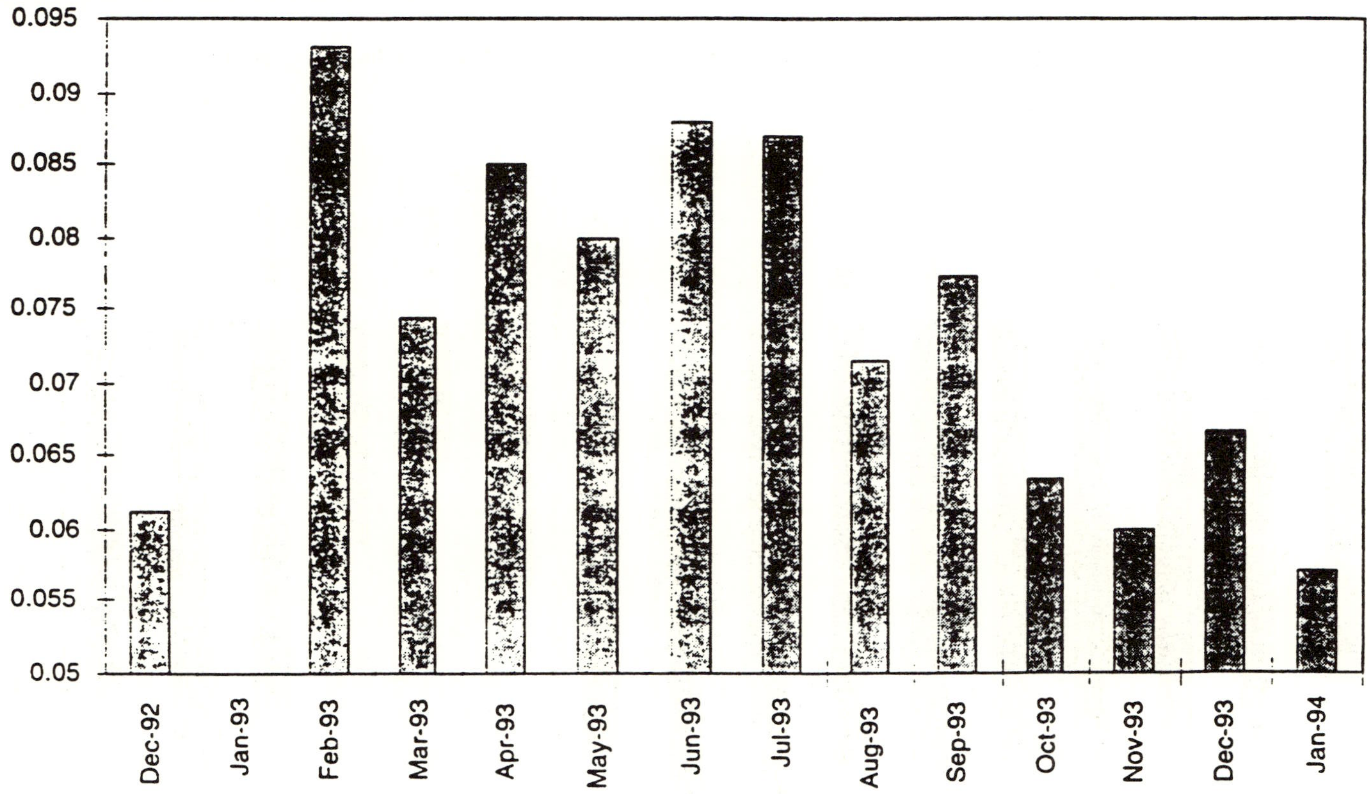

Note: Monthly data.
Source: Eesti Pank, several issues.

Case 1. ***Chart 8.*** Estonia: Ratio of Total Loans to Laons Past Due to Deposit Money Banks from December 1992 to January 1994 government—according to the traditional view—risked a debilitating flight to currency and foreign exchange.

The Scope of the Financial Crisis

The crisis of 1989 was the second banking crisis of the decade.[48] In contrast to the crisis of 1980-82, the 1989 crisis was fundamentally a case of public sector (primarily central bank) debt distress coupled with the government's loss of access to international credit markets. In August of 1989, the financial system was in a precarious position. Non-performing loans stood at 27 percent of the banking system's total loan portfolio, with a significantly higher ratio recorded for government-owned banks (32%) compared to private banks (9%).[49]

Bank deposits at the Central Bank were equal to 62 percent of the total deposits of the financial system.[50] At the same time, "loans and other credit" had fallen from 78 percent of the total assets of the consolidated financial system in June 1982 to 46 percent in December 1988.[51] Total interest bearing liabilities of the central bank reached a peak of 37.1 percent of GDP in the first quarter of 1989.[52]

Thus, the government and the central bank faced a growing debt servicing burden. Given the internal erosion of demand for money and debt instruments denominated in domestic currency, this burden could only be financed at higher and higher interest rates.[53] The rising cost of borrowing money increased public sector borrowing requirements. All of the government's attempts to generate a public sector primary surplus sufficient to pay for its combined external and internal accumulated debt obligations failed.[54] Since the state itself had reached the limits of its debt capacity and external debt repudiation was ruled out, the only alternative was to explicitly repudiate a portion of its internal debt.[55]

The immediate trigger for the December 1989 crisis was the government's decision to free the foreign exchange market and to remove all price controls. This provoked a sudden price increase and lead to sudden bank deposit withdrawals.[56] When banks were unable to meet the demands of their customers, the government declared a banking holiday in late December which lasted until early January.[57]

The Distress Resolution Plan from 1989

During this banking holiday, the government implemented the "BONEX Plan." This plan forced the conversion of virtually all domestic commercial bank 7-day time deposits in private and public banks into a combination of cash (up to the equivalent of US $500) and US $ 3.5 billion of BONEX (external) government bonds. These dollar denominated bonds had a maturity of 10 years, carried a 2-year grace period, and paid an interest rate of LIBOR plus a small spread.[58] Technically the conversion worked as follows: the treasury purchased commercial banks' voluntary and compulsory holdings of seven day interest bearing central bank and national treasury obligations in return for Bonex bonds. These were then used by the commercial banks to make the conversions. The conversion eliminated the impact of this large domestic debt on the public sector borrowing requirements.[59] But it also meant a unilateral write down of public sector debt to the private sector since Bonex bonds traded at a discount.

While the government addressed this source of the public debt distress, it only gradually took on action on public banks which still carried large amounts of doubtful loans on their balance sheets.[60] Despite their significant portfolio of nonperforming loans, public banks are perceived by the public to enjoy an implicit government guarantee arising from their state ownership.[61] These banks accounted for 40.9 percent of all financial system deposits and 39.6 percent of all financial system assets at the end of 1991.[62]

The Argentine government actions served to reinforce the weak precedents set during the banking crisis of the early 1980s by once again imposing losses on depositors.[63] The Bonex plan imposed losses on time deposit holders throughout the system. The Bonex scheme transformed bank deposits into government bonds which immediately traded at a discount of almost 2/3 and did not pay interest for at least 24 months.[64] However, the Bonex conversion provided depositors with tradable claims therefore avoiding the additional cost for depositors of having their deposits frozen for an extended period of time. According to estimates, after the inflation and debt conversion, overall private sector depositors and holders of currency lost nearly 70 percent in real terms of the value of their claims in the financial sector.[65]

The Economic Impact of the Financial Resolution Plan:

Macroeconomic Indicators

Although the Argentine government adopted a resolution mechanism that imposed losses on depositors throughout the banking system, this decision did not derail economic recovery. While real GDP growth had been small or negative through much of the 1980s (−6.2% in 1989), real output did not decline any further during 1990, posting a 0.1 percent growth rate for 1990. GDP growth accelerated after 1990, reaching 8.9 percent for 1991 and 8.7 percent in 1992.[66] However, industrial production was more volatile in the immediate aftermath of the crisis: it bottomed out in March 1990, posted a sharp increase over the next two months to dip again. A sustained increase in industrial production started in January 1991 (see Chart 1).[67]

Total real loans hit a low in September 1990 and started to rise moderately thereafter (see Chart 2a). However, as chart 2a shows, the resolution mechanism adopted did not derail lending to the private sector which began

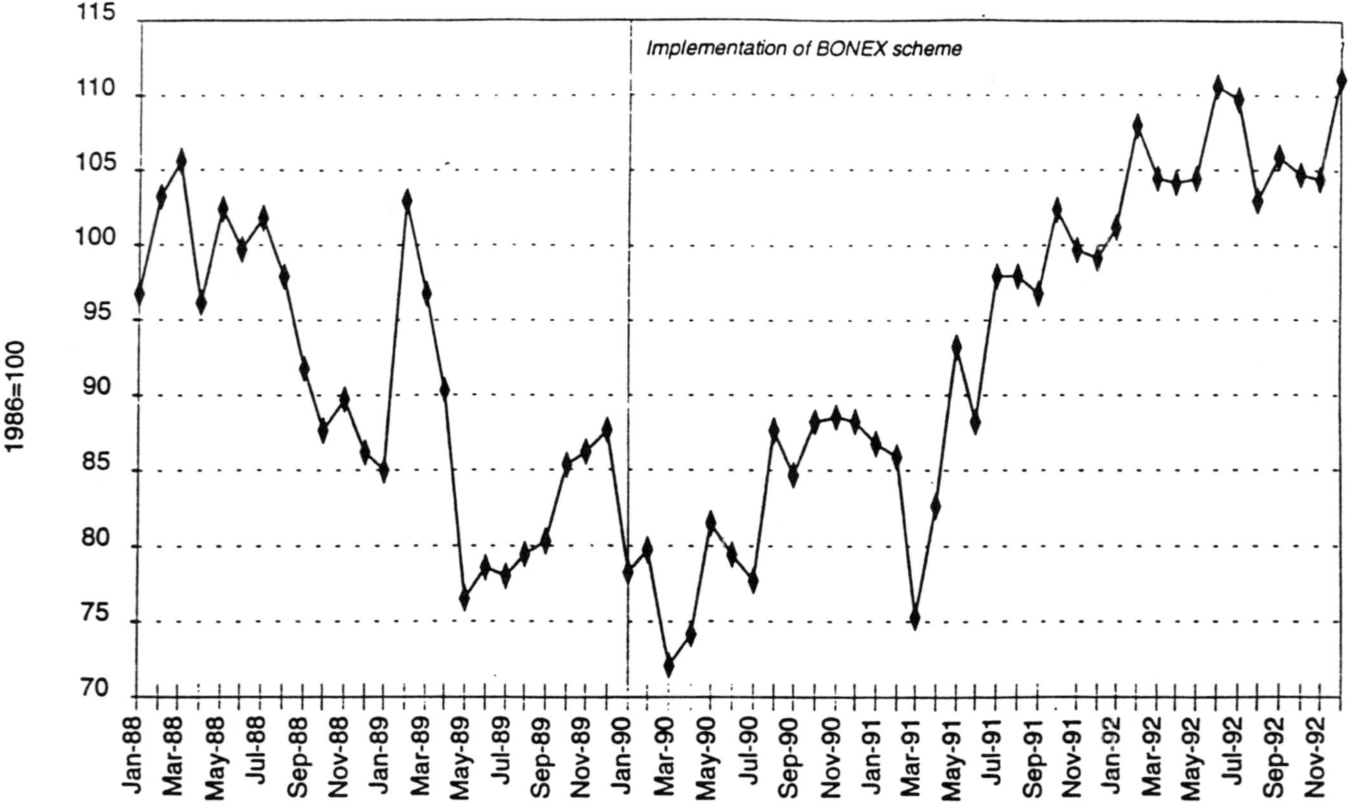

Note: Monthly seasonally adjusted data.
Source: Central Bank of Argentina, Carta Econimica, several issues.

Case 2. ***Chart 1.*** Argentina: Industrial Production Index 1988-92

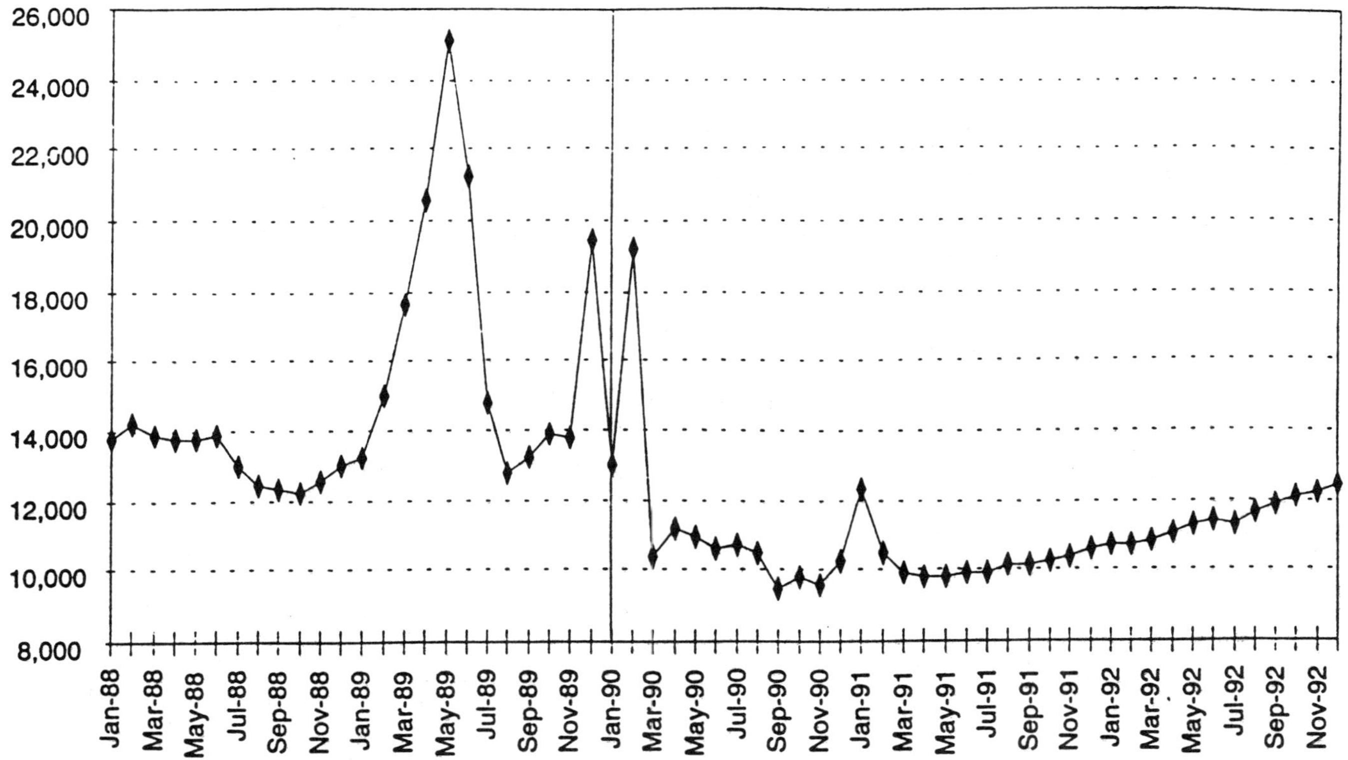

Note: Monthly data.
Source: World Bank, BESD.

Case 2. ***Chart 2a.*** Argentina: Total Real Loans of Deposit Money Banks from 1988 to 1992

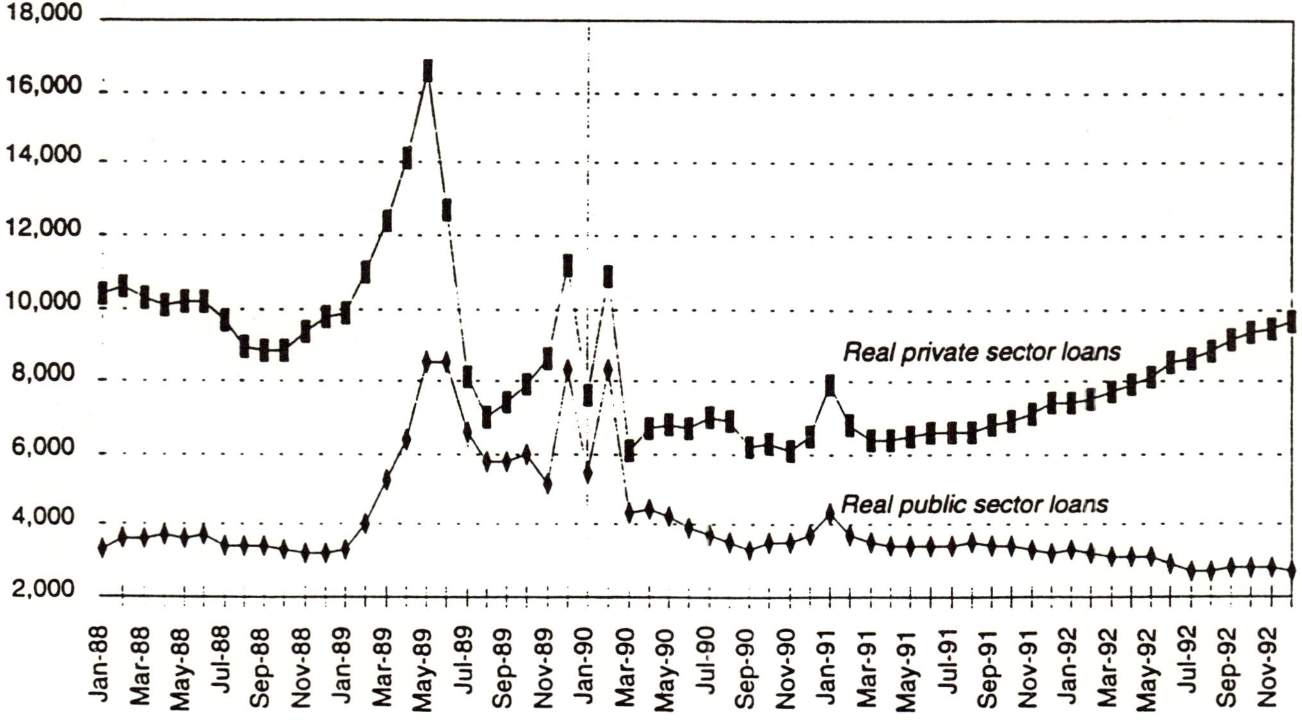

Note: Monthly data.
Source: World Bank, BESD.

Case 2. ***Chart 2b.*** Argentina: Real Private and Real Public Sector Loans of Deposit Money Banks from 1988 to 1992

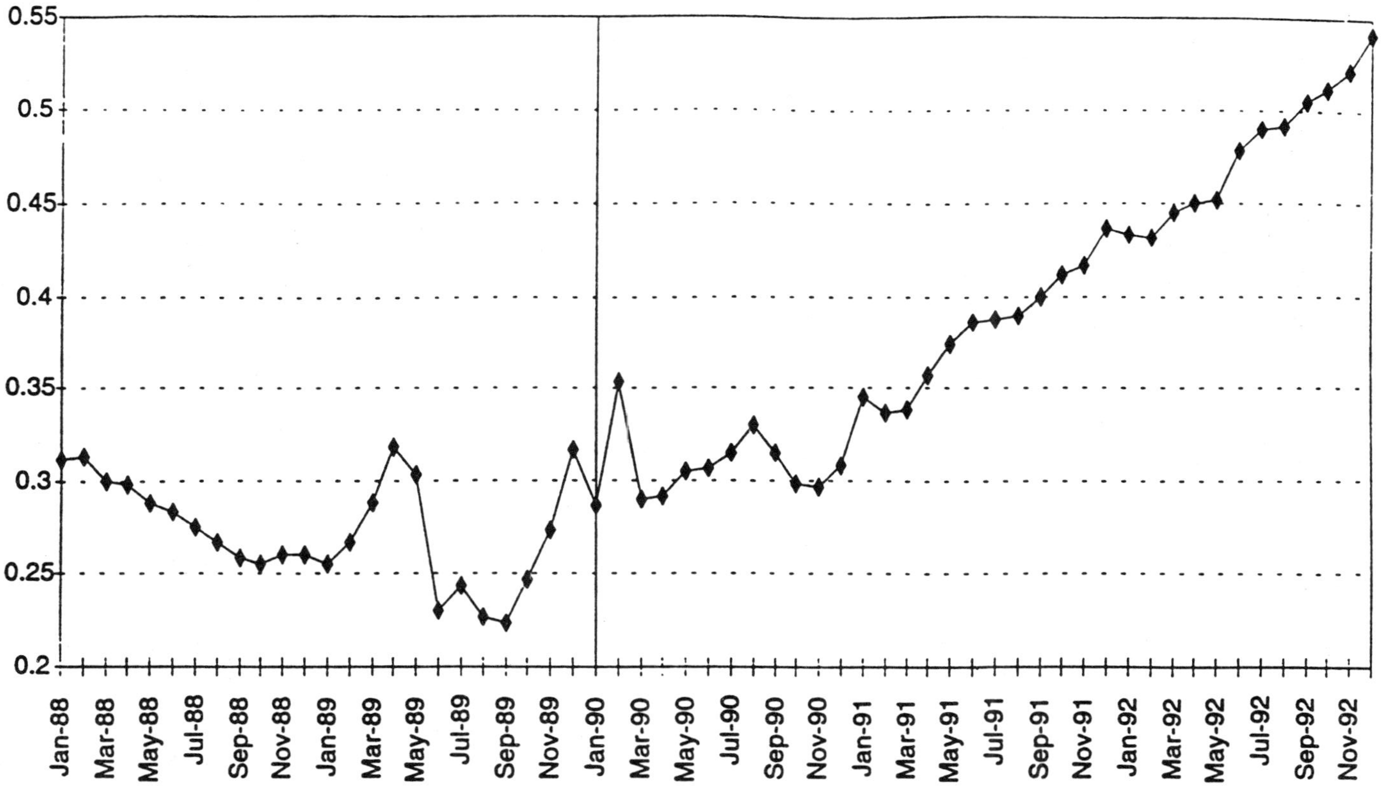

Note: Monthly data.
Source: Central Bank of Argentina, Boletin Estadistico, Several issues

Case 2. ***Chart 3.*** Argentina: Ratio of Private Sector Loans to Total Assets of Deposit Money Banks from 1988 to 1992 to rise again in April, three months after the Bonex conversion. The slower recovery of total real lending was caused by a significant fall in lending to the public sector which declined continuously after February 1990. The Bonex plan did not derail deposit money banks' shift into private sector lending which had already began in October 1989. The ratio of private sector loans to total assets of deposit money banks continued to rise albeit at a more erratic path in the immediate aftermath of the crisis (see chart 3).

Rather than setting off a flight to currency, the imposition of losses on time deposit holders put an end to the sharp decline of the deposit to currency ratio which bottomed out in December 1989 (see chart 4a/1 & 4a/2). Deposits did in effect flow back into the system after January 1990: savings & time deposits rose from real A$ 2.2 billion to nearly 6 billion during 1990.[68] Total real deposits of deposit money banks started to rise three months after the conversion plan was implemented (see chart 4c). These developments suggest that the governments' action reduced depositors' uncertainty. The Bonex conversion of January 1990 also put an end to a sharply declining deposit to reserve ratio. It rose moderately in the immediate aftermath of the crisis indicating that banks' uncertainty was also reduced (see chart 4b/1 & 4b/2).

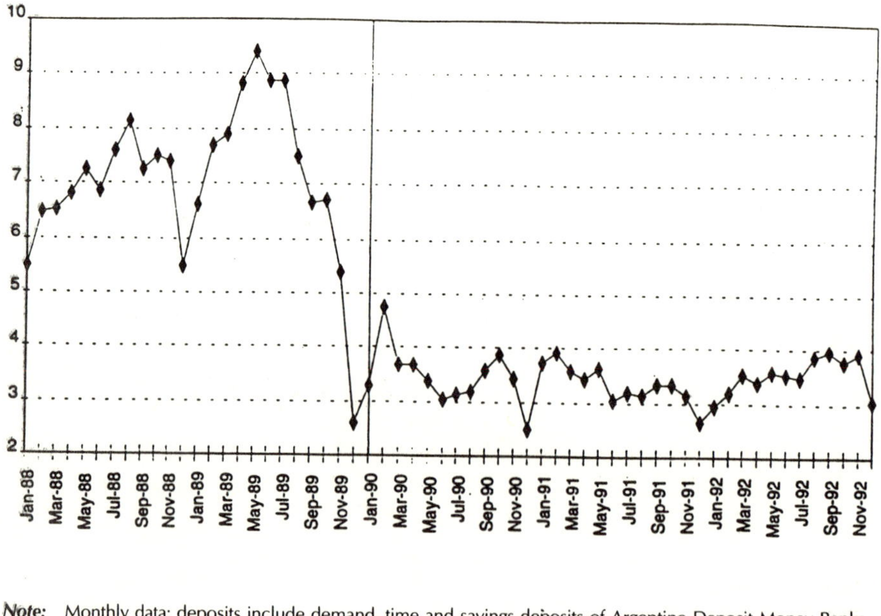

Note: Monthly data: deposits include demand, time and savings deposits of Argentine Deposit Money Banks.
Source: World Bank, BESD.

Case 2. *Chart 4a/1.* Argentina: Deposit To Currency Ratio from 1988 to 1992

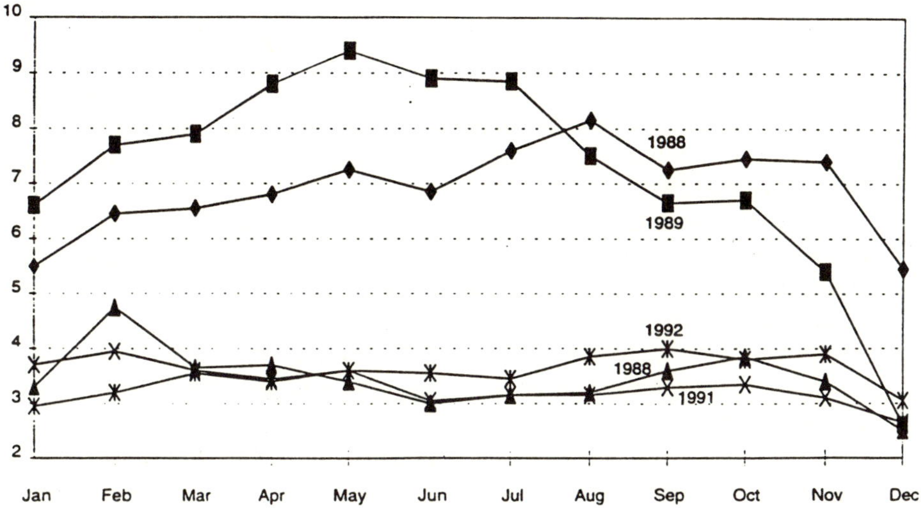

Note: Monthly data.
Source: World Bank, BESD.

Case 2. *Chart 4a/2.* Argentina: Deposit To Currency Ratio from 1988 to 1992

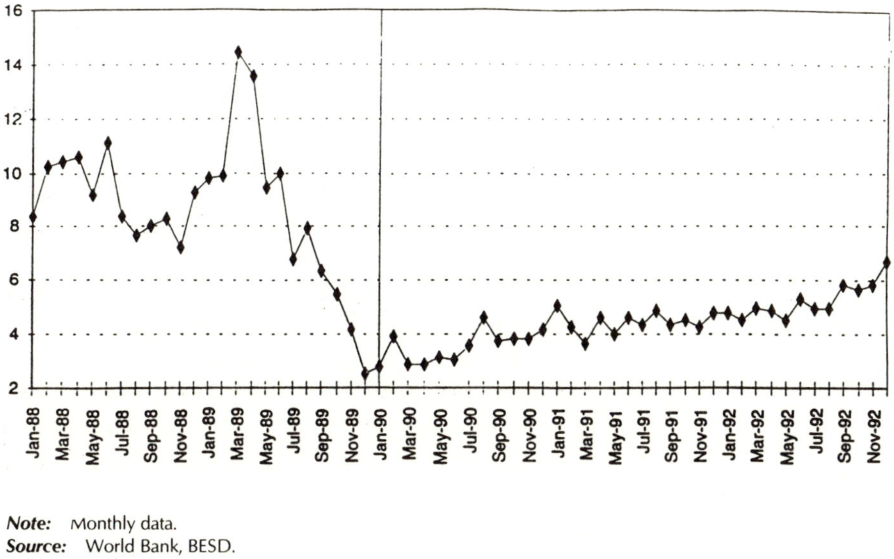

Note: Monthly data.
Source: World Bank, BESD.

Case 2. *Chart 4b/1.* Argentina: Deposit to Reserve Ratio of Deposit Money Banks from 1988 to 1992

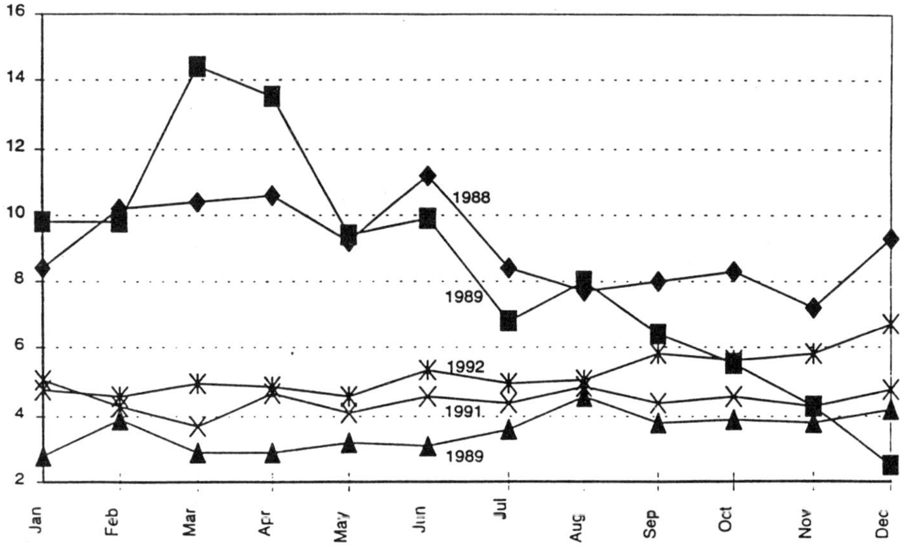

Note: Monthly data.
Source: World Bank, BESD.

Case 2. ***Chart 4b/2.*** Argentina: Deposit to Reserve Ratio from 1988 to 1992

Complementary Monetary Policy Actions

The Bonex plan reduced the money supply by eliminating short term deposits. Furthermore, it allowed the government to finance part of its debt by effectively selling Bonex to private bank account customers rather than by inflating the money supply by issuing new currency.[69] Furthermore, the Argentine government effectively stopped rediscount subsidies to the financial sector which it had previously provided through a multitude of channels.[70] The central bank pursued a tight monetary policy in the immediate aftermath of the conversion. As a consequence, real high-powered money continued its sharp decline in the immediate aftermath of the conversion. After the government announced fiscal reforms in March 1990, the central bank eased its tight monetary policy, and subsequently real high-powered money rose modestly (see Chart 5).[71] Real M2 bottomed out in March 1990 and rose steadily during the rest of the year (see Chart 6).

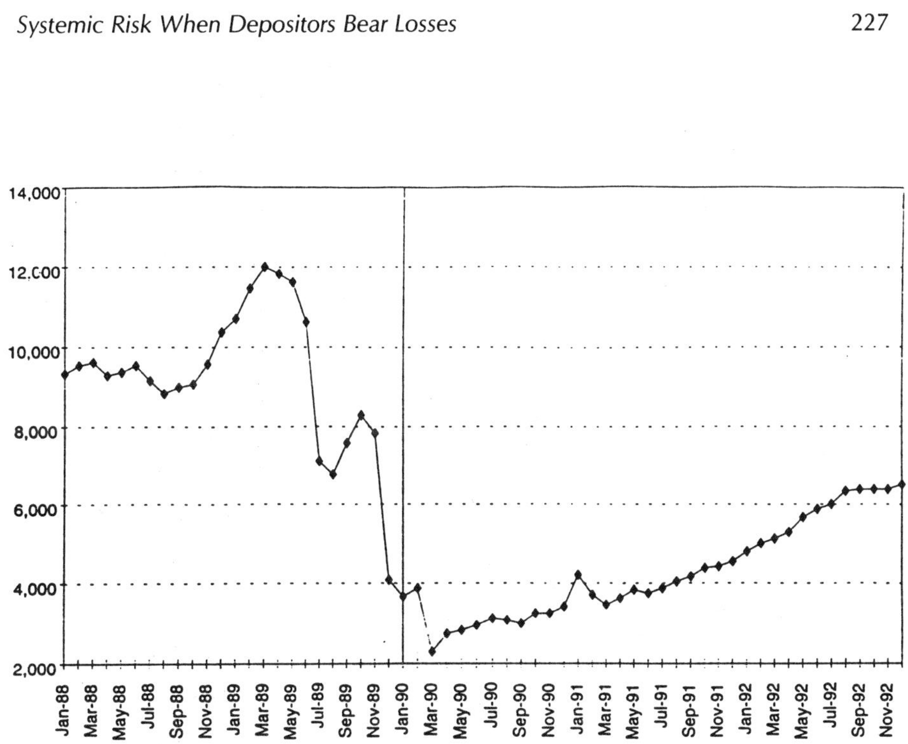

Note: Monthly data.
Source: World Bank, BESD.

Case 2. ***Chart 4c.*** Argentina: Development of Total Real Deposit Money Banks' Deposits from 1988 to 1992

The Malaysian Banking Crisis of 1985 to 1987

The magnitude of the financial crisis problem was smaller in Malaysia than in the other four countries; the insolvent Deposit Taking Cooperatives accounted for only 3.3 percent of all financial system deposits while undercapitalized (and perhaps insolvent) commercial banks accounted for another 4.4 percent of all financial system deposits. However, the Malaysian case study is of interest for at least two reasons: First of all, the government intervened early in the crisis, this is at a point when it was confined to a rather small segment of the financial sector and had not yet developed into a system wide insolvency. Secondly, although Malaysia is a country with a high level of intermediation and as such can be assumed to be particularly concerned about the stability of its financial system, the government decided to impose some losses on depositors and did not rush to guarantee deposits.

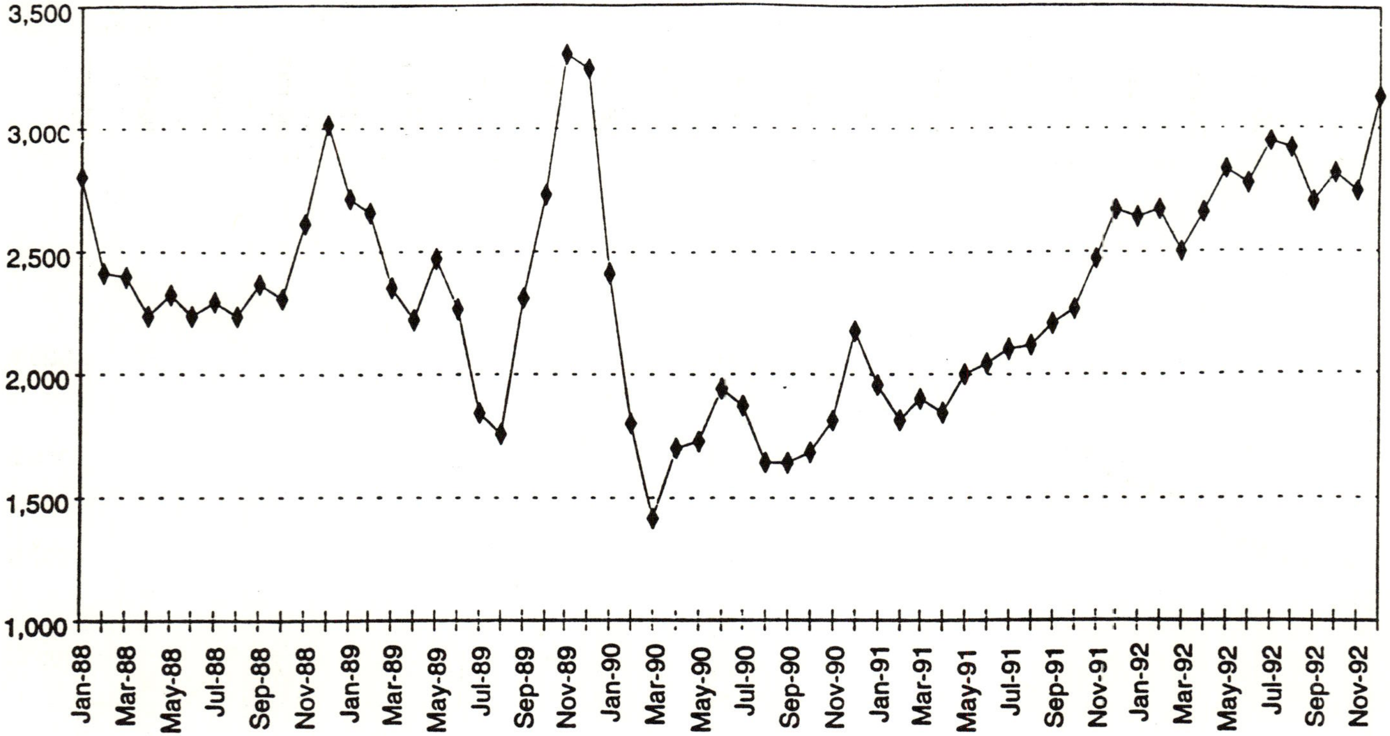

Note: Monthly data.
Source: World Bank, BESD.

Case 2. ***Chart 5.*** Argentina: Real High-Powered Money from 1988 to 1992

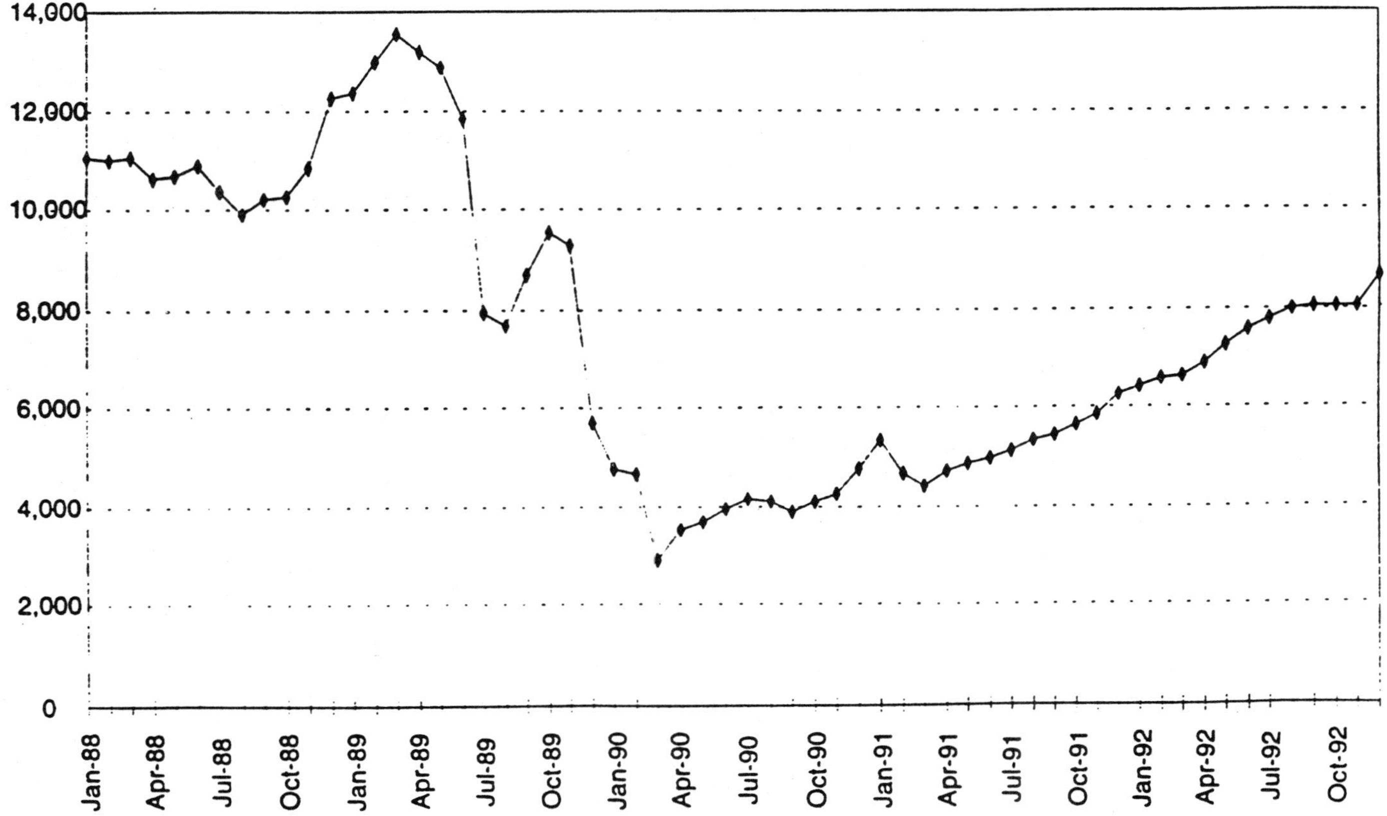

Note: Monthly data.
Source: World Bank, BESD.

Case 2. ***Chart 6.*** Argentina: Real M2 from 1988 to 1992

The Scope of the Financial Crisis

In 1985, the Malaysian economy entered on a recession marked by a significant slowdown in inflation[72] brought on by tighter monetary policy, deteriorating terms of trade caused by falling commodity prices,[73] and plummeting securities and property prices. The combination of tight liquidity, low inflation and a precipitous decline in share and property prices brought a sharp contraction in cash flow for Malaysian companies causing serious problems.

These developments spilled over to the financial sector and loan loss provisions and interest-in-suspense grew, cutting into bank profits across the board.

In mid-1985, rumors about "Public Bank", Malaysia fourth largest commercial bank, sparked a run on its branches.[74] In September a small illegal deposit taking institutions, Setia Credit and Leasing, failed generating further, isolated runs on several licensed finance companies. The panic withdrawals subsided.[75] In December however, the collapse of Pan Electric, a large publicly listed company led to a three-day closure of the Kuala Lumpur and Singapore stock exchanges and a run on a medium-size finance company which was associated with Pan-electric shareholders. After the Bank Negara provided liquidity assistance and stepped in and changed the management, the run abated.[76]

The decline in asset values had serious impacts on 4 of 47 finance companies and 4 of 38 commercial banks accounting for 6.7 percent of financial system deposits.[77] The three commercial banks in which the central bank finally injected capital accounted for 4.4 percent of all financial system deposits at the end of 1986.[78] More serious problems were faced by 32 of the 35 authorized deposit taking cooperatives (DTCs)[79] which accounted for 3.8 percent of all financial system deposits, and the 33 illegal deposit-taking institutions (DTIs).[80] Excluding the illegal DTIs, the affected institutions had total deposits of M$ 9.4 billion accounting for 10.4 percent of total deposits of the banking system. In the aggregate, these forty institutions reported pre-tax losses of $ 3.1 billion during the period 1985 to 1987, with banks and finance companies reporting M$ 1.7 billion and with DTCs reporting M$ 1.4 billion. These reported losses were equivalent to 4.7 percent of GNP or 3.4 percent of total deposits in 1986.[81]

Depositors' nervousness continued to spread to DTCs, banks, finance companies and finally culminated on July 23, 1986, in the suspension of payments by Kosatu, a large DTC with M$ 156 million in deposits.[82] Other DTCs were soon facing problems in meeting the deposit withdrawal of their creditors.[83] According to Sheng, at that point there was danger that these isolated bank runs would spread over to the finance companies and commercial banks causing a "systemic financial failure".[84] The distress resolution plan which was implemented in the following period of time dealt with 25 of the

35 deposit taking cooperatives[85], the cooperative central bank[86], the 4 commercial banks and the 4 finance companies.

The Distress Resolution Plan at the Crisis Point in July 1986

The Restructuring of the Financial Institutions. On August 8, 1986, the central bank announced the suspension of 24 DTCs of the 33 DTC's in financial distress and froze their deposits of M$ 1.5 billion which accounted for 1.8 percent of total system deposits at the end of August 1986.[87] On November 10, the government issued a "White Paper", a restructuring plan for these DTC's which was later implemented in a modified form and carried out in three stages.[88] According to the White Paper, only 3 of the credit cooperatives were found solvent as of August 8, 1985 and only 60 percent or M$ 889.7 million of deposits were reckoned recoverable.[89]

Stage one involved the removing of the freeze on the deposits of 11 cooperatives with total deposits of M$ 191 million which had relatively small capital deficiencies. They received loans at concessional rates from the central bank, and reached agreement with their appointed banks or finance companies to take over their assets and liabilities. Furthermore, it was agreed that depositors would not accrue interest on their funds. (no further information available on nature of soft loans)[90] Stage two involved the group of 12 DTCs with moderate or heavy losses. They were absorbed into a single licensed finance company, Tai Shen, which was purchased by the government for this purpose for M$ 8 million.[91] Stage three involved the largest DTC, with deposits of M$ 549 million. The Koperatif Serbaguna Malaysia (KSM) had an asset backing of about 50sen per $M 1 deposited.[92] The net assets and deposit liabilities of the KSM were taken over by Magnum Corporation Berhad (MCB), a large publicly listed company, and its licensed finance company subsidiary, (MFB).[93] Altogether the rescue of 24 DTCs, involving deposits of M$ 1.5 billion, required M$ 1 billion in loans from the central bank as well as M$23.4 million incurred in the investigations and receivership.[94]

There was no formal deposit insurance scheme in effect at the time of the crisis and the government did not grant a guarantee to depositors to make them whole. Instead it adopted the following policies for dealing with depositors of the insolvent DTCs: The 85,000 depositors of the 11 cooperatives with relatively small capital deficiencies saw the maturity of their deposits extended for up to five years and suffered the loss of foregone interests on their deposits (January 1987).[95] Depositors of these institutions received their first partial cash repayment of up to 10-20% in January 1987.[96]

The depositors of the group of 12 deposit cooperatives with moderate to heavy losses received their principal through a combination of cash payments spaced over 5 years and equity in a licensed financial institution which would absorb all the assets and liabilities of the 12 DTCs (December 1987).[97] At a minimum, depositors received cash payments equal to at least 50 percent of their deposits. Where asset value permitted, cash payments were greater. Besides having their deposits frozen, depositors of these 12 DTCs would bear losses if the share prices decreased on flotation. In order to enable the acquiring financial institution to meet the partial repayments of funds to depositors, the government extended soft loans totaling M$ 333 million at 1 percent interest and additional M$ 160 million at commercial interest rates (January 1988).[98] The cash payments were to be made until December 1989.[99]

The 166,000 depositors of Koperatif Serbaguna Malaysia were repaid in full on a 50:50 basis, the cash to be paid in stages between 1987-1989, and the remainder initially in the form of irredeemable convertible, unsecured stock of MCB, which took over net assets and deposit liabilities of KSM. The loan stock would be non-interest bearing for the first 2 years and would be convertible into MCB ordinary shares at a predetermined rate over 2 years from 1989-91 (January 1988). Magnum Finance received soft loans of M$ 280 million and commercial loans of M$ 150 million so that it could satisfy the 50 percent cash payout of depositors.[100]

At the beginning of 1988, the central bank intervened in the Co-operative Central Bank with deposits of M$ 1.5 billion which accounted for 1.6 percent of total system deposits in 1987 and 320,262 members (262 credit cooperative societies and 320,000 individual members). Its 1987 audited accounts showed accumulated losses of over M$ 726 million, and a capital deficiency of MS$ 652 million.[101] The CCB was placed in receivership and the government made available a standby facility of M$ 323 million to meet its liquidity needs.

In the case of the 4 illiquid but possibly "solvent" commercial banks,[102] the central bank followed four basic steps. First, it required the institutions to recognize all losses and interest-in-suspense immediately, rather than deferring the losses by stretching them over time. Second, management was replaced, by revamping the Board of Directors, appointing a reputable professional banker to serve as chief executive, and then allowing the new Board to take necessary steps to stem losses and to restore profitability. Third, existing shareholders were required to inject as much new capital as possible through rights issues, while the central bank supplemented the proceeds with enough capital to meet the minimum capital adequacy requirements. The total pre-tax losses of the three banks in which the central bank eventually injected capital were recorded at M$ 1.203 billion. This loss was born by the existing shareholders.[103] The existing shareholders subsequently injected M$ 159 million in equity through a rights issue, Bank Negara injected M$ 672 million and M$ 401 million was injected in the form of subordinated loans.[104]

Additional Policy Measures. In the immediate aftermath of the crisis, the central bank continued to put into place a number of regulatory changes designed to strengthen the structure of the banking system and its own regulatory powers to enforce these standards and improve intervention options.[105] The main changes consisted of the prohibition of loans to the directors and staff of finance companies. In 1987, the central bank raised the minimum capital adequacy requirements from 7.4% at the end of 1984 to 8.1% at the end of 1987.[106]

Political Issues

The final draft of the resolution plan which involved 13 DTCs with moderate to heavy capital deficiencies was completed in January 1988 after a more than 18 months long and heated debate about the appropriate resolution mechanism. After the central bank intervention into the DTCs in August 1986, the government established a commission which was supposed to make recommendations for the resolution mechanism to be adopted.[107] Their recommendations were partially incorporated in the government's draft of a white paper which was published in November 1986. The white paper met with harsh criticism not only from opposition parties but also from parties in the ruling government front coalition. The Malaysian Chinese Association[108], a member of the ruling coalition was especially vocal. It demanded a government guarantee and full refund of deposits for the 588,000 Chinese depositors.[109] The depositors of the two DTCs which were earmarked for liquidations organized demonstrations.

These forces finally won significant concessions from the government. However, the government stood firm on its "no full cash refund policy" and at no point in the process fully guaranteed the deposits. For depositors at the least insolvent institutions, losses took the form of foregone interest. Depositors at other institutions saw a portion of their deposits converted to equity whose value was ultimately determined by the performance of the underlying loan portfolio.

The Economic Impact of the Financial Resolution Plan

Macroeconomic Indicators

Despite adopting a resolution mechanism which imposed some losses on depositors at a large number of institutions, the economic recovery which had began at a slow pace in 1986 (1.2%) was not derailed by the banking crisis and subsequent restructuring of the Malaysian banking system. On the contrary, real GDP growth accelerated in 1987, increasing at an annual rate of 5.3%.[110] Although a strong seasonal pattern characterizes the Malaysian Industrial Production Index, it can be noticed that Industrial Production dropped slightly greater than usual in November of 1986 (White Paper

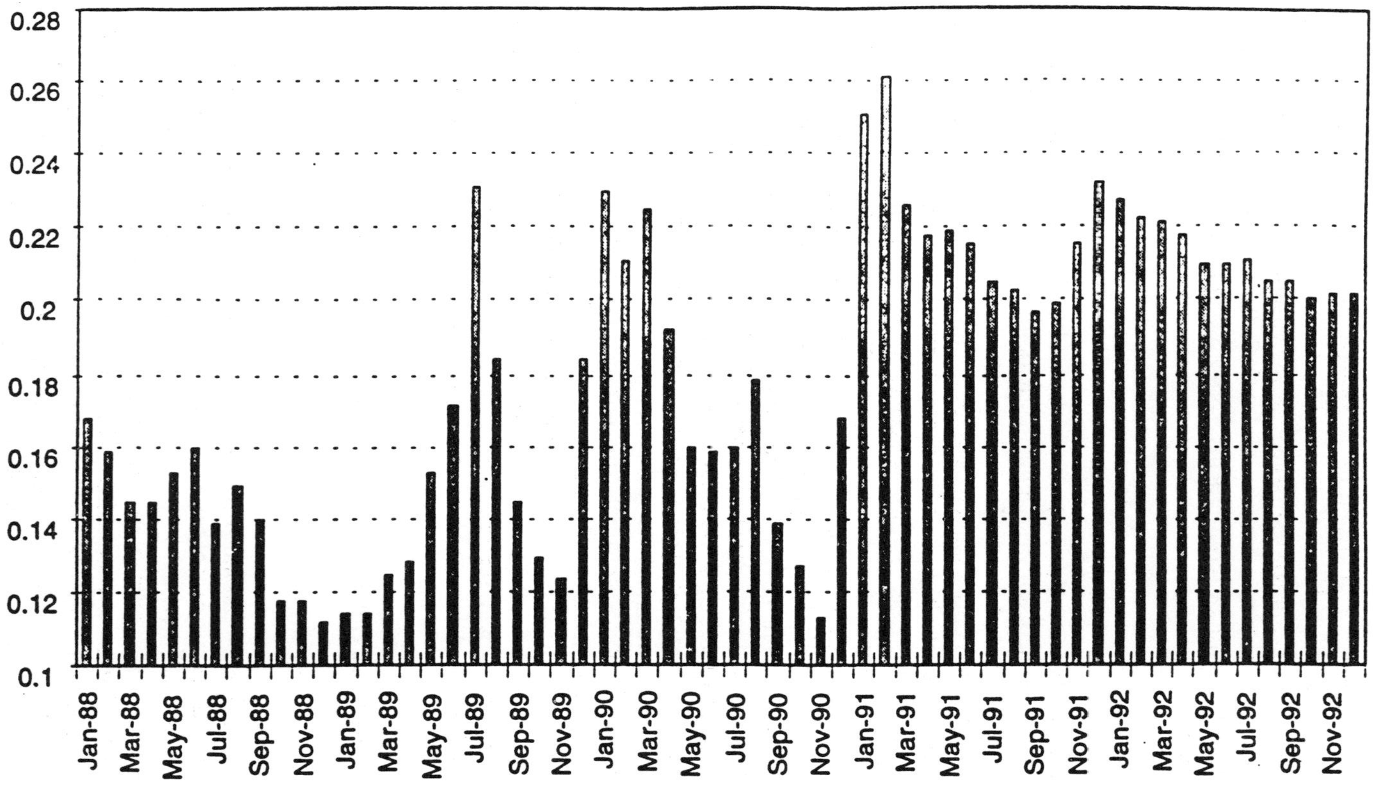

Note: Monthly data.
Source: Central Bank of Argentina, Boletin Estadistico, several issues.

Case 2. ***Chart 7.*** Argentina: Capital to Asset Ratio of Deposit Money Banks from 1988 to 1992

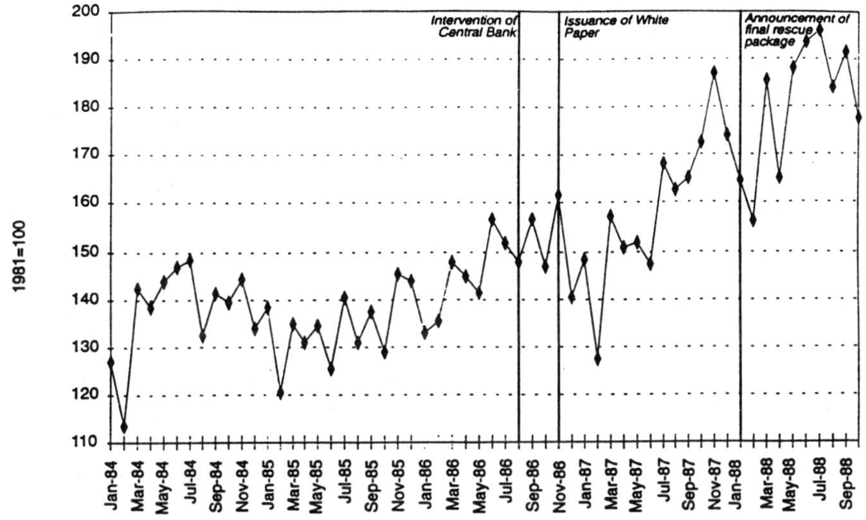

Note: Monthly data.
Source: Central Bank of Malaysia.

Case 3. ***Chart 1a.*** Malaysia: Industrial Production Index From 1984 to 1988

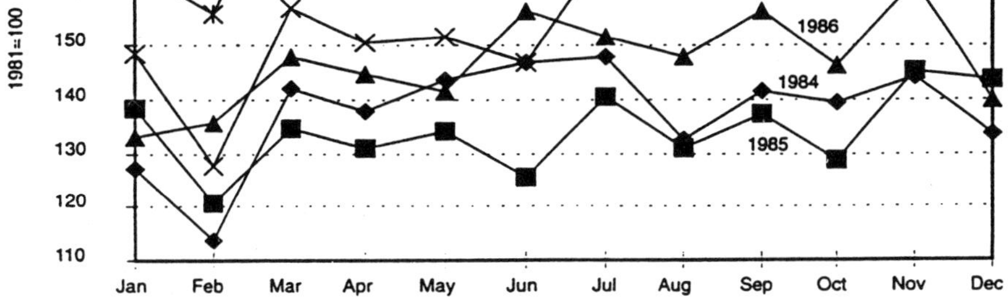

Note: Monthly data.
Source: Central Bank of Malaysia.

Case 3. ***Chart 1b.*** Malaysia: Industrial Production Index From 1984 to 1987

Publication) and experienced stronger than usual fluctuations for the first half of 1987. But all in all, Industrial Production continued to rebound after the central bank intervention in the banking system and achieved a higher rate after July 1987. (See Chart 1a, 1b)

While industrial production was largely unaffected, there was a clear but modest contraction in lending in the aftermath of the crisis. In real terms, total loans of deposit money banks and other financial institution declined moderately during the rest of 1986 and the first half of 1987. But by mid-1987, real loans outstanding were rising steadily and by January 1989 at a faster pace than pre-crisis levels. (See Chart 2) Furthermore, the share of commercial banks and finance companies in the loan market remained stable during that period. (See Chart 3a, 3b) However, there is a shift in the loan to asset ratio of commercial banks and finance companies. In the period after the banking crisis, the loan to asset ratio for commercial banks fell from 68.7 percent from July 1986 where it had reached its highest level to under 59.6 percent in December 1989. During the same period, the loan to asset ratio of finance companies increased slightly. However, this shift in commercial banks' loan to asset ratio did not detail the recovery.

Erratic and seasonal movements in the deposit to currency ratio reduce its usefulness as an indicator of public confidence in the financial system. (See Chart 4a, b, c). But there is a secular decline in the deposit to currency ratio observable in the immediate aftermath of the central bank's intervention and the publication of the White Paper. This decline was spurred by a rise in public's currency holdings which were not offset by rising nominal total deposits. Total deposits even decreased slightly in some months, but these decreases are not large relative to decreases observed in the precrisis period. The fall in the deposit to currency ratio must be seen against the backdrop of very low inflation which limited the public's opportunity costs of holding currency. The price level showed little growth in 1986 and 1987 with an inflation rate of 0.6% and 0.8% respectively.[111] Although the drop in the currency to deposit ratio is a sign of depositors' nervousness, the deposit to currency ratio never fell below its 1983 level in spite of low inflation rates and did not lead to a significant contraction in total real M2 which can be seen as sign of general public confidence in the banking system (See Chart 6a).

Complementary Monetary Policy Actions

Before the culmination of the crisis, the central bank tried to provide liquidity to the banking system by lowering statutory reserve and liquidity requirements of commercial banks.[112] In addition to these measures, the legislation enacted in the immediate aftermath of the crisis allowed the central bank to place deposits with banks and finance companies and to purchase Negotiable Certificates of Deposits from banks and finance companies.[113] Real M2 remained almost stable in this period (Charts 5a and 5b).

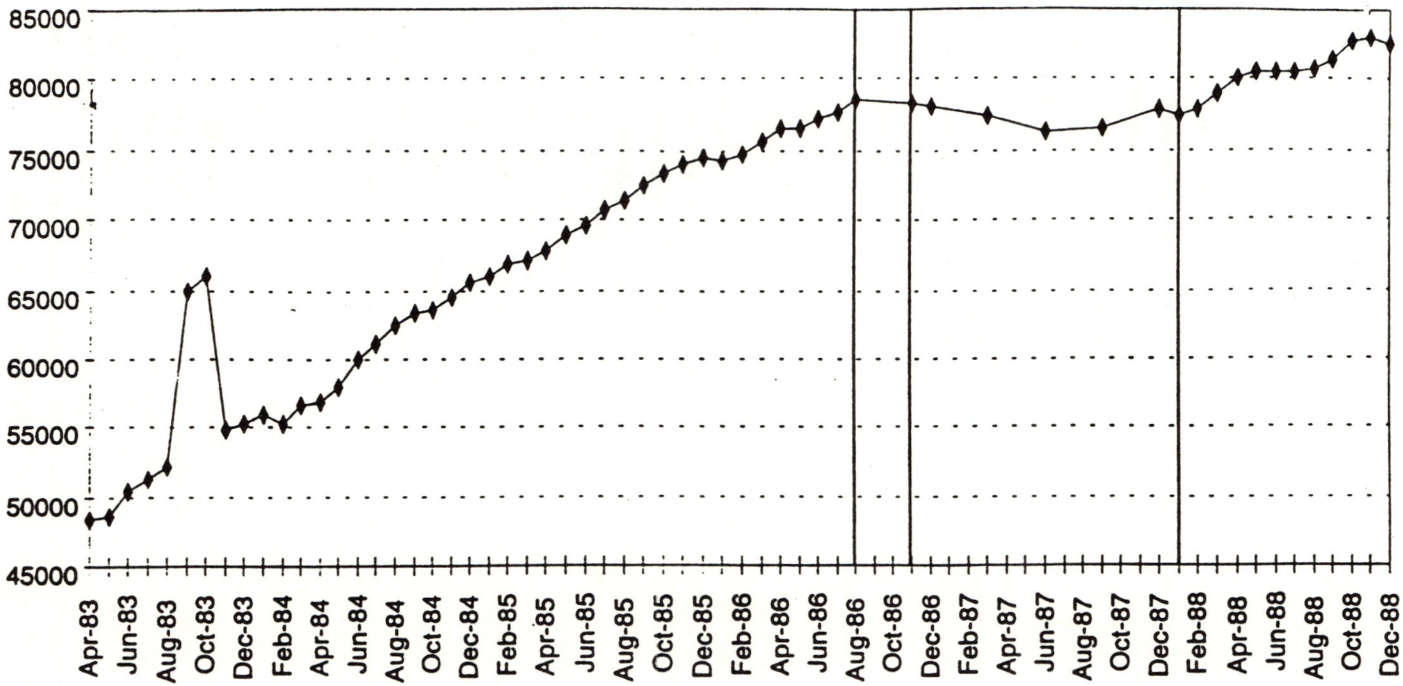

Note: Monthly data.
Source: World Bank, BESD.

Case 3. ***Chart 2a.*** Malaysia: Real Private Sector Loans of Deposit Money Banks and Other Financial Institutions from 1983 to 1988

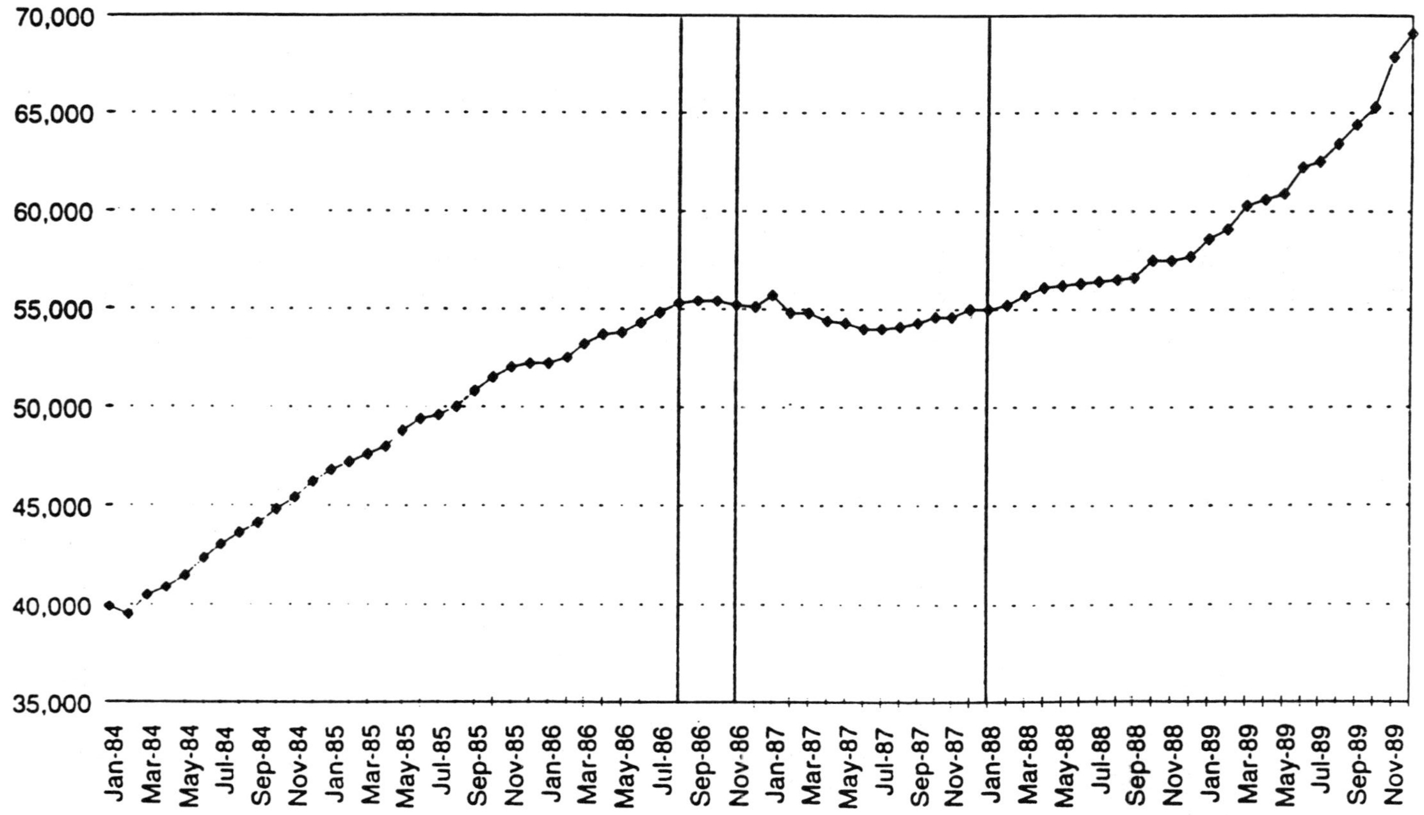

Note: Monthly data.
Source: World Bank, BESD.

Case 3. ***Chart 2b.*** Malaysia: Real Private Sector Loans of Deposit Money Banks from 1984 to 1989

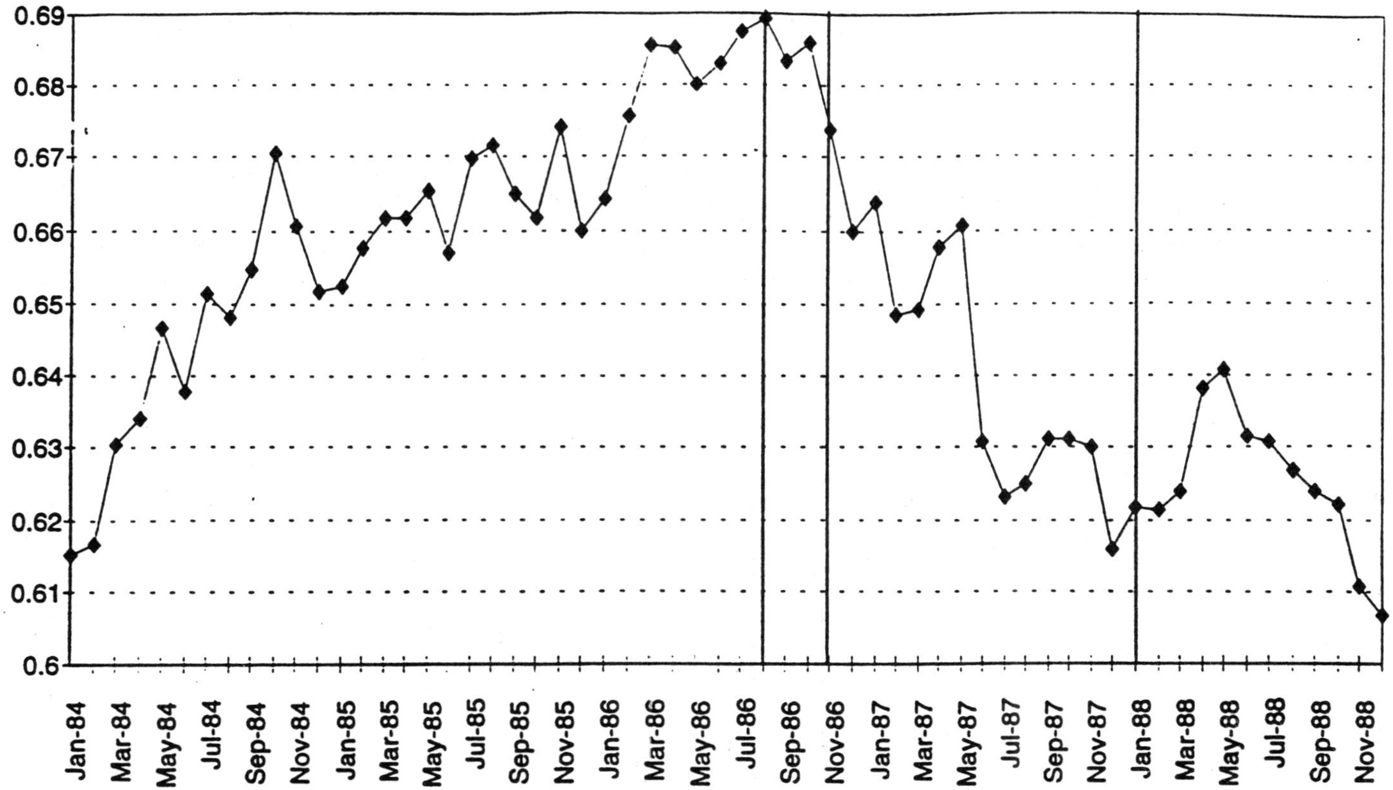

Note: Monthly data.
Source: Central Bank of Malaysia.

Case 3. ***Chart 3a.*** Malaysia: Loan to Asset Ratio of Commercial Banks from 1984 to 1988

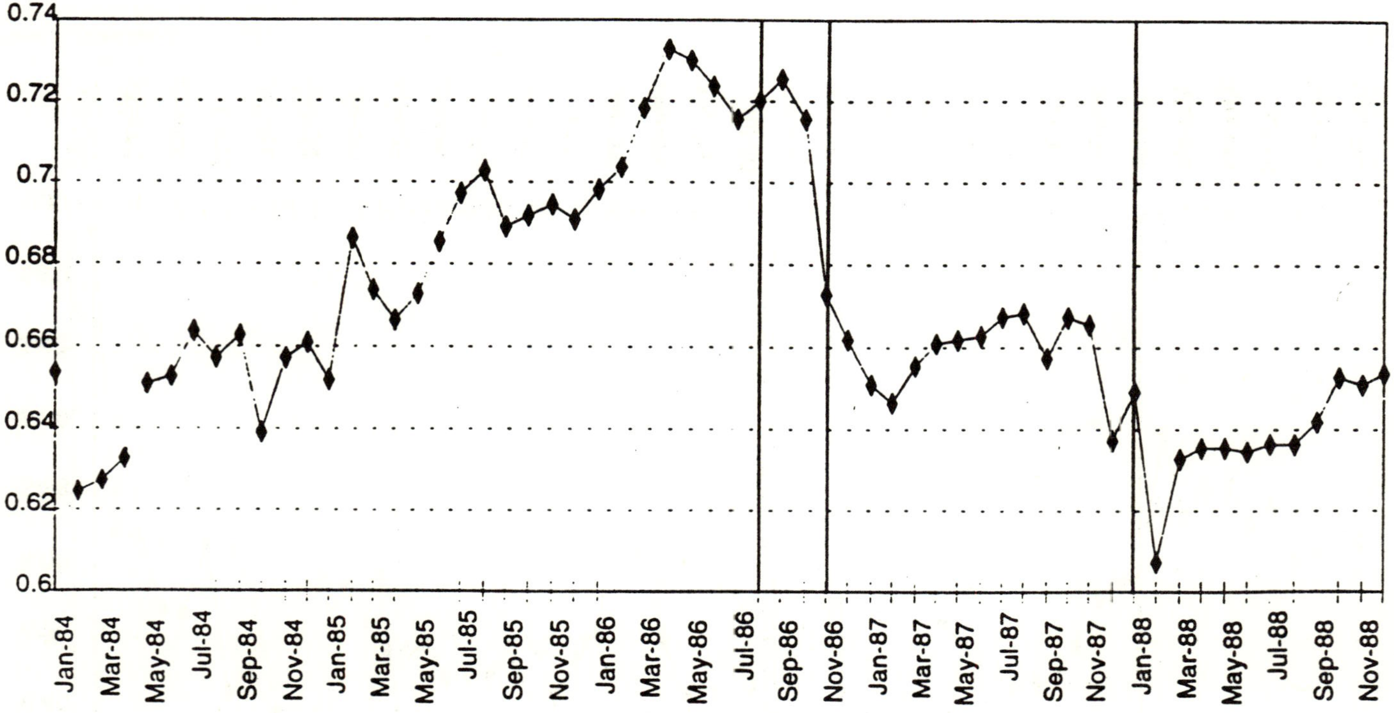

Note: Monthly data.
Source: Central Bank of Malaysia.

Case 3. ***Chart 3b.*** Malaysia: Loan to Asset Ratio of Finance Companies from 1984 to 1988

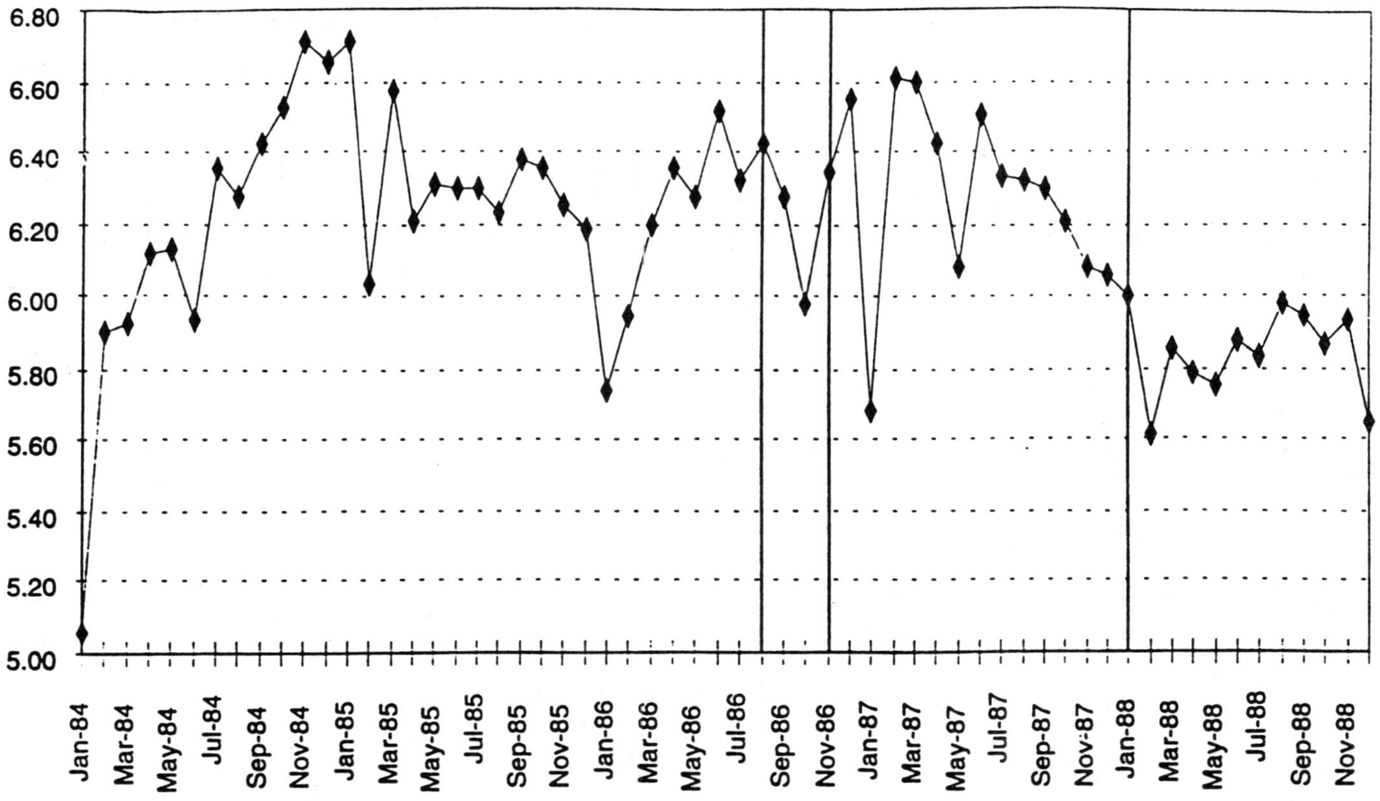

Note: Monthly data.
Source: World Bank, BESD.

Case 3. ***Chart 4a/1.*** Malaysia: Deposit to Currency Ration from 1984 to 1988

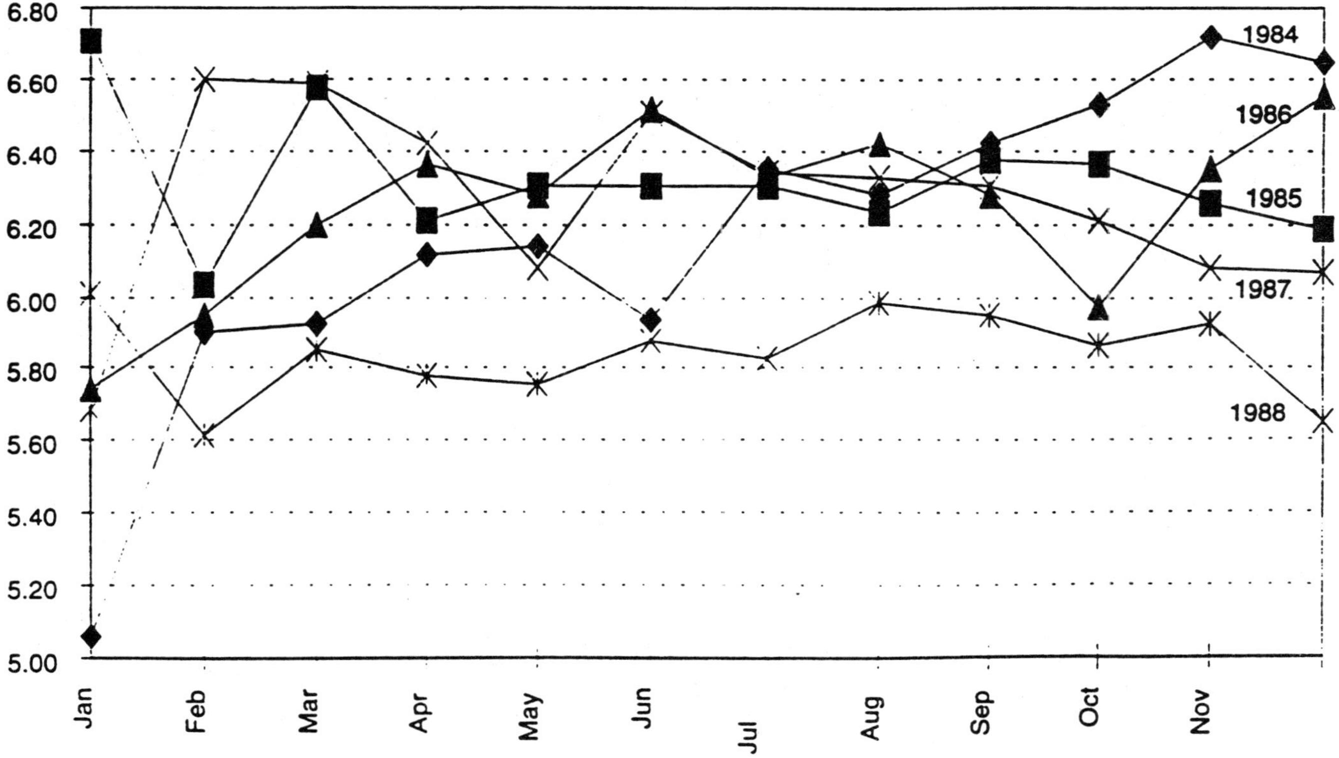

Note: Monthly data.
Source: World Bank, BESD.

Case 3. ***Chart 4a/2.*** Malaysia: Deposit to Currency from 1984 to 1988

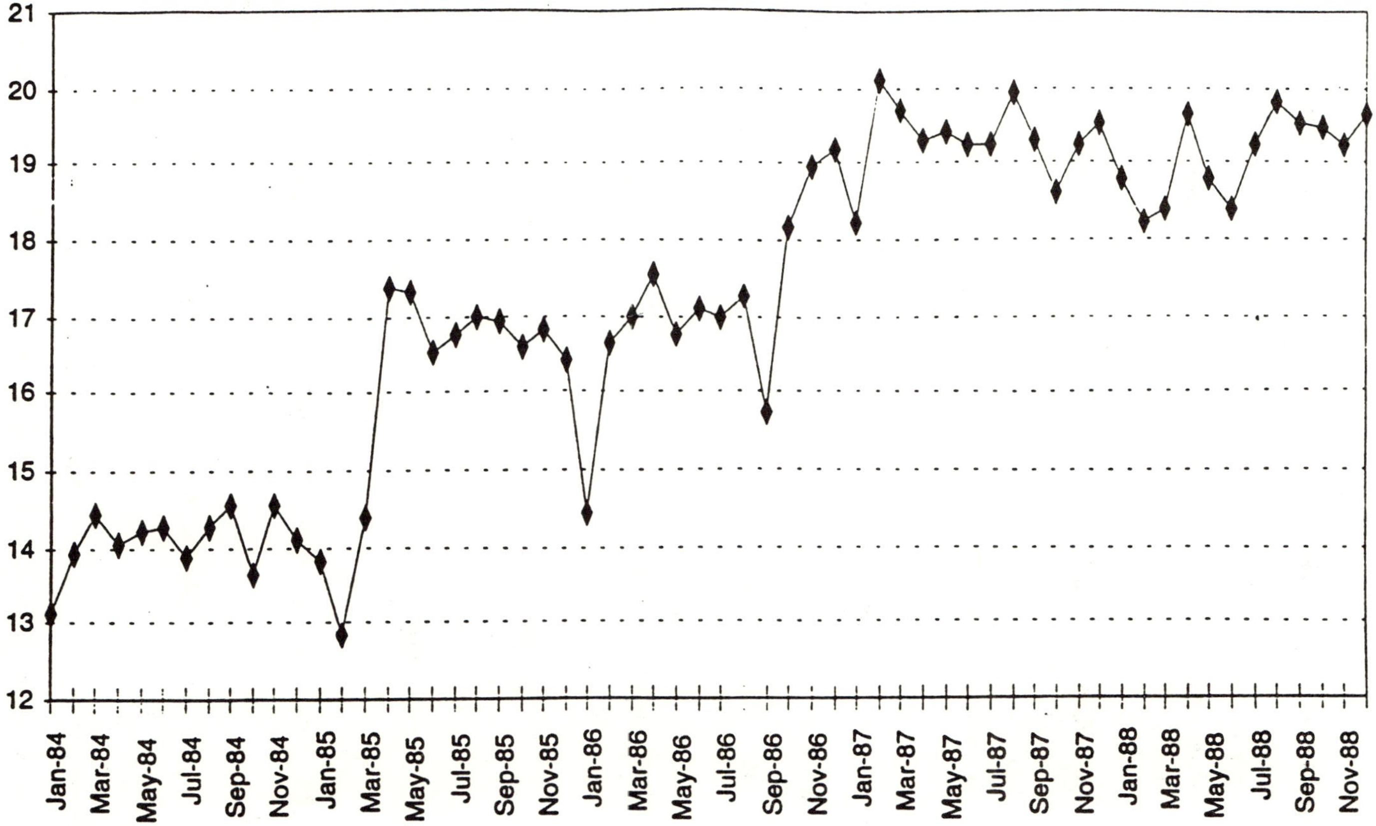

Note: Monthly data.
Source: World Bank, BESD.

Case 3. ***Chart 4b/1.*** Malaysia: Deposit to Reserve Ration from 1984 to 1988

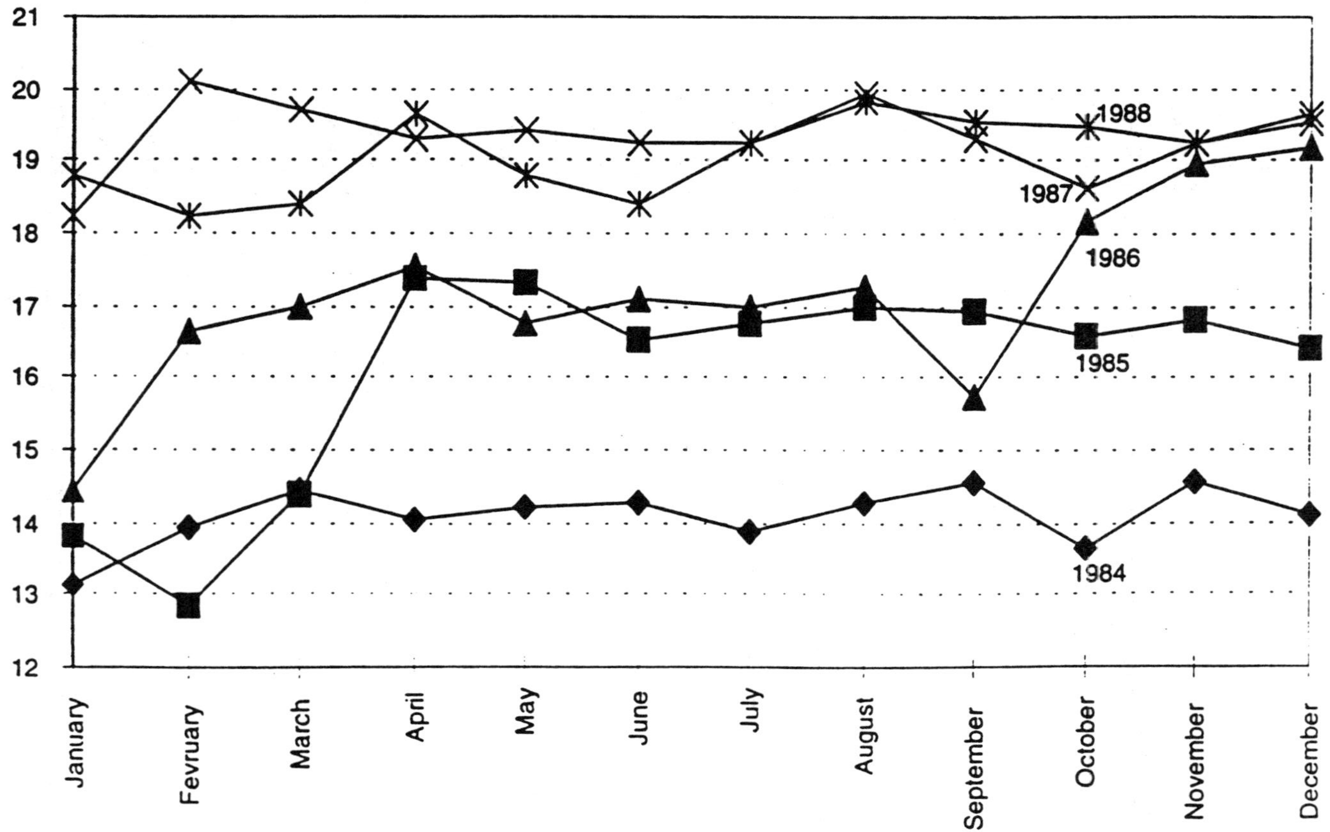

Note: Monthly data.
Source: World Bank, BESD.

Case 3. ***Chart 4b/2.*** Malaysia: Deposit to Reserve Ratio from 1984 to 1988

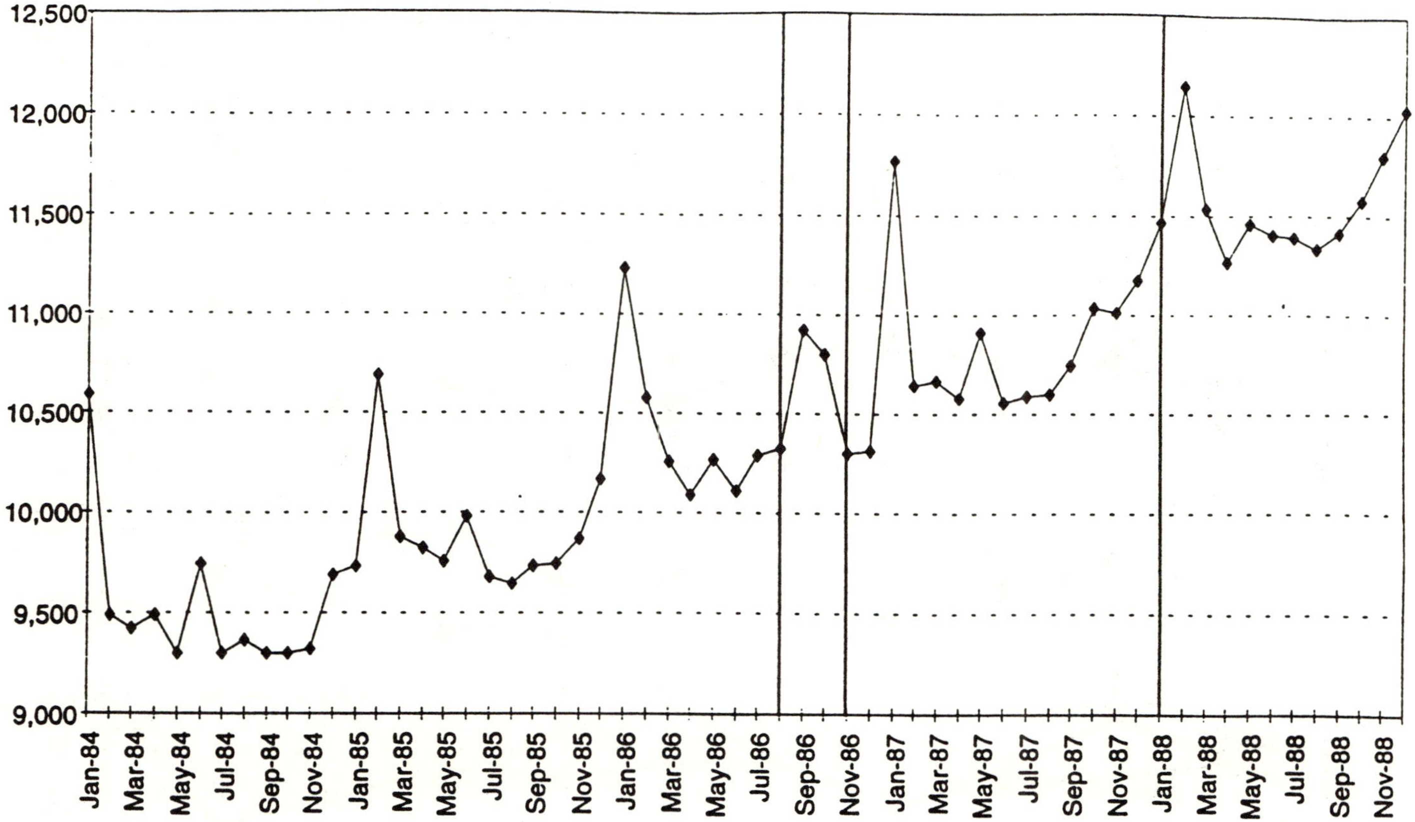

Note: Monthly data.
Source: World Bank, BESD.

Case 3. ***Chart 5a.*** Malaysia: Real High-Powered Money from 1984 to 1988

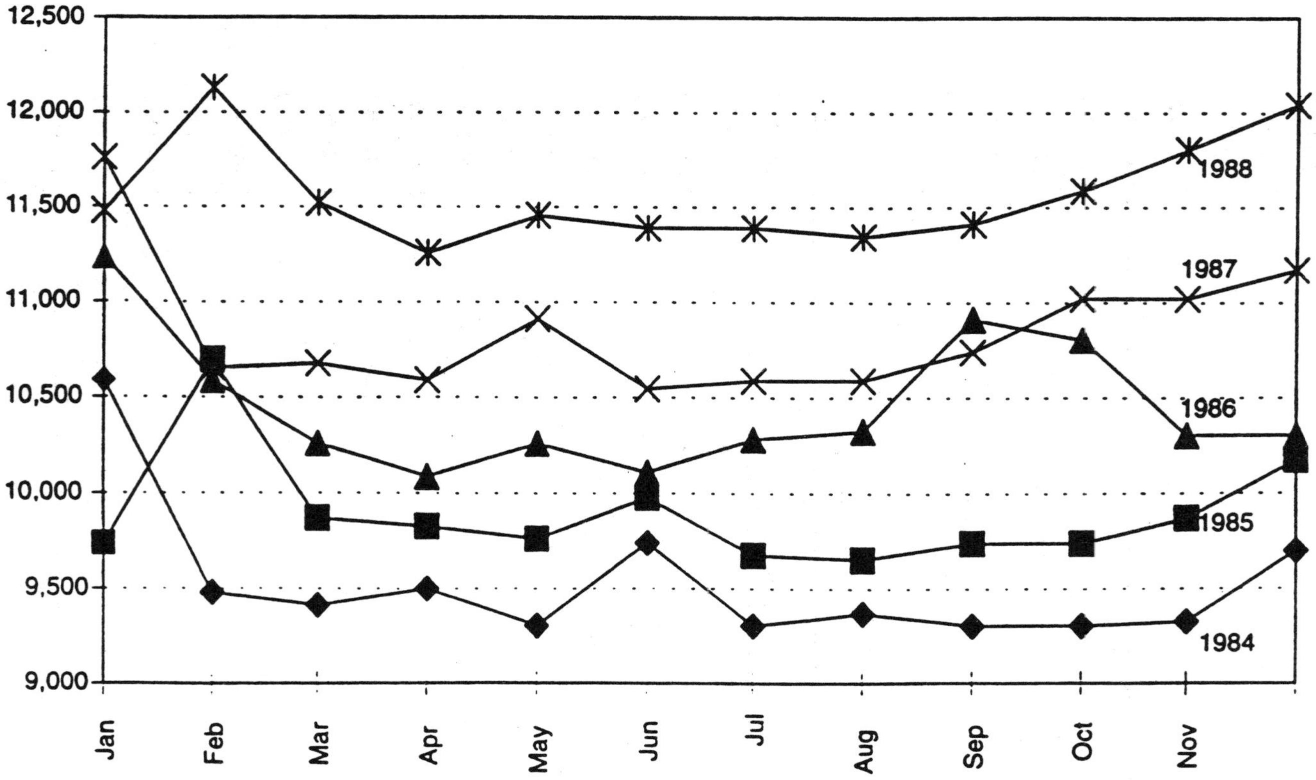

Note: Monthly data.
Source: World Bank, BESD.

Case 3. ***Chart 5b.*** Malaysia: Real High-Powered Money from 1984 to 1988

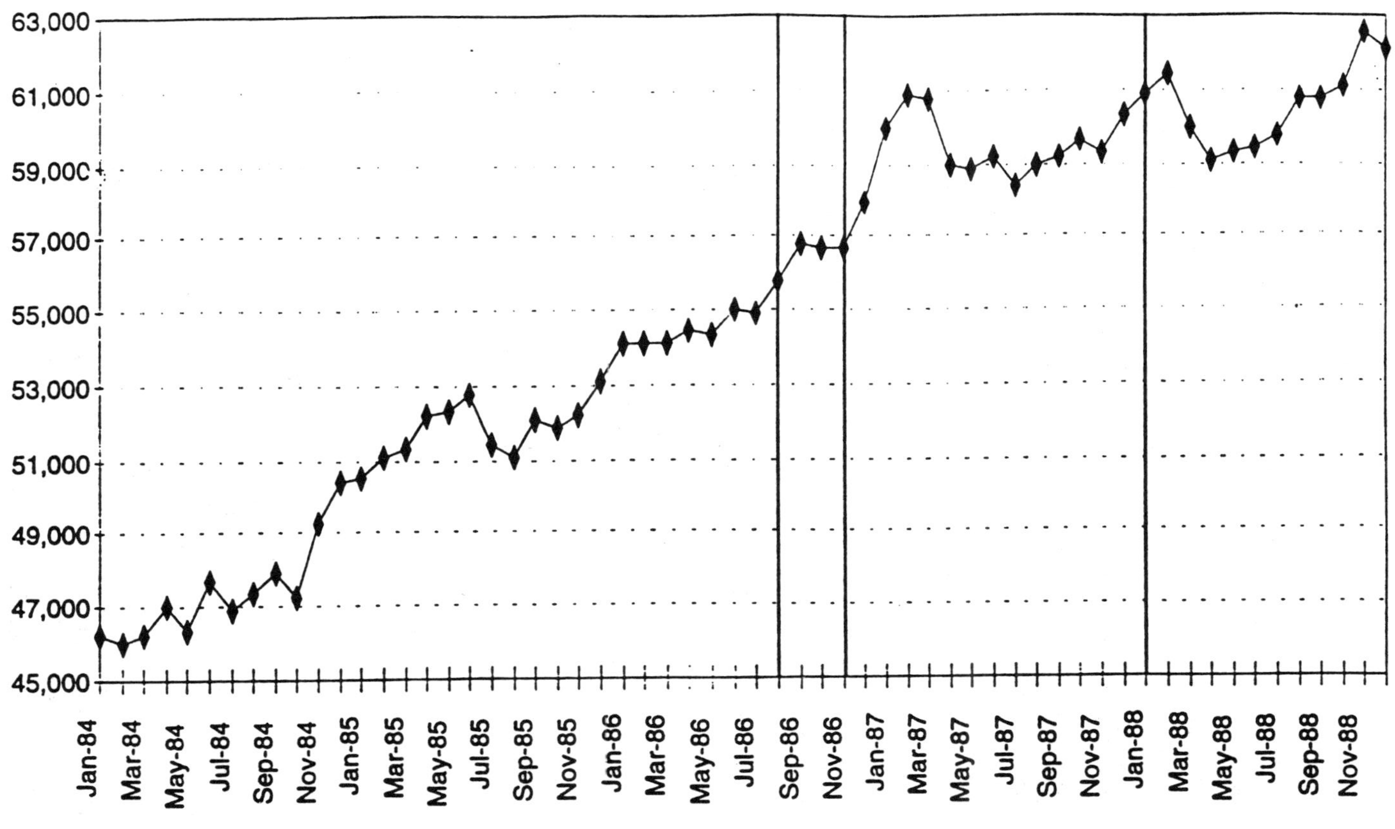

Note: Monthly data.
Source: World Bank, BESD.

Case 3. ***Chart 6a.*** Malaysia: Real M2 from 1984 to 1988

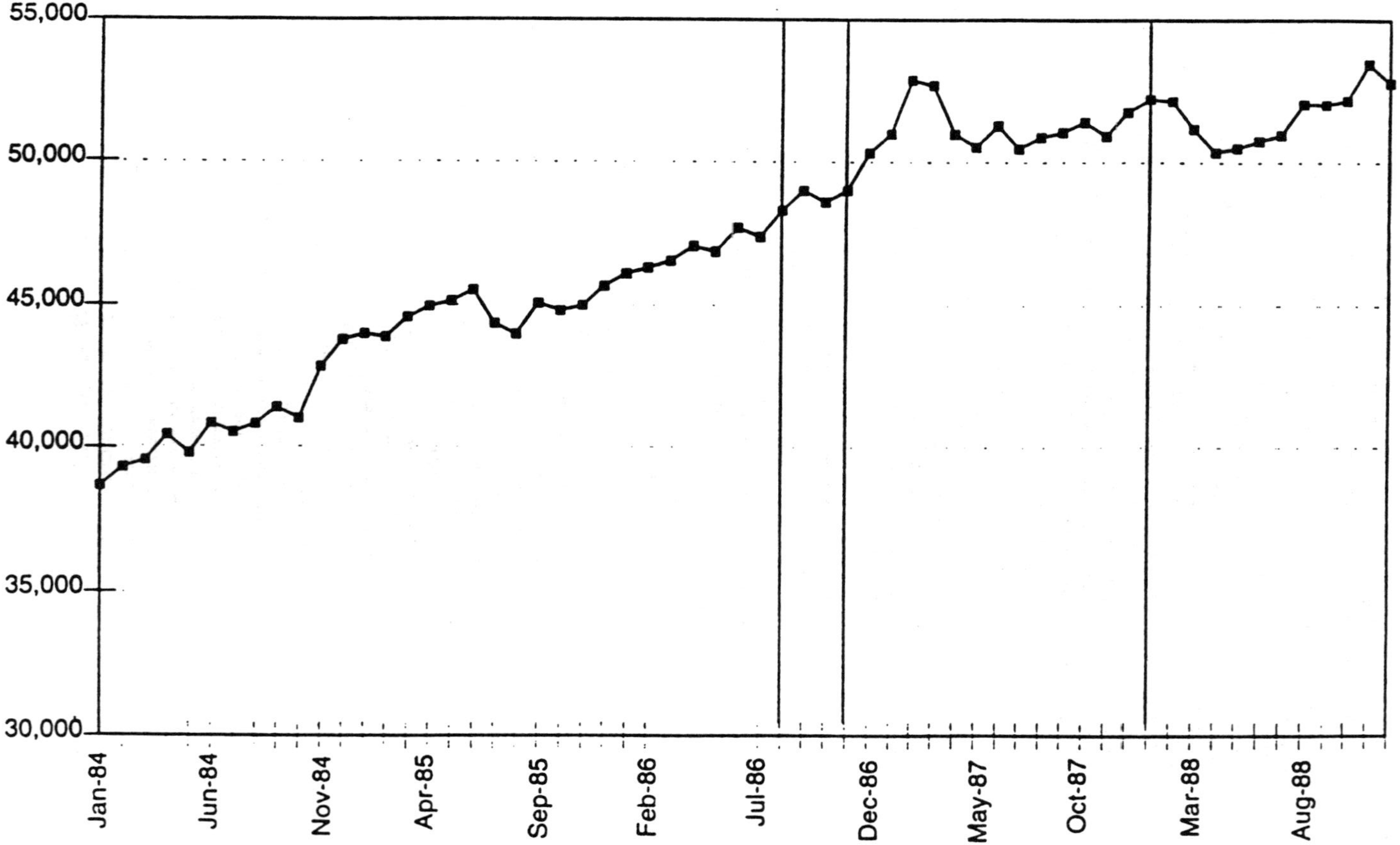

Note: Monthly data.
Source: World Bank, BESD.

Case 3. ***Chart 6b.*** Malaysia: Real Deposit

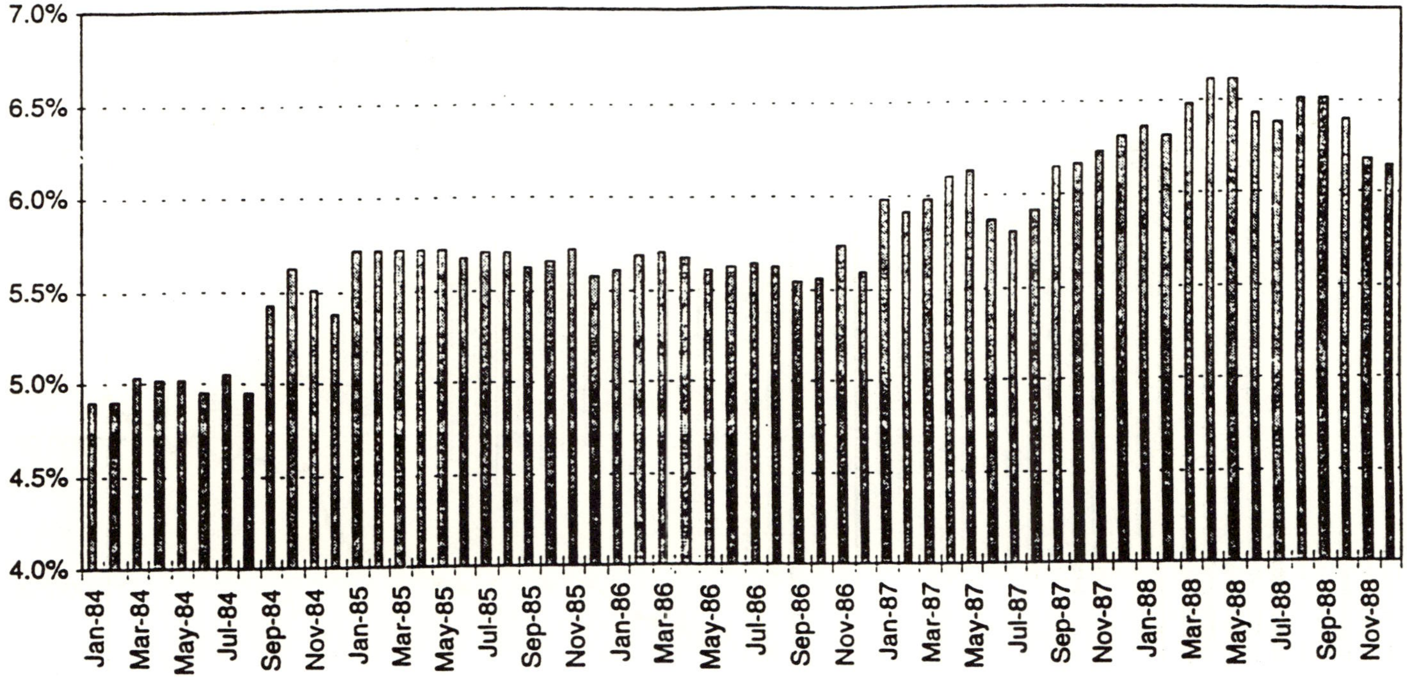

Note: Monthly data.
Source: Central Bank of Malaysia.

Case 3. ***Chart 7a.*** Malaysia: Capital to Asset Ratio of Commercial Banks from 1984 to 1988

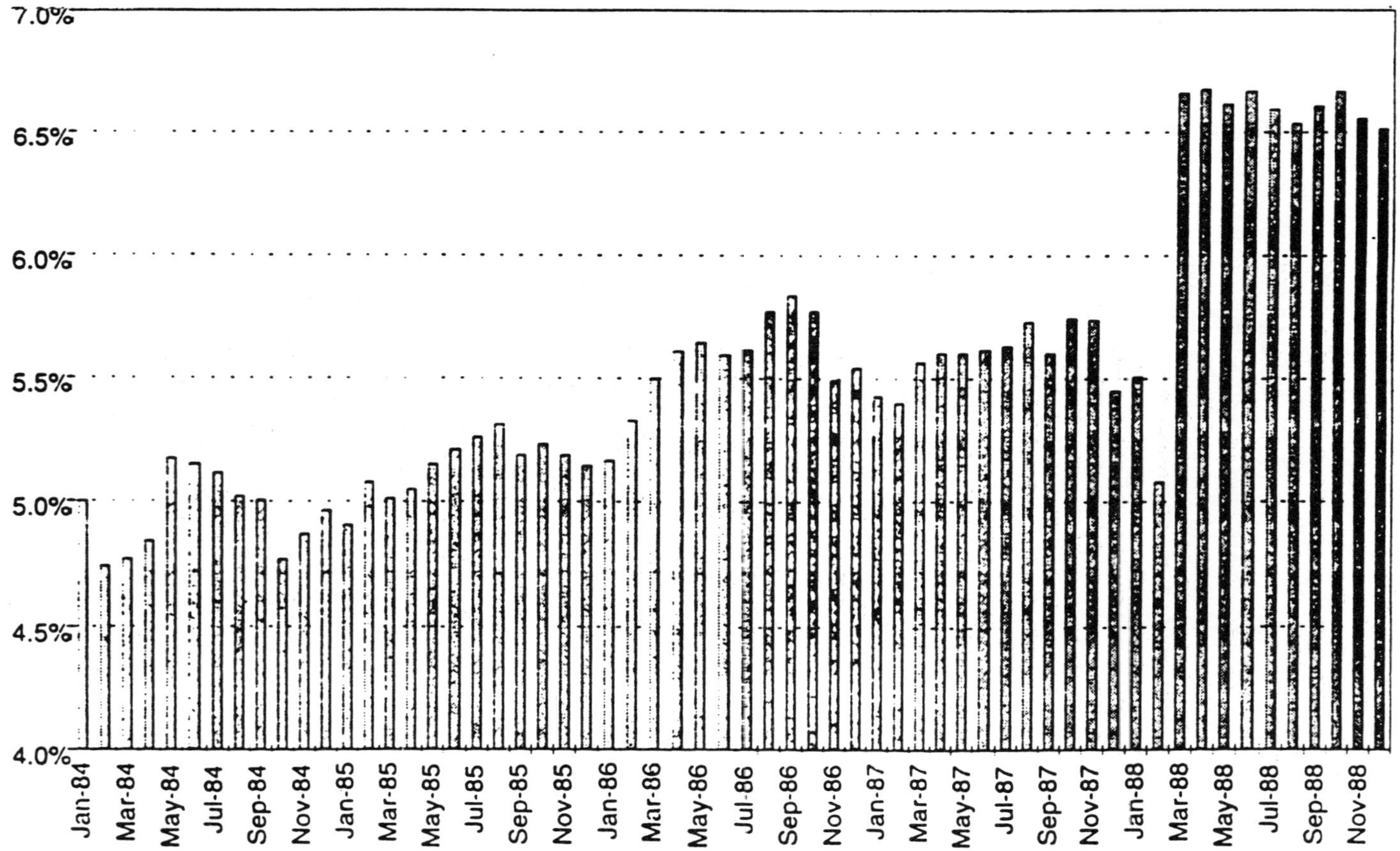

Note: Monthly data.
Source: Central Bank of Malaysia.

Case 3. ***Chart 7b.*** Malaysia: Capital to Asset Ratio of Finance Companies from 1984 to 1988

Japan 1946

The Japanese case study is of significant interest for at least three reasons. First, the insolvency crisis was systemwide. Second, the government decided to take a comprehensive approach and chose a restructuring mechanism which set correct incentives for bank management and depositors. Third, the Japanese government imposed losses on large depositors while protecting small deposits thus establishing the precedent of not bailing out all depositors.

Scope of Financial Crisis

In August 1945, Japan surrendered unconditionally to the Allied Forces ending World War II. Japan was then placed under the indirect administration of the Allied powers until the San Francisco Peace Treaty came into effect in 1952.[115] Under strong pressure from the Allied forces, the government decided in August 1946 to stop war indemnities payments. It decided not to pay wartime compensation that it owed munitions companies, not to honor government guaranteed bonds, and not to compensate banks for the losses due to uncollectible government mandated loans to munitions companies.[115]

According to a government estimate from October 2, 1946, the discontinuation of war indemnities imposed losses of 91.8 billion yen on the government sector, equivalent to 19.4 percent of Gross National Expenditure in fiscal year 1946.[116] Losses due to the suspension of wartime compensation for munitions companies were appraised at 66.9 billion Yen, the losses on government guaranteed bonds which were mostly held by financial institutions were gauged at 19.8 billion Yen and loses due to suspension of compensation for losses arising from government-ordered loans were estimated at 5.0 billion Yen.[117]

This decision had severe adverse effects on the asset quality of private financial institutions.[118] The losses on government mandated loans to munition companies were borne by the banking system. In addition to that, financial institutions incurred heavy indirect losses through the repudiation of government debt to munitions companies which consequently had to default on some of their bank loans and on their government guaranteed bonds which were mainly held by banks. The major banks were especially affected by this decision. War related loans accounted for 85 percent of Yasuda Bank's loan portfolio, 92 percent of Misubishi Bank's, 86 percent of Sumitomo Bank's, and 93 percent of Teikoku Bank's respectively.[119] All in all, the "special losses" for the 64 ordinary and special banks amounted to 23.1 billion Yen in 1948 which was equivalent to 16.5 percent of banking system deposits as of August 1946. The losses for the 10 savings and trust banks were recorded at 3 billion Yen which was equivalent to 2.1 percent of banking system deposits.[120]

The proclamation of the discontinuation of war indemnity payments was accompanied by an announcement of a restructuring program for the financial system in order to counterbalance the severes adverse repercussions that the decision would generate for the banking system.

2. *The Financial Crisis Resolution Plan from August 11, 1946*

Before the implementation of the financial crisis resolution plan, the Japanese government had put into place several measures which were aimed at decelerating the inflation and stabilizing Japanese banks which were facing increasing deposit withdrawals due to the accelerating inflation. It froze bank deposits on February 17, 1946, and limited cash withdrawals to monthly living expenses.[121] The blocking of deposits was followed by a partial currency conversion which allowed each individual to exchange only 100 Yen of old Yen for new Yen. At the same time, notes in circulation of denominations above 5 Yen not deposited with financial institutions ceased to be legal tender. According to Tsutsui, almost 46 billion Yen of deposits entered the financial system.[122]

On August 11, 1946, the restructuring program began in earnest. The first step was to freeze the balance sheets of all financial institutions and then separate them into an old and a new account. Those assets that were expected to be uncollectible because of the suspension of wartime compensation were allocated to the old account which was expected to go through reorganization. Also assigned to the old account were the bank's capital plus retained earnings, bank debentures, and a certain amount of the frozen deposits or so called "second line deposits".[123] In the aggregate, roughly 40 percent of total financial system deposits were ascribed to the old account.[124] These liabilities of the old account were at risk of being canceled if the recoveries from munitions companies proved insufficient.[125]

The assets of the new account consisted of cash, government and municipal bonds, credits against the government other than bonds, interbank loans, and other assets specified by the Finance Minister. The liabilities of the new account included the unrestricted deposits and the rest of the frozen deposits the so called "first line frozen deposits". Eventually, the Japanese government and the Allies agreed not to cut into new deposits if the financial institution was rendered insolvent after the merging of the old and new account.[126]

The financial institutions were permitted to continue operations using the new account. Differences between assets and liabilities in one account were recorded as an unsettled account against the other; if the liabilities of the new account surpassed its assets, the difference was entered as a credit against the old account. Furthermore, a bank had to pay compensation from the new account to the old account if it used assets from the old account.[127]

The second step of the restructuring program comprised the marking down to market of the assets in the old account.[128] Since a number of banks realized during the reevaluation process that they did not have to cancel all second-line frozen deposits, they were allowed to transfer these deposits into first line frozen deposits in December. However, no major bank could make an interim payment because of their dismal loan portfolio.[129] In January 1948, after completing the reevaluation of their assets, the financial institutions submitted their reorganization plans to the Ministry of Finance which gave its consent in May 1948.[130]

The restructuring process was completed in July 1948 after the old and new accounts had been merged and the losses due to the suspension of wartime compensation had been canceled out.[131] Losses were written off from the liability side according to the following priorities: (realized) capital gains on assets and other profits in the old account, retained earnings in the old account, up to 90 percent of the bank's capital, up to 70 percent of the second-line frozen deposits that exceed 5 million Yen per account, up to 50 percent of the second line frozen corporate deposits that exceed 1 million Yen per account. Up to 30 percent of the second line frozen corporate deposits that exceed 100 thousand Yen per account. Up to 70 percent of the remaining second line frozen deposits, the remaining 10 percent of the capital, the remaining 30 percent of the second line frozen deposits, and finally second line frozen deposit designated for tax payments.[132]

If following this market-to-market, total assets were less than total liabilities, the government offset the difference by injecting additional funds. All in all, the government injected 16.4 billion Yen into the financial system.[133]

After the restructuring process was completed, depositors gained renewed access to their frozen accounts. (but depositors could withdraw money from frozen deposits earlier[134] Many banks had to issue new equity in order to replenish their capital base.[135] Although the Japanese government was concerned about the willingness of the public to buy the shares, most issues were well subscribed.[136]

There was no formal deposit insurance scheme in effect at that time and losses were partly borne by depositors. Thus, the government established the precedent of not bailing out depositors.[137] In the aggregate, deposits amounting to 17.9 billion Yen or roughly 12.8 percent of all financial system deposits as of August 1946 were canceled against the special losses of banks. The losses incurred by individual depositors varied from 17 percent to 100 percent of the old account. As a general rule, losses to depositors of large banks amounted to 60 to 70 percent of the old account while depositors of regional banks suffered smaller losses. The heaviest losses were incurred by depositors of savings banks and trust companies.[138]

However, although creditors initial losses in 1948 were rather heavy, many were able to later recapture a large part of their money. The 1948 write down of banks' deposits and capital were based on very cautious estimates of the value of loans to munitions companies which later proved to be too pessimistic. Therefore, the majority of banks were able to pay back all the canceled deposits including the interest in the following years.[139] (unclear whether depositors received the same interest on second-line frozen deposits as on first line frozen deposits)[140]

As a result of marking to market the assets of the old account, 1.8 billion Yen of bank capital were written down to cancel out the losses. In 66 of the 74 ordinary, special, and savings banks as well as trust companies, shareholders lost at least more than 90 percent of their equity holdings.[141]

The Economic Impact of the Financial Crisis Resolution Plan

Macroeconomic Indicators

After the end of the war, Japan's economy was faced with two major challenges: the war had destroyed 25 percent of productive assets as well as 30% of transportation related durable goods and infrastructure[142] and the hyperinflation of 1946 and 1947 had eradicated much of the financial wealth in the economy.[143] Although the restructuring program involved imposing

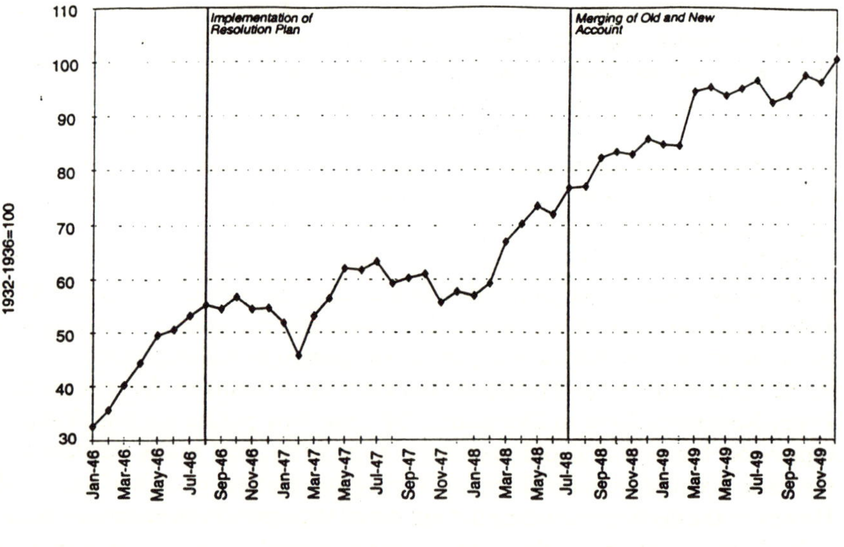

Note: Monthly data.
Source: Japan Statistical Yearbook, various issues.

Case 4. ***Chart 1a.*** Japan: Industrial Production from 1946 to 1949

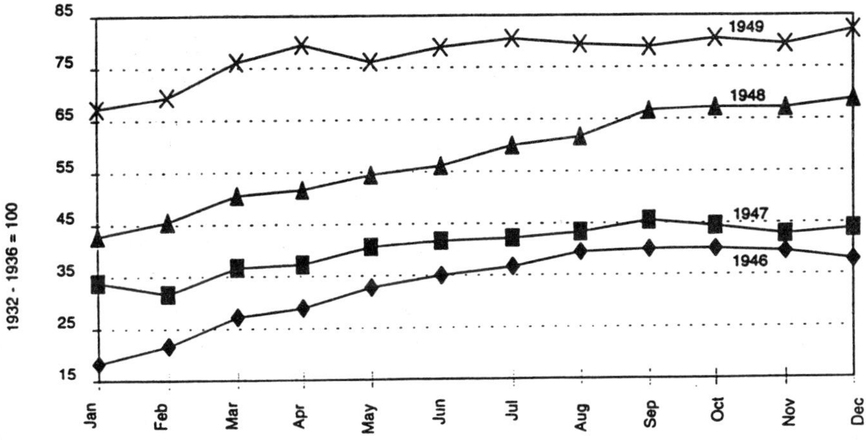

Note: Monthly data.
Source: Japan Statistical Yearbook, various issues.

Case 4. ***Chart 1b.*** Japan: Industrial Production Index from 1946 to 1949

losses on depositors, it did not derail the recovery of industrial activity. However, macroeconomic activity remained volatile during the first year and a half after the splitting of the balance sheet into an old and new account. From August 1946 to December 1946, industrial production stayed more or less stable. After a short relapse, it increased steadily until July 1947, dipping afterwards modestly. After December 1948, it showed a sustained increase (see Chart 1a and 1b).

Real total loans outstanding sharply declined in the immediate aftermath of the separation of the old and new account and bottomed out in October 1947 (see Chart 2a). But as Chart 2b shows, the sharp decline in real credit from the banking sector in that period was caused by the repayments of loans in the old account which outpaced the creation of loans in the new accounts. From November 1946 to December 1947, the only period for which separate figures on the new and old account are available, real loans outstanding in the new account remained nearly steady fluctuating in a narrow margin. However, the decline in lending did not derail the recovery of economic activity.

Real total loans from the banking sector started to grow moderately after October 1947, except for a short relapse from July to September of 1948. A portion of this decline can be attributed to the merging of the old and the new account in July of 1948 with the write down of loans in the old account (see Chart 2a).

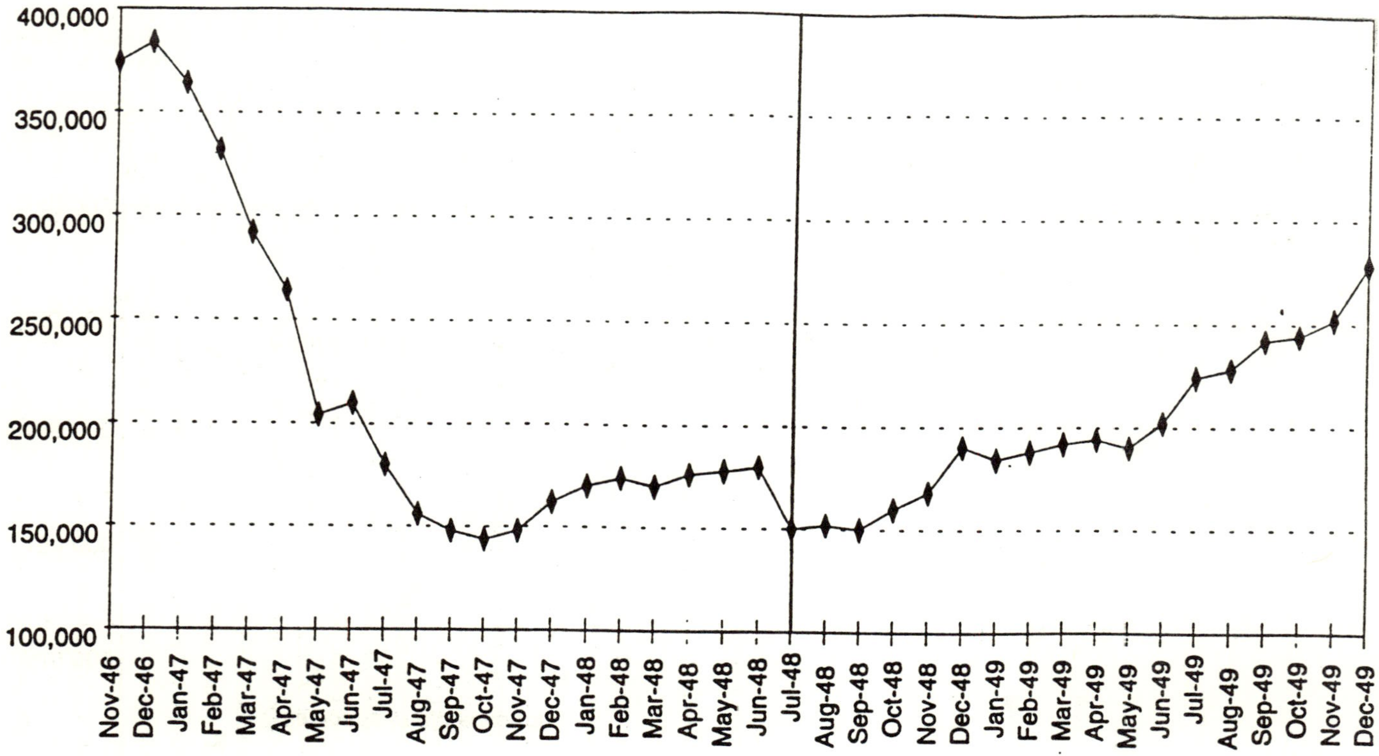

Note: Monthly data, adjusted for inflation by the Consumer Price index.
Source: Statistical Yearbook of Japan, several issues.

Case 4. ***Chart 2a.*** Japan: Development of Real Loans of All Banks from 1946 to 1949

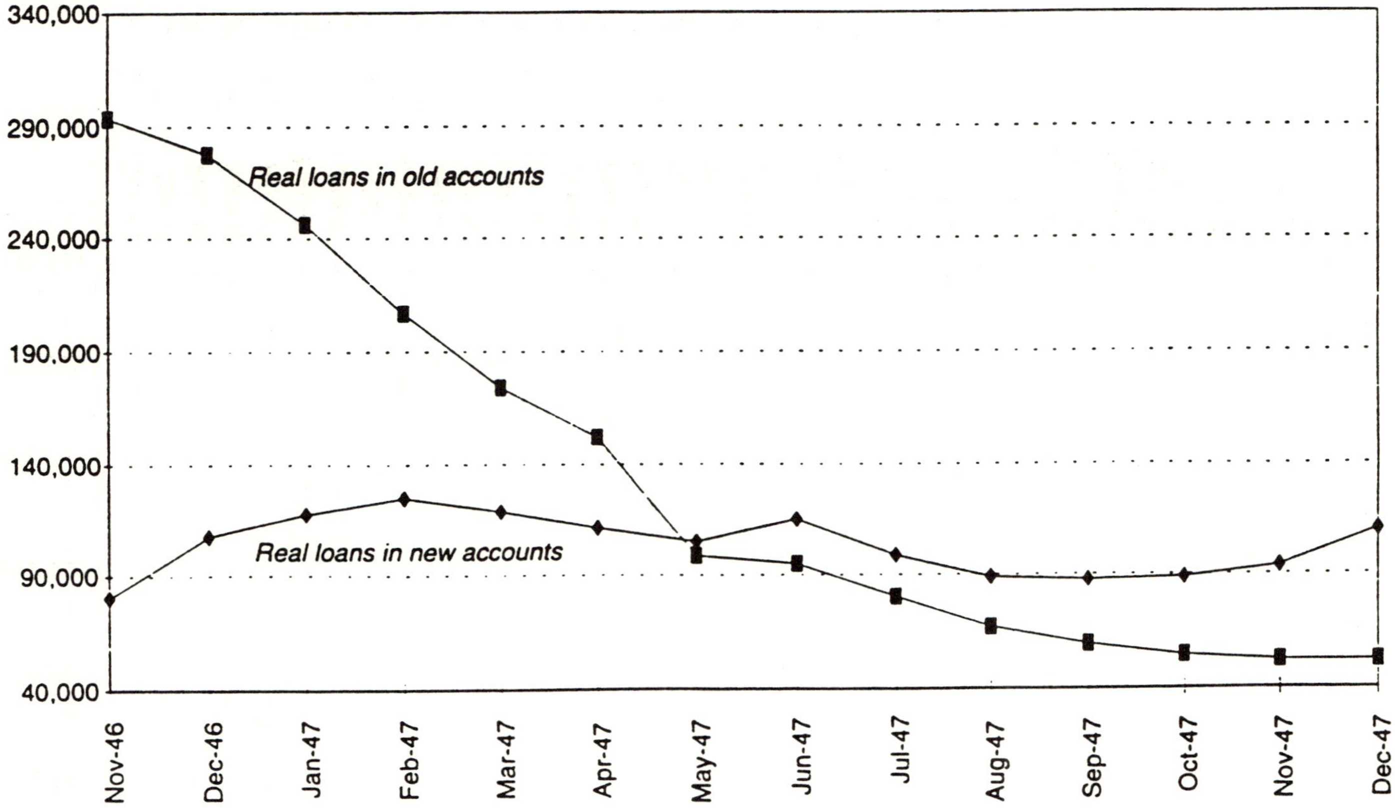

Note: Monthly data.
Source: Statistical Yearbook of Japan, several issues.

Case 4. ***Chart 2b.*** Japan: Development of Real Loans in the Old and New Accounts of Japanese Banks from 1946 to 1949

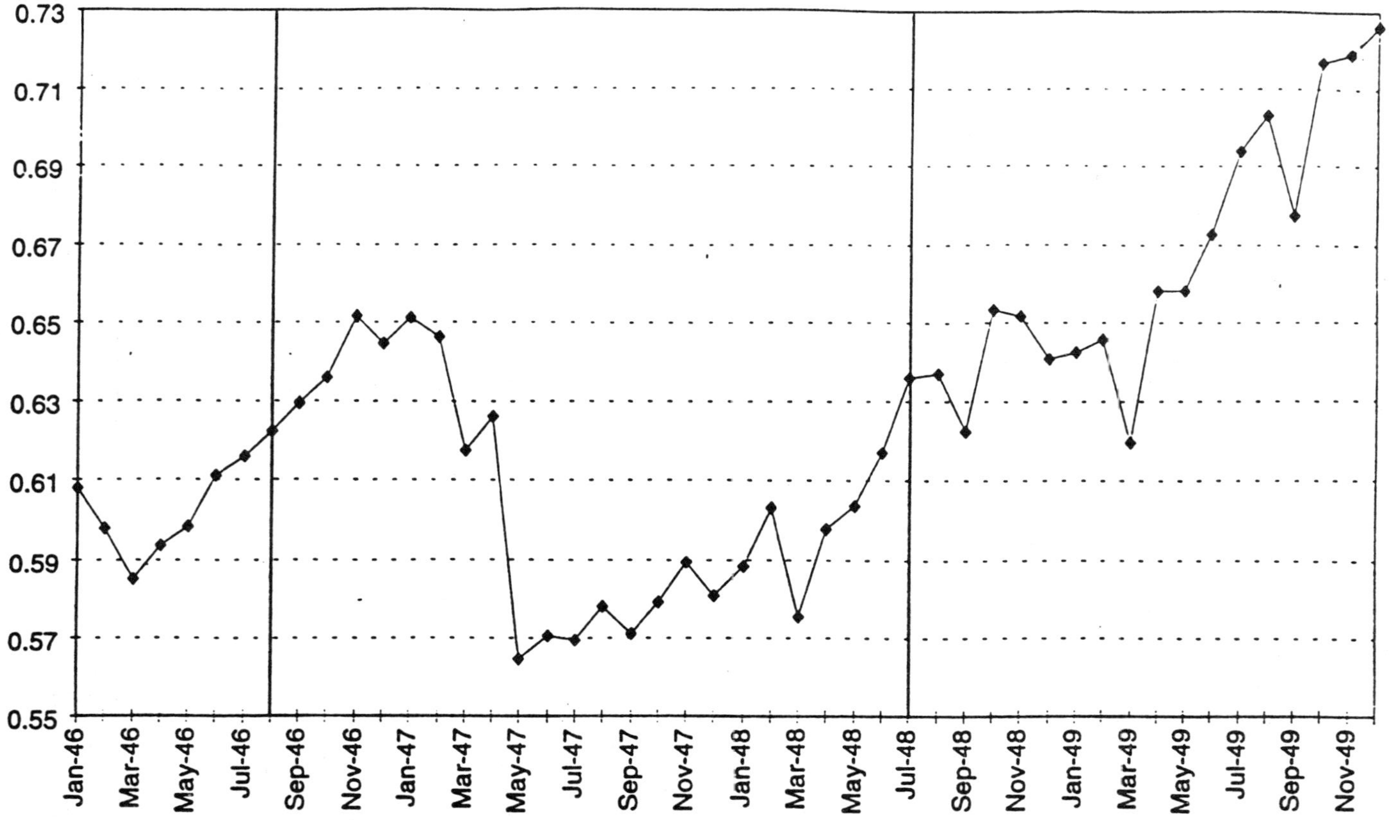

Note: Monthly data.
Source: Central Bank of Japan, Statistical Yearbook, several issues.

Case 4. ***Chart 3a.*** Japan: Ratio of Loans to Total Assets of All Banks from 1946 to 1949

Besides the loans which were provided by the banking sector, additional funds were channeled to the private sector via the Reconversion Finance Bank (RFB) which was founded in January 1947.[144] Its outstanding loan balance grew rapidly and by March 1948, it held 25% of all outstanding financial system loans.[145] The RFB supplied financing for the "priority production" of the coal, iron, steel, fertilizer, electric power, ocean shipping, and textile industries.[146] In March 1949, with the implementation of the "Dodge Line" which was aimed at curbing the inflation and implementing a balanced budget, new lending operations were finally suspended.[147]

The loan to asset ratio of Japanese banks rose in the immediate aftermath of the separation of the balance sheet indicating that the resolution mechanism employed did not have an adverse impact on loan preferences (see chart 3b). New loans to total asset continuously rose in the time after the implementation of the restructuring measures while old loans to total assets declined. The decline in the total loan to asset ratio can therefore be attributed to a decline in the old loan to asset ratio (see Chart 3a).

Since data on currency held by the public were not collected for this period, we constructed a deposit to currency issue ratio which was corrected by banks' holdings of cash. March 1946 which represents the first point in time for which

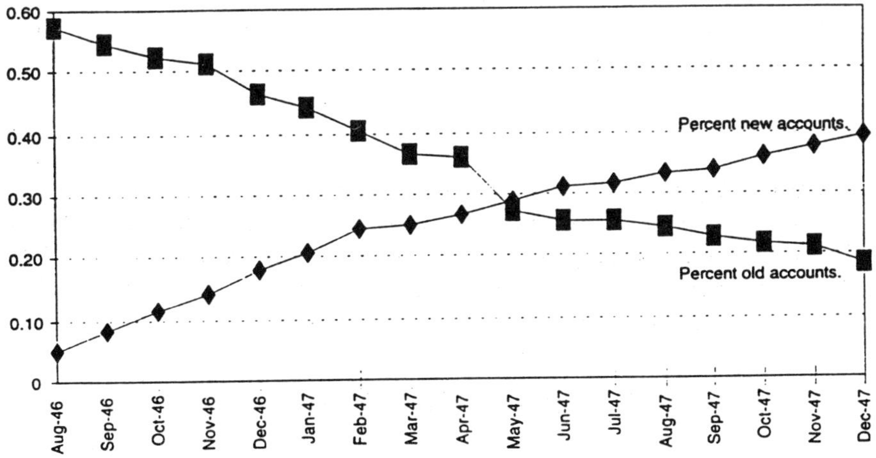

Note: Monthly data.
Source: Central Bank of Japan, Statistical Yearbook, several issues.

Case 4. ***Chart 3b.*** Japan: Loan to Asset Ratio in Old and New Accounts from 1946 to 1947

data are available cannot be taken as a benchmark. The ratio at that point in time is artificially high because of the implementation of the anti-inflationary program which, as explained earlier, forced all money back into the banking system.[148] However, the modified deposit currency ratio is also low when compared to the deposit currency ratio for 1939. Moreover, it continued to fall after the implementation of the comprehensive restructuring program. The continued decline in the deposit currency ratio may have been the result of deposit interest rate ceiling which sharply reduced the opportunity cost of holding currency. The modified deposit to currency ratio bottomed out in December 1947 and started to rise moderately thereafter (see Chart 4) indicating a reduction in depositors' uncertainties.

The decline in the modified deposit to currency ratio is caused by a decline in deposits. As Chart 4c shows, real total bank deposits fell sharply in the immediate aftermath of the separation of the old and new account. This fall was not only caused by a decline in the real value of old deposits, but as Chart 4c demonstrates, the real value of new deposits do not begin to grow until April 1947. Between May 1947 and October 1947, when real deposits bottomed out new deposits flowed into the banking system. However, these inflows were outpaced by inflation and by the decline in old deposits (see Chart 5). After October 1947, real total deposits rose except for a short downswing in July 1948. This downswing can partly be attributed to the write down of deposits due to the merging of the old and new account and real total deposits resumed to grow in October 1948.

Monetary Policy Measures

During the initial phase of the restructuring program, the Bank of Japan did not accommodate the fall in the deposit to currency ratio. The sharp fall in real M2 only ended in September 1947. From September 1947 until June 1948, the monetary authorities did not allow the money supply to fall any further and M2 was stable. It resumed its fall in September 1948.

III. THE UNITED STATES 1933

From the 1930 to 1933, the US banking system was plagued by a series of bank failure waves forcing 9,096 banks to suspend operations.[149] The total number of banks declined from 24,633 at the end of 1929 to 14,523 at the end of June 1933.[150] The US case is of particular interest for our study because it illustrates the importance of adopting a comprehensive resolution approach to an insolvency crisis when imposing losses on depositors. Prior to March 1933, the government's policy, which included imposing losses on depositors

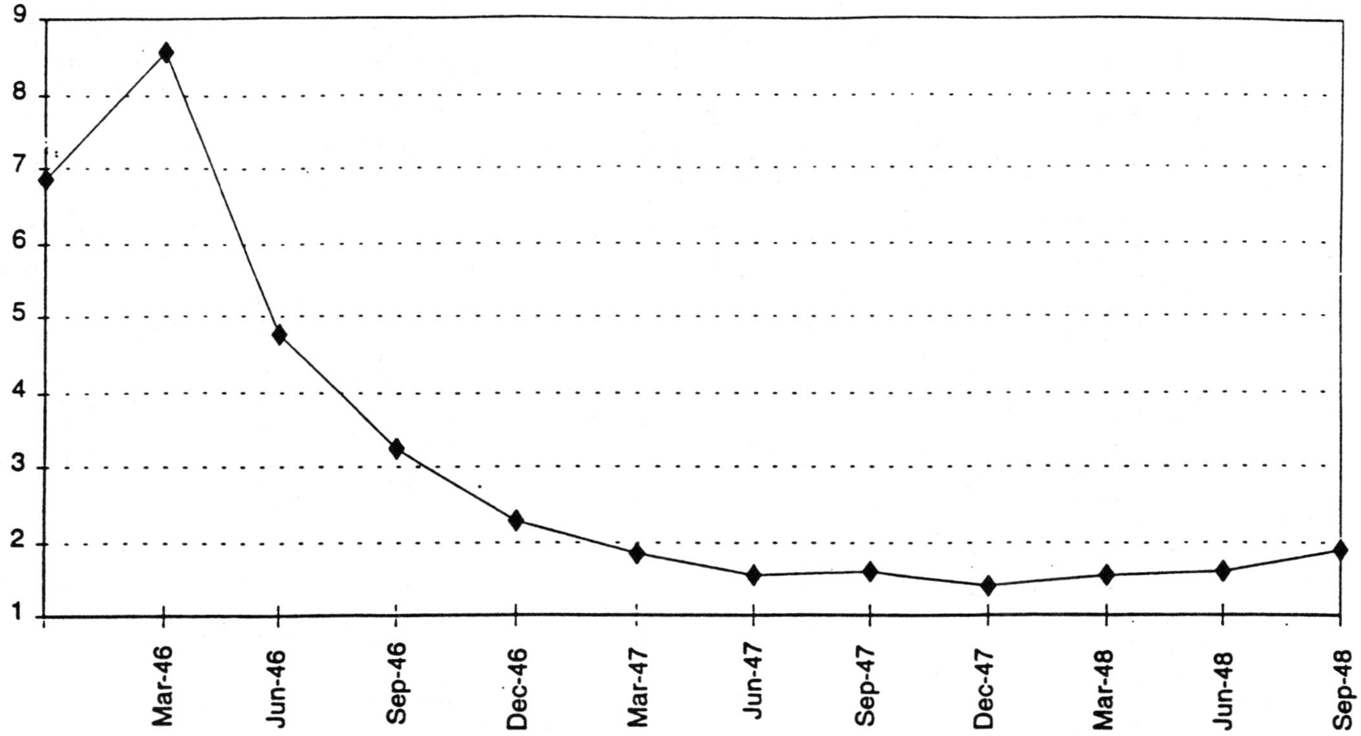

Note: Quarterly data; modified currency is currency in issue corrected by banks' cash holdings.
Source: Teranashi, 1991, p. 48; Central Bank of Japan, Hundred Year Statistics.

Case 4. ***Chart 4a.*** Japan: Deposit to Modified Currency Ratio from 1946 to 1948

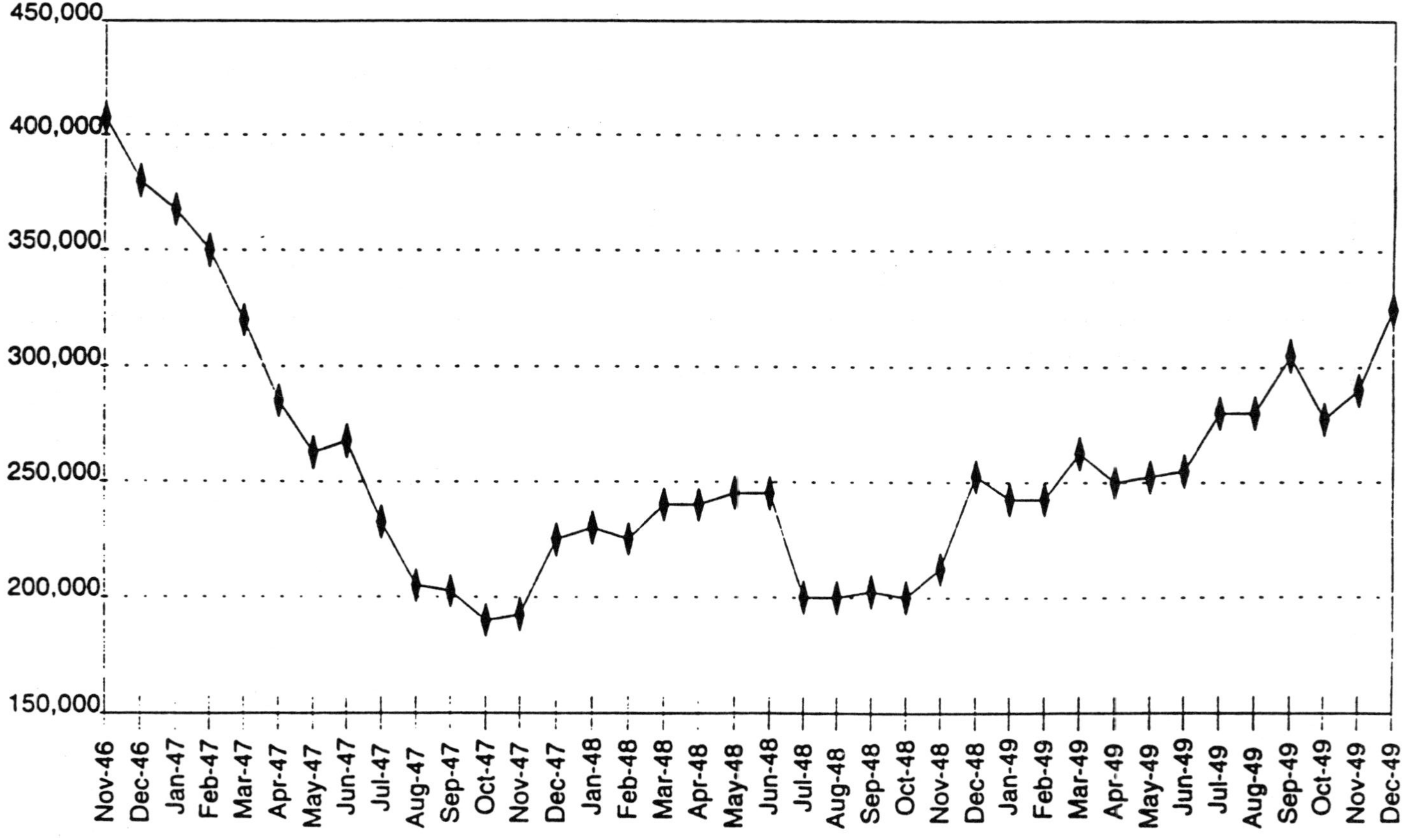

Note: Monthly data adjusted by the Consumer Price Index.
Source: Japan Statistical Yearbook.

Case 4. ***Chart 4b.*** Japan: Development of Real Deposits from 1946 to 1949

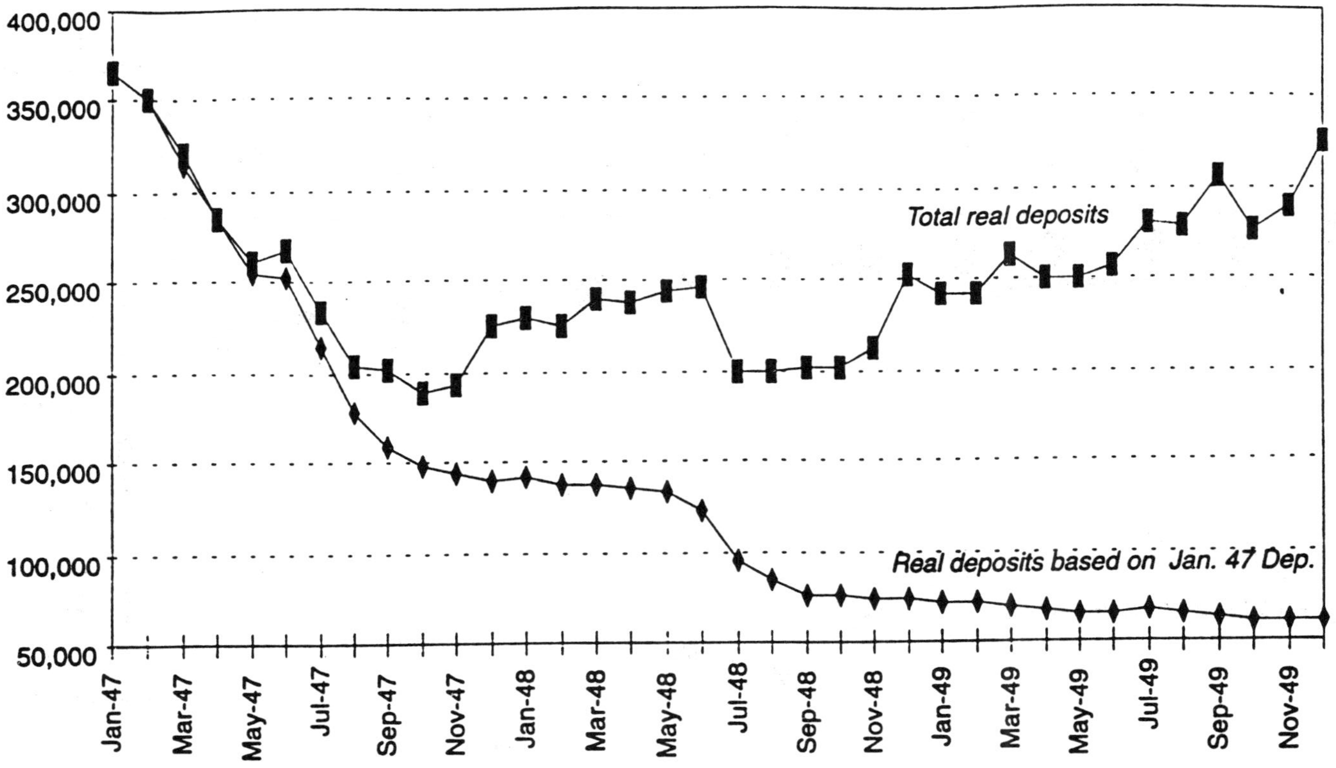

Note: Monthly data.
Source: Japan Statistical Yearbook, several issues.

Case 4. ***Chart 4c.*** Development of Real Deposits in Japan from 1947 to 1949

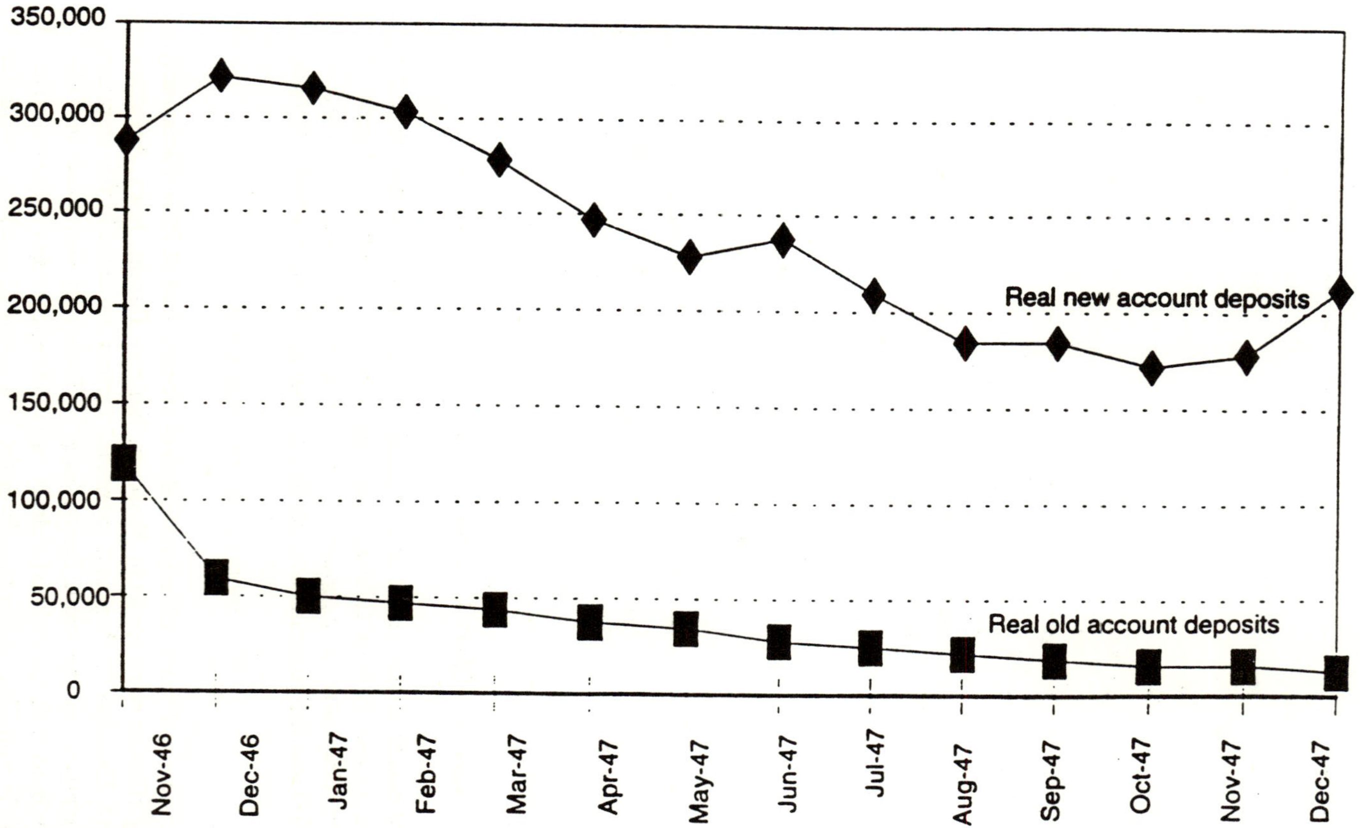

Note: Monthly data.
Source: Japan Statistical Yearbook, several issues.

Case 4. ***Chart 4d.*** Japan: Development of Real Old and Real New Account Deposits from 1946 to 1947

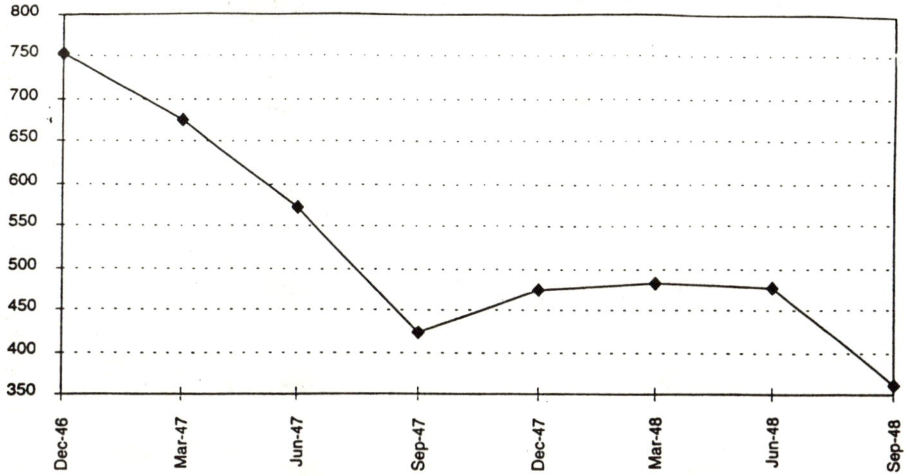

Note: Quarterly data.
Source: Central Bank of Malaysia.

Case 4. ***Chart 5.*** Japan: Real M2 from 1946 to 1948

and might best be characterized as piecemeal and haphazard, was not successful in putting an end to bank failure waves and in restoring public confidence to the system. Only after the adoption of a comprehensive resolution approach in March 1933 was the government successful in ending the waves of bank failures.

The Scope of the Financial Crisis

The first wave of bank failures started in the second half of 1930. Particularly adversely effected were banks in Missouri, Indiana, Illinois, Iowa, Arkansas, and North Carolina.[151] Real and monetary factors are cited in the literature for the increase in the bank failure rate.[152] The crisis continued in 1931. Although bank failures declined sharply early in the year, they picked up again in March. In mid-July, the instability of the U.S. financial markets was further aggravated by the closing of the Kreditanstalt, Austria's largest commercial bank and the subsequent closing of banks in Germany that had repercussions on the US banking market.[153] In addition, further pressure on bank reserves was exerted by an outflow of gold. Britain's departure from the gold standard in September 1931 and the anticipation of similar actions by the US led several central banks and private holders convert to their dollar denominated assets in the New York money market to gold.[154] Between August 1931 and January 1932, 1,860 banks with deposits of $1.5 billion suspended operations.[155]

In 1932, bank failure subsided modestly.[156] 1,453 banks out of an average 18,720 failed in 1932.[157] In response to the banking crisis, Congress passed several pieces of legislation aimed at improving the situation of the banks.[158] In addition to these measures, the Federal Reserve conducted large scale open market purchases in early 1932.[159]

In early 1933, however, a new wave of bank failures emerged. These failures were mainly attributed to four factors: growth in the number of insolvent banks due to monetary factors, real factors, and inadequate supervision and the misvaluation of the exchange rate.[160] Increasingly, regulators declared statewide bank holidays.[161] Finally, President Roosevelt proclaimed a nationwide bank holiday on March 6, 1933 which lasted until March 15, 1933. During this time, the banking system was completely shut down.

After the bank holiday, the 11,878 banks allowed to continue their operations held 87.3 percent of all commercial bank deposits. The 5,430 banks that were not allowed to reopen on an unrestricted basis after March 15, 1933 had a deposit base of US $ 3.4 billion which was equivalent to 12.7 percent of all commercial bank deposits.[162] Of the 5,430 banks which were not allowed to reopen after March 15, 1933, 1,621 were member banks holding US $2.867 billion in deposits accounting for 9.13% of all commercial system deposits.[163]

By December 1934, 1,088 banks accounting for 4.7 percent of financial system deposits that had not been allowed to reopen, had been reorganized under old or new charters or merged with other national banks had been reorganized under old or new charters or merged with other national banks; 30 went into voluntary liquidation. 294 representing $US 152 million (0.5% of commercial bank deposits as of March 15, 1933)[164] were placed into receivership and 5 with 0.3 percent of total deposits of the 1,417 banks remained unlicesened.[165] The 2,172 banks which were finally closed down accounted for 8 percent of commercial bank deposits.[166]

The Distress Resolution Plan at the Crisis Point of 1933

The Emergency Banking Act of 1933

Under the authority of the Emergency Banking Act, President Roosevelt issued a proclamation on March 9, 1933, continuing the Bank holiday and an Executive Order on March 10, 1933, empowering the Secretary of the Treasury to issue licenses to member banks to reopen. Every member bank was directed to apply for a license to reopen to the Federal Reserve Bank of its district. They would serve as agents of the Secretary of the Treasury in granting licenses. The Executive Order also empowered state banking authorities to reopen their sound banks that were not members of the Federal Reserve System.[167]

Under the Emergency Plan, national or state member of nonmember banks deemed insolvent were not allowed to reopen.[168] The plan called for the Comptroller to appoint a conservator for solvent but undercapitalized national banks.[169] The conservator's objective was to work out a reorganization plan that was subject to the Comptroller's approval and could only be put into effect with the consent of 75 percent of the bank's depositors and other creditors or with the consent of two-thirds of the stockholders or by a combination of the two.[170] Only those depositors and creditors whose claims were not fully compensated were given the right to oppose or reject the proposed plan.[171] Furthermore, these banks were allowed to resume operations on a restricted basis. The comptroller could direct conservators to allow payment to the depositor of parts of existing deposits that he deemed safe to release. In addition to this, subject to the approval of the comptroller, the conservators could receive new deposits available for immediate withdrawal without restriction and segregated from other liabilities of the bank.[172]

An Executive Order issued on March 18, 1933 dealt with state banks. It granted state banking authorities permission to appoint conservators for unlicensed state member banks which were solvent but undercapitalized when consistent with state law.[173] State bank commissioners were left free to take action on nonmember state banks. Where there was no provision for the equivalent of conservatorship, it was necessary for state banks, member or nonmember, to be either licensed or placed in the hands of receivers. Some states passed statutes patterned after the Federal Bank Conservation Act, and other relied on their various "stabilization" or "dictator laws".[174]

Additional policy measures consisted of strengthening the capital base of banks.[175] For example, in order to strengthen its capital base, national banks were permitted to issue non-assessable preferred stock to be sold to the public or to the Reconstruction Finance Corporation (RFC).[176] The RFC was also permitted to buy similar issues from state member banks. In 1933, the RFC bought a total of over $1 billion in 6,139 national, state member, and nonmember bank capital issues - one third of the total equity of all banks in the US in 1933.[177] The understanding was that capital would be retired out of about one half the net earnings of the banks after payments of dividends or interest on RFC capital.[178]

The treatment of depositors followed policies in earlier banking failures; they received no direct government support. In all of 1933, depositors lost US $

540 million, 15 percent of deposits in all suspended banks or $ 2.15 per $ 100 of adjusted deposits in all commercial banks.[179] In order to accelerate the process of liquifying deposits in open and suspended banks, the RFC lent US $187 million to open banks for distribution to depositors. It also lent over US $ 900 million to closed banks.[180] Bank shareholders losses amounted to US $ 0.9 billion according to an estimate of the Federal Reserve.[181]

Monetary Policy Measures of the Emergency Banking Act

The Emergency Banking Act provided for two different sets of monetary policy measures to respond to the insolvency crisis. The first set of measures included changes in the monetary standard to halt the overflow and hoarding of gold. To that effect, banks and nonbanking institutions were in effect prohibited from making gold payments unless permitted by the Secretary of the Treasury under license. The order also narrowly limited foreign exchange dealings.[182] On April 5, 1933, an Executive Order required all holders of gold, including member banks, to deliver their holdings of gold coin bullion, or certificates to Federal Reserve Banks on or before May 1, 1933.[183]

The second set of policy measures was aimed at strengthening the Federal Reserve's ability to respond to liquidity crises by granting wider rediscounting power to the Federal Reserve Banks and widening the possibility of the Federal Reserve to issue Federal Reserve notes in emergencies.[184] The Act further allowed any Federal Reserve Bank to deposit any direct obligation or any notes, drafts, bills of exchange, or bankers' acceptance with the Treasury as securities against which emergency issues of Federal Reserve Bank notes could be issued.[185]

The Economic Impact of the Financial Crisis Resolution Plan

Macroeconomic Indicators

While the measures of 1933 included imposing losses on depositors, the accompanying restructuring and cleanup of the U.S. banking system in March 1933 put an end to bank runs that had plagued the system for the preceding three years and set the economy back on a path to growth after three and a half years of decline. After the commencement of the comprehensive program, there was an immediate rebound in industrial production (see Chart 1). The recovery was uneven, but economic activity never again dipped down to the levels that had prevailed in 1932 and 1933. However, industrial production remained volatile in the immediate aftermath of the crisis. The reopening of the banks was followed by a rapid rise in industrial production until July 1933, but fell then again.[186] From April 1933 to December 1933, industrial production was running 15 percent above the preceding years.[187] However, industrial production did not rise continuously until late 1934.

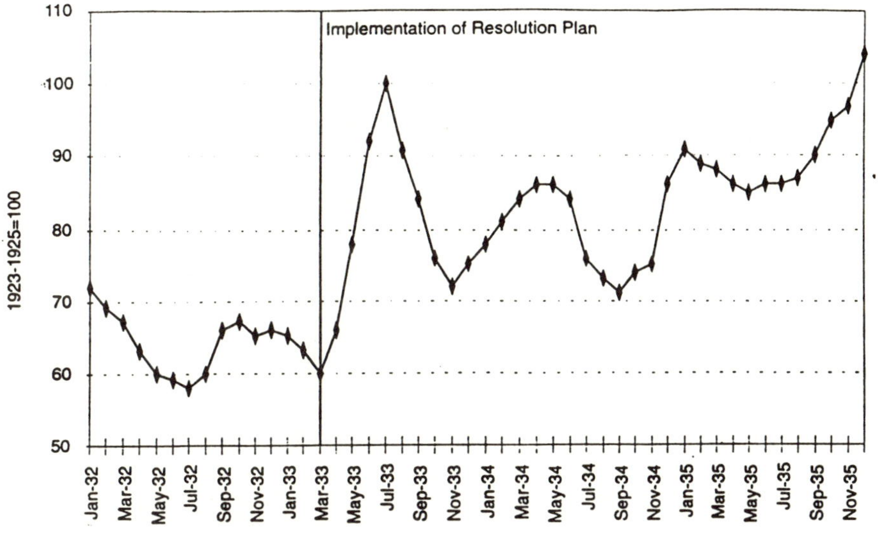

Note: Monthly figures seasonally adjusted.
Source: Board of Governors, Federal Reserve Bulletin, several issues.

Case 5. ***Chart 1.*** United States: Industrial Production Index from 1932 to 1935

Bank lending took longer to recover. Real total lending declined further in 1933, although at a sharply decelerating pace. It bottomed out in the second half of 1935 (see Chart 2a). The ratio of loans to total assets also continued to decrease markedly in the immediate aftermath of the restructuring of the banking system. Between 1933 and 1935, the ratio of loans to total assets fell from 43 percent to 34 percent (see Chart 3). To the extent the decline was exogenous, it would have been a drag on growth. Nevertheless, modest economic recovery continued.

Although the policy measures implemented included imposing losses on depositors, deposits started to flow back into the banking system immediately after the Bank Holiday came to its conclusion. Two weeks after the bank holiday, nearly 1 billion dollar had returned to banks.[188] This led to a sharp increase in the deposit to currency ratio in April 1933 and through the rest of 1933 and 1934 and reversed the trend of a sharply deceleration of the ratio in the period before the Bank Holiday. This development suggests that the governments' actions succeeded in restoring public confidence into the banking system (see Chart 4).[189]

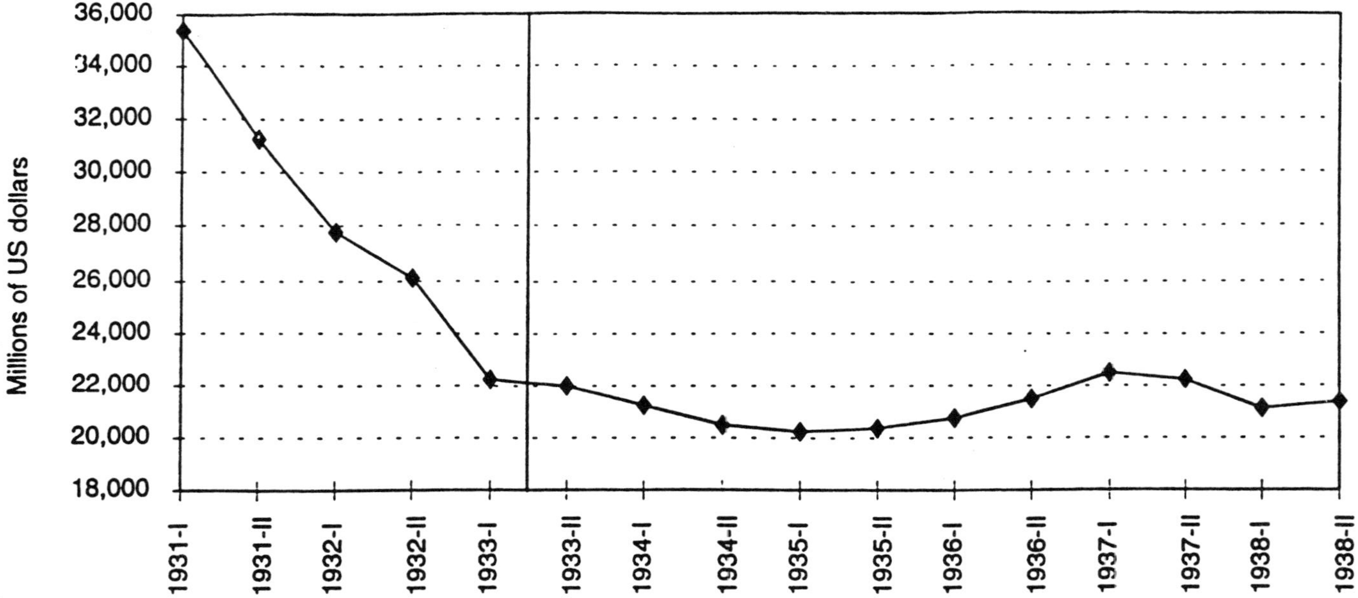

Note: Half-year data.
Source: Board of Governors, Federal Reserve Bulletin, several issues.

Case 5. ***Chart 2a.*** United States: Outstanding Loans of all Commercial Banks from 1930-38

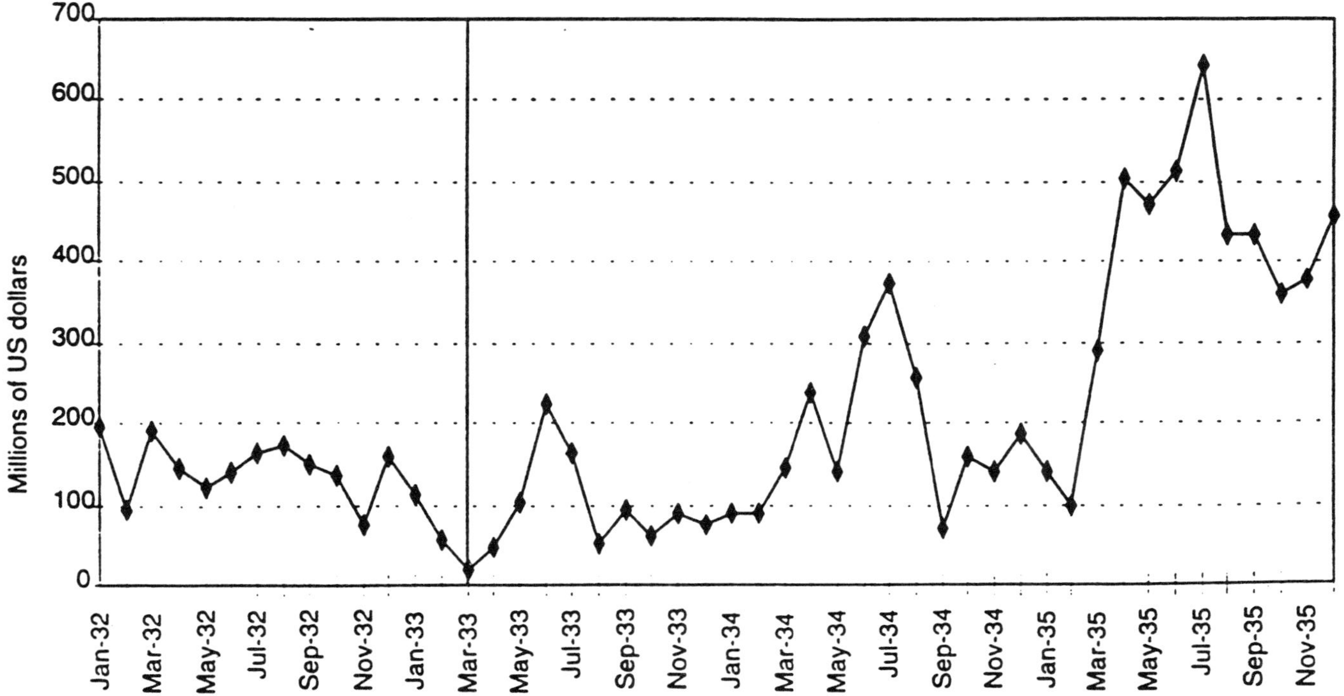

Note: Monthly data.
Source: Board of Governors, Federal Reserve Bulletin, several issues.

Case 5. ***Chart 2b.*** United States: Total Capital Issues from 1932 to 1935

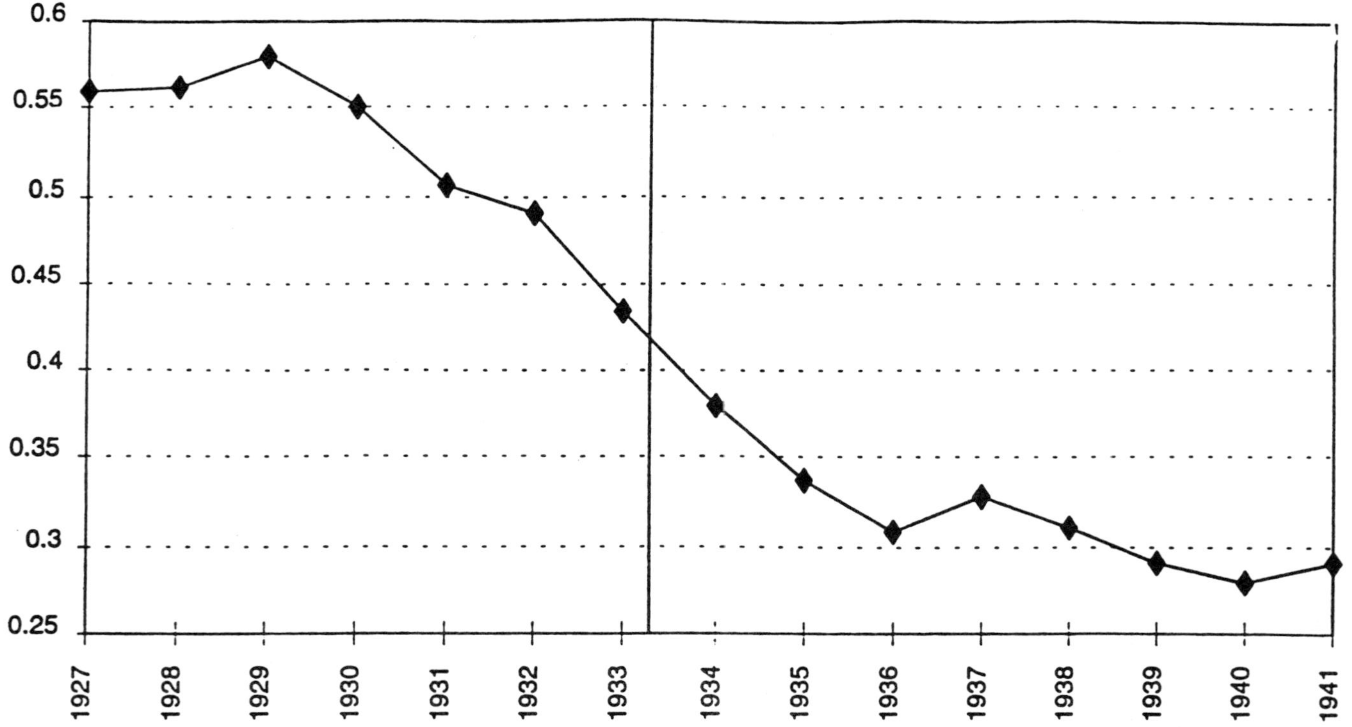

Note: Annual data.
Source: Board of Governors, All Bank Statistics, 1955, pp. 53-55.

Case 5. ***Chart 3.*** United States: Loan to Asset Ratio of All Banks from 1927 to 1941

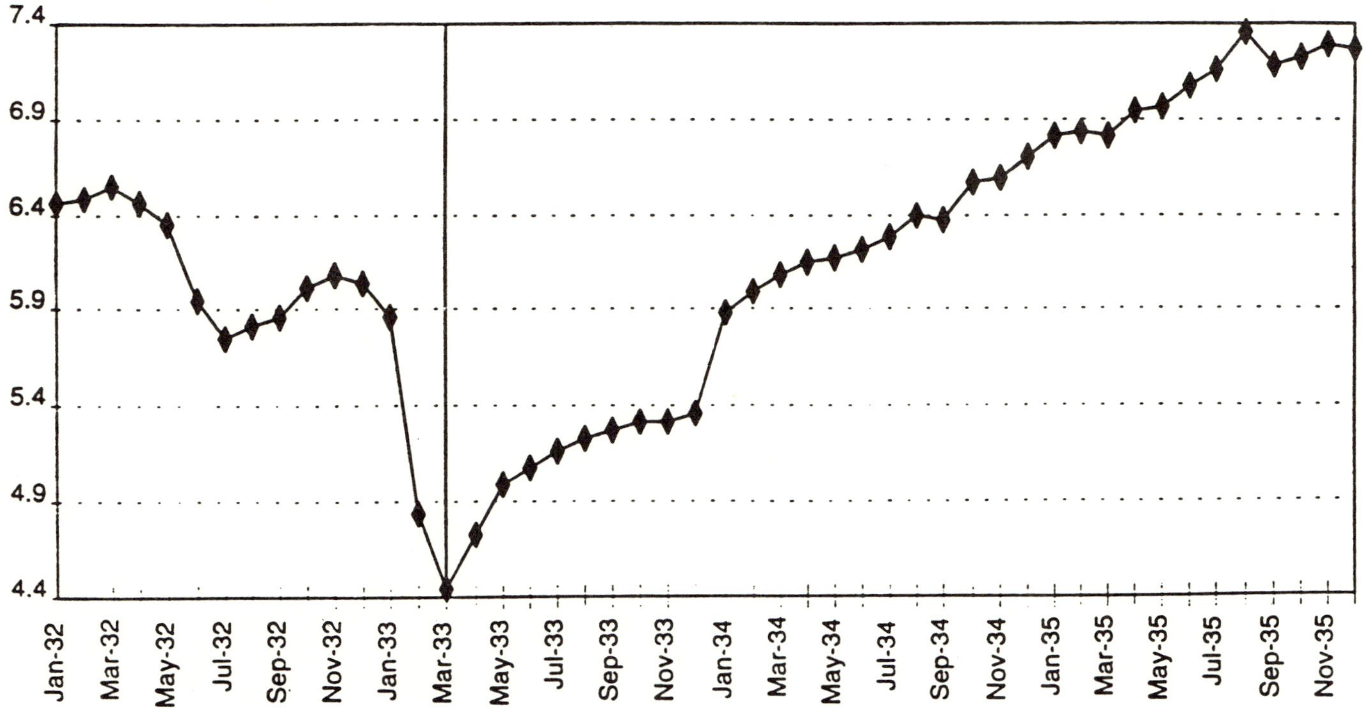

Note: Monthly seasonally adjusted data.
Source: Friedman, Schwartz, 1971, pp. 803, 804.

Case 5. ***Chart 4.*** United States: Deposit to Currency Ratio from 1932 to 1935

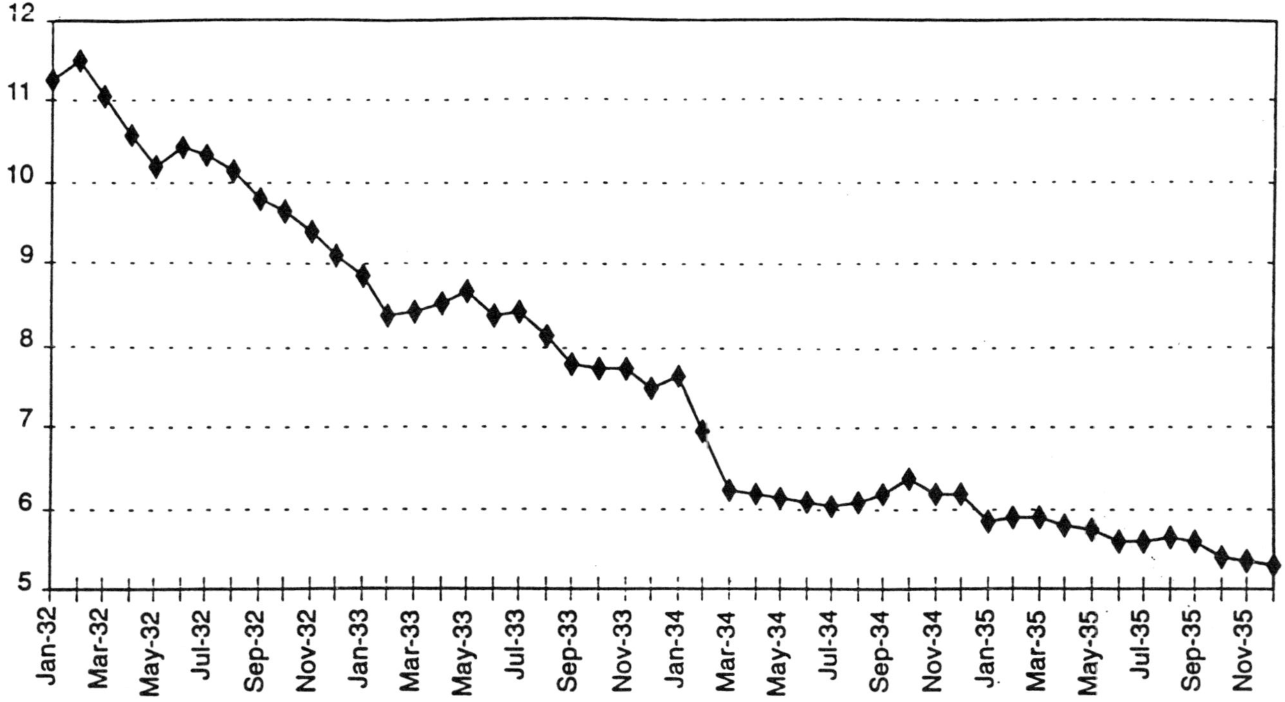

Note: Monthly seasonally adjusted data.
Source: Friedman, Schwartz, 1971, pp. 803, 804.

Case 5. ***Chart 5a.*** United States: Deposit to Reserve Ratio from 1932 to 1935

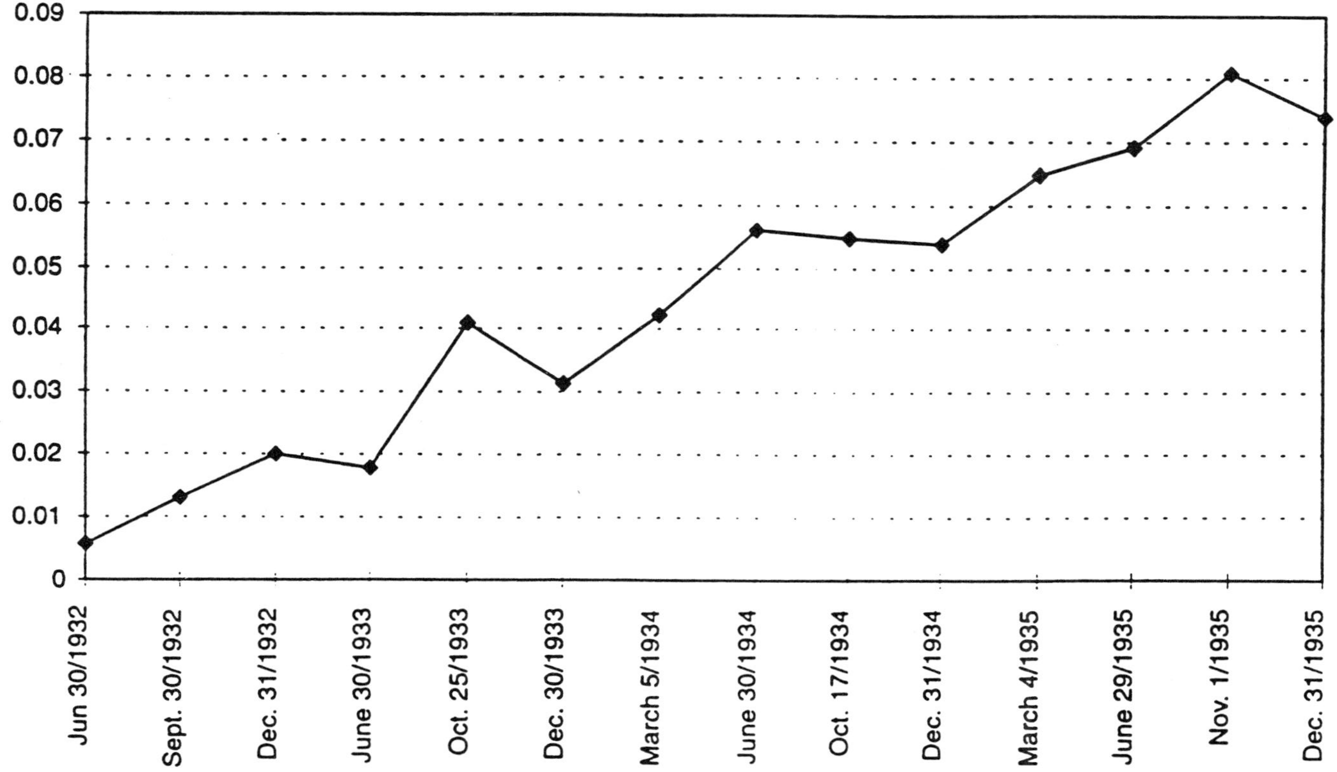

Note: Call Date data.
Source: Board of Governors, Banking and Monetary Statistics, 1943.

Case 5. ***Chart 5b.*** United States: Ratio of Excess Reserves to Total Deposits of All Member Banks from 1932 to 1935

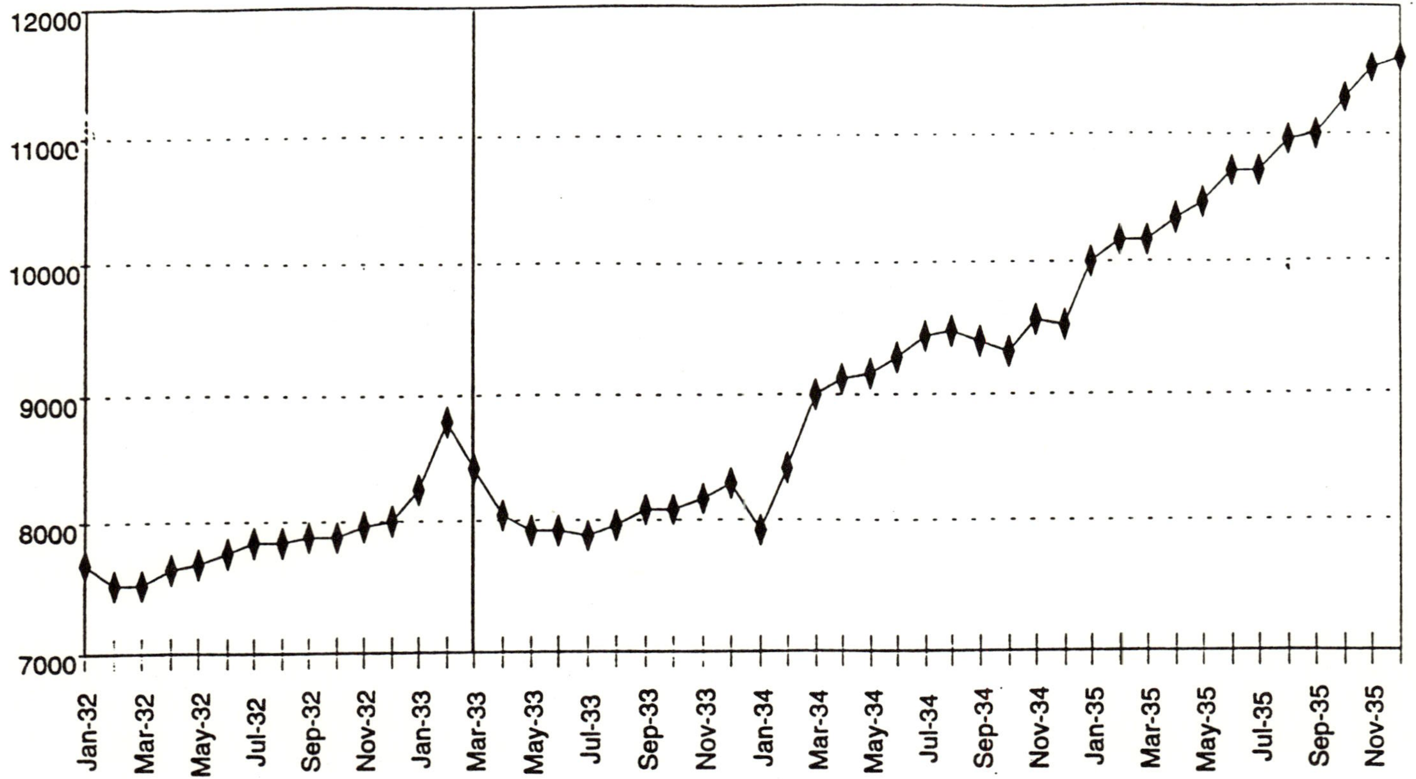

Note: Monthly seasonally adjusted data.
Source: Friedman, Schwartz, 1971, p. 803-804.

Case 5. ***Chart 6.*** United States: High Powered Money from 1932 to 1935

The deposit to reserve ratio did not recover in the aftermath of the bank holiday. The deposit to reserve ratio rose only modestly until May 1933 but then resumed a decline which continued through 1933, despite unchanged reserve requirements (see Chart 5). This indicates that banks remained uncertain and preferred to hold excess reserves in order to be able to meet increased depositors' withdrawals.

Complementary Monetary Policy Actions

The restructuring program rather than monetary policy would appear to deserve most of the credit for the initial phase of the recovery. In the period following the Bank Holiday, the Federal Reserve System did not adopt an expansionary course by trying to alter the quantity of high powered money by either open market operations or rediscounting. Outstanding Federal Reserve credit (including bills discounted, bills bought, U.S. government securities and others) even declined in the months following the Bank Holiday. It only started to rise again in August 1933 and reached its March 1933 level by December of 1933 (see Chart 7a).[190] This downward trend in outstanding Federal Reserve credit (which was not compensated for by an increase in currency outstanding; Chart 7b) was reflected in a continuing decrease of high-powered money until May 1933. It then remained almost stable during the rest of 1933.[191] These policies largely off-set the increase in the money multiplier generated by increasing public confidence. As a result, M2 after having fallen modestly in April 1933 did not rise significantly but remained stable during 1933 (see Chart 8).

IV. CONCLUSIONS

The major conclusion of this study is that financial systems are not as fragile as commonly thought. We find that when losses are imposed on depositors in a comprehensive fashion there are little or no adverse macroeconomic consequences. Our second conclusion is that the imposition of losses when done in a comprehensive fashion is generally not followed by a significant flight to currency (the sole exception being Japan which artificially reduced the attractiveness of deposits by setting deposit rates so low that there was little opportunity cost to holding currency). Our third conclusion is that the imposition of losses on depositors does not always cause banks to react by reducing lending. Indeed, the contraction in lending that occurred in the U.S. after 1933 does not seem to have occurred in any of these other cases. Finally, these case studies suggest that it is possible to impose losses on a bank's depositors and still have the bank continue operating on a going concern basis.

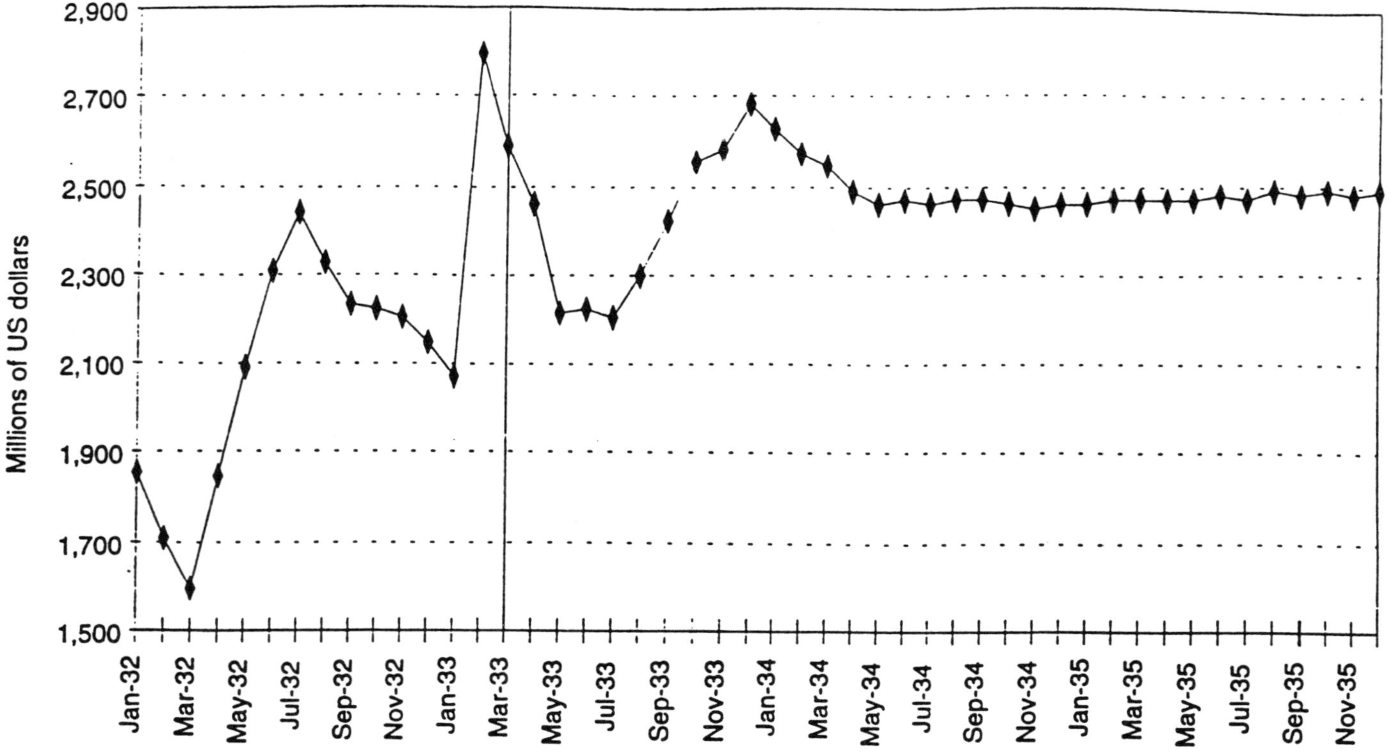

Note: Monthly data: Reserve Credit outstanding consists of bills discounted, bills bought, U.S. Government securities others.
Source: Board of Governors, Banking and Monetary Statistics, 1943, p. 376.

Case 5. ***Chart 7a.*** United States: Reserve Bank Credit Outstanding from 1932 to 1935

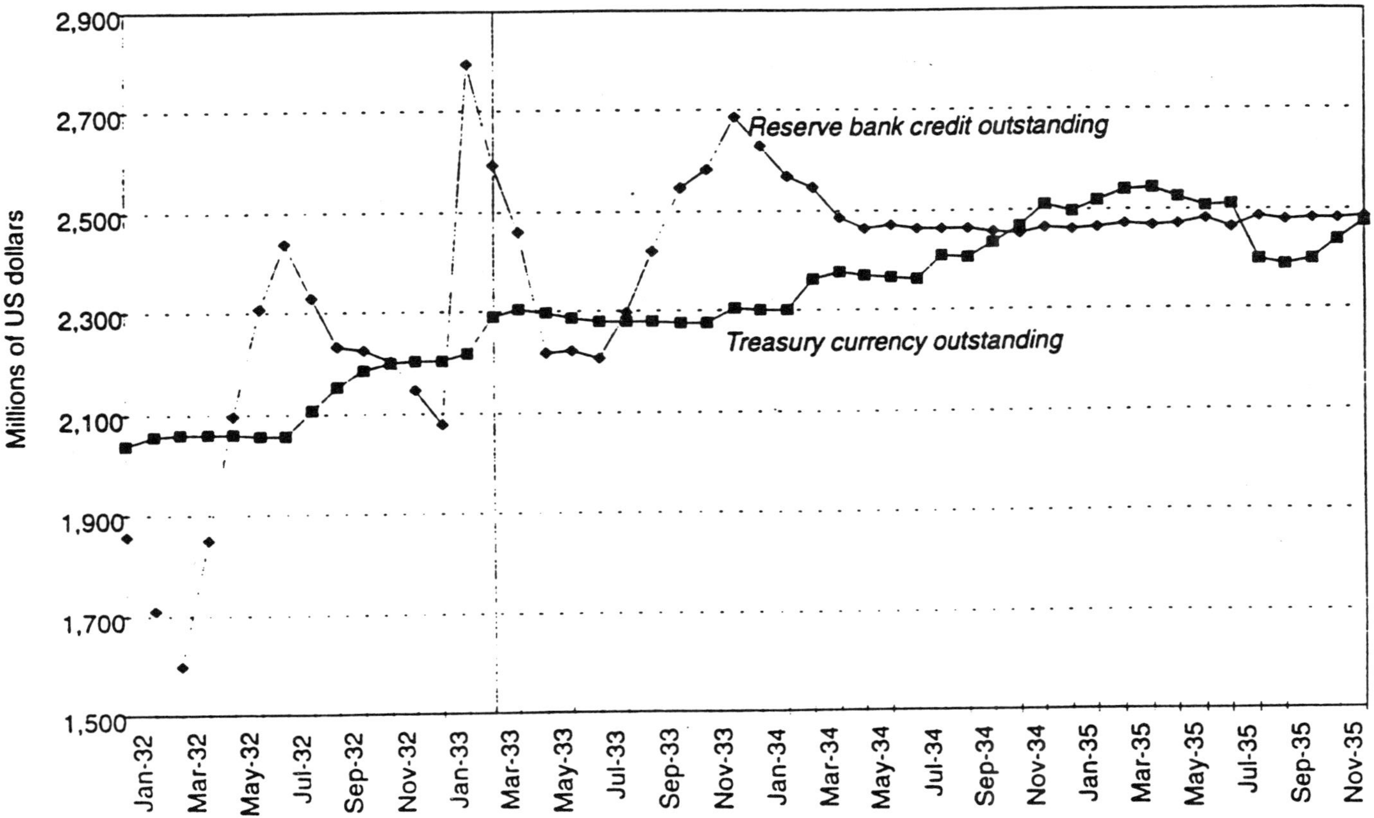

Note: Monthly data.
Source: Board of Governors, Banking and Monetary Statistics, 1943, p. 376.

Case 5. ***Chart 7b.*** United States: Reserve Bank Credit Outstanding & Treasury Currency Outstanding from 1932 to 1935

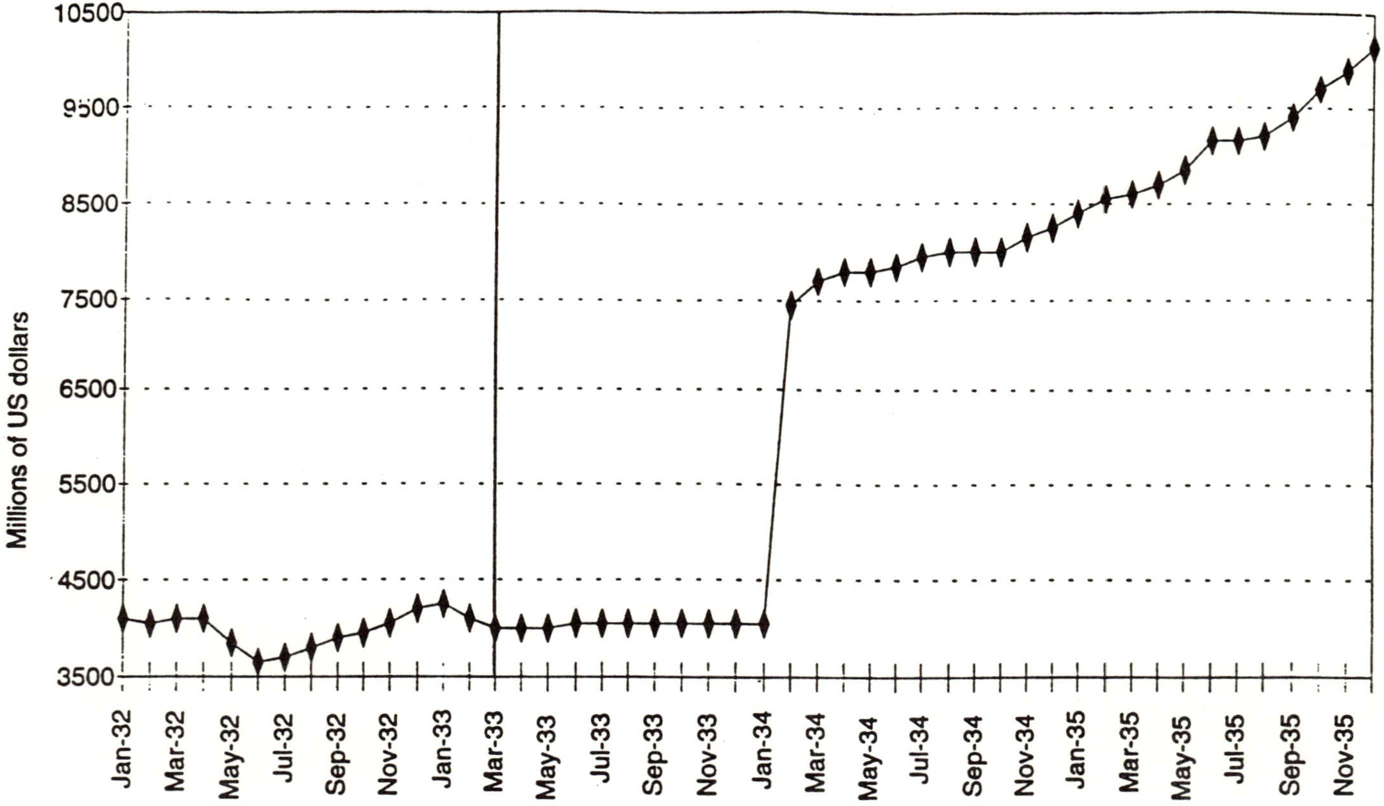

Note: Monthly data: Gold stock includes only gold held by the Treasury.
Source: Board of Governors, Banking and Monetary Statistics, 1943, p. 363.

Case 5. ***Chart 7c.*** United States: Gold Stock from 1932 to 1935

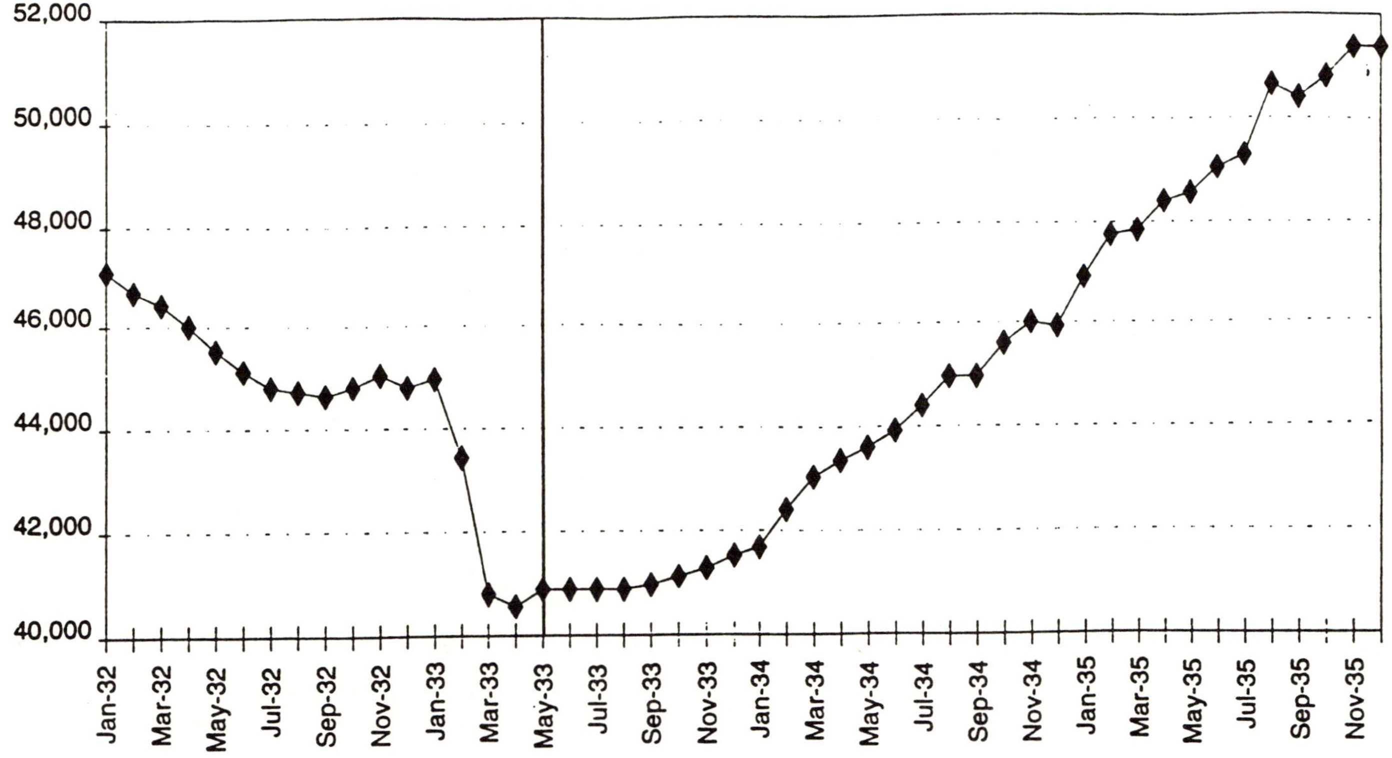

Note: Monthly seasonally adjusted data.
Source: Friedman, Schwartz, 1971, pp. 713, 714.

Case 5. ***Chart 8a.*** United States: M2 from 1932 to 1935

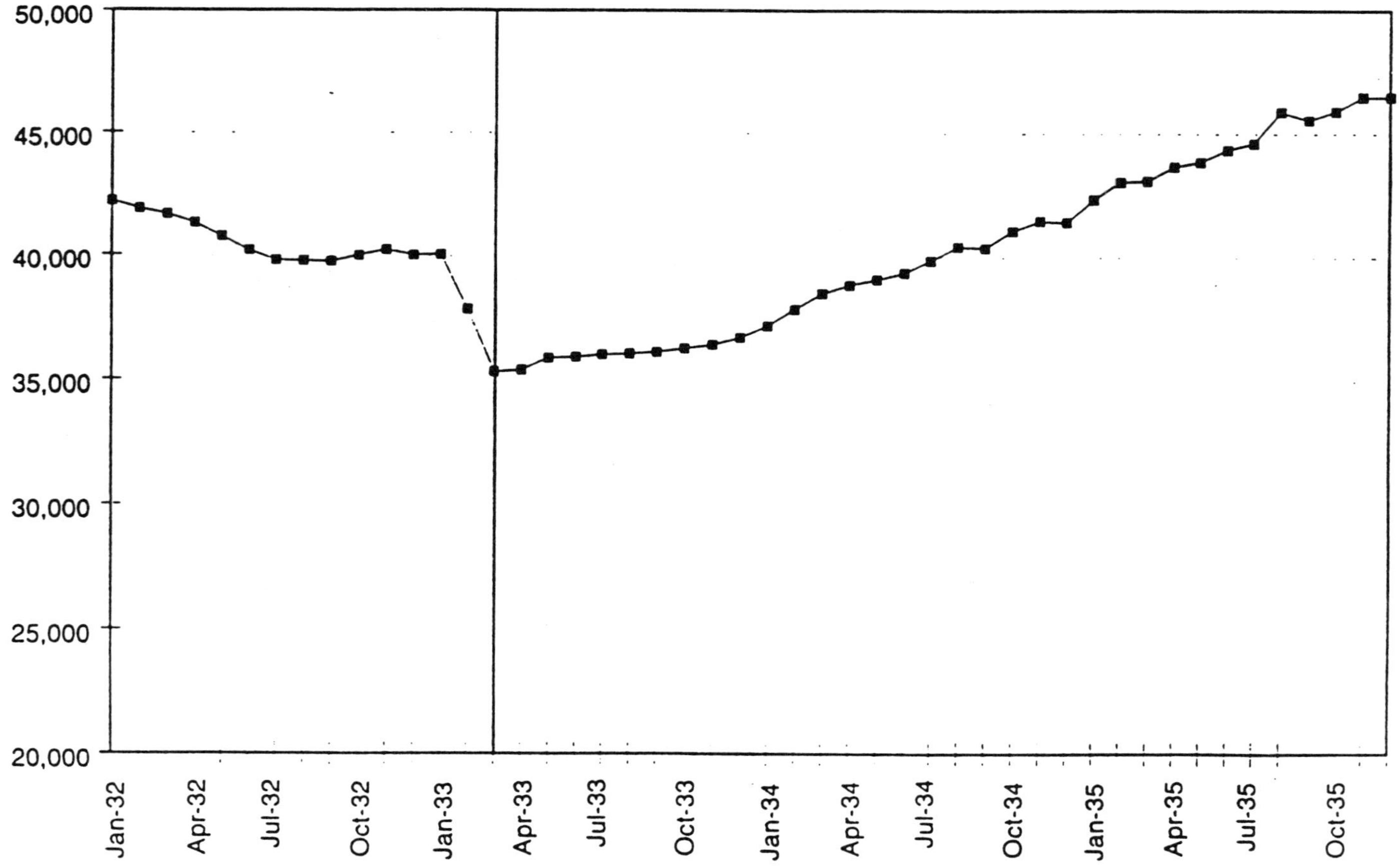

Case 5. ***Chart 8b.*** United States: Deposits

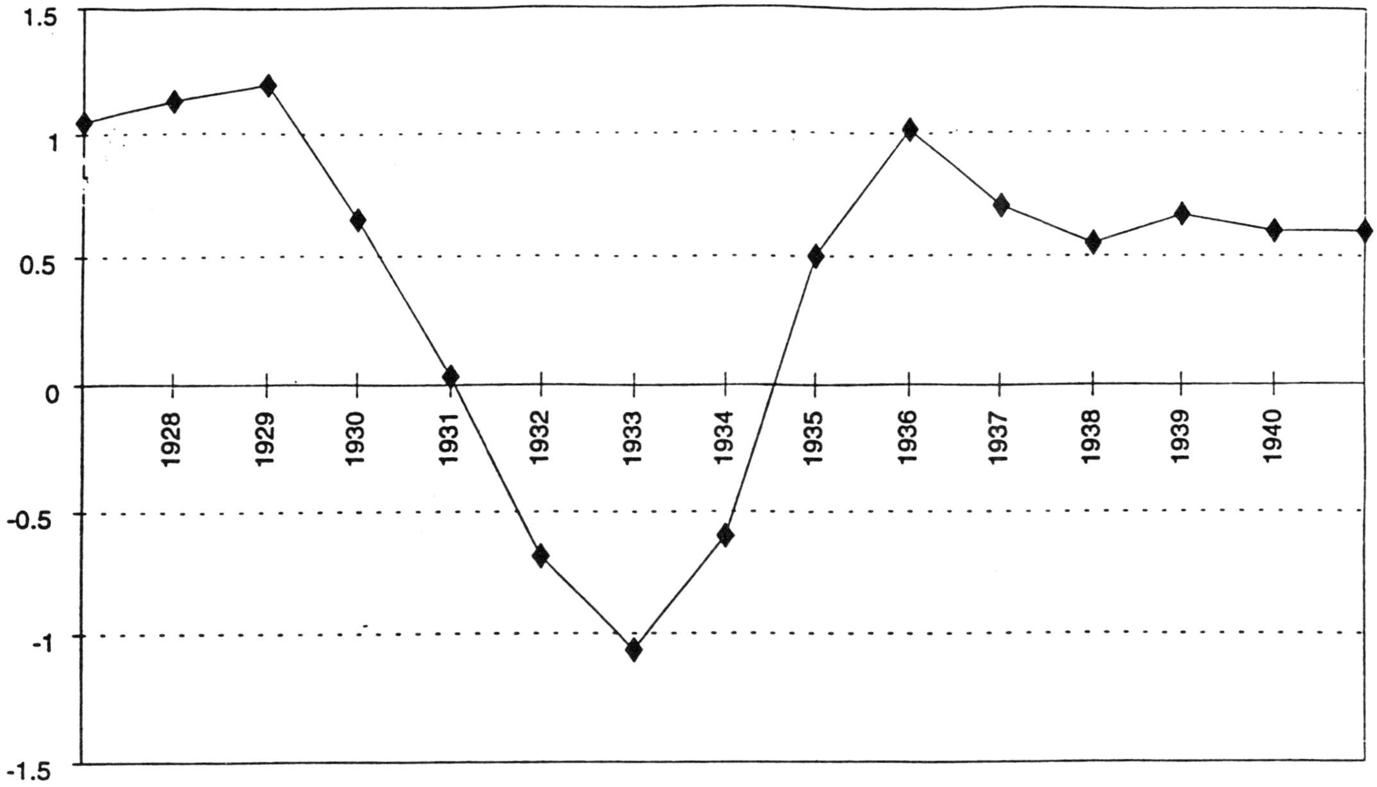

Note: Annual data.
Source: Board of Governors, Banking and Monetary Statistics, 1943, p. 263.

Case 5. ***Chart 9a.*** United States: Return on Assets b. t. of Member Banks from 1927 to 1941

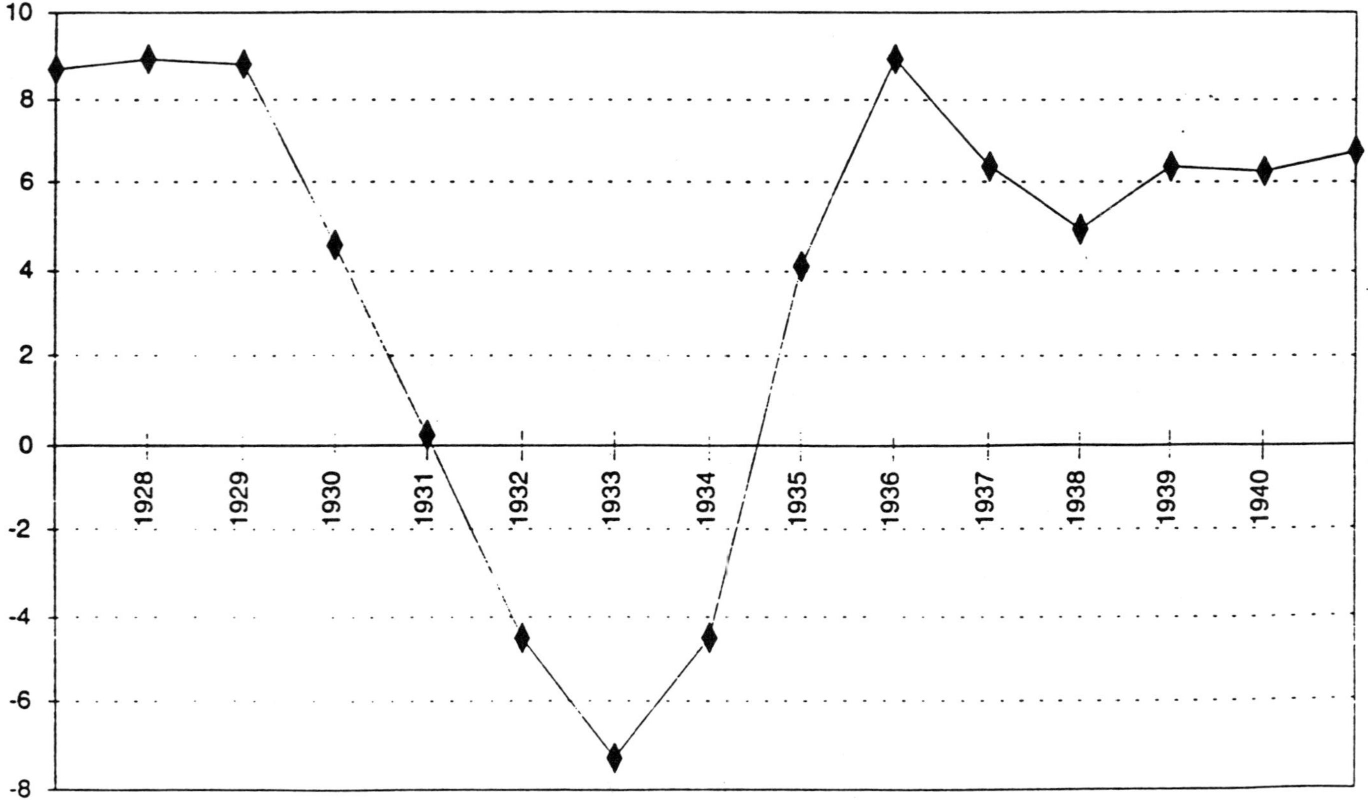

Note: Annual data.
Source: Board of Governors, Banking and Monetary Statistics, 1943, p. 262 ff.

Case 5. ***Chart 9b.*** United States: Return on Equity b.t. of Member Banks from 1927 to 1941

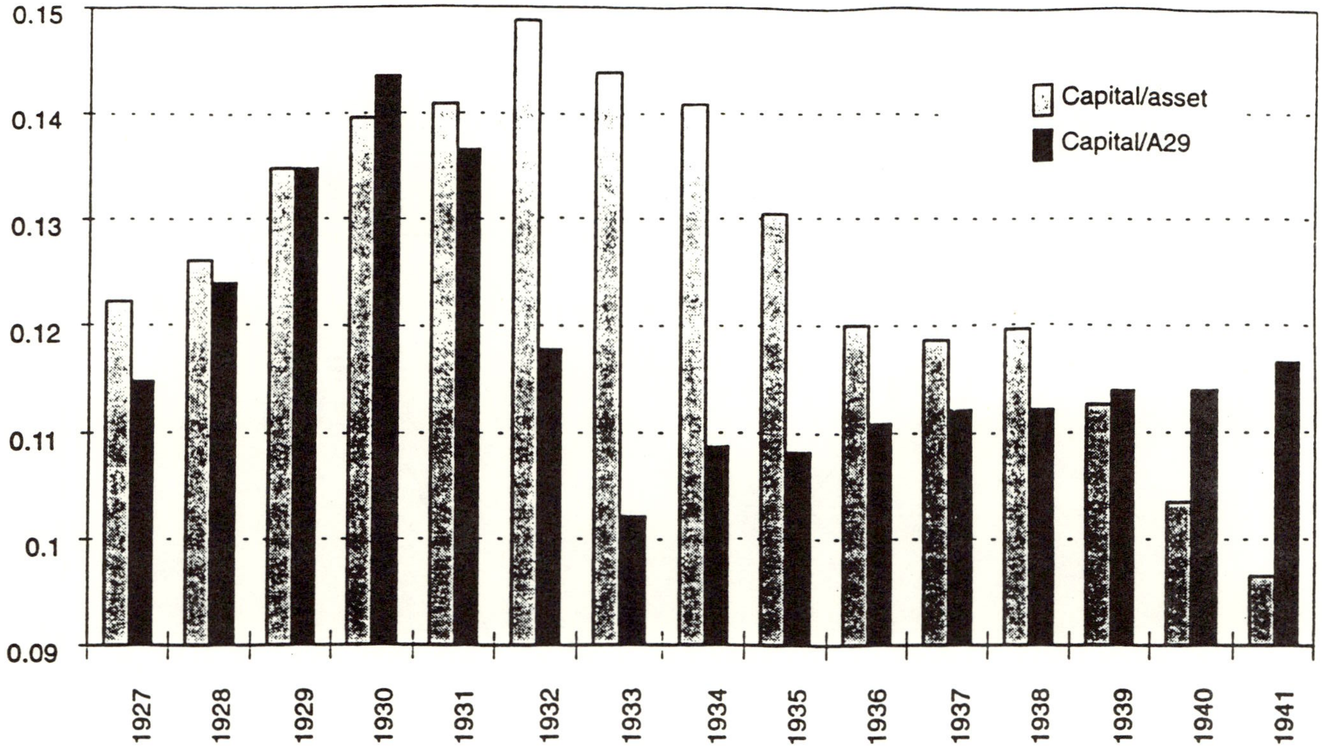

Note: Annual data.
Source: Federal Reserve Board, All Bank Statistics, 1955, pp. 53-55.

Case 5. ***Chart 10.*** Capital to Asset Ratio of All US-Banks 1927-1941

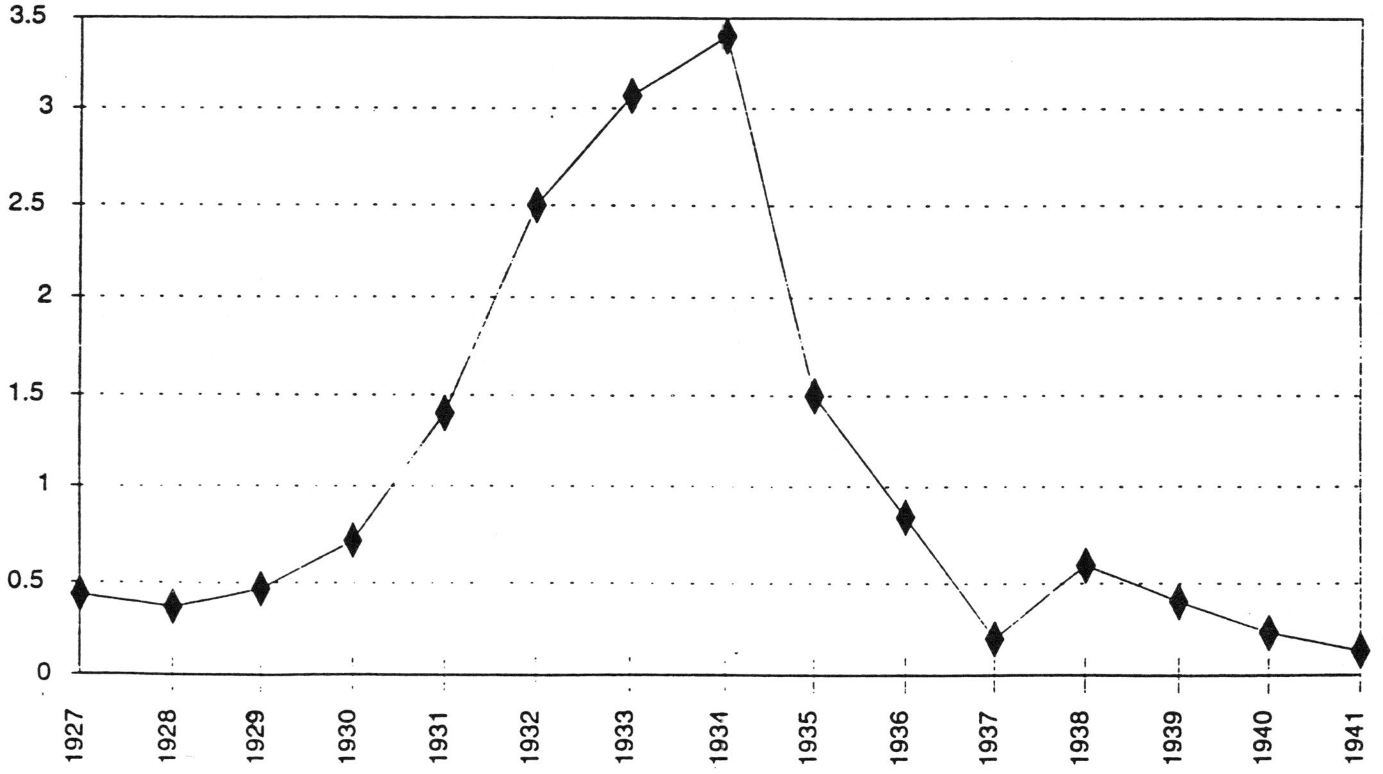

Note: Annual data.
Source: Federal Reserve Board, All Bank Statistics, 1955, p. 262.

Case 5. ***Chart 11.*** United States: Ratio of Net Losses on Loans to Total Loans of Member Banks from 1927 to 1941

While the policies adopted by these countries to deal with financial distress vary in a number of important dimensions, a number of common elements are discernible.

- Comprehensive action against depositors at all troubled banks stabilizes the system, reducing depositor uncertainty and increasing supervisory credibility.
- Policies specifically targeted towards solvent, but undercapitalized banks helped increase public confidence.
- After marking deposits to market, deposits were liquified in order to minimize the macroeconomic impacts.
- Many banks were restructured rather than liquidated.

The extent to which other countries might expect to obtain similar outcomes by pursuing similar policies is a matter still open to debate. However, our sample is heterogenous with respect to the size of the problem, the rate of inflation, the level of per capita income, the fiscal position of the government, the importance of the financial system to the economy, the sophistication of the legal system, and the size of the preceding decline in GPD. Perhaps the only two common elements are that all five countries were operating more or less as democracies at the time of the financial distress and that all five countries were willing to consider a set of policies that are dismissed by most policymakers.

NOTES

1. Herbert Baer was a financial economist at the World Bank and Daniela Klingebiel is a doctoral candidate at Albert-Ludwigs Universitat, Freiburg, Germany. The authors wish to thank Takeo Hoshi for providing us with guidance and information concerning the restructuring of the Japanese banking system and John Hansen for providing us with information and guidance on the restructuring of the Estonian banking system. The authors also wish to thank Gillian Garcia and George Kaufman for comments on earlier drafts. Any errors are the responsibility of the authors. This paper was in the process of being revised at the time of Baer's death and is being published in its unrevised form.

2. Sheng, 1992, Chapter VIII, p. 1.

3. *Policy Research, Adjustment in Africa: Reform, Results and the Road Ahead.* The World Bank: Washington, 1993, p. 411.

4. *The Economist*, August 27th, 1994, p. 63.

5. Half of the money has gone in financial assistance to eight commercial banks which the Venezuelan Central Bank then decided to close down. *The Financial Times*, June 16, 1994.

6. Policymakers placing heavy emphasis on empirical evidence could rightfully argue that opponents of government funded recaps have marshalled little evidence to support their arguments.

7. Where govenments have adopted policies of high inflation or severe financial repression, concerns about the welfare of the population at large are of dubious credibility since the government has already demonstrated a willingness to appropriate financial wealth.

8. Indeed, in some cases, the recapitalization may provide a mechanism for indirectly looting the government treasury.

9. See Calorimis 1993.

10. See for example C.T. Conover's, Comptroller of the Currency, justification for bailing out Continental Illinois of Chicago, USA, in his testimony before Congress: "In our collective judgement (director of FDIC, Chairman of Federal Reserve Board and Secretary of Treasury) had Continental failed and had been treated in a way in which depositors and creditors were not made whole, we could very well have seen a national if not an international financial crisis the dimension of which were difficult to imagine." *Hearings before the Subcommittee on Financial Institutions Supervision, Regulation and Insurance of the Committee on Banking, Finance, and Urban Affairs*, 1984, p. 287 f.

11. Direct empirical evidence on the macroeconomic impact of large scale merger and or acquisition of insolvent banks is lacking. However it is not clear why these transactions can preserve informational capital.

12. For the U.S. see Friedman and Schwartz (1963). For Japan see Hoshi, Kashyap, and Loveman (1993) and Hoshi (1994). For Argentina see Giorgio and Sagari (forthcoming). For Malaysia see Sheng (forthcoming). For Estonia see Hansson (1994).

13. See Baer and McElravey (1993) for some evidence on this point.

14. Under a currency board there is no scope for a central bank to manipulate interest rates or credit levels and very limited scope to act as lender of last resort.

15. The currency reform unified the exchange rate and reduced buy-sell spreads, cutting revenues from foreign exchange trading. According to Eesti Pank, 76.1% of commercial bank revenues were based on exchange rate differences. This had fallen to 14.7% in the second half of 1992. Eesti Pank, Quarterly Review, 1993:1, p. 38.

16. The currency board principle prohibited the Bank of Estonia from giving soft credits to banks, except in the context of a well defined banking crisis (Hansson, 1994, p. 9ff). For further details see Bennett, 1993.

17. Estonia. Informal Study of the Enterprise and Financial Sectors, The World Bank, April 1993, p. 16.

18. World Bank, Estonia. Informal Study of the Enterprise and Financial Sectors. World Bank. April 1993, p. 46.

19. World Bank, *Memorandum: Joint Mission* October 1992, p. 12.

20. World Bank, Estonia-Informal Study, 1993, p. 16. The open crisis began when UBB froze the accounts of government owned firms on November 6, 1992. See for further detail: Hansson, p. 11.

21. The Foreign Exchange Bank was hived off with four other banks from the Gosbank (State Bank) in the Former Soviet Union in 1987. See for more detailed information: Hansson, 1994, p. 6.

22. Hansson, 1994, p. 11.

23. Eesti Pank, Quarterly Review, 1993:1, p. 19. The claims of Tartu's creditors were ranke in the following order: deposits made for November 17, wage claims aof bank staff, deposits made before November 17, and capital. Hanssson, 1994, p. 12.

24. The BoE Board wanted to merge the two banks with no change in the ownership structure. The banks' depositors were to be given the alternative to either take a contingent claim on VEB deposits or a fixed discount in exchange for these deposits. The government objected to this proposal because it regarded the direct purchase of deposits as too costly for the budget, and the unchanged ownership structure as too favorable to bank owners. Hansson, p. 12. The solution presented by the IMF was also rejected as among other things as too costly. The IMF suggested to merge all three banks into a single unit, wipe out shareholders' equity and reduce all deposits by a common proportion.

25. The solution could go into effect after the Estonian parliament approved the creation of the VEB fund and the emission of government bonds on January 20, 1993.

26. Buyuske and Rhyne, 1993, p. 21. See for a detailed description of the restructuring mechanism: Hansson, 1994, p. 13. and *Euromoney*, "New Central Bank Leads the Way." June 1993, p. 164 f.

27. Buyuske and Rhyne, 1993, p. 21. But NESJB already reopened on Januray 25 with the support of a 87 million EEK liquidity loan extended from the BoE. On February 8, UBB was formally liquidated and integrated into NEJSB. Hansson, 1994, p. 14.

28. Since the Estonian banking system is a fragmented banking system, depositors at the three commercial banks were Estonian corporations. Private households hold their savings in the Savings Banks which are guaranteed by the government. See Estonia-Informal Study of the Enterprise and Financial Sector, World Bank 1993, p. 47, 51.

29. World Bank, Estonia-Informal Study, 1993, p. 47.

30. By April, liquidators of Tartu Bank were able to unfreeze 50% of deposits after the first auction had taken place. See Hansson, p. 12.

31. Hansson, 1994, p. 12.

32. World Bank. Estonia-Informal Study, 1993, p. 19.

33. Hansson, 1994, p. 13.

34. Hansson, 1994, p. 3.

35. In January 1993, the minimum capital requirement rose from 500,000 EEK (ca. US $ 40,000) to 6 million EEK (US $ 500,000) and in January 1994 to 15 million EEK (US-$ 1.2 million). Existing banks were given a year to reach this threshold. Hansson, 1994, p. 4.

36. The relatively small bank Revalia (53.1 million EEK of assets which is equal to 1.26% of all commercial bank assets) entered a court-managed liquidation proceeding, following its acute liquidity crisis which was brought on by non-performing loans to shareholders in March of 1993. See "Revalia Bank Declared Bankrupt", April 1994. Byske and Rhyne, 1993, p. 22. According to Hansson, another small bank has also been forced into bankruptcy without bailing out of depositors. Hansson, 1994, p. 1.

37. The prerequisites for obtaining a new banking lincense were the following: a bank had to had minimum capital of at least 6 million kroon, "its accounts must be in order," and it had "to meet basic requirements" of Estonia's central bank. Eesti Pank, 1993:1, p. 31. However, some question need to be raised about the success of this relicensing process. The central bank had to close down two banks relatively shortly after they had been regranted their licenses. Hansson, 1994, p. 1.

38. Eesti Pank, 1:1993, p. 32.

39. See Eesti Pank, 1993:3. p. 24-35.

40. Rules will be tightened further. The commercial bank law draft envisions a partial write down required after 30 and 60 days of non-payment and a complete write down following 90 days of delayed payment. See for further detail: Hansson, 1994, p. 3.

41. Numbers according to John Hanson, World Bank. The central bank showed some skepticism towards official numbers pointing out that "the data of the Estonian Statistics department cover just one part of the Estonian economy for the most part which is reducing production. A large part of the non-state sector, which is increasing its output, has not been documented at all." Eesti Pank: 1993:2, p. 11.

42. See for more detail: Hansson, Sachs, 1994, p. 19. See also, Eesti Pank, 1993:2, p. 12 f.

43. Numbers according to World Bank, ECA staff.

44. John Hanson, World Bank.

45. The fall in the deposit to reserve ratio is caused by a steep increase of banks' non-interest bearing excess reserve holdings. This is reflected in a sharp decline in the deposit to excess reserve ratio (see chart 4c).

46. The scale of assistance that the central bank can grant to weak banks is confined to its excess foreign exchange reserves. Bennett, 1993, p. 456.

47. The kroon was pegged to the Deutschmark at an exchange rate of eight to one. The Central Bank is not allowed to devalue the kroon (this right is given to the parliament). Hansson, 1994, p. 8.

48. Argentina experienced two financial crisis in the decade of the 1980s, in 1980 to 1982 and in 1989. During the 1980s, the financial sector was continously restructured: during 1981 to 1988, the Central Bank intervened in, liquidated or forcibly merged roughly 10% of all financial institutions of the banking system each year. 168 institutions were closed during that period of time. Numbers according to Giorgio and Sagari, 1992, p. 1.

49. World Bank, *Financial Sector Review*, 1989, p. 16.

50. This ratio fluctuated widely and had jumped to 95% in May of the same year. The central bank holdings of bank deposits arose from two sources: reserve requirements: first, conventional unremunerated and remunerated reserve requirements which vary with deposit levels and second, forced investments which do not vary with deposit levels. Unrenumerated reserves are set at 88.5% of demand deposits, remunerated reserve requirements are set at 25% of savings deposits and between 0 and 5% of time deposits, depending on maturity. Unrenumerated bank reserves were on average 14% of total deposits in 1989. In October 1989 forced deposits amounted to 42% of October 1989 deposits. The central bank paid approximately the average market deposit interest rate plus a spread (which was 1% in October 1989) on the forced the investments. The major difference between forced investments and reserve requirements was that forced investment balance would be unavailable to banks even when their deposit base declined, World Bank, Financial Sector Review, 1989, p. 6; World Bank, Argentina-From Insolvency to Growth, 1993, p. 180.

51. Numbers according to: Giorgio. Sagari, 1992, p. 8. In addition to reserve requirements and forced investment with the Central Bank, commercial bank voluntarily hold short-term paper and an assortment of government bonds. See for a detailed analysis of the condition of the banking system at the brink of the 1989 crisis: World Bank, Financial Sector Review, 1989.

52. Giorgio, Sagari, 1992, p. 20.

53. According to Beckerman in July 1989 domestic debt totalled US $ 7 billion. Assuming nonthly interest rates of 5% and monthly GDP running at US $ 5 to $ 6 billion, the monthly interest bill of US $ 350 million was 6 to 7% of monthly GDP. Beckerman, 1992, p. 22.

54. See for a detailed analysis of public distress cycle: Beckerman, 1992, p. 23. *The World Bank Financial Sector Review*, 1989, pp. 17 ff.

55. For a detailed analysis of causes and development of the "public debt distress" and the different stabilization plan aimed at solving this situation during the 1980s see Beckerman 1992 and Smith, 1992. For an analysis of the condition of the banking sector during the 1980s see: The World Bank. "Argentina's Banking Sector: The Need for Reform", 1986.

56. These action were implemented by the govenment as it became obvious that its "BB stabilization plan" had failed. This "BB plan" was put in place by the new Menem govenment which came into power in July 1989. It was aimed at curbing hyperinflation that had run since February. The measures of this plan included a sharp devaluation of the austral, a massive increase in public service prices, and agreement by the largest industrial enterprises to freeze output prices as long as public service prices remained unchanged and the commitment for a tight monetary policy in order to hold the paralled and official exchange rates equal and fixed. Initially the plan worked with inflation failing to single-digit monthly rates and falling interest rates. But in mid-October, the austral started to move downward in the parallel market inducing expectation of further devaluations which in turn led to bank deposit withdrawals and rising interest rates. For more detail see Beckerman, 1992, p. 1ff and Smith, 1992, pp. 42-44.

57. Miller, 1993, p. 478. The occurrence of a bank holiday was not unsual to the Argentine public. According to Giorgio and Sagari, there had been 8 bank holidays in the first half of 1989. Giorgio and Sagari, 1992, p. 18.

58. Beckermann, 1992, p. 24 and Giorgio and Sagari, 1992, p. 20. The accounting exchange rate was A$ 1,800 per Dollar.

59. Beckermann, 1992, p. 2, 24.

60. 35.76% of loans to their largest clients of national public banks and 51.42% of loans of provincial and municipal banks were of doubtful status compared with less then 5% for all categories of private banks as of December 1992. But this ratio of doubful loans to total loans to the largest clients improved for public banks over the next year and was recorded at 17.8% for national public banks, 48.4% for state and municipal public banks, and 5.4% for private banks at the end of 1993. Numbers According to: Central Bank of Argentina. *Indicadores del Sistema Financiero*, Several Issue. Nevertheless, the publicly-owned housing and development banks which were long subject to political influence and dependent on government financial support are undergoing major restructuring. See The World Bank. "Argentina: From Insolvency to Growth." Washington 1993, p. 20. Public banks lent priamrily to provincial governements and public enterpirces and to a lesser extent they provided subsidized credits to favored priate firms. The high non-performing loan to loan ratio resulted from a lack of commercial considerations and government interventions in public banks' lending decisions. World Bank, "Argentina: Capital Market Study," June 1994, p. 3.

61. World Bank, Junuary 1993, p. 68. The assumption that an implicit deposit insurance scheme exists for public banks was vindicated when La Rioja, a state provincial bank failed and the government assumed the liabilities of the bank. World Bank, *Argentina: Capital Market Study*, June 1994, p. 9.

62. Public banks include national, provincial, and municipal public banks which are categorized as public commercial banks. Not included in this ratio are savings banks and savings and loans institutions. Private commercial banks accounted for 54.7% of all financial system deposits and 35.7% of all finacial system assests at the end of 1991. Numbers computed according to Central Bank of Argentina. Estado de las Entidades Finacieras del 31 Deciembre de 1991. Marzo de 1992.

63. But in 1982, the government limited depositors' losses by retroactively increasing the size of deposits being covered under the scheme and larger deposits were still covered up to 90%. However, the government did not bail out foreign currency deposit holder. See for an extensive discussion: Thomas Balino. "The Argentine Banking Crisis of the 1980" In V. Sundararajan. Thomas Balino. *Banking Crisis: Cases and Issues*. International Monetary Fund, 1991, pp. 58-112.

64. But partly because of policy uncertainties and exemptions given by the government on deposit-conversion to withdrawasls of up to A$ 500,000, senior citizen and deposits for wage and tax payments, slightly more than half of deposits was still available to depositors at the end of December 1989. Giorgio. Sagari, 1992, p. 20.

65. Giorgio and Sagari, 1992, p. 20.

66. The World Bank, *Argentina: Rebuild Capital Markets*, April 1994, p. iii.

67. In January and February 1990, the exchage rate and the price level remained extremly volatile, rising at average levels of 70 to 80%. It settled down in early March when the government announced substantial fiscal measures and after a month during which the central bank had pursued an extremely tight monetary policy. Beckermann, 1992, p. 25.

68. World Bank, *Argentina: From Insolvency to Growth*, 1993, p. 330.

69. Miller, 1993, p. 478.

70. Especially the public banks enjoyed this subsidy since they received approximately 78.5% of the rediscounts granted by the central bank. World Bank, *Argentina-From Insolvency to Growth*, 1993, p. 226.

71. Over the first two months of 1990, the exchange rate and the price level remained extremely volatile, rising at average monthly rates of 70 to 80%. In March 1990, after the announcement fo substantial fiscal measures, the inflation rate eased to about 10 to 15%. Beckerman, 1992, p. 25.

72. The inflation rate measured by the consumer price index fell from 3.9% in 1984 to 0.3% in 1985. Numbers according to Sheng, 1992a, p. 6.

73. Beginning in the second half of 1985, world wide commodity prices dropped sharply. E. g. crude oil fell 62% from their peak and oil prices fell 57%. Sheng, 1992a, p. 7.

74. These rumors were prompted by the failure of Overseas Trust Bank in Hongkong on June 6, 1985. With assets of 5.4 billion MS as of June 30, 1984, the Public Bank held 8.6% of all banking system assets. The collapse of Overseas Trust Bank caused also repercussion in the management of the seventh larges commercial bank, the "Perwira Habib Bank", which sacked its top executives. See for a more detailed account: *Far Eastern Econonomic Review*, 20 June 1985, p. 10. Ebid. *The Rot Spreads Further*, 27 June 1985, pp. 88-89.

75. Sheng, 1992a, p. 13.

76. Sheng, 1992a, p. 13. *Far Eastern Economic Review*, December 19 and 226 1985.

77. Numbers according to Sheng, 1992b, p. 231.

78. Commercial banks had expanded their loans in the property sector from 26% in 1980 to 36% in 1986 and incurred heavy losses form falling property prices. Vittas, 1992, p. 16. Numbers according to Sheng. 1992b, pp: 224. 231.

79. The 32 DTCs under investigation or by supervision of the Central Bank accounted for M$ 3.1 billion in deposits (and estimated 77% of the total deposits of all 38 of Malaysia's and Sabah's DTCs) by the end of 1987 or 3.4% of total system deposits). Numbers according to Sheng, 1992a, p. 17 and World Bankd, BESD Data Set. The investigations of the central bank later came to the conclusion that the DTCs "were heavily mismanaged and undercapitalized, with overcommitments in long-term and speculative assets, such as land and shares." Bank Negara, 1988, p. 45.

80. The 33 illegal DTIs involved 8,000 depositors and M$ 46 million of deposits accounting for 0.05% of total system deposits at the end of 1986. Source for basic numbers: Sheng, 1992b, p. 231 and World Bank, BESD data base.

81. Total deposits comprised commercial banks and finance companies as well as DTCs. Numbers according to Sheng, 1992b, p. 232.

82. Sheng, 1992b, pp. 195-237, p. 213. According to the Far Eastern Economist, Kosatu was among the ten largest credit cooperatives, with 72 branches and 14,000 members. The central bank stepped in when post-dated cheques issued to depositors were dishonored and it had become clear that Kosatu was in danger of imminent failure. Far Eastern Review, Cooperatives Purged, 21 August 1985, p. 50-51.

83. One of the 23 credit cooperatives which was later suspended lost 200 million MS from July 23 until August 8, 1985. *Far Eastern Economic Review*, 21 August 1985, p. 50.

84. Sheng, 1992a, p. 1.

85. According to the Far Eastern Economic Review, Malaysia's 35 Deposit Taking Institutions had deposits of over 4 billion MS. 19 of them were taking deposits without the required prior authorization from the Registrar-General of Cooperatives. *Far Eastern Review, the Entagled Web of Deposit Cooperatives*, 1 April 1987, p. 22.

86. The Central Cooperative Bank was one of three cooperative banks which worked as a kind of central bank for the deposit taking cooperatives. As such, the Central Cooperative Bank was allowed to accept deposits from individuals and companes. Upt ot the cental bank intervention, it was supervised by the central bank, but by the Cooperative Development Department in the National and rural Development Ministry. *Far Eastern Review, Cooperative Efforts*, 1 October 1987, p.

87. Numbers according to: *Far Eastern Economic Review*, "The 50:50 Solution," 2 October 1986, p. 225 and World Bank, BESD Data Base. *Far Eastern Review,* 21 August 1986, p. 59. According to the Far Eastern Review, the central bank was criticized from the opposition parties for not reacting faster to the heavey and sustained deposit withdrawal that the cooperatives were facing. The timing, however, might have been, as they specualte, dictated by the general elections

which were called by the prime Minister on July 18 to be held on August 3, 1986. "At least a quarter of the suspended DTCs were closely linked with the Malaysian Chinese Association (MCA), the second largest party in the ruling National Front." *The Far Eastern Review*, "The Tangled Web of Deposit Taking Cooperatives," April , 1987, p. 23. Ibid, Get on Your Mark, 31 July, 1986, p. 8-9.

88. The passing of the "Essential Regulations" in July 1986 allowed the central bank to intervene in the DTCs and DTIs and restructure them. See for a copy of the "Essential Regulations". Bank Negara Malaysia, Annual Report 1986. Kuala Lumpur 1987. See for a more detailed analysis: Sheng, 1992b, p. 221. See for a detailed description of the rescue effort of the DTCs: Bank Negara Malaysia, *Annual Report 1987*. Kuala Lumpur 1988, pp. 43-50.

89. Far Eastern Economic Review, 20 November 1986, p. 103. The restructuring mechanism outlined in the "White Paper" was partially based on recommendations made by the "Action Committe on Cooperatives" which was appointed by the government to draft a restructuring plan. The committee was chaired by the central bank and consisted further of representatives from the government and the private sector. See for further detail: Sheng, 1992b, p. 225.

90. Sheng, 1991a, p. 27. These 11 DTC's had asset backing averaging 95M cents for each dollar and accounted for 15% of total frozen DTC deposits. *Far Eastern Review*, "Cooperative Venture," 25 June, 1987, p. 58.

91. *Far Eastern Economic Review*, "Cooperative Restructuring," 11 February 1988, p. 52.

92. During the restructuring process, the three or four proposals on the future of KSM were submitted to the receivers. This interest was largely attributed to KSM's controlling 30% stake in the conglomerate Multi Purpose Holdings. See for Details: Far Eastern Review, Cooperative Venture, 25 June 1987, p. 58.

93. These 12 cooperatives held 47.4% of the frozen deposits and had asset backings from 10 to 69 cents on MS. *Far Eastern Review*, 16 July 18, p. 58.

94. Sheng, 1992a, p. 28. Furthermore, the government also decided to change the cooperative laws to limit cooperatives to take only specific deposits from their members, not savings and fixed deposits. Sheng, 1992b. p. 226. They were furthermore barred from accepting non-member deposits.

95. Sheng, 1992b, p. 227. It is difficult to estimate the total losses depositors incurred through foregone interest since their are no numbers available on when the acquiring bank or finance company completed the repayments. Interest rates on fixed deposits (1-12 months) were between 6% to 7% and on savings deposits 6%. They dropped singificantly to 2 to 4.25% for fixed term deposits and 3% form savings deposits in 1987. (Mode values) Central Bank, *Statistical Monthy Bulletin*, several issues.

96. *Far Eastern Review*. "New Year's Resolution," 29 January 1987, p. 129.

97. This scheme represents a signifant modification from the original "White Paper" which had earmarked two DTCs for liquidation and according to Sheng stated "as a matter of principle, the public would not be responsible for the large losses arising from bad management and depositors would be able to receive the amount of their asset backing of their respective DTC." Sheng, 1992a, p. 26.

98. *Far Eastern Economic Review*, "Cooperative Rstructuring." 11 February 1988, p. 52.

99. Depositors received a partial refund in February 1988, 18 months after their deposits were frozen. *Far Easten Review*, 11 February 1988, p. 52.

100. *Far Eastern Economic Review*, 11 February 1988, p. 52. Sheng, 1992a, pp. 26-28.

101. *Asian Wall Street Journal*, January 18, 1988. Sheng, 1992b, p. 214. The depositors of the CCB were uninsured.

102. According to Sheng, these banks has an average capital to asset ratio of 2.8% at the end of 1986. Compare Sheng, 1992a, Key Data on Ailing Commercial Banks, p. 24. Also, the *Far Eastern Economic Review* and *The Asian Wall Street Journal* do not mention that these banks were insolvent at the time of the intervention.

103. Contemporary sources do not clarify the point whether the commercial banks were insolvent at the time of their recapitalization or not.

104. Sheng, 1992b, p. 224.

105. Sheng, 1992b, p. 220. It is further important to point out that the central bank introduced uniform guidelines in the height of the recession in 1985 for financial institutions on the treatment of non-accrued income or interest-in-suspense which forced these institutions to immediately acknowledge their losses. Sheng, 1992a, p. 14. But this measure was watered down in July 1986 when the central bank decided to leave it to "the discretion of a bank's board of directors to decide when a loan had become un-performing and therefore, when to suspend the inclusion of interest as income. Far Eastern Economic Review, 31 July 1986, p. 66. In addition, the 1985 amendments to the banking legislation had included limits and the imposition of penalties on bank staff who exceed their authorized lending limits, and the powers given to the cental bank to lend or to purchase equity in financial institution in distress. See for a list of 1985 changes in the banking law: Bank Negara Malaysia, *Annual Report 1986*. Kuala Lumpur 1986, pp. 40f. See for a enumeration of 1986 changes: Bank Negara Malaysia, 1986, p. 42.

106. Sheng, 1992a, p. 21.

107. See for a moe detailed account: Sheng, 1992b, p. 225 ff.

108. But the MCA's close association with several of the insolvent DTCs made it vulnerable to protests from disenchanged depositors. As the Far Eastern Review reports," A riot nearly ensued on 16 November when MCA delegates attacked a group of some 50 depositors and two DPA MPs who were picketing the headquarters of the MCA on te morning of the party' general assembly." *Far Eastern Review*, 27 November 1987, p. 75.

109. *Far Eastern Review, Depositors Strike Back*, 27 November 1986, p. 75. Ebid, New Year's Resolution, 29 January 1987, p. 48.

110. GDP figures according to Sheng, 1992a, p. 6

111. Figures according to Sheng, 1992b, p. 196.

112. The Central bank had lowered statutory reserve requirements from 5 to 4% and to 3.5% of total eligible liabilities (April 15, 1985. Bank Negara, Annual Report 1985, p. 77) and liquidity requirements for commercial banks were reduced from 20% to 18.5% of total eligible liabilities in February 1986 and further reduced to 17% in October 1986. Central Bank of Negara, *Annual Report 1986*, p. 34. See also: *Far Eastern Review: Offering Light Relief*, 30 October 1986, p. 53. It is further important to note that the central bank was proscribed by law from acting as a lender of last resort for the DTIs and DTCs. Sheng, 1992a, p. 20.

113. Compare Bank Negara. *Annual Report 1986*, p. 43.

114. The Japan Development Bank. *The Japan Economic Research Institute*, 1994, p. 123.

115. Fuji Bank, 1961, p. 191. On November 24, 1945, the Allied forces had sent an order to the Japanese government to discontinue payments "upon any claim arising from the production or supply of war materials, from war damage or from the construction or conversion of war plants" except into blocked account supervised by the Allies. See for further detail: Adams, 1964, p. 177. Quotes cited after cid. Adams, 1964, p. 180. According to Tsutsui, with the cancellation of war indemnity payments the Supreme Command of the Allied Froces wanted to "break the financial bonds of war years" and "allow banking and industry to organize on a peacetime basis." Tsutsui, 1988, p. 25. The Supreme command and the Japanese government later agreed that the payments could be nominally made by the Japanese "to preserve the facade of good faith". Furthermoe, centain private sector creditors were exempted from the tax, creating a loophole which eventually allowed for the disbursement of 18 billion Yen in payments. See Tsutsui, 1988, p. 29. The discontinuation of war indemnity payments was passed into law in October 1946. Teranashi, 1991b, p. 23.

116. Hoshi, Kashyap, Loveman, 1994, p. 20.

117. Hoshi, 1994, p. 1.

118. In addition to that, the balance sheets of financial institutions carried loans and securities from outside Japan had to be condidered mostly uncollectible. Tsuitsui, 1988, p. 23.

119. See for further detail: Hoshi, 1994, p. 25.

120. Hoshi, 1994, p. 24. The Ministry of Finance. *The Financial History of Japan: The Allied Occupation Period 1945-1952.* Volume 13: Finance (2), Tokyo, 1983, p. 303. In August 1946, total banking system deposits amounted to 139.8 billion Yen. Numbers according to: Statisitcs Bureau of Prime Minister's Office and the Executive Office of the Statistics Commission, 1949, p. 554.

121. Hoshi, 1994, p. 4. In July 1946, 86% of bank deposits were frozen.

122. These new deposits were used by major banks to reduce their debt ot the Bank of Japan. See for further detail: Tsutsui, 1988, p. 28 ff. Adams, 1964, p. 178.

123. The frozen deposits were separated into first and second line frozen deposits according to the following rules: all individual deposits under 3,000 Yen were assigned to first line frozen deposits. Deposit account holders exceeding 3,000 Yen could decide whether they wanted to transfer 15,000 Yen for one household with each financial institution or 4,000 Yen for each household member up to a totoal of 32,000 Yen into first line frozen deposits. Corporations' and other bodies' deposits of up to 15,000 Yen were moved into first line frozen deposits. The remaining rest of the deposit became second line frozen deposits and therefore at risk of being cancelled out against losses. The second line frozen deposits further included 'special deposits' which included indemnity payments (wartime insurance payments, payments for the wartime liquidation of enterprises and payments for military supplies) already made by the Japanese government. Fuji Bnk, 1961, p. 191 f.

124. After the separation of the old and new account, 18% of all deposits in banks were free deposits, 42.3% were first line frozen deposits, 13% second line frozen deposits and 26% were special blocked deposits. In the aggregate, 67 billion Yen were put in the old accounts and 73 billion were put in the new account. But depositors were allowed to use their second line frozen deposits to pay some taxes and to pay back the bank loans that were collateralized by second line frozen deposits. Furthermore, the government started a savings campaign in November 1946, and among other measures, allowed depositors to open time deposit accounts to which they could partly transfer their old account deposits. Consequently, second line frozen deposits fell from 67 billion Yen in August to 14 billion in December 1947. Executive Office. Japan-Statistical Yearbook. Nihon Statistics Association, 1952, p. 554. Adams, 1964, p. 185. As Hoshi (1994) points out, the portion of deposits which were put in the old account could differ among the financial institutions. Yasuda Bank transferred 52.7% of its deposits into the old account, Mitsubishi 60%, Sumitomo 76%, and Mitsui Bank 83%. According to Hoshi "this probably reflects the high proportion of corporate deposits". Hosi, 1994, p. 25.

125. See Table 1, Hoshi 1994, p. 41.

126. Tsutsui, 1988, p. 31.

127. Hoshi, Kasyap, Loveman, 1994, p. 10.

128. According to Hoshi, the government initially wanted to take a three step approach: At first, industrial firms would give their estimate of losses due to the repudiation of wartime compensation to their creditors. The second step would then include the restructuring of financial institutions' balance sheet based on the estimates provided by the industrial firms. And finally, the industrial firms would reestimates their losses, using the information on deposit recoveries supplied by financial institutions and other industrial firms. But since anti-trust emasures deferred the reorganization of the industrial fims and the Allied Supreme Command and the Japanese government considered the speedy reorganization of the financial system as paramout, the banks marked down to market their balance sheet items without the firms' loss estimates. See Hoshi, 1994, for further detail. Hoshi, 1994, p. 5 and 6.

129. Hoshi, 1994, p. 7

130. The delay in the approval was caused by Supreme Command of the Allied Forces which had ordered the Japanese government to assign bank debentures to the old account and not as

originally envisioned by the Japanese government to the new account. Thus, the financial institutions had to resubmit their restructuring plans which were retroactively approved as of March 31, 1948. Hoshi, 1994, p. 8, 22.

131. Fuji Bank, 1961, p. 197.

132. Hoshi, 1994, p. 8.

133. According to Hoshi, just one ordinary bank needed government assistance. Main receivers of government help were agricultural banks and insurance companies. Hoshi, 1994, p. 9

134. According to Teranashi, 1991c, the Japanese government had relaxed limitations on deposit withdrawals before the point in time. Teranashi, 1991c, p. 27.

135. Creditors which had suffered losses during the restructuring period enjoyed the first priority to buy "a certain (what is that dependent from) amount of shares at par value". Then priority was given to the following groups in declining order: former shareholders, former employees of the institutions, local residents and the general public. Hoshi, 1994, p. 9

136. According to Hoshi, the main reason for this positive outcome can be found in "fortunate stock market condition". After the long closing of the stock market after the war, "people were eagerly waiting for the reopening of the Tokyo Stock Exchange." Hoshi, 1994, p. 9.

137. This was a change in policy compared to the government policy in the banking crisis in 1927. In the banking crisis of 1927, banks received extensive rescue credit by the Bank of Japan and according to Teranashi "it is believed that one reason for the severity of the financial crisis in 1927 was increased risk-taking by banks that were rescued in 1920 and 1922 and who were again anticipating rescue credits." Teranashi, 1991a, p. 329.

138. Numbers according to Ministry of Finance (1983), pp. 303f.

139. Technically, banks created "reconciliation accounts" that where higher than expected returns from loans to munition companies were registered. In July 1948, the Japanese parliament passed the "Financial Institution Reconstruction and Reorganization Act" which stipulated that the profits of the "reconciliation account" should be returned to creditors whose claims were wiped out through the reorganization process. But before the creditors could be repaid, the government compensation was to be paid back including interest. Since the firms' reorganization took a very long time, final estimates of the "reconciliation account" were completed as late as in 1959. In the end, only one out of all 64 banks failed to pay back all cancelled deposits and five reimbursed interest on the cancelled deposits. For a more detail account see: Hoshi, 1994, pp. 10ff.

140. The Japanese government implemented interest rate regulations effective from Dec. 1947 which impose an interest rate cap on deposits and short-term loans. The interest rate on deposits was linked to the official discount rate and had further be approved of the "Interest Adjustment Council". Since these caps were much lower than the inflation rate, depositors incurred heavy real losses. (For example, the annual consumer price inflation rate was 82.7% in 1948 whereas the official discount rate was set at 5.11% for the same period. (see Table)) See for details: The Japan Development Bank, *The Japan Development Institute*, 1994, p. 109.

141. Ministry of Finance, 1983, p. 303f.

142. Hoshi, Kashyap, Loveman, 1994, p. 8.

143. The wholesale price inflation rate was recorded at 364% and 195% for 1946 and 1947 respectively. The inflation rate for consumer goods ran at 115% in 1947. Numbers according to: The Bank of Japan. *Hundred Year Statistics of the Japanese Economy*, Tokyo 1966, p. 77, 81.

144. The Reconversion Finance Law was passed in October 1946. Its was supposed to provide funds required for economic reconstruction and to mitigate the blow to the economy due to the cancellation of war indemnity payments. Until the Reconstruction Finance Banks started its operation, the Industrial Bank acted on its behalf and advanced 4 billion to the private sector. The coal industry absorbed 40% of these credits and the fertilizer industry was the next main recipient. Adams, 1964, p. 183.

145. Fuji Bank, 1961, p. 193.

146. In the more than two years of its existence, the RFB provided 74% of the funds for capital investment. For the major industries mentioned, it provided 84% of capital investment funds and 16% of the total working capital. See for further detail: World Bank, 1994, p. 127 f.

147. Since the financing of the RFB ended in an increase in notes issue, the RFB contributed considerable to the accelerating inflation. Originally, the funds of the RFB were to be supplied by the government. In the end, most of the funds were raised by Reconversion Finance Bonds of which the most part 69% were eventually taken over by the Bank of Japan which monetized them. Adams, 1964, p. 184.

148. In February 1946, financial system deposits were frozen. Deposit withdrawals were limited to living expenses. The deposit freeze was followed by a partial currency conversion which force money backed into the system since notes in circulation above 5 Yen ceased to be legal tender.

149. Numbers according to Friedman & Schwartz, 1971, p. 438.

150. Board of Governor, 1943, p. 16.

151. Friedman, Schwartz, 1963, p. 308, 309. In November and December, 608 banks failed with US$ 550 million in deposits, among them the Bank of the United States with US $ 200 million in deposits, the largest commercial bank (by deposit size) ever to have failed. Banks in rural areas where persistent problems in the agricultural sector left them with poorly performing loan portfolios were particularly adversely effected. Conditions in the agricultural sector were futher worsened by the passage of the Smoot-Hawley tariff in June 1930 which led to a sharp decline in the demand for agricultural exports. See for further detail on the banking crisis in 1930: White, March 1984, p. 119-138, p. 126.

152. There are conflicting hypothesis about the causes of the crisis in 1930. Whereas Friedmand and Schwartz (1963) cite monetary factors as the primary culprit, Temin (1976) views the declining economy as the main reason for the increase in the bank failure rate. Friedman and Schwartz state that the loss in confidence spreading from the failure of the bank of the United States is the decisive factor behind the increased failure rate of banks. They blame the Federal Reserve for not stemming the contraction of the money stock by providing adequate high powered money to the system. According to Temin, the origins of the banking crisis lay in the real sector and were not caused by monetary disturbances. White, 1984, in his analysis of the competing interpretation comes to the conclusion that real and monetary factors caused the increase in the bank failre rate: "The weakening of assets and the lack of easy credit put the squeeze on all banks, and many weak ones were doomed." White, 1984, p. 137. He further points to federal and state regulations as a contributing factor to the crisis. These regulations restricted branch banking and thus created small unit banks with relatively undiversified loan portfolios. White, 1984, p. 119 ff. Temin, 1976, pp. 106 ff.

153. As a consequence of a yearlong standstill agreement among commercial banks not to press for repayment of short-term international credit, a large amount of US commercial bank short term obligations were frozen. Futhermore, the commercial bank depositors became more and more uneasy about the failure of world famous institutions. Friedman & Schwartz, 1963, p. 314.

154. From mid-September to the end of October, the gold stock declined by US $ 725 million-its average 1929 level. According to Friedman and Schwartz, this added pressure on banks because the Federal Reserve did not offset the effect of external gold drain on high-powered money with open market purchases. Friedman, Schwartz, 1917, p 315 f. See also: Eichengreen, 1992, p. 293f.

155. Friedman, Schwartz, 1971, p. 317.

156. See for a more detailed account: Friedman & Schwartz, 1971, pp.

157. In 1931, 2,293 banks out of an 20,940 suspended operations. Friedman & Schwartz, 1971, p. 438. Source for number of banks: Board of Governors of the Federal Reserve, System. 1943, p. 16.

158. For a more detailed account of the legislation considered before Congress see: Burns, 1986.

159. Friedman & Schwartz, 1971, p. 322. According to Eichengreen, 1992, although these open market purchases relieved some pressure from the system, they failed to stabilize industrial production because they were anticipated by the business community to be only temporary and did not signal a sustained increase in demand and a permanent improvement in business conditions." Eichengreen, 1992, p. 315.

160. The incoming Roosevelt administration was perceived by the public as leaning towards a devaluation of the dollar in order to restore U.S. prices to pre-Depression levels. American in the position to obtain gold or foreign currency and foreigners started to liquidate their dollar assets in order to avoid capital losses. See for further detail: Eichengreen, 1992, p. 323. The growing insolvency problem in the US banking system in 1933 is generally credited to the cumulative affects of mounting economic and financial difficulties. The bank capital positions were weakened by falling bond prices and a rising rate of loan default. Futhermore, in late 1932, Congress critical of the RFC tendency to aid large banks forced the RFC to release information on its lending activities. This led to unease in the public which started to withdraw its funds from the banking system. The Federal Reserve did not counterbalance the loss of reserves banks were facing with open market operations. Therefore, Friedman & Schwartz blame the Federal Reserve for a not more vigourous pursuit of open market operations to ease bank liquidity problems and prevent further bank failures. Friedman & Schwartz, 1963, p. 332ff. For further discussion on the 1933 banking crisis see Kennedy, 1973 and Temin, 1976. For a survey of the literature on the importance of monetary and real sector issues in causing the Great Depression see Calomiris, 1992.

161. On February 11, 1933, a Bank Holiday is declared in Louisana, On Febrary 14, in Michigan, on February 27, in Maryland. American Banker, Several Issues, February 1933. In Februrary. Congress freed national banks from penalties of restructing or deferring withdrawals according to the terms of holidays in the state. Friedman, Schwartz, 1963, p. 324. By March 3, held of the states had implented bank holidays.

162. Friedman, Schwartz, 1963, Table 13, p. 423. Numbers seasonally adjusted. Among the banks not allowed to reopen were 14 of the nations 200 largest banks. *American Banker*, March 20, 1933.

163. Friedman & Schwartz, 1963, . 424. According to Friedman and Schwartz, not seasonally adjusted commercial bank deposits amounted to US $31.4 billion. In Dec. 1932, 6,816 member banks held 79.8% of total commecial bank deposits. The 10,986 non-member banks accounted for 20.2% of commercial bank system deposits. Numbers according to: Federal Reserve Board, 1943, p. 20ff.

164. Number according to Friedman & Schwartz, 1963, p. 423.

165. Comptroller of the Currency, Report, Washington 1934, p. 1.

166. Calculated from Friedman, Schwartz, 1971, p. 427 in conjunction with table 13, p. 423, and Table 13, p. 423.

167. *Federal Reserve Bulletin*, March 1933, p. 119.

168. Encouraged for 18 months to operate with instrinsically impaired capital position, they (banks) found the Federal and State authorities insisting that they take their losses and then open only if there was anything left." American Banker, March 15, 1933, p. 1. According to Upham & Lamke, although there was "tremendous pressure upon the authorities to get the banks open, and the relatively short time in which it was one, some error of judgement were to be expected (..) only a few banks were relicensed which were in an unsound condition." 221 relicensed banks suspended operations until December 1933, 15 national and state member banks and 206 non-member banks, indicating that state supervisors were laxer in relicensing procedure. The low failure rates of relicensed banks must also be judged in the context of RFC's capital injections. Upham & Lamke, 1934, p. 49.

169. All in all, a conservator was appointed for 1,088 of the 1417 unlicensed national banks which were assumed to be solvent but undercapitalized. For more details on concervators see Upham and Lamke, 1934, p. 49. The conservator had powers which were similar to a receiver.

According to the American Banker" the real difference between a conservator and a receiver is that by the new law a great deal of red tape is done away with, and the conservator can make available good assets quickly for depositors, and has more power in proceeding with plans to reorganize the bank. American Banker, March 15, 1933, p. 3

170. Board of Governors of the Federal Reserve Board, *Annual Report 1933*, Washington 1934, p. 2, 23.

171. Emergency Banking Act, Title II, Sect. 207. Reprinted in: Board of Governors of the Federal Reserve System, *Federal Reserve Bulletin*, March 1933, p. 116.

172. Emergency Banking Act: Title II, Section 207, reprinted in: Board of Governor of the Federal Reserve Board, Federal Reserve Bulletin, Marh 1933, p. 116. Those were payable on demand, bore on interest and were designed to provide depository services which otherwise would have been unavailable. See Upham & Lamke, 1934, p. 51.

173. Board of Governors, Federal Reserve Bulletin, March 1933, p. 119.

174. The dictator law give the state banking commissioner dictorial power in emergencies, with his acts subject only to review by the governor. The ultimate power is thus resting with the state's chief executive. American Banker, March 22, 1933, p. 1. Upham and Lake, 1934, p. 50. See for example: "Comstock (Governor of Michigan) to reopen Non-Member Banks, Uses Dictator's Powers to Open State Financial Institutions". *American Banker,* March 23, 1933, p. 1. "New Banking Laws Extend Powers of Utah Commissioner", *American Banker*, April 4, 1933, p. 1. *"Tennessee Bill Allows* Conservator Method of Savings Its State Banks". *American Banker*, April 12 1933, p. 1. "Would Change Florida Banking Laws to Paralell National", *American Bankers,* April 18, 1933.

175. This was permitted by section 304 of the Emergency Banking Act. Board of Governors, Federal Reserve Bulletin, March 1933, p. 117. In some states, state banks were not eligible for a RFC purchase of preferred stock. Therefore some state banking laws were changed to enable state banks to comply with federal provisions. *American Banker,* March 30, 1933.

176. Prior to that time, the equity issues of national banks and most state banks were subjet, to double liability. See Macey and Miller, 1991.

177. Friedman, Schwartz, 1963, p. 427-428. See for an analysis of the political economy of the RFC's actions: Krozner, 1994.

178. Friedman, Schwartz, 1963, p. 427, footnote 4. See for a detailed account on the RFC: Upham & Lamke, 1934, p. 125 ff. Jone, 1951. Olson, 1980, Todd, 1992.

179. Friedman & Schwartz, 1963, p. 438, p. 438. We have not been able to find statistics on losses at banks were closed until the Bank Holiday of March.

180. These loans were secured by the best assets of those institutions. Friedman, Schwartz, 1963, p. 427-428.

181. *Federal Reserve Bulletin*, September 1937, p. 897. Total capital accounts of all banks in the US amounted to 7.4 billion in 1933 according to all Banks Statistics, Washington 1959, p. 53.

182. On March 10, 1933, an executive order extended the prohibition for banks to make gold payments or deal in foreign exchange which came into effect with the declaration of the Bank Holiday. Friedman, Schwartz, 1963, p. 462.

183. The expiration date was later set as January 17, 1934. Friedman & Schwartz, 1963, p. 463 ff.

184. See Emergency Banking Act, section 407, reprinted in: Board of Governor of the Federal Reserve System, March 1933, p. 118; Board of Governor of the Federal Reserve System, 1934, p. 38.

185. Emergency Banking Act, Title IV, Section 401. The passage of the Robinson-Steagall made non-member state banks eligible for this new currency on March 23, 1933. *American Banker*, March 25, 1933, p. 1.

186. The cause for July's sharp decline is not clear. Some observes have argued that it was caused by unfulfilled expectations of a more expansionary monetary policy.

187. Eichengreen, 1992, p. 342. According to Eichengreen, the recovery of the American output "was not more sustained because the stimulus lent by policy was so limited." The Fed did not increase the money supply with extensive open marken purchases and the foreign demand for US exports recovered significantly. In his view "output recovered strongly in the immediate aftermath of the suspension of convertibility, reflecting investors' hopes that a comprehensive package of expansionary measures would be adopted. It fell back subsequently when it became apparent that American's departure from the gold standard had not inaugurated a new area of monetary expansion. Eichengreen, 1992. p. 344.

188. American Banker, March 25, 1933, p. 3. According to bankers' accounts, this return in currency was largely in the form of vault cash. Since the dollar devaluation did not follow immediately after the banking crisis but in mid-April, there was speculation that american capital had fled the system in the interim period despite foreign exchange restrictions. See; "How much capital took flight?", *American Banker*, April 27, 1933.

189. However, since the dollar devaluation had not yet taken place and foreign exchange restriction on the purchase of gold were in place, the opportunity cost of holding currency increased.

190. According to Friedman, Schwartz, the Federal Reserve System employed the Federal Reserve credit outstanding as a tool to sterilize gold movement and to prevent erratic short term changes in high powered money. Friedman, Schwartz, 1963, p. 504.

191. At the beginning of 1934, high powered-money started to increase remarkedly. According to Friedman & Schwartz this increase in high-powered money can largely be attributed to treasury purchases of gold. They proved expansionary to the quantity of high-powered money because the treasury paid for them by printing gold certificates and either adding them to its cash balances or depositing them at one of the Federal Reserve Banks. See Friedman, Schwartz, 1971, p. 506.

REFERENCES

Adams, T. M. *A Financial History of Modern Japan*. Tokyo 1964.

Baer, H. and John N. McElravey. "Capital Shocks and Bank Growth-1973-1991. In *Federal Reserve Bank of Chicago Economic Perspectives* 1993.

Bernanke, B. "Nonmonetary Effects of the Financial Crisis in the Propagation of the Great Depression." *American Economic Review*, 1983, 73, 257-276.

The Bank of Japan, Statistics Department. *A Hundred Years of Statistics of the Japanese Economy*, July 1966.

Balino, Thomas. "The Argentine Banking Crisis of the 1980." In V. Sundararagan. Thomas Balino (Eds.), *Banking Crisis: Cases and Issues*. International Monetary Fund, 1991, pp. 58-112.

Beckerman, Paul. "Public Sector Debt Distress in Argentina, 1988-1989". World Bank. Policy Research Working Paper No. 902, May 1992.

Bennett, Adam. "The Operation of Estonia's Currency Board," IMF Staff Paper 40, no. 2, June, pp. 451-470.

Board of Governors of the Federal Reserve System. *Banking and Monetry Statistics*, Washington 1943.

Burns, Helen M. *The Banking Community of New Deal Banking Reforms*, 1933-1935, University Press of Kenntucky 1973.

Buyuske, Gail and Elisabeth Rhyne. "Estomia's Emerging Financial System: Progress and Prospects," August 1993.

Calomiris, Charles. "Regulation, Industrial Structure, and Instability in U.S. Banking." In Michael Klausner and Lawrence J. White (Eds.). *Structural Change in Banking*. Homewood, IL: Business One Irwin (1993).

Calomiris, Charles W. "Did Monetary Factors Caused the Great Depression, Draft, " July 1992.

Calomiris, Charles and W. Gary Gorton. "The Origins of Bank Panics." in Glenn Hubbard (Ed.) *Financial Markets and Financial Crisis* Chicago: University of Chicago Press (1991).

Calomiris, Charles W. and Charles M. Kahn. "The Role of Demandable Debt in Structuring Optimal Banking Arrangements." *The American Economic Review*, June 1991, pp. 497-513.

Eichengreen, Barry J. *Golden Fetters. The Gold Standard and the Great Depression.* New York: Oxford, 1992.

Euromoney, "New Central Bank Leads the Way," June 1993.

The Financial History of Japan: The Allied Occupation Period, 1945-1952. Volume 13: Finance (2), Tokyo, 1983.

Friedman, Milton and Anna Schwartz. *A Monetary History of the United States, 1867-1960.* Princeton, University Press 1963.

Fuji Bank. *Banking in Modern Japan,* Tokyo 1961.

Gertner, Robert and David Scharfstein. "A Theory of Workouts and the Effets of Reorganization Law." *Journal of Finance*, 46, 4, Sept 1991, pp. 1189-1222.

Giorgio, Louis and Silvia B. Sagari. "Argentina: Financial Crisis and Restructuring in the 1980s." In Andrew Sheng (Ed.), *Bank Restructuring. Techniques and Experience.* forthcoming.

Gorton, Gary. "Clearinghouses and the Origins of Central Banking in the US." *Journal of Economic History*, 42 (June 1985), pp. 177-194.

Hanson, Ardo. "Reforming the Banking System in Estonia," Draft, February 1994.

Hanson, Ardo and Jeffrey D. Sachs. "Monetary Institutions and Credible Stabilization: A Comparison of Experiences in the Baltics." April 1994.

Hearings before the Subcommittee on Financial Institutions Supervision, Regulation and Insurance of the Committe on Banking, Finance, and Urban Affair, 98th Congress, Inquiry into Continental Illinois Corporations and Continental National Bank, September 18 and 19 and October 4, 1984, p. 287 f.

Hoshi, Takeo, Anil Kashyap and Gary Loveman. "Lessons from the Japanese Main Bank System for Financial Reform in Poland." EDI Working Papers. No. 94-18. World Bank, 1994.

Hoshi, Takeo. "Cleaning up the Balance Sheets: Japanese Experience in the Post-War Reconstruction Period." Unpublished Paper, April 1994.

The Japan Development Bank, The Japan Development Institute. *Policy Based Finance. The Experience of Post War Japan.* World Bank Discussion Papers No. 221. Washington 1994.

Kaufman, George G. "Are Some Banks too Large To Fail? Myth and Reality" *Contemporary Policy Issues.* Volume VIII, October 1990, pp. 1-14.

Krozner, Randall S. "The Political Economy of the Reconstruction Finance Corporation's Bail-Out of the U. S. Banking System During the Great Depression," Draft, April 1994.

Miller, Geoffrey P. "Politics of Deposit Insurance Reform: The Case of Argentina" In: Federal Reserve Bank of Chicago. *FDICIA: An Appraisal, Proceedings of the Annual Conference on Bank Structure and Competition.* Chicago: Federal Reserve Bank of Chicago 1993. pp. 473-489.

Myers, Stewart C. "Determinants of Corporate Borrowing," *Journal of Financial Economics* 5 (1977), pp. 147-175.

Sheng, Andrew. (1992a). "Malaysia: Bank Restructuring, 1985-1988," in Andrew Sheng (Ed.). *Bank Restructuring: Techniques and Experience.* World Bank Draft, 1992 (a), Chapter VII, p. 1. Washington 1992.

Sheng, Andrew. (1992b). "Bank Restructuring in Malaysia," 1985-1988. In: Vittas, 1992.

Sprague, O.M. *History of Crisis Under the National Banking System*: Washington: O.S. Government Printing Office (1910). Reprinted by Augustus M. Kelley Publishers.

Tsutsui, William M. *Banking Policy in Japan. American Efforts of Reform During the Occupation.* Routledge, 1988.

Teranashi, Juro (1991a). Financial System and the Industrialization of Japan: 1900-1970" *Banca Nazionale de Lavoro Quarterly Review*. No. 174. Septembe, pp. 308-341.
Teranashi, Juro. (1991b). "Financial System Reform After the War. Hitotsubashi Univesity," Discussion Paper Series A No. 244, 1991.
Teranashi, Juro. (1991c). "Inflation Stabilization with Growth-The Japanese Experience During 1945-1950." Hitotsubashi University, Discussion Paper Series A No. 243, 1991.
Temin, Peter. *Did Monetary Factors Cause the Great Depression?* New York 1976.
Upham, Cyrill B. and Edwin Lamke. *Closed and Distressed Banks. A Study in Public Administration*. Washington: Brookings Institution, 1934.
Vittas, Dimitri (Ed.). *Financial Regulation. Changingg the Rule of the Game*. EDI Development Studies, World Bank: Washington 1992.
White, Eugen Nelson. "A Reinterpretation of the Banking Crisis of 1930." *Journal of Economic History*. Volume 46, No. 1, (March 1984), p. 119-138.
World Bank, Estonia-Memorandum: Joint Mission October 1992, p. 12.
World Bank, "Estonia-The Transition to a Market Economy," 1993.
World Bank, Estonia. "Informal Study of the Enterprise and Financial Sectors," The World Bank, April 1993, p. 16.
World Bank. "Argentina's Banking Sector: The Need for Reform", 1986.
World Bank, "From Insolvency to Growth, 1993."
World Bank, "Financial Sector Review-Argentina," 1989.
World Bank, "Report on Argentina," 1993.
World Bank, "Argentina: Capital Market Study," June 1994.

COMMENT ON TRANSNATIONAL ASPECTS

Daniel E. Nolle

There are three major questions students of international aspects of systemic risk would like to have answered. First, what have been the experiences of different countries in facing and dealing with systemic events (actual or potential), and what general insights can we draw from these? Second, what regulatory mechanisms are in place, and how have/would regulators respond to an event with possible cross-border systemic consequences? Finally, what are the linkages between national banking systems that could serve as likely conduits for contagion to spread? The Baer and Klingebiel paper and the Goldstein paper deal with the first two question, and leave us poised to inquire into the third.

The Baer and Klingebiel paper provides an empirical investigation of the issue of possible systemic consequences of the widespread imposition of losses on depositors as a result of a banking system crisis. Their research finds that it is not necessarily the case that imposing losses on depositors results in a systemic event. Baer/Klingebiel take aim at the conventional wisdom that holds that a government funded recapitalization of banks during episodes of wide spread insolvency is the surest and most practical way to avoid a systemic event. This line of reasoning holds that the failure of government to recapitalize insolvent banks will result in what Baer/Klingebiel call "systemic risk", defined

Research in Financial Services Private and Public Policy, Volume 7, pages 303-308.

ISBN: 1-55938-244-9

as "a sharp decline in macroeconomic activity resulting from shifts in the willingness of the public to hold banking system liabilities."[1] Because they look across countries, across time, and across stages of economic development the conclusions they draw are compelling.

Baer and Klingebiel rely heavily on circumstantial information and qualitative judgement in categorizing and measuring the events and consequences surrounding banking crises in Estonia (1992), Argentina (1989), Malaysia (1986), Japan (1946), and the United States (1933). This is not to say, however, that the method and scope of their research is flawed. Indeed, they do an admirable job of imposing clarity and order on their descriptions of each episode, their discussions of the resolution mechanisms, and their evaluation of the outcomes. Were no larger issues addressed or general conclusions drawn, that work would be a substantial contribution in itself.

In fact, Baer and Klingebiel do pull together their wide-ranging analyses to draw three significant conclusions. First, the imposition of losses on depositors did not have an impact of systemic proportions in the five episodes they examine. However, the important corollary is that the outcomes depended on the nature of the restructuring plans. Key elements were that policymakers took a comprehensive approach to the crisis, and allowed only well-capitalized institutions to remain open. Finally, Baer/Klingebiel conclude that banks can be successfully restructured even if their depositors suffer losses. These findings have important implications. If there are reasonably well-defined circumstances under which losses can be imposed on depositors, then it would not be impractical to reduce the official safety net of deposit insurance. Doing so, of course, reduces the incentives for banks to take excessive risks, hence *reducing* systemic risk.

Whether or not the Baer and Klingebiel work is useful in reforming deposit insurance schemes, the lessons it teaches could be useful to policymakers in a number of "emerging market" economies. Authorities in several of those economies are in the unenviable position of seeing a global reevaluation of their growth prospects, and hence a substantial slowdown in capital inflows, coupled with a weak banking system. The research of Baer and Klingebiel provides considerable guidance on how to "bite the bullet" in the event of widespread banking system insolvency.

Goldstein's paper moves to the realm of "transnational aspects" of systemic risk, providing a transition from the "comparative international" viewpoint of the Baer and Klingebiel piece. Keeping in mind the ground rules he sets for himself—namely, that he does not intend the paper to be comprehensive—Goldstein nevertheless selects four important cross-border dimensions of systemic risk for investigation:

1. the international transmission of asset price changes;

2. liquidity strains in various economies in the event of international financial market turbulence;
3. strenghts and weaknesses of "the" international supervisory and regulatory framework; and
4. international aspects of payments systems.

Conceptually, the first two topics are closely related to each other, and could be considered as "international marketplace" factors, while the third and fourth topics could be group together as "international supervision, regulation, and payments systems" issues.

While it is beyond Goldstein's scope to draw a detailed map of the conduits by which national banking and financial markets are connected, he does consider the degree to which asset price changes can be transmitted globally, and therefore gives us useful preliminary information on some possible scenarios for the transmission of turbulence across borders.[2] Indeed, with the peso/emerging markets crisis unfolding at the time of this writing, his starting point seems particularly prescient:

> Suppose, for example, that a major industrial country implemented a significant and somewhat unexpected change in monetary policy. Wouldn't increased integration then mean that the sharp change in interest rates in the initiating country would quickly be reflected elsewhere, possibly inflicting sizeable losses on those market participants at home and abroad who had wrong-footed positions or imperfect hedges? (p. **).

Obviously, recent experience tells us that the answer to this question is an unequivocal "yes," but Goldstein gives us a feel for why this is so. Summarizing recent work he and Michael Mussa have done, Goldstein (p. *) explains that international financial integration is "considerably higher than it was a decade ago," and "has proceeded farthest for those liquid, financial instruments traded in major financial centers," though for equities the recent pace of global integration has not been nearly as rapid.[3] Indeed, Goldstein explains briefly the nature of remaining frictions between national capital markets, focusing on firms' internal financing and the still large role of domestic savings in financing domestic investment.

Another "international marketplace" factor Goldstein considers is the degree to which there are international differences in the liquidity of financial markets. Reviewing the ERM crises of fall 1992 and summer 1993, Goldstein explains that those crises were exacerbated when market participants tried to retrench in currencies less widely traded than marks, yen, or dollars (e.g., Swedish krona, ECUs, the lira), and in small OTC options markets. This sort of "crowding a narrow exit" phenomenon was also evident in smaller European government bond markets as the tightening of interest rates begun in the United States in early 1994 reverberated across many financial markets in the ensuing months. Goldstein's point is that, in addition to systemic risk which arises as a consequence of the greater interconnectedness of markets, there is risk associated with the fact that the "diameter" of the financial "pipes" running through different markets varies from large liquid markets to smaller, less liquid markets. He cautions that, though it is technically difficult to measure, risk management programs need to take account of international differences in liquidity.

Goldstein lists significant differences in payments systems among (and within) countries which make coordination across borders difficult. Nevertheless, there is a growing consensus that well-coordinated international linkages between national systems are crucial both to promote effective economic relations, and to manage a large potential source of systemic risk. Goldstein outlines a number of measures in which central banks are currently engaged that will reduce friction within domestic payments systems, including a move to a real-time gross settlement system, and interbank netting schemes.

Efforts underway to regulate, or at least monitor, international bank and nonbank activities are reviewed by Goldstein. He devotes a good deal of attention to nonbank activities which are not regulated, or subject only to light regulation (in particular hedge funds and derivatives dealers), concluding that public policy is most appropriately (and probably most successfully) aimed not at limiting risks from these activities, but rather insuring that participants understand the risks they undertake. He does not give us concrete suggestions for policy action, but his discussion of the pros and cons of relying on private market monitoring versus explicit regulation sets the parameters for future debate.

Goldstein also brings the discussion to bear on international coordination of banking supervision, making two key points.[4] One, which those advocating reform of deposit insurance schemes would clearly applaud, is that regardless of the degree of international cooperation and goodwill, little real progress will be made on reducing systemic risk until banks are forced to "internalize much of the externalities associated with excessive risk taking" (p. *).

A second observation on international banking supervision Goldstein makes is that, unlike the case of nonbanks, a good deal of coordination and cooperative effort exists between bank supervisors from many countries. Certainly the strides made by the Basle process are substantial. However, we would be ill-advised to believe those efforts implied that all, or even most, of the larger issues surrounding international supervisory cooperation and coordination have been resolved. Indeed, one need only look to national markets to find examples of the substantial difficulties involved in coordinating not only the actions, but even the points of view of multiple regulatory authorities.[5] To expect an easier go of it in an international context is patently unrealistic. At a minimum, the fact that there are honest difference of opinions across countries on the role of the banking industry, as well as fundamental differences on what the appropriate mission for supervision should be virtually guarantee that a complete meeting of the minds among regulators from different countries is not attainable. Acknowledging this "state of nature" need not, however, discourage efforts to make real progress. Instead, a realistic approach to international supervisory coordination would have as its key elements the necessity of regular reminders of the honest differences of opinion on fundamentals, and a willingness to accept a "muddling through" attitude in the absence of complete agreement.

In any case, perfect coordination has its hazards, as we are reminded by the story of the two hunters. Having bagged a deer, they began dragging it back by its hind legs, and intensely awkward procedure which continually entangled the unfortunate creature's antlers in the underbrush. When a passing woodsman suggested they instead drag deer by the antlers, the two hunters happily seized upon the idea. They carried on in a spirit of brotherly cooperation, the one hunter observing how much easier was the present mode of transporting the carcass. "However," said the second hunter, "we're getting further and further away from the car." If policymakers set manageable targets for themselves, and can profit from the kinds of insights provided by the Baer/Klingebiel and Goldstein papers, the hunt for reasonable measures to deal with international systemic risk stands a good chance of winding up in the right place.

ACKNOWLEDGMENT

The views expressed in this paper are those of the author alone, and do not necessarily reflect those of the Office of the Comptroller of the Currency or the Department of the Treasury.

NOTES

1. Baer and Klingebiel therefore see the "risk" involved not as a measure of the likelihood of the macroeconomy being affected, but rather the degree to which it would be affected. Despite this somewhat awkward use of the term "systemic risk", clearly the target of their research is significant and warrants careful attention. Nevertheless, the issue of the definition of systemic risk is not a trivial one, and has come under intense scrutiny. See especially Bartholomew and Whalen (this volume).

2. See Kaufman (1994) for a thorough review of the theory of, and empirical evidence on bank contagion. Kaufman focuses largely on banking events in the United States, but his approach could serve as a model for an investigation of the possible international character of contagion.

3. Mussa and Goldstein (1994) give empirical evidence on the extent to which capital markets are globally integrated.

4. Benston identifies the two key aspects of international coordination of banking supervision: "harmonization," defined as "enactment and enforcement of regulations that similarly affect banks in related countries," and "cooperation" which "requires only that banking authorities exchange information" (p. 206). After a comprehensive review of arguments for both harmonization and

cooperation, Benston concludes that "public-interest reasons do not provide support for international harmonization of banking regulations" (p. 222), but that there is limited support for the realization of benefits from greater cooperation.

5. For example, it is well known that recent efforts in the United States to reorganize and rationalize federal bank and thrift supervision have met with little success.

REFERENCES

Benston, George J., "International Harmonization of Banking Regulations and Cooperation Among National Regulators: An Assessment," *Journal of Financial Services Research,* 8, 4, September 1994, pp. 205-225.

Kaufman, George G., "Bank Contagion: A Review of the Theory and Evidence," *Journal of Financial Services Research*, April 1994, pp. 123-150.

Mussa, Michael, and Morris Goldstein, "The Integration of World Capital Markets." In *Changing Capital Markets: Implications for Monetary Policy*. Federal Reserve Bank of Kansas City, 1994.

PART IV

ADDRESSING SYSTEMIC RISK

IS SYSTEMIC RISK DEAD?

Richard Scott Carnell

Concern over systemic risk raises important issues about the adequacy of our existing framework for supervising depository institutions. In short, is systemic risk dead? And if not, why not?

In the course of this century, Congress has enacted the Federal Reserve Act, the Banking Acts of 1933 and 1935, the Financial Institutions Supervision Act of 1966, the International Lending Supervision Act of 1983, the Financial Institutions Reform, Recovery, and Enforcement Act of 1989, and the Federal Deposit Insurance Corporation Improvement Act of 1991 (FDICIA). If, with such a broad array of regulatory measures in hand, we have still not eradicated systemic risk,[1] is there something fundamentally flawed in our approach to the problem? I know that many of the academics here would answer the last question with resounding "Yes," but I will postpone my own response until later in the discussion.

As for whether systemic risk is dead, I would have to answer in the negative. But its survival does not necessarily indicate massive shortcomings in the existing regulatory framework or even a need for additional tools. It does suggest that our future success in keeping systemic risk to tolerable levels will depend on how well we use the supervisory tools we already have.

Research in Financial Services Private and Public Policy, Volume 7, pages 311-315.

ISBN: 1-55938-244-9

To illustrate the point, consider a familiar analogy. In the mid-1980s and again this past year, some critics of the prevailing monetary policy asked, "Is inflation dead?" The critics implied that inflation was indeed dead and that the Federal Reserve could therefore safely turn its attention to stimulating the economy. Whatever one's judgment about current monetary policy, there is a very real sense in which inflation never dies. The inflation rate remains subject to unexpected supply shocks, such as those OPEC imparted in the 1970s. More broadly, because in the long run the money supply strongly influences the general level of prices, inflation will remain dormant only while money growth remains subdued. It is like a blaze that is never finally extinguished, requiring constant vigilance to prevent it from rekindling. Furthermore, because monetary policy actions affect the inflation rate only after a substantial lag (variously estimated at between 18 months and three years), one cannot prevent inflation by acting only after the inflation rate actually begins to accelerate.

Similarly, systemic risk, although currently under control, remains a latent threat awaiting only an unexpected shock or a gross policy error to show its ugly face. That it rarely manifests itself twice in exactly the same form compounds the challenge of controlling it.

As for the adequacy of our basic regulatory framework for containing systemic risk, there are at least two possible conclusions. One is that the existing framework provides the necessary policy tools to keep systemic risk at an acceptably low level, albeit with no guarantee that we will always use those tools appropriately. The other is that the regulatory framework is fundamentally flawed, and it is just a matter of time until bitter experience demonstrates the need for a massive revision of legislation currently on the book to deal with systemic risk.

I would argue that, at least as concerns the banking system during the remainder of this decade, the former conclusion is closer to the mark than the latter. That is to say, we have the tools necessary to limit systemic risk, and are likely to use them appropriately. I base this judgment on a step-by-step evaluation of the tools we have, how they have been used in the past, and what the prospects are for their use in the future.

Certainly, the Federal Reserve Act put in place the key policy tool for containing a banking crisis. By creating a central bank with lender of last resort responsibilities, Congress intended to assure that healthy, well-managed banks with good assets could always obtain liquidity in time of crisis. Toward that end, Congress gave the Federal Reserve System wide latitude in determining what could serve as acceptable collateral for loans from the discount windows of the regional Federal Reserve banks. This lending capability, combined with the Fed's later development of open market operations, should have sufficed to contain all but the most severe cases of systemic risk associated with exogenous shocks.

The new system failed its first real test, in the 1930s. Yet that failure is now widely understood to have resulted not from any basic deficiency in the arsenal of policy tools available to combat the crisis, but from failure to use those tools effectively. As Friedman and Schwartz have documented at great length, the Fed ignored lessons about appropriate central bank behavior known since the time of Walter Bagehot, and stood aside as the nation's banking system collapsed.

For those who weren't satisfied with having a lender of last resort to combat systemic risk, the Banking Act of 1933 included a second major response to such risk: federal deposit insurance. If runs were a key channel for transmitting adverse effects from poorly managed, failing banks to otherwise healthy banks—a notion that recent research has called into question—then deposit insurance should play an important role in confining the effects of failures to the institutions immediately involved.

From 1934 through the early 1980s, deposit insurance received credit for dramatically stabilizing the banking system. Bank failures declined to the minuscule rate of fewer than ten per year, almost all involving small banks that failed through fraud or malfeasance. More recently, scholars have emphasized that the weakest banks had virtually all closed by 1933, and that the economy strengthened greatly with the onset of World War II. But whatever the reason, runs—a familiar feature of earlier banking crises—essentially disappeared.

During the 1980s, bank failures accelerated sharply, marked first by defaults on farm loans and later by losses on commercial real estate. This might seem to belie the adequacy of the tools available to regulators. But once again, the fault lay less in the tools than in how they were used. Regulators seemingly forgot hard-won lessons—known to bankers and regulators alike—about the perverse incentives of deposit insurance and the dangers of capital forbearance. Thrift regulators allowed institutions to operate for a decade or longer after becoming book-value insolvent—a national disgrace, and one which greatly exacerbated the losses those institutions caused to the taxpayers. Although banking regulators did not carry forbearance that far, they received just criticism for the inequity of treating some institutions as "too big to fail," and for such lapses as permitting banks to increase their commercial real estate exposure just as other lenders were leaving the market.

Why, then, do I believe that the existing array of supervisory and regulatory tools should prove adequate to deal with systemic risk? First of all, despite major shortcomings in supervisory policy, the banking and thrift crises of the 1980s never threatened such a breakdown of the system as occurred in the 1930s. On the contrary, the payment system functioned without interruption, runs remained basically nonexistent, and credit remained generally available, albeit with some painful tightening in some regions and economic sectors.

Second, the Fed's prompt reaction to the stock market crash of 1987, when it took extraordinary measures to assure that liquidity was available to the market, suggests that the central bank has learned its lessons well since the 1930s. It also deserves good marks for gradually withdrawing the excess liquidity after the crash had run its course.

Third, and just as importantly, 1991 saw two crucial additions to the tools available to regulators for dealing with banking crises: *the instructions for using the other tools, together with an improved set of incentives*. These came in the form of FDICIA's prompt corrective action and least-cost resolution provisions. Prompt corrective action requires regulators to impose increasingly stringent restrictions and requirements on an institution as its capital declines below required levels—with the goal of resolving the institution's problems at no loss or minimal loss to the deposit insurance fund. Least-cost resolution curtails too-big-to-fail policies by generally requiring the FDIC to resolve failed or failing institutions using the method least costly to the deposit insurance fund.[2] Exceptions can be made only if necessary to avoid "serious adverse effects on economic conditions or financial stability," and then only if proposed by two-thirds majorities of both the Federal Reserve Board. The legislative history indicates that Congress intended this exception "for those rare instances in which the failure of an institution could threaten the entire financial system."

Prompt corrective action codified supervisory principles regulators had known for decades, but which they had a tendency to discard under pressure. By tying mandatory supervisory intervention—including resolution—to an institution's capital position, FDICIA limited regulators' discretion to prolong and ultimately increase the agony associated with depository institution failures. And in so doing, it helped counteract the old incentives to practice forbearance and overextend the federal safety net.

The initial results of prompt corrective action and least-cost resolution are positive. With capital deficiencies now carrying clear and fairly predictable consequences, banks and thrifts have corrected those deficiencies—so much so that today an undercapitalized institution is a lonely outlier. Fewer institutions are getting into trouble, and those that ultimately fail are imposing even smaller losses on the FDIC. And one no longer hears all that loose talk about not needing to concern oneself with an institution's credit quality because the institution was too big to fail. The potential for problems at sick institutions to spread to healthy institutions—insofar as it existed—is further reduced.

But that is not cause for complacency. We need to remain vigilant against the natural tendency to forget the lessons of a crisis once the crisis subsides. If institutions have federal deposit insurance, they should also have real capital. And we should not let an institution be walled off from market discipline by the perception that it is too big to fail.

I question whether any institution is really too big to fail, especially if we understand "failure" as being broader than liquidation. As we all know, some very large banks have failed in an economic sense. Of course, "too big to fail" refers not to the economic concept of failure, strictly defined, but to the regulatory recognition of that failure. Just as there is a difference between a student failing a course and the professor recognizing that failure by giving the student an "F," there is an equally sharp distinction between the failure of a bank and its recognition and resolution. Thus, even though some banks are too big to liquidate without unduly disrupting the financial system, regulators' adherence to a clearly stated rule in reorganizing banks, wiping out existing stockholders' claims, and giving haircuts to uninsured creditors will serve the economic functions of failure.

In concluding, I would like to return to the question posed earlier as to whether our regulatory framework, as presently constituted, is fundamentally flawed. My judgment that it should prove adequate to deal with systemic risk is an evaluation of only one dimension of performance. If alternative ways can be devised to achieve that same end that also enhance the financial system's competitiveness, efficiency, progressiveness, and responsiveness to social goals, we should certainly explore them. A variety of suggestions for substituting market discipline for formal government supervision come to mind in this context. But that is a question that goes far beyond the scope of these comments.

NOTES

1. Systemic risk is the risk of a sudden, unexpected, and widespread collapse of confidence in the financial system, with potentially large effects on the real economy.

2. For a detailed discussion of the incentive effects intended in FDICIA, see Carnell, "A Partial Antidote to Perverse Incentives: The FDIC Improvement Act of 1991," *Annual Review of Banking Law*, vol 12 (1993), pp. 317-71.

SYSTEMIC RISK AND THE REGULATORY AGENCIES

Susan M. Phillips

I. INTRODUCTION

There are numerous definitions of systemic risk, but as a central banker I am uncomfortable with most of them. Especially within the financial community, the term 'systemic risk' seems to have become synonymous with any large-scale disruption to the efficient or normal functioning of financial markets. Moreover, the notion of efficiency is in the eyes of the beholder. Such definitions seem to miss the obvious evidence that the United States—and perhaps the global—financial system has been extremely resilient when shocked. Large losses for some or re-evaluation of positions by others do not necessarily mean systemic risk.

It seems to me that the salient characteristic of systemic risk is the potential to affect real macroeconomic activity. Certainly, the initial impetus might be a cascading or failure originating from a single financial shock. Or, it may be associated with a generalized loss of confidence in a class of financial institutions. In either situation, holders of financial assets may become extremely risk averse—they hold back and liquidity in financial and credit

Research in Financial Services Private and Public Policy, Volume 7, pages 317-322.

ISBN: 1-55938-244-9

markets could be impaired. What *is* certain is that the causal factors of such incidents are unpredictable in advance and that a given shock can have different effects depending on the economic environment.

II. DEVELOPMENTS INCREASING THE POTENTIAL FOR SYSTEMIC DISRUPTIONS

Over the past 10 or 15 years, a number of economic developments have had important implications for systemic risk. Perhaps the most profound development has been the increased speed and force by which disturbances can be transmitted among financial markets, both domestically and internationally. In part, this development reflects improvements in technology that permit the instantaneous dissemination of information. A second factor is the globalization of financial markets. In addition to technological advances, this reflects the expansion of international trade, the deregulation of financial markets, and the growing importance of institutional investors seeking the potential benefits of international diversification. Globalization has led to a virtual explosion in the volume of foreign exchange and cross-border securities transactions. Both involve significant settlement risk. Increasingly, such transactions are being funneled through a relatively small set of intermediaries that provide custody and settlement services. Globalization also makes it increasingly likely that the resolution of a significant financial disruption will require close co-ordination and co-operation among public and private sector authorities in multiple countries. I don't believe that this element of systemic risk or its resolution have received sufficient attention.

Another related development is the exponential growth of derivatives markets. The ability to hedge foreign exchange, interest rate, and other market risks more easily has been a further impetus to the integration and globalization of financial markets. But while derivatives have worked to improve overall market efficiency, their growth also carries potential implications for systemic risk. Because market-makers typically hedge their derivatives positions on spot and forward markets and on futures exchanges, they are heavily dependent on their own access to credit and on the liquidity of the markets. This dependence was illustrated during the 1987 stock market crash.

Derivative market-making tends to be highly concentrated in relatively few large firms having a global reach. These dealers need sufficient capital to take large positions. They also need the technical expertise as well as the information processing and communications systems to manage credit, settlement, market, and liquidity risks globally. In the unlikely event that such an institution should fail, finding a liquidator to manage these complex risks would be a challenge.

The rapid growth in off-balance sheet activities also raises questions about transparency. Because accounting and disclosure standards for off-balance sheet activities have failed to keep pace with recent market developments, there are questions about the ability of traders and investors to evaluate the riskiness of potential counterparties having sizable derivatives positions. Indeed, the lack of transparency is, I think, one reason that market makers in the derivative markets have been subject to such wild rumors. Until there is better public disclosure of relevant information, the public may overreact in a time of market stress.

III. ADDRESSING SYSTEMIC RISK

In this changing environment, our traditional public policy instruments for containing financial disruptions may have become less effective. Open market operations and discount window lending, while still critical tools for providing central bank liquidity and bolstering public confidence, may not be well-suited to addressing fundamental credit quality concerns. Moreover, the adequacy of the backstop provided by the federal deposit insurance system may be less certain for several reasons: (1) the greater importance of non-banks in the financial system, and (2) recent statutes that give depositors preference over other creditors and that restrict the FDIC's ability to protect uninsured creditors at failed depositories.

Because of concerns about financial market globalization and systemic risk, there is a renewed focus in the United States and abroad on improving the resiliency of the financial system so that both the probability and likely severity of financial shocks are reduced. But public authorities have been extremely reluctant to broaden the government safety net, reflecting the obvious moral hazard concerns. To the extent financial risks are borne by the public sector, practitioners themselves have little incentive to develop and implement effective risk management systems. Yet, ultimately, private agents are in the best position to monitor, limit, and manage their own risk exposures. For these reasons, public policy efforts have focused on three areas: (1) improving risk management practices used by institutions; (2) improving the infrastructure of payments and settlement systems; and (3) improving financial disclosure and accounting practices, especially for off-balance sheet activities. To the extent we are successful in these efforts, we may be able to do as much to reduce systemic risk in the 1990s as deposit insurance did in the 1930s.

IV. IMPROVING RISK MANAGEMENT

Despite the growing importance of nonbank firms in the financial system, banks retain a central role. As bank supervisors, we have a fundamental obligation to ensure that banking organizations are not a source of systemic risk. We have taken numerous important actions toward this end over the past several years. First, under the auspices of the Basle Committee on Banking

Supervision and the G-10 Central Bank Governors, great strides have been made in enhancing consolidated supervision of internationally active banking organizations and ensuring that, on a uniform basis, banks are adequately capitalized for the risks they assume. Risk-based capital requirements for credit risk are already in place, and there are ongoing efforts to incorporate market risk as well. In addition, to reduce credit risks associated with derivatives activities, the Basle Accord has been amended to provide incentives for banks to utilize legally enforceable bilateral netting agreements.

Within the United States, the supervisory process has been strengthened, among other things, to encourage greater discipline in the banking industry. On-site examinations play a critical role in the supervision of banks, and an increasingly important element of our examinations is an assessment of the adequacy of internal risk management systems. Internationally, a similar approach has been adopted by the Basle Supervisors Committee and the International Organization of Securities Commissions. Both have issued coordinated documents stating similar principles or promoting sound internal risk management for banks and securities firms. In recent years, the U.S. banking agencies have taken steps to strengthen the training and capabilities of examiners in the risk-management areas, particularly with regard to derivatives.

Various provisions of the 1991 FDIC Improvement Act (FDICIA) reinforce these supervisory initiatives. Annual full-scope, on-site examinations of major banks are now required. Risk-based deposit insurance premiums and prompt corrective action policies have encouraged banks to increase their regulatory capital levels.

U.S. and foreign authorities have also worked to enhance both their own and practitioners' understanding of risk management issues. The results of these supervisory, regulatory, and educational initiatives are quite evident. Within the last few years, we have observed substantial payoffs in terms of increased use of bilateral netting, margining arrangements, marking positions to market, and collateral agreements among counterparties. In addition, we have observed generally improved management of market risks at bank and nonbank institutions alike. I expect these trends to continue.

V. IMPROVING INFRASTRUCTURE

United States and foreign authorities also have been working to reduce the magnitude of settlement risks. One effort has sought to reduce legal uncertainties regarding he enforceability of bilateral netting agreements, including so-called close-out agreements. Such agreements have the potential to lower settlement risk dramatically by reducing both the number and amount of payments that must be made compared to settlement on a gross, transaction-by-transaction basis. Within the Unites States, an important provision of FDICIA now ensures the validity and enforceability of bilateral netting arrangements among financial institutions. Work is also proceeding along similar lines in several other countries. This process has been hastened by the amendment to the Basle Accord, mentioned earlier, which permits banks to recognize the benefits of netting for capital purposes only if they can demonstrate the enforceability of their netting agreements in all relevant jurisdictions.

On a second track, we are striving to reduce the duration of settlement risk through improvements to payment and settlement systems. Within the United States, for example, settlement risk associated with CHIPS payments has been reduced by the implementation of 'same-day' settlement, limitations on bilateral and multilateral settlement exposures, as well as collateral and enhanced loss sharing arrangements. In addition, to lower operational barriers to reducing Herstatt risk, the Federal Reserve recently announced that it will expand the operating hours of Fedwire from the current 10 hours to 18 hours, beginning in 1997. Steps also are being taken by other central banks to develop or improve their real-time payments systems.

VI. TRANSPARENCY

To manage counterparty risks effectively, market participants need timely and accurate information about the financial conditions of potential counterparties. Similarly, in order to respond effectively to potential financial disruption, supervisors and central banks need such information. One unfortunate consequence of the rapid pace of financial innovation in recent years is that financial accounting and disclosure practices have not kept pace, especially in the area of off-balance sheet activities. The lack of market transparency is of concern to policymakers and practitioners around the world.

From a regulatory standpoint, efforts are under way to improve the available information on banks' off-balance sheet exposures. In 1994, all Reports filed by U.S. banks collected new information on derivatives held for trading purposes and on nonperforming derivatives contracts, to supplement information already required on notional amounts and replacement cost. In addition data on derivatives positions and associated risks, including detailed disclosure of fair values, net credit exposures, and breakdowns of trading revenues. The FASB has adopted a similar standard, FAS 119, for firms filing GAAP financial statements.

However, these are only first steps toward improving the reporting of off-balance sheet instruments. Much more is needed, particularly in the area of *quantitative* disclosures about an individual firm's risk management objectives and policies and whether their policies actually achieve the objectives. A framework for such disclosures was recently laid out in a discussion paper prepared by a working group of the G-10 central banks chaired by Peter Fisher of the Federal Reserve Bank of New York.

VII. CONCLUSIONS

In closing, I would note that large-scale financial crises have not occurred in the United States since the 1930s. There actually have been numerous major shocks that *could* have been destabilizing—such as interest rate and exchange rates fluctuating more widely, the 1987 stock market crash, the recent problems of S&Ls and banks, and the failure of a major securities firm. Through all, the financial system has shown remarkable resiliency.

This has not been happenstance, but reflects, I believe, private and public sector efforts to strengthen the financial system. Clearly, the advent of deposit insurance and improvements to date in the financial infrastructure have been significant developments. Equally important have been improvements in risk management systems at the level of individual firms. Over time, as real and financial risks in the economy have evolved, so too has the sophistication of the systems used by major financial institutions to limit and manage risk exposures. Ultimately, these risk management systems have been, and will continue to be, the front line of defense against systemic disruption.

An additional factor contributing to the resiliency of our financial system has been the effectiveness of public institutions responsible for dealing with systemic risks. In addition to insisting that the infrastructure be improved and that banks adopt effective risk management techniques, liquidity has been provided to the system when needed. When potentially destabilizing shocks have occurred, they have been successfully contained, at least partially because of regulators' understanding of the systemic risks involved and their knowledge of financial markets and relevant market participants.

Looking ahead, as we strive to further strengthen the global financial system, we will need continued work and cooperation among public and private sectors internationally. With this commitment, I think the outlook is good for the development of markets and risk management capabilities that limit systemic risks while supporting a dynamic and growing world economy.

REGULATORY RESPONSES TO THE POTENTIAL FOR SYSTEMIC RISK IN THE FINANCIAL SECTOR

Mark J. Flannery

I accept the possibility that systemic risk *may* exist in the United States and other countries, but I know no appropriate, universal definition of "systemic risk". I take the phrase to mean a type of externality whereby one (financial) firm's failure can induce failures elsewhere, to the extent that the financial system's overall efficacy is impaired for at least a short period. I further presume that systemic risk is an important policy concern because (if) the financial system's impairment may impose real costs on the economy, in the form of either financial firms' bankruptcy costs or nonfinancial firms' impaired ability to undertake profitable activities.

Systemic risk exposures are most frequently discussed in connection with the large-value payment system, foreign exchange (FX) dealings, or the market for OTC derivatives. In these markets, a few firms regularly undertake very large transactions with a small number of counterparties, apparently creating the potential for several defaults should one large market participant fail. Systemic risk occurs if a liquidity or solvency problem at one financial firm

Research in Financial Services Private and Public Policy, Volume 7, pages 323-336.

ISBN: 1-55938-244-9

may impair other firms' abilities to fulfill their obligations. Problems can be transmitted via two avenues. First, one firm's failure may leave others illiquid: counterparties remain solvent, but have insufficient "good money" to satisfy their obligations. Potential liquidity problems tend to be more important in the payments system than in the derivatives market. Second, some firms may have had sufficiently large, undiversified credit exposures to the failing entity that they are themselves rendered insolvent. Solvency issues tend to be more prominent in the derivatives market discussions of systemic risk.

I. CAUSES OF POTENTIAL SYSTEMIC RISK

I begin by describing the private contracting features which can give rise to systemic risk. Consider, first, the simple transaction of purchasing a newspaper on the way out of Washington's Metro system. This transaction benefits both parties (in the sense of providing consumer surplus) without involving any risk. Why? Because the cash purchase simultaneously exchanges the commodity for "good money". In our personal lives, most of us take for granted this type of "delivery versus payment" (DVP) transaction. The defining aspect of systemic risk, however, is that extremely large transaction volumes *do not* involve DVP. Instead, market conventions specify that a commodity or security is delivered before final payment is made.[1] The seller thereby extends credit to the buyer and these credit extensions are the root cause of systemic risk concerns.

An example can help clarify the implications of this particular type of credit risk. Consider "spot" FX transactions, which (paradoxically) settle one day after the trade, when the market convention requires that each currency be delivered in its "home" country. For example, a dollar-yen trade between National Westminster and Deutsche Bank will have Deutsche Bank deliver yen in Tokyo and NatWest deliver dollars in New York (usually over CHIPS). Both payment must be made by close of business on the "value date", but the close in Tokyo predates the New York close by 14 hours. Because Deutsche Bank must pay out yen (up to) 14 hours before it is scheduled to receive the promised dollars, it bears *credit risk* (that NatWest will be unable to pay) on the full transaction amount. This risk is commonly called "Herstatt risk", in reference to the 1974 failure of Bankhaus Herstaff.[2] (NatWest's default would also expose Deutsche Bank to additional *foreign exchange risk*, because the default leaves Deutsche Bank short dollars, relative to its planned position.) Many other financial transactions also involve substantial amounts of credit risk. Equity trades generally settle with a multi-day lag[3], and mortgage-backed securities settlement may take several months. Swaps and many other "derivatives"[4] involve still more credit risk because they entail a potentially lengthy *stream* of counterparty payments following the trade date. Thus derivatives transaction can involve quantitatively (though not qualitatively) more counterparty risk than spot FX or interbank payments do.

Credit risk exposure in the payments and derivatives trading systems generates two distinct, though related, risks for the trading parties: liquidity risk and default risk, and regulatory oversight must distinguish between the two. Liquidity risk represents the possibility that a *solvent* firm will be unable to deliver promised "good funds". Given the time required to liquidate some of its assets (or to issue additional liabilities for cash), the troubled firm *could* honor its obligations. For the present, however, the illiquid firm's creditors may themselves be rendered illiquid. By contrast, default risk represents the possibility that a firm will be unable to honor its total obligations, including those related to the payments system or the derivatives market. Defaulting firms do not have the resources to satisfy all their outstanding obligations.

Note that illiquidity does not necessarily imply that a firm is insolvent, nor must insolvency be accompanied by illiquidity. An illiquid firm might become insolvent if it suffered large "fire sale losses" while converting assets into the good money required to satisfy its near-term debts. (This is Goodhart's (1990) primary justification for a government-operated lender of last resort.) An insolvent firm might still be able to "settle" its near term obligations. The potential for confusing illiquidity with insolvency complicates the market's (and regulators') most appropriate response to any type of payment difficulty.

Sound management practice generally requires that default risks be well diversified. Credit risk associated with the payments and interbank trading systems may be unusual—and hence warrant special regulatory attention—if some important traders must be highly exposed to the risk of default by a single counterparty. For example, it is frequently observed that the market for OTC swaps in the United States is quite concentrated.[5] If one dealer were to fail, therefore, many counterparties would potentially suffer losses. Furthermore, since the swaps dealers trade fairly heavily among themselves (as do FX traders), several dealers could plausibly have a large exposure (compared to his/her own capital) to one which fails. The fact that bilateral exposures are not widely known confounds the problem further: the combined with incomplete information about their extent means that one dealer's failure may generate extensive changes in financing costs or availabilities for its potential counterparties throughout the financial sector.

II. ALTERNATIVE INSTITUTIONAL SETTLEMENT PROCEDURES

Despite the fact that the payments system and OTC derivatives trading arrangements presently bundle credit with the exchange of goods and securities, one can readily imagine alternative institutional arrangements which require less credit for any given set of transactions. One way to eliminate all bilateral credit extension would be to expand use of the simple newspaper example: to require simultaneous exchange of the commodity and the good money (DVP; also known as "real-time gross settlements"). This approach has been implemented by the Swiss Interbank Clearing (SIC) system. "Bilateral netting" arrangements—under which counterparties exchange only the net value of all their trades over a single day—can also reduce the credit required to support large trading positions (McAndrews and Roberds, 1994; Mengle, 1990; Cody, 1990; Gilbert, 1992; Cohen and Roberds, 1993; Emmons 1994; Schoenmacher, 1994). "Multilateral netting"—under which each trader nets his obligations to a *group* of other traders—can bring still further reductions in the credit components of financial trading, although at the cost of involving unrelated parties in one trader's credit problems.[6] Futures clearinghouses are essentially institutional trading arrangements which mutualize (effectively via multilateral netting) and collateralize the credit aspects of financial transaction (Moser, 1994; Baer, France and Moser, 1994). Some OTC trades apply the clearinghouse techniques: counterparties can (and do) post collateral in connection with their net debit positions (as they presently do on CHIPS and for Fedwire transactions involving problem banks), and the ISDA has developed standard contract arrangements for periodic marking-to-market of net payment obligations of interest rate and currency swaps.

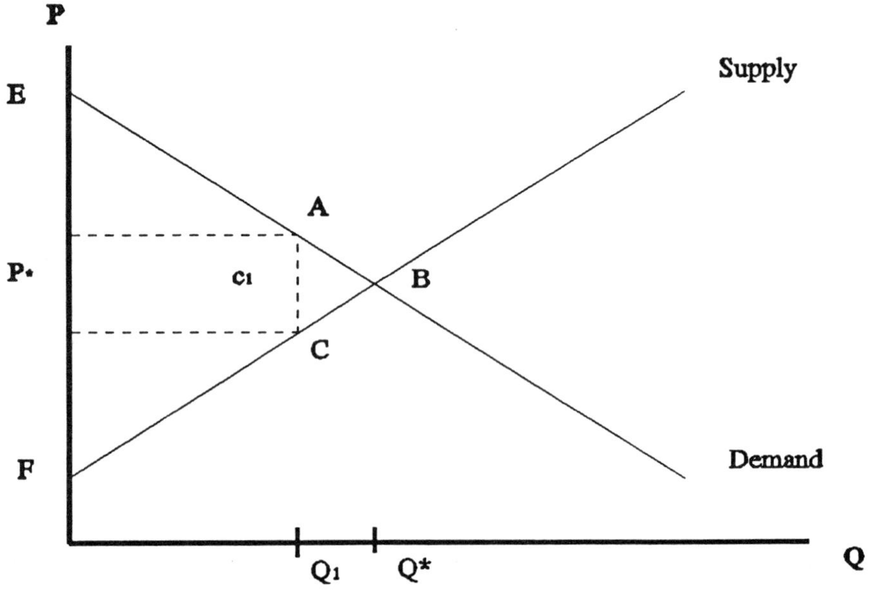

Figure 1.

The social benefits of lower credit risks are illustrated in Figure 1, which describes investors' aggregate desire to trade a particular security. The horizontal axis measures quantity traded, while the vertical axis measures price (e.g., the dollar price of deutschemarks). In a frictionless world, the equilibrium market price would be P*, at a traded volume of Q*. This equilibrium constitutes a social optimum because all traders who value the security at P* or higher will actually own it, while the investors who value the security at P* or lower will be able to sell it.[7] Transaction costs reduce the social welfare produced in this market by imposing a "wedge" between the seller's and buyer's perceived prices. In particular, a transaction cost of c_1 will reduce the equilibrium quantity traded to Q_1, depriving traders of the consumers' surplus triangle ABC. If c_1 is indeed the irreducible cost of transacting, Q_1 represents the socially optimal level of trading in this commodity: any further trading volume costs more (c_1) than the total consumer surplus generated.

Transaction costs include both real resource cost and the counterparty risks associates with the trade's settlement procedures. Consider, for example, the "Herstatt risk" in a dollar-yen FX trade. The dollar buyer recognizes that she may not be paid dollars even after delivering the promised yen. Hence, the FX transaction has an expected credit cost equal to the counterparty's probability of default (during the interval between close of business in Tokyo and in New York) times the trade's principal amount. In general, the magnitude of this transaction cost component reflects both the counterparty's credit worthiness and the time lag between payment in one currency vs. receipt of the other.

Several important points follow immediately from Figure 1:

a) Private traders will seek to minimize transaction costs in order to attain further consumer surplus in the region ABC. Traders will therefore seek institutional arrangements that minimize the net cost of counterparty risk (that is, expected default losses less the cost of settling trades in the specified manner). Given a particular set of market arrangements, investor can also lower their transaction costs by modifying their trading behavior as a counterparty's perceived credit quality changes. In particular, suppose one trader's credit quality declines. Other traders would perceive an increase in the cost of transacting with this firm, and would hence shift their trading volume to other, safer counterparties.[8]
b) If the government could lower the social cost of transactions below what private parties can accomplish, it could improve social welfare.
c) A government policy of *subsidizing* trades will *reduce* social welfare, despite that fact that it increases the amount of trading (hedging, risk-spreading). To see this, imagine an extreme policy of having the government pay all transaction costs. In Figure 2, traders would earn a surplus of EBF, while the government would bear transaction costs

of c_1Q^*. The *net* surplus in this market is smaller than the amount in Figure 1 when traders bear their own transaction cost.[9] This inefficiency obtains whether the government subsidizes out-of-pocket transaction costs or absorbs counterparty risk (e.g., through a subsidizing lender of last resort).

III. WILL PRIVATE MARKET ARRANGEMENTS BE SOCIALLY OPTIMAL?

A benevolent dictator would undertake a careful cost/benefit analysis of the alternative settlement arrangement for each type of transaction (underlying security), and seek to implement the system providing the greatest net social benefits. While there is no reason for all traded securities to settle in the same fashion,[10] all cost-effective steps should be taken to reduce the net cost of coping with settlement failures. Under some circumstances, economic theory implies that market allocations and institutional arrangements can mimic the decisions of a benevolent dictator, and therefore maximize social welfare. In the context of payments systems and financial settlements, three possible situations could make the market's chosen arrangements socially sub-optimal.

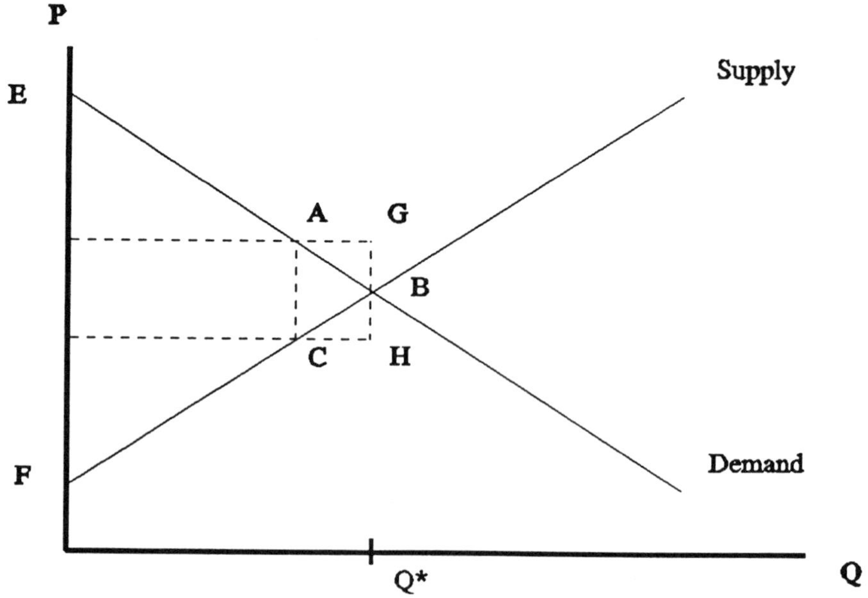

Figure 2.

Conjectural Guarantees

If government stands ready to avoid a payments system or derivatives-related failure (e.g., by providing the funds to effect settlement when a private firm cannot), market arrangements may be inefficient. As indicated in Figure 2, private investors will trade excessively when government absorbs some counterparty risk. (That is, the marginal trades' social cost will exceed their private benefits.) The government's willingness to absorb credit losses would also blunt private incentives to design institutions and structure trading patterns that minimize credit risk exposures. In this equilibrium, government regulators would accurately belive that traders tolerate unreasonable credit risks because they rely on government to subsidize counterparty defaults in some states of the world. To the extent that a conjectural guarantee blunts private incentives to control or price risk, regulation should seek to replace the lost private controls (Flannery, 1994).

Legal/Administrative Uncertainties

Theoretical analyses of optimal contract design are based on the notion that payment and contracting efficiencies will reflect the legal liabilities imposed on the contracting parties.[11] The optimal trading and payment arrangements for interbank transactions often imply no single "best" arrangement (Mengle, 1990). But even theoretically optimal contracts would be subject to nontrivial uncertainties about their legal enforceability. Two broad problems arise. First, it is sometimes unclear how courts will interpret various types of netting arrangements when one party has defaulted and/or sought bankruptcy protection. Second, many payment and contracting issues involve more than one country's laws. Legal uncertainty tends to increase the perceived costs of transacting, which reduces welfare (*ceteris paribus*) in Figure 1.

Information Asymmetries

Whenever credit risk is an important component of transaction costs, traders must understand the credit quality of their counterparties in order to evaluate a trade's full economic effect. When one trader assumes a potentially large credit exposure, other traders will want to know about it promptly and reliably. But this information is difficult to obtain. First, the net exposure to individual counterparties can change quickly. Second, an institution with (actual or potential) large bilateral exposures can only be evaluated when the condition of *its* counterparties is known. Finally, the lack of accurate, universal accounting conventions makes "full disclosure" problematic even in situations where all the parties wish to effect it. The cost of maintaining timely information on all counterparties' credit condition can obscure the full implications of a particular firm's failure. As extensively evaluated by Calomiris (1994), this situation can generate systemic risk: traders suspect that one firm's failure has left others weakened, but they cannot promptly ascertain which other firms have been hurt. In this context, the government's ability to function as lender of last resort (LLR) may enhance social welfare.

IV. HOW SHOULD REGULATORS "ADDRESS" SYSTEMIC RISK ISSUES?

The preceding analysis suggests two broad roles for government policy in assuring the efficiency of interbank payment and derivatives markets: establishing a reliable contracting environment and providing a LLR facility. In defining them, I do not mean to imply that either is appropriate, but only that government intervention *may* improve economic efficiency. A complete analysis of the cost and benefits would be required to establish that any specific government action would improve social welfare.[12]

First, governments can help establish a known, reliable framework within which private traders can operate. This facilitation, which may be justified by coordination problems among private parties, has two natural components.

Because large bank failures are rare, all traders must bear some legal uncertainty until an actual failure has allowed the courts to interpret various legal and contractual arrangements.[13] Governments can work to clarify the *legal status* of interbank financial arrangements such as netting and the right of offset. Because a large firm's failure will almost surely involve several nations' legal systems, central banks and governments should encourage and facilitate the involvement of international groups like the BIS and Group of Thirty.

b) Governments can help to develop and define *industry standards* for information presentation and disclosure.[14] Free-rider and coordination problems among private members of a club or clearinghouse may inhibit their ability to design and enforce optimal standards, and government mandates can sometimes improve the situation.'

Second, government can operate a formal LLR facility, which affects the private costs of trading and making payments in interbank markets. Because liquidity and credit risks are logically separable, I consider two distinct examples of salutary LLR actions.

LLR Response to a Pure Liquidity Problem

Consider first the case of a solvent, but illiquid, firm which cannot fulfill its payment obligations at close of business. (I discuss below how the analysis is made more complex if such firms are not easily identified.) The firm's counterparties would willingly accept an IOU in settlement today,[15] except for the fact that they might be relying on payment from this firm to fulfill the good money promises they have made to others. An illiquid firm's settlement failure generates problems when its creditors are not indifferent between payment in good funds today vs. tomorrow. This preference for immediate cash could arise from either reserve requirement considerations or market concern over a creditor's solvency.

The illiquid firm could settle in good funds if it could sell some of its assets. However, the number of same-day buyers for any type of asset is limited late in the business day.[16] For similar reasons, a pre-negotiated line of credit from other private lenders may not substitute perfectly for direct access to central bank money: where would the lenders obtain good funds on short notice at the close of business? Because the LLR has unique access to central bank money late in the business day, it should stand ready to lend on the security of good collateral in order to permit an illiquid, solvent institution to honor its end-of-day settlement obligations. Promising to provide liquidity to solvent firms eliminates a risk that the private sector would otherwise have to bear, which reduces the (social) transactions cost wedge in Figure 1. Since the central bank is the only entity which can provide liquidity at day's end, its refusal to do so would raise transactions costs and prevent the market from making socially desirable trades.

LLR Response To An "Important" Firm's Insolvency

If an illiquid firm is also insolvent, the LLR should not lend even on a secured basis.[17] But what of *that* bank's creditors? If all creditor firms' exposures to the insolvent firm were known with certainty, there would be no role for the LLR beyond that associated with simple liquidity provision (as above). However, when a large banking firm fails, market participant may take a while to evaluate the implications for other firms. Even if information about other firms' exposures to the insolvent firm were not known with certainly, market investors would remain willing to lend to all illiquid firms on the basis of their *expected* ability to repay—provided that all other potential lenders were believed to be equally ignorant. Information asymmetry among lenders could cause the market for loans to contract or collapse entirely. A relatively uninformed lender would expect to suffer adverse selection (i.e., a "lemons" problem) in lending at a rate which reflects the average anticipated incidence of insolvency. She would rationally raise her required loan rate or withdraw from the private debt market ("flee to quality") until the crisis had abated. In this situation, some solvent firms would be unable to pay off their maturing short-tem obligations (such as commercial paper) without issuing new debt. A government LLR can enhance social welfare by standing ready to lend at rates which reflect the (objective) expected default rates.[18] So long as government has no worse information about borrowers' solvency than private lenders, there will be no subsidy associated with such lending.[19]

LLR: Conclusions

Provided that financial markets continue to settle at discrete times (e.g., daily), a government-operated LLR should lend freely to solvent firms without much regard for collateral (see also Bagehot, 1894). Applying this rule in particular circumstances can be complex, especially since the LLR may be operating under severe time pressure. If the LLR's behavior implicitly subsidizes borrowing firms, we will have excessive credit risks generated by market trading and payment arrangements. Consequently, the LLR may choose to charge a penalty rate, on the assumption that some solvent-looking borrowers will default. Similarly, the LLR may reasonably require collateral if solvent firms can more readily supply it, or it might mandate collateral for certain types of interbank transactions as a means of minimizing the need for LLR intervention.[20] Regardless of these details, however, it is hard to understand how incomplete disclosure of the LLR's intentions could be optimal: such ambiguity adds to the perceived cost of dealing in interbank markets (see Figures 1 and 2), while distorting the incentives of private traders to devise institutional arrangements that minimize and control counterparty (and hence, perhaps, systemic) risks.[21]

V. BANK SAFETY AND SOUNDNESS REGULATION

Federal regulators are, appropriately, concerned that insured banks' derivatives business—either as an end-user or as a dealer—may expose them to excessive risks. For example:

> The Federal Reserve's regulatory concerns regarding derivatives activities relate principally to their volume and complexity, which affects both the ability of examiners to evaluate a bank's activities and the ability of management, itself, to identify, understand, and control the risk management process (Federal Reserve Board, 1993, p. 328).

Regulators clearly need to examine and regulate individual banks' activities, because deposit insurance and other government guarantees subsidize private firms and encourage risk-taking (Flannery, 1994). For this purpose, however, derivatives-related risks must be evaluated the same way as credit, interest rate, liquidity, and other risks are. In particular, the level of derivatives exposure *per se* is not nearly so important as how that derivatives risk complements the firm's overall position. Like a bank's derivatives counterparties, examiners should concentrate on an institution's management skills and systems, seeking to ascertain whether the bank can assess and manage its derivatives risk exposures adequately. Derivatives risks and management abilities should be easier to evaluate once the legal and accounting infrastructures have been carefully established.

CONCLUSIONS

Financial regulators are appropriately concerned with the private sector's management of large credit risk exposures. The potential for such exposures in the large dollar payment system and derivatives trading makes these institutions a proper object of regulatory scrutiny, particularly since the regulators' conjectured responses to a crisis can importantly affect the type and extent of feasible trades and transactions. Regulatory authorities should assure that the legal and informational frameworks associated with the financial activities are adequately designed and clearly understood. Central banks can also reduce the private (and social) costs of making payments and trading risks by providing limited "lender of last resort" services. The central bank should stand ready to provide liquidity to solvent firms on short notice, while avoiding situations where it is likely to provide subsidies on account of adverse selection in its lending. The anticipated "lender of last resort" actions should be clearly specified *ex ante*. By contrast, the role for *direct* government intervention in the payments and OTC derivatives markets seems quite limited. While regulatory examiners must understand and limit insured banks' overall risk exposures, limiting the activities of informed, individual banks or their customers seems unwarranted when the overall financial system is reasonably sophisticated and the legal and accounting systems permit adequate disclosure of the relevant information.

NOTES

1. A financial transaction is generally comprised of three distinct components: the trade, clearing, and settlement. (See, e.g., Perold 1994). A "trade" occurs when two parties agree to exchange a security for value. "Clearing involves the "back office" function of confirming tht both parties had agreed to the same terms, and "settlement" constitutes the security's delivery and associated payment. Because clearing takes time, there is a delay between the trade and its final settlement. There is no apparent need for delivery and payment to occur at different times, although it usually does.

2. Before CHIPS initiated same-day settlement in October 1981, Herstatt risk involved *more* than a full calendar day. Since 1981, the longest credit risk exposure—associated with a dollar-yen trade—is 14 hours.

3. Presently 5 business days in the U.S., and longer elsewhere.

4. Such over-the-counter (OTC) derivatives include forward FX transactions, interest rate and currency swaps, OTC options, forward rate agreements (FRAs) and many others.

5. See Abken (1994) and the references therein. In setting policy, regulators must determine whether the existing concentrations reflect some intrinsic feature of the market-making process, or simply the private sector's conjecture that regulators will not permit a large firm failure in this sector.

6. Any type of netting can involve either a single type of financial security (e.g., provide for the net payment of FX or equity or check-clearing amounts due, or the net payment on interest rate swap payments), or can offset payments due across a range of financial contract types.

Multilateral netting examples include the depository arrangements (Depository Trusts Company and National Securities Clearing Corporaton) currently in place for settling equity trades (Stigum, 1988).

7. When the "commodity" being traded is a FX or swap contrat, the value to each party can depend in part on his own endowments. The ability to trade risks increases the efficiency of risk-bearing, which can have important effects on real savings/investment decisions. Merton (1994), for example, therefore argues that extensive derivatives trading enhances social welfare.

8. The resulting loss in trading revenues constitutes a form of market discipline that reinforces the trouble firm's incentives to reverse its decline.

9. To see this, note that the additional consumer surplus generated by the government's absorption of transaction cost (ABC) is smaller than society's additional transaction costs (AGHC) under this arrangement.

10. For example, one cost of the SIC system of DVP with no daylight overdrafts is alleged to the the risk of a payment system "gridlock". This risk may be easier to deal with in the Treasury market (where good collateral is readily available) than elsewhere in the payments system.

11. Consider a relatively simple, international example. Nonbank X wishers to pay nonbank Y. How does X "discharge" his debt? Clearly, X can hand currency to Y, but with large dollar amounts (and geographic separation between X and Y) this is impractical. More commonly, X will instruct a bank (B_x) to pay funds into the account of Y at B_y. This transfer will frequently involve further intermediary banks. Suppose that X can employ either the expensive, but highly reliable B_{x1}, or the cheaper, less reliable B_{x2} to undertake its funds transfer. Similarly, suppose that the selected bank can employ either an expensive, reliable intermediary B_{z1} or a cheaper, less reliable B_{z2} as the intermediary through which funds are advanced to B_y. What determines the route by which payment is made?

If X remains liable to Y until Y has received good funds, X has the incentive to consider the reliability of B_x. And if B_x remains liable to X until Y receives good funds, B_x similarly has and appropriate incentive to select a dependable route through which to direct payments. However, if law, regulation, or courts fail to assign accountability in this manner, X and/or B_x will have limited incentives to choose the most socially efficient payments mechanism, and Y will suffer higher credit risk exposure than it would under alternative liability rules.

12. For example, Goodfriend and King (1988) and others argue that a LLR has perverse incentives which lead it to subidize insolvent firms. If true, this must be counted as a cost of government intervention.

13. The risk that particular contract terms will be invalidated in court is not necessarily diversifiable for a single trade who takes a large aggregate position in some security. Even most *laissez faire* writers recognize that enforcing private contracts is an appropriate government responsibility.

14. For example, the Federal Reserve apparently had an important effect on the banking system's recognition of the credit risk associated with their payments operations. See Flannery (1988), pp. 268-289.

15. If each of the illiquid firm's creditors were itself widely known to be solvent, they should also be able to "settle" at day's end by getting their creditors to extend credit for another day.

16. Even if he illiquid firm *could* find same-day buyers, its solvency may be threatened if it must sell many assets at "fire sale" prices (Goodhart, 1990; Benston *et al.*, 1986).

17. If the LLR lends on good collateral, it effectively places itself ahead of other, unsecured creditors if the borrower ultimately fails. FDICIA generally forbids the Fed from lending to firms that are not certified (by their primary regulator) to be solvent.

18. I first heard this interpretation of LLR financing from Charles Goodhart, in a 1993 conversation. The basic idea has been modelled by Bernanke and Gertler (1990) and Calomiris and Hubbard, 1990: when some shock reduces a firm's equity value, market investors may become unwiling to lend funds, except at a (high) rate which reflects adverse selection and moral hazard.

19. The government's exposure to adverse selection problems when it operates as LLR is a problem which warrants further study. Goodfriend and King, (1988) discuss this cost of discount window lending.

20. For example, the Fed was unwilling to provide CHIPS with a Fedwire settlement account unless CHIPS members agreed to post collateral which would be available to the Clearinghouse in the event of a settlement failure. While having marketable collateral at close of business is not equivalent to having central bank money, the presence of $3.4 billion in marketable securities permits the Fed to provide substantial liquidity without subsidizing risky private firms. Presumably, posting collateral is socially costly; if it were not, all CHIPS (and other) payments would optimally be fully collateralized.

21. Investor uncertainty about the Fed's LLR funds provision can either raise or lower private incentives to control their trading risk exposures, according to whether market investors under- or over-estimate the Fed's future level of support to the market.

REFERENCES

Abken, Peter A., "Over-the-Counter Financial Derivatives: Risky Business," Federal Reserve Bank of Atlanta *Economic Review* (March/April 1994), pp. 1-22.

Baer, Herbert L, Virginia G. France, and James T. Moser, "Opportunity Cost and Prudentiality: An Analysis of Futures Clearinghouse Behavior," The World Bank, Policy Research Working Paper 1340 (August 1994).

Bagehot, Walter, *Lombard Street*, London: Kegan Paul, Trench, Trubner & Co., 1894.

Benston, George J., Robert A. Eisenbeis, Paul M. Horvitz, Edward J. Kane, and George G. Kaufman, *Perspectives on Safe & Sound Banking: Past, Present, and Future*, Cambridge: The MIT Press (1986).

Bernanke, Ben, and Mark Gertler, "Financial Fragility and Economic Performance," *Quarterly Journal of Economics* (February 1990), pp. 87-114.

Calomiris, Charles W., "Is the Discount Window Necessary? A Penn Central Perspective," Federal Reserve Bank of St. Louis *Review* (May/June 1994) pp. 31-56.

Calomiris, Charles W., and R. Glen Hubbard, "Firm Heterogeneity, Internal Finance, and Credit Rationing," *The Economic Journal* (March 1990), pp. 90-104.

Cody, Brian J., "Reducing the Costs and Risks of Trading Foreign Exchange," Federal Reserve Bank of Philadelphia *Business Review* (November/December 1990), pp. 13-23.

Cohen, Hugh, and William Roberds, "Towards the Systematic Measurement of Systemic Risk," Federal Reserve Bank of Atlanta Working Paper Series, WP-93-14 (October 1993).

Emmons, William R., "The Payments System, Delegated Monitoring, and Banking Safety Nets," Working paper, Dartmouth College (November 1994).

Federal Reserve Board of Governors, "Responses to Questions on Financial Derivatives Posed by Congressman James A. Leach." In *Safety and Soundness Issues Related to Bank Derivatives Activities–Part 3*, Hearing before the Committee on Banking, Finance and Urban Affairs, House of Representatives, One Hundred Third Congress, First Session (October 6, 1993), pp. 282-381.

Flannery, Mark J., "Corporate Finance, Market Discipline, and Bank Supervision." *The Declining? Role of Banking*. Proceedings from the 30th Annual Conference on Bank Structure and Competition, Federal Reserve Bank of Chicago (May 1994), pp. 313-330.

Flannery, Mark J., "Payments System Risk and Public Policy." In William S. Haraf and Rose Marie Kushmeider (Eds.) *Restructuring Banking & Financial Services in America*. Washington, D.C.: American Enterprise Institute for Public Policy Research (1988), pp. 261-287.

Gilbert, R. Alton, "Implications of Netting Arrangements for Bank Risk in Foreign Exchange Transactions," Federal Reserve Bank of St. Louis *Review* (January/February 1992), pp. 3-16.

Goodfriend, Marvin, and Robert G. King, "Financial Deregulation, Monetary Policy, and Central Banking." In William S. Haraf and Rose Marie Kushmeider (Eds.), *Restructuring Banking & Financial Services in America.* Washington, DC: American Enterprise Institute for Public Policy Research (1988), pp. 216-253.

Goodhart, Charles, *The Evolution of Central Banks.* Cambridge: The MIT Press (1990).

McAndrews, James, and William Roberds, "Banks, Payments, and Coordination," Working paper, Federal Reserve Banks of Philadelphia and Atlanta (August 1994).

Mengle, David L., "Legal and Regulatory Reform in Electronic Payments: An Evaluation of Payment Finality Rules." In David B. Humphrey (Ed.), *The U.S. Payment System: Efficiency, Risk and the Role of the Federal Reserve.* Boston: Kluwer Academic Publishers (1990), pp. 145-195.

Merton, Robert C., "Financial Innovation and the Management and Regulation of Financial Institutions," Working paper, Harvard Business School (September 1994).

Moser, James T., "Origins of the Modern Exchange Clearinghouse: A History of Early Clearing and Settlement Methods at Futures Exchanges," Federal Reserve Bank of Chicago Working Paper Series, WP-94-3 (April 1994).

Perold, Andre F., "The Payments System and Derivative Instruments," Working paper. Harvard Business School (October 1994).

Schoenmaker, Dirk, "A Comparison of Net and Gross Settlement," London School of Economics Financial Markets Group Special Paper (May 1994).

Stigum, Marcia, *After the Trade.* Homewood: Dow Jones-Irwin, (1988).

MISSING ENTAILMENTS IN PUBLIC-POLICY DEFINITIONS OF SYSTEMIC RISK

Edward J. Kane

In policymaking applications, poor definitions are not harmless. Nor are good definitions arbitrary. A conscientious economic modelbuilder must employ definitions that promise to develop insightful theorems and instructive policy implications.

This theme was sounded in the first session of this conference by Phil Bartholomew when he observed that our ability to deal with a real-word problem is constrained by how we define that problem conceptually. Entailments we leave out of our definitions of systemic risk limit our policy perspective. They cut back on how much of the problem we actually perceive. The masking effects of perspective limitation can be illustrated by considering how effectively a museum curator can cover up weaknesses in a sculptor's work by placing a statue within a niche located in a narrow and poorly lit corridor.

Operative definitions of systemic risk have metaphorical roots. This morning's speakers held themselves to metaphors that entail a tightly restricted time frame: falling dominos, failing power grids, and stationary elephant parts.

Research in Financial Services Private and Public Policy, Volume 7, pages 337-346.

ISBN: 1-55938-244-9

Metaphors, like analogies and parables, seek to conceptualize difficult issues and problems in terms of structural relationships we already understand. The essence of metaphorical reasoning is to characterize the aspects of one problem in terms of a second and simpler problem.

Simple biological and engineering metaphors for a banking system underlie policy pronouncements about how to define systemic risk. My goal is to show that each of these metaphors offers instructive entailments that self-congratulatory assessments of regulatory performance systematically neglect. I contend that the unexplored portions of standard public policy metaphors for systemic risk pose regulatory problems whose perception has been distorted by incentive conflicts for which society has yet to formulate a satisfactory solution.

I. INCOMPLETE USE OF ENGINEERING AND BIOLOGICAL METAPHORS

By a *system*, regulators mean an integrated network of parts that together perform an identifiable function. In discussions of financial regulation, *systemic risk* concerns the chance of a system breakdown or devolution. A system may break down in two ways: (1) in a contagious conflagration in which damage spreads unchecked across the component parts of the network or (2) in a disintegration or deterioration of particular connections that link individual parts.

The distinction between conflagration risk and deterioration risk may be illustrated by envisioning a sound system composed of a tuner, phonograph, CD player, tape deck, preamplifier, amplifier, and speaker. Conflagration would occur if a voltage surge (say, from a lightning strike) were to travel through the system and burn out all components. Disintegration may occur as the result of gradual decay or from a sudden breach in an electrical line or connection somewhere in the system.

Conflagration risk is managed by erecting barrier controls to lessen the degree of component unification so as to contain damage individual parts incur form spreading contagiously to other system components. Deterioration risk is managed in two ways: by identifying and renewing poorly performing or deteriorating parts and by erecting tandem or fail-safe connections designed to keep the system working when fragile linkages rot or burn out. A neglected entailment of this engineering metaphor is that strategies for containing conflagration risk can easily increase the system's exposure to deterioration risk and *vice versa*. To manage systemic risk means to strike an appropriate balance between conflagration risk and deterioration risk. An appropriate balance is unlikely to be struck when the all-too-real risk of slow deterioration is set aside by definition.

Biological metaphors liken the financial system to an assemblage of body parts that perform some vital function. In this conception, systemic risk is represented as exposure to disease or paralysis. As in the engineering metaphor, system breakdowns may occur through contagious conflagration or through a slow or sudden breaking apart of connective tissues. When using this metaphor, regulatory policymakers instinctively cast themselves in the care-giving role of *emergency-room doctors*. Regulators downplay complementary entailments for fostering patient health in everyday situations.

Financial policymakers fail to assign roles in either metaphor to the full cast of potential *causative agents* for system breakdown. Policymakers have obsessed on the possibility that the equivalent of exogenous voltage surges and biological poisons will suddenly damage institutions and markets that lie within their jurisdiction. This obsession has led them to underplay the importance of policies designed to facilitate the renewal and adaptation of regulatory systems to ongoing technical change. They have failed to make the positive goals of promoting efficient evolution of the financial system over time coequal with the negative objective of avoiding occasional breakdowns.

Exploring the biological metaphor can clarify that policy discussions fail either to envisage the conflicts of interest that actual doctors are known to face or to address systemic breakdowns that correspond to slow-working parasites and dietary deficiencies. Exploring the engineering metaphor can clarify that all too often turf-protecting regulators resist the retirement of defective and obsolete components known to lie within their jurisdiction. The S & L insurance mess illustrates both entailments. For decades politicians and regulators allowed a financial plague to spread slowly to taxpayers from insolvent institutional parasites, parasites with whom more than a few supervisory officials had bonded professionally.

Today, technological change requires managers of financial institutions and regulatory agencies to adapt their enterprises in painful ways. The costs of delaying efficiency-promoting adaptation are seldom immediately visible to the public at large. Clever accounting maneuvers can hide these costs and roll them forward to be recognized on a successor's watch.

Around the world, incentive defects in public service help to shape the range of deterioration risks that financial systems face. In their willingness to delay the treatment of slowly progressing disorders, financial regulators may themselves be likened to virulent parasites that are willing to see their institutional host sicken fatally as long as they can expect to relocate themselves with another host before the last rites need to be administered. Proposals to fold the OTS into the OCC and SAIF into BIF exemplify the opportunistic process of bureaucratic migration.

Regulators often act on *poor information* and with *poor motivation*. Regulators face perennial conflicts of interest between hidden agendas of personal and bureaucratic gains on the one hand and the promotion of their overt societal mission on the other. Far from admitting weakness, most regulators seek to convince us that their efforts play a critical role in system survival. In the most self-congratulatory rhetoric, an inherently unstable financial system is repeatedly kept from self-destruction only by the vigilance and energy of selfless public officials.

Such utopian self-images lead regulators in most countries and agencies to view the technologically driven globalization of financial markets and institutions as spreading conflagration danger rather than effecting beneficial forms of renewal and adaptation. They discern a growing threat of system breakdown in the increased integration of world finance and fail to celebrate the simultaneous loss-control benefits that go with replacing defective and obsolete parts and forging stronger and expanded linkages between a more diverse set of system components. Top regulators typically work far harder at preserving their autonomy and supporting the markets and institutions that lay within their purview than they work at building a more resilient and more transparent financial system.

II. THE ACCOUNTABILITY-RESISTANCE HYPOTHESIS

Where society should want barrier controls is between financial-institution activities and taxpayer loss exposures. Such a separation can be enhanced by policies that expand private risk-sharing arrangements. Dropping the assumption that government officials faithfully optimize taxpayer welfare allows economists to explain persistent supervisory and regulatory breaches in taxpayer protection as equilibrium phenomena rather than isolated mistakes. What we may call the Accountability-Resistance Hypothesis holds that the renewal of worn-out and obsolete parts in supervisory information, monitoring, and enforcement systems is routinely sabotaged to serve personal and bureaucratic ends.

Congressional acceptance of this hypothesis is signalled by the Depositor Preference Act of 1993 and the Prompt Corrective Action (PCA) and Least Cost Resolution (LCR) provisions of FDIC Improvement Act of 1991 (FDICIA). The value of this legislation to taxpayers is emphasized by Rick Carnell.

Unreconstructed forms of accountability resistance may be discerned in two other regulatory systems: the system of Risk-Based Capital (RBC) Supervision for G-10 Banks and the regulatory system for monitoring derivatives risk.

Risk-Based Capital Supervision: Let us address weaknesses in the RBC system first. There is nothing wrong with the idea that bank capital should increase commensurately with bank risk exposure. Corporate-finance theory interprets requirements for ownership capital at insured banks as implicit deposit-insurance premiums that help to control the moral hazard to which the insurer's reserves are exposed (Buser, Chen, and Kane 1981). But if they are to neutralize risk-taking exposure, supervisors cannot set capital standards operative definitions of capital and risk exposure, and procedures for monitoring compliance arbitrarily. System components must be made commensurate with those a well-capitalized private guarantor would impose.

It is desirable for bureaucratic decision about operative standards, conceptual definitions, and monitoring procedures to be tested econometrically against premiums estimating from capital-market experience and to be shown by economic analysis to have an appropriate impact. Running such tests should be the first priority of economists working in regulatory employ.

The RBC system cannot pass these accountability tests. Economic analysis and selected accounting theorists such as Chambers, (1981), and Wolnizer, (1987) conceive a bank's capital position as the sum of tangible and intangible opportunity-cost values (positive and negative) for all potential sources and uses of cash flows. This criterion shows that RBC capital definition lacks economic content. The RBC system conceives of bank capital as composed of mere "tiers" of accounting liability. Tier-one capital represents the accounting value of stockholder equity (i.e., net worth); tier-two capital is the aggregate value of a few other accounting liabilities. Tier-two items consist of two kinds of claims: (a) those on which contractual payments can be interrupted without triggering default (e.g., preferred stock and subordinated debt): and (b) reserve accounts against which accountants might easily charge losses that might accrue (e.g., unallocated reserves for loan losses). Even though mark-to-market accounting principles are beginning to displace historical-cost valuation in generally accepted accounting principles, banking regulators continue to profess a disinclination to let unrealized or "paper" losses impact tier-one capital (Meredith, 1994). Just last month, federal banking regulators decided not to incorporate into regulatory measures of capital unrealized losses on securities holdings that are now accounted under FASB 115.

RBC definitions of risk exposure also lack economic content. The RBC system measures risk as a sum of exposures attributable to on-balance-sheet values and selected off-balance sheet positions. Exposures assigned to the particular risks the system recognizes come from weights that carry an arbitrary assessment of default risk. The risk weighting scheme recognizes only four risk tranches. The tranches employ weights of 0 percent, 20 percent, 50 percent, and 100 percent respectively.

Finance theory assesses item risk at the margin and sees it as originating and evolving not just with default risk, but with many sources. Although the RBC scheme is eventually supposed to find ways to incorporate time variation, asset-concentration risk and interest-rate risk into the mix, authorities have made negligible progress toward formulating satisfying measures of these important risk exposures.

The RBC norm for when a bank's capital is adequate is not economically satisfying either. Regulators arbitrarily regard bank capital as adequate if two test are met: (1) tier-one capital equals at least 4 percent of the aggregate value of risk-weighted positions and (2) overall capital reaches 8 percent of this total. Relative to the leverage restrictions that would be implied by market-imposed risk premiums, it is virtually certain that capital allocations on some assets will prove too high and others too low. Burdens from overweighted assets can be avoided either by asset sales or by restructuring, securitizing, or otherwise participating out cash flows. This means that the gross opportunity-cost burden of positions a bank retains is not likely even approximately to counterbalance the loss exposure that bank operations impose on deposit-insurance reserves. This perspective helps us to understand why, as the system settled into place, few important banks failed to record substantially more accounting capital than the minimum values dictated by the risk-weighted formulas. It also clarifies why monitoring designed to assure conformance with RBC standards need not prevent taxpayers from facing loss exposure in BIF and why the PCA and LCR requirements of FDICIA are not redundant.

Bank Activity in Derivative Instruments: Further corroboration for the accountability resistance hypothesis can be found in the reluctance of federal regulators to empower complementary mechanisms for private loss sharing that could help control the derivatives risk exposures at U.S. banks. Three mechanisms exist by which federal bank regulators could enlist the self-interest of private market participants to help them monitor and limit the nontransparent loss exposures that bank derivatives positions pass through the federal safety net. Without appealing to covert bureaucratic motives such as lessening accountability and controlling regulatory turf, it is hard to explain how persistently top U.S. banking regulators have resisted opportunities for increasing transparency by introducing additional private surveillance mechanisms.

Three market-based surveillance mechanisms exist. The most effective device would be to insist that dealing in derivative contracts by any insured bank take place through a separately capitalized swap subsidiary. To intensify the degree of intercorporate capital separation, the extent to which a parent bank or bank holding company could mirror or guarantee the swap subsidiary's performance obligations would have to be sharply limited. Under this corporate structure, private rating agencies and counterparties would have a strong incentive to insist that the parent corporation transfer enough economic capital explicitly to the subsidiary to credibly bond its ability to perform its obligations under outstanding derivatives contracts (Figlewski, 1994). For institutions with substantial loss exposures in swaps, the transparency of these explicit capital transfers to the subsidiary would straightforwardly and continuously alert bank regulators of the extend to which parent capital was supporting the organization's swap book. Improved transparency for capital deficiencies would make weakness in the consolidated banking entity easier to observe and make bank regulators more accountable for delays in demanding organization-wide recapitalization when it is needed.

Far from empowering market participants to undertake this form of private loss-sharing and bank surveillance, federal regulators have discouraged it. For example, on November 19, 1992, after receiving indications that their proposals would be rejected, Citibank and Continental Illinois withdrew application in which they had formally asked the Office of the Comptroller of the Currency for permission to spin off their bank's swaps book in this fashion (Kantrow, 1992). It was widely asserted that concerns about the overall adequacy of capital at these banks made regulators reluctant to earmark capital to bond this narrow class of risk.

A second way to increase private loss-sharing and monitoring for derivatives positions would be to develop a globally enforceable contracting protocol for netting derivative obligations within a voluntary "ring" of derivatives dealers. Far form assigning urgent staff priority to solving this problem, bank regulators have treated the practical difficulty of perfecting universally enforceable derivatives contracts as if it were a defensible excuse for inaction. But private initiatives have been forthcoming. The Chicago Board of Trade has proposed a multilateral clearinghouse for swaps. The private International Swap and Derivatives Association (ISDA) has developed a cross-product master netting agreement covering a wide range of forwards, swaps, options, and other derivative contracts. It is estimated that the ISDA netting agreement is used frequently by 70 percent of swap dealers. The agreement provides for the sharing of a single net closeout amount when one counterparty defaults on covered for the sharing of a single net closeout amount when one counterparty defaults on covered derivatives contracts (Hendricks, 1994). For ISDA members, a major purpose of establishing this agreement is to convince regulators that covered contracts are enforceable enough to make it reasonable to apply risk-based capital requirements to the marked-to-replacement-cost value of *net*—rather than gross—derivatives positions (Thomasula, 1994). Still, the enforceability of the ISDA protocol is known to be imperfect in at least two ways. First, the ISDA agreement does not assure that individual counterparties truly have the legal capacity to enter the contracts being netted. Second, in the United States, the FDIC claims authority to curtail the covenanted right of counterparties under the agreement to terminate a contract in the event of a bank failure.

In the natural course of events, at least a few netting rings may be expected to evolve over time into a full-fledged derivatives exchange (Moser, 1994). The third mechanism for enhancing private surveillance would be for financial regulators to insist that by a specified date all or most classes of derivatives contracts must trade on an exchange. The obligations undertaken by clearing members of an exchange go beyond clearinghouse commitments in two ways.

First, clearing members guarantee counterparty performance on all traded contracts. Second, this guaranted gives clearing members strong incentives to contract for the informational transparency necessary to monitor and control nonperformance risk on the exchange. These monitoring and control efforts lead to private performance bonding that is enforced in part by a transparent and frequent marking to market (eventually perhaps in real time) of the value of each counterparty's open positions in exchange contracts. It is both instructive and ironic that, to assure the lawfulness of less transparent OTC dealing in derivatives contracts by U.S. banks, Congress was persuaded to enact the Futures Trading practices Act of 1992 (FTPA). This low authorizes the Futures Trading Commission (CFTC) to exempt bank dealing in derivatives retroactively from exchange-trading requirements that would otherwise seen to have applied to bank dealers Mitchell (1993). Prior to the passage of the FTPA, some OTC swap participants were uncomfortable in relying on the authority of safe-harbor criteria for over-the-counter trading asserted in CFTC statements of policy. It is hard to understand CFTC willingness to surrender its natural jurisdiction over derivatives products without introducing concepts like shirking and turf-protecting pressure from banking regulators.

III. IMPLICATIONS FOR POLICY STRATEGY

My theme is that the more important form of systemic risk is deterioration risk and that the timely renewal of worn-out and obsolete parts of the financial regulatory system remains hampered by defects in the incentives faced by officials responsible for adapting this system over time. Regulated institutions use political clout and structural adaptation to resist needed changes. Regulators respond to political pressure and routinely use disinformation to resist efforts to shrink their domains and to make them more accountable. As a result, financial regulatory strategies known to better serve societal interests prove unduly slow to win adoption.

The current system routinely empowers government regulators to resist the expansion of powers by institutions outside of their specialized supervisory domain. But an entry-facilitating strategy of regulatory renewal could be adopted. Such a strategy would set costs of private entry and exit into individual financial activities as low as two other societal objectives allow: (1) maintaining confidence in financial contract performance and (2) tempering the severity of macroeconomic fluctuations. An entry-facilitating strategy could better confront obsolescence risk in the regulatory system and more reliably transmit healthy market discipline both to financial institutions and to state, federal, and foreign regulators that back these institutions up.

To strengthen the economic pressure transmitted to federal regulatory enterprises, government budgetary restraints could be adapted to make federal players in the market for regulatory services more competitive. Information-reporting protocols could be designed to make the efficiency of individual regulatory efforts more transparent. In turn, budgetary rules incorporating more transparent measures of governmental performance could be used to assure that efficient regulatory enterprises expand and inefficient ones contract.

Accomplishing these tasks would lower entry barriers for private financial institutions by making it easier to displace incumbent competitors and their specialized regulators from traditional activities. Around the world, the exit of inefficient deposit institutions, regulators, and economic models has been retarded by governmental information and budgeting systems that support failing competitors. Routinely providing subsidies to crippled firms makes financial markets less contestable globally. It does this by increasing the cost for new or foreign firms and regulators to use technological advances to secure competitive footholds that can open fail-safe tandem connections in global markets.

As popular memory of the S&L insurance mess and Continental-Illinois debacle has faded, regulators have begun to put a self-congratulating spin on their collective performance during these disheartening episodes. These self-serving reassessments underscore how closely the principal-agent problems that taxpayers face with regulatory resemble those that parents face with children.

The comic strip *Calvin and Hobbes* treats the difficulty of controlling an unprincipled child as a daily source of amusement. A particularly instructive interchange begins with Calvin's mother singing his praises: "Why look! You made your bed without even being told to! That's wonderful, Calvin." Once she leaves the room, Calvin's stuffed tiger Hobbes can speak. He observes: "Gee, your mom is sure nice when you help her." Calvin replies: "Yeah. That's the reason I usually don't. I like mom to be impressed when I fulfill the least of my obligations."

ACKNOWLEDGMENT

The author wished to thank Richard C. Aspinwall, Benjamin Esty, and James Moser for helpful comments on an earlier draft of part of this analysis.

REFERENCES

Buser, S. A. Chen, and E. Kane. "Federal Deposit Insurance, Regulatory Policy, and Optimal Bank Capital." *Journal of Finance*, 36 (March 1981): 51-60.

Chambers, R. J., *Foundation of Accounting*. Geelong: Deakin University Press, 1991.

Figlewski, S. "The Birth of the AAA Derivatives Subsidiary. *Journal of Derivatives*, 1 (Summer 1994): 80-84.

Hendricks, D. "Netting Agreements and the Credit Exposures of OTC Derivative Portfolios." *FRBNY Quarterly Review*, 19 (Spring 1994): 7-18.

Kantrow, Y. "Continental, Citi Scrap Plan to Form Swaps Units." *American Banker*, 157 (Dec. 17, 1992): 1 and 12.

Meredith, R. "Regulators Seeking a Way to End Paper Losses from Mark-to-Market." *American Banker*, 159 (June 10, 1994): 2.

Mitchell, D. "CFTC Exemptions for Swap Agreement and Hybrid Instruments." *Review of Banking & Financial Services*, 9(May 5, 1993): 87-93.

Moser, J. "Origins of the Modern Exchange Clearinghouse: A History of Early Clearing and Settlement Methods at Futures Exchanges." Working Paper No. 94-3, Federal Reserve Bank of Chicago 1994.

Thomasula, D. "Eased Swaps Capital Rules Proposed by Basel Panel." *American Banker*, 159 (July 27 1994): 1 and 16.

Wolnizer, P. W. *Auditing as Independent Verification*. Sydney: Sydney University Press 1987.

PART V

KEYNOTE ADDRESS

RETHINKING SYSTEMIC RISK

Eugene A. Ludwig

I. INTRODUCTION

If economics is the dismal science, as Malthus said, on the face of it, the topic of this conference may be among the most dismal. Failure to address this issue in a thoughtful and fact-based manner has very serious costs for our financial system and our economy.

Happily, an abundance of excellent scholarship over the past two decades gives us a better basis for identifying and dealing with systemic risk. In particular, as I will discuss in greater detail later, recent academic research has called into question some of the most cherished beliefs of regulators concerning the fundamental importance of systemic risk as a justification for detailed regulation of depository institutions. It is important that, as policy makers concerned with systemic risk, we be familiar with this scholarship and use it to guide our actions. That, of course, is the purpose of this conference. So it is particularly gratifying to have so many important academics and policy makers here to participate in these proceedings.

Systemic risk has been a central concern for me from the day I was nominated almost two years ago. At that time, I laid out four goals that have since become the pillars of my agenda for my term as Comptroller:

Research in Financial Services Private and Public Policy, Volume 7, pages 349-356.

ISBN: 1-55938-244-9

- First, to ensure the safety and soundness of the national banking system.
- Second, to promote banks' ability to compete.
- Third, to improve the efficiency and effectiveness of OCC supervision.
- And finally, to ensure fair and equal access to financial services for all Americans.

It should be clear that understanding, identifying and planning for systemic risk are central to achieving all four goals. I am committed to increasing safety and soundness and to lowering risk to our financial systems. Careful and thoughtful analysis incorporating the finest scholarship, such as we see here today, is necessarily helpful in that endeavor.

II. DEFINING SYSTEMIC RISK

Regrettably, there is no clear agreement on what constitutes systemic risk, how it manifests itself, or oven the extent to which regulators ought to be concerned about it. The phrase "systemic risk" means different things to different people. Congress, bank supervisors, and economists all struggle over the basic nature and quantitative significance of this shadowy concept. Indeed, one important result of this conference may be to further the process of de-mystifying systemic risk.

That would be a significant result, because the need to minimize systemic risk is often cited as a key reason for banking regulation. In many respects, it becomes the rationale that cannot be denied. Why have the regulators taken a particular action? To minimize systemic risk, they may say. And how exactly will this particular action minimize systemic risk? The answer to that question is often wrapped in obscurity.

For purposes of my remarks here today, I would like to adopt the provisional definition of systemic risk used in this morning's presentation by Phil Bartholomew and Gary Whalen. That is, systemic risk is characterized by "a sudden, usually unexpected, collapse of confidence in a significant portion of the financial system with potentially large real economic impacts."

III. TRADITIONAL VIEWS OF SYSTEMIC RISK

For many years, systemic risk has come to be associated with the fallout from bank failures. The conventional wisdom has held that the social costs associated with the failure—or, more precisely, the liquidation—of a very large bank, or a large number of smaller banks, would be prohibitive. Therefore, such occurrences ought to be prevented at all cost. Indeed, the following scenario—what I will all the specter of the 1930s—has become one of the most familiar ghosts to haunt many of us in the business of regulating banks.

Here's the scenario. The failure of a large institution or a number of smaller institutions results in losses to uninsured depositors and/or other institutions holding balances at the failed banks. Seeing this, and lacking the information to judge whether their own institutions are solvent, uninsured depositors at other banks withdraw their deposits as a protective measure—the phenomenon of contagion. With their reserves greatly reduced, the affected banks stop making new loans and liquidate securities. Fearing additional runs, still more banks cut back on their lending in order to build up their excess reserves.

The end results are a general credit stringency, a shrinkage of the money supply, a decline in economic activity, increased default on loans, and further bank failures. Just how bad conditions ultimately become in this scenario depends on your assumption about the behavior of regulators, how well the central bank fulfills its role as lender of last resort, and a host of other variables. In every case, however, the general picture is one of a financial system seriously disrupted, with adverse effects extending far beyond the shareholders, depositors, and creditors of the original failing bank.

This specter of the 1930s has for some time permeated the structure of bank regulation. Now, no one who lived through the collapse of the banking system between 1929 and 1933 and the accompanying economic upheavals would welcome a repetition of those events. At the same time, we should not forget that the terrible dimensions of that debacle were the result, at least in large part, of a combination of external events and policy errors that need not be repeated.

These include the government's failure to replenish the reserves of the banking system depleted by runs, the widespread tendency among regulators to approach the banking crisis as just retribution for bankers' sins in the 1920s, the onset of depression in Europe after the failure of the Credit Anstalt in Austria, and the passage of the Smoot-Hawley Act in 1930. The short-run effects of all these developments were magnified by the fact that they occurred in a world without deposit insurance. If even one or two of the major policy errors were avoided in a future banking crisis, one could reasonably argue that the outcome in terms of damage to the system would be considerably milder.

I do not intend in any way to minimize the potential seriousness of systemic risk stemming from bank failures. Quite the contrary—it is my firm belief that we need to face up to the full range of possibilities now, when there is relative calm in the banking industry, and to plan for a wide range of contingencies. Now is the time to confront the ghost of the 1930s and finally lay it to rest. By doing so, we can avoid the ad hoc policy approach that too often has characterized the regulators' actions during times of crisis.

IV. INCREASED COMPETITION

In some respects, Congress and the bank regulators have already begun to take actions to dispel this ghost. The system of bank regulation built up in the aftermath of the Depression was designed to protect depository institutions and limit competition. But in the 1970s and early 1980s, Congress and the bank regulators took several steps toward dismantling this system. Restrictions on bank competition—most notably, restriction on deposit interest rates—were relaxed and then eliminated altogether. Within a relatively short time, banks and thrifts pushed into more competitive markets.

Unfortunately, in beginning to remove competitive restrictions on depository institutions, the government failed to provide for minimizing the costs of a higher rate of bank failures. Of course, higher failure rates were inevitable. It is axiomatic in economic analysis that more competitive markets mean lower profits and a higher incidence of failure. The cost of bank failures were addressed, albeit somewhat belatedly and perhaps somewhat imperfectly, when Congress enacted the Financial Institutions Recovery, Reform and Enforcement Act in 1989 and the FDIC Improvement Act in 1991. In the case of FDICIA, Congress consciously tried to limit the costs of bank failures by systematizing the process of exit from the banking industry.

V. BIASES IN THE PERCEPTION OF SYSTEMIC RISK

One of the difficulties in carrying on a rational public debate about competition and systemic risk in the banking system stems from the widely varying ways in which the public experiences the benefits of competition and the costs of bank failures. A banking crisis like that of the 1920s and 1930s is an extremely visible event, announced by headlines and followed continuously by the press as long as it lasts. If accompanied by a depression in real economic activity—regardless of whether it is the cause or the effect—the crisis may also be associated in the public mind with tangible, personal economic harm.

It is scarcely surprising, then, that both the general public and its representatives in Congress often judge regulators by their success in limiting systemic risk. In the minds of the great majority who do not attend conferences like this one, limiting systemic risk means limiting bank failures.

By contrast, the benefits of enhanced competition and efficiency take the form of small reductions in price or improvements in the quality and variety of banking services over an extended period of time. It may require sophisticated econometric techniques to measure the benefits from particular liberalizations of regulations or changes in market structure. In these circumstances, the typical consumer of financial services may have trouble believing that there really are such benefits.

The reaction to the banking and thrift crises of the 1980s gave ample evidence of how the public viewed the costs and benefits of banking competition. At the first sign of trouble, many critics of the recent course of banking regulation were ready to repeal the full array of deregulatory measures—measures adopted only after decades of research and political infighting. It is discouraging that many critics did not adequately, to my mind, consider other obvious explanations for the crisis, such as mispriced deposit insurance, the indiscriminate capital forbearance practiced in the thrift industry, or the risk concentrations in loan portfolios encouraged by branching restrictions.

VI. NEW RESEARCH ON SYSTEMIC RISK

Fortunately, virtually every misconception regarding risk in the banking system that I have cataloged to this point has been the subject of intense academic research over the past two or three decades. In many cases, this research has discredited popular fallacies accepted as unquestioned truth for more than 50 years.

Skepticism toward traditional views of bank regulation dates back at least to the 1950s, to the work of David Alhadeff, a pioneer in applying the industrial organization approach to the financial sector. Alhadeff questioned the prevailing view, expressed by one well-known regulatory official, Howard Crosse, that "a bank failure is a community disaster whenever and wherever it occurs." He noted that the failure of the sole local manufacturing firm might be a more serious problem for many one-employer towns than the failure of the local bank—a view stated independently at about the same time by former OCC economist and FDIC Research Director Paul Horvitz. Alhadeff called for a reassessment of policy toward entry of new banks into the banking system.

Shortly thereafter, in a little-heralded article that is still well worth reading, Dale Tussing of Syracuse University made the fundamental distinction—albeit without using the term—between systemic risk on the one hand and the risk of individual bank failure on the other. He noted that there are two key linkages that justify "the long-standing policy of avoiding bank failure": the linkage "between the failure of an unsound and/or poorly managed bank and the failure of other banks," and the linkage between a bank failure and its effects on "depositors, borrowers, and third parties." Tussing argued that public policy could permit increased competition and freedom of judgment in banking—even when it led to increased bank failures—if a system could be devised to break these two linkages. Many of the proposals for supervisory and regulatory reform advance in recent years, including the prompt corrective action provisions of FDICIA, seek to do precisely that.

Another important example of academic research that has discredited fallacies about systemic risk is the chapter on "The Great Recession" in Friedman and Schwartz's *Monetary History of the United States from 1867 to 1960*. Their work probably has done more than any other research to call into question prevailing views regarding the relationship between the banking collapse and the Great Depression, as well as the connection between individual bank management, the behavior of the bank regulators, and the bank failures.

Citing evidence that there had been no observable deterioration in banks' *ex ante* credit standards in the 1920s, Friedman and Schwartz argued that the banking collapse was much more a consequence of faulty regulatory policy and an inadvertently tight monetary policy than of any tendency toward excessive risk-taking by banks. Research in the early and mid-1960s largely laid to rest the notion that excessive competition for deposits had led to excessive risk-taking by banks and large numbers of bank failures in the early 1930s. It's worth noting, however, that, as late as 1966, Congress was still trying to limit competition by depository institutions when it extended interest rate ceilings on deposits to cover savings and loan associations as well as banks.

Finally, one of the most exciting developments in banking research in the past decade has been the reexamination of U.S. banking history in the 19th century using modern finance theory and current statistical techniques. The picture that emerges calls for revision of many of the impressions conveyed by traditional histories of U.S. banking and by many current texts on money and banking. Among the findings that are most relevant to our present concern with systemic risk are those that relate to the resilience and rationality of financial markets. The traditional view of baning panics in the 19th century has emphasized the susceptibility of markets to irrational behavior—for example, the notion that the flimsiest rumor often motivated depositors to run on a bank. Without totally dismissing that idea as a logical possibility, George Benston and George Kaufman concluded in a recent survey of the historical evidence that depositors, far from being indiscriminate in their behavior, "run on particular banks for specific, well-documented reasons..."

Edward Kane had reached a similar conclusion several years earlier with respect to the runs that occurred in 1985 on institutions insured by the Ohio Deposit Guarantee Fund. Equally or more important, the historical evidence calls into question the notion that banking markets are fragile, contrary to the repeated assertion of a number of highly regarded scholars over the past several decades.

VII. OBSTACLES TO INCORPORATING RESEARCH INTO REGULATORY PRACTICE

Although many questions regarding the nature, significance, and policy implications of systemic risk remain unanswered, researchers have made substantial progress toward understanding this phenomenon, whose prevention or minimization many view as the major goal of banking regulation. One consequence of this progress is the emergence of a gap between current bank supervision practice and the body of thought on policy toward systemic risk widely accepted by the academic community. This gap is most evident in the agencies' continued reliance on detailed supervision of bank product offerings and lending policies and the examination process to control bank risk-taking—an approach that has been supported in large measure by Congress. Witness recent legislative proposals on derivatives.

There are at least three important reasons why practice tends to lag behind academic research in the area of banking regulation. First, there is an understandable skepticism on the part of those responsible for formulating and implementing regulatory policy toward ideas that they view as radical and untested—particularly when they are the ones hauled before congressional committees to explain why a large bank has failed. Second, there has not been enough time for state-of-the-art academic research to be verified by professional peer groups and to became widely known to the regulatory community. And finally, to date, academics have failed to provide reasonably accurate and reliable estimates of the magnitudes of the probabilities of events and the associated costs and benefits under alternative regulatory approaches.

Nonetheless, there are surely many areas of banking regulation and supervision where we can work to narrow the gap between current academic thought and regulatory practice in ways that will reduce systemic risk and increase the effectiveness of our financial system.

VIII. CONCLUSION

What this all boils down to is a number of specific findings that fly in the face of traditional regulatory thought. Specifically, systemic risk caused by bank failures appears to be less common than generally supposed. The occasions on which it has been associated with serious economic effects were also marked by major policy errors. Bank runs are typically motivated by accurate information about the condition of particular banks—not by rumors or general uncertainty following bank failures. Contagion has been both rare and, generally, highly localized. Financial markets are less fragile than many of us had been led to believe, and runs and failures can be a source of long-run discipline on bank risk-taking.

Please don't misunderstand me. I am *not* saying that we should not be concerned about individual bank failures. Believe me, bank failures do concern me and our agency a very great deal indeed. What I am saying is this: isolated bank failures do not appear necessarily to generate the kind of systemic risk about which bank supervisors have traditionally been concerned. And, it that is the case, we need to gain a better understanding of the ways in which banks are tied to each other and to the banking system as a whole in order to identify the real risks that can affect the entire banking system.

We may also need a better understanding of the interrelationships between banks and the broader financial markets. For example, how are banks affected by events in the insurance industry? Conversely, how do events in the insurance industry affect banks? What about events in the commodities industry or the securities market or the bond market? Do we need a broader approach to limiting systemic risk for banks—one that embraces the entire financial industry?

These are questions to which bank supervisors do not have answers today, but to which they will need answers in the not-too-far-distant future. As banks gain more freedom to compete in a broader range of activities, we and they must understand how these activities will affect not only individual institutions but the entire financial market and the economy as a whole. Only then can we be certain that bank supervision is effective in minimizing systemic risk. Only then can we be certain that bank supervision truly serves the public interest.

Advances in Pacific Basin Business, Economics and Finance

Edited by **C. F. Lee,** *Rutgers University*

Volume 1, 1995, 370 pp. $73.25
ISBN 1-55938-737-8

CONTENTS: PART A: MACROECONOMICS. Outlook for Japan-EC-United States Political-Economic Relations, *Richard J. Sweeney.* New Economic Policies for the U.S., *John Clark Francis.* Japan and the Threat of Laura Tyson, *Jeremiah J. Sullivan.* An Overview of Recent Economic Development in China, *Wuu-Long Lin and Thomas P. Chen.* Linkage Effects of Foreign Enterprises on Chinese Economy: Problems and Prospects in the 1990s, *Peter C. Y. Chow.* Linkage Effects of Foreign Enterprises in China: Problems and Prospects - Comment, *Chao-Nan Liu.* Financial System in China, *Frank C. Jen.* Trade Policy of Taiwan, *Rong-I Wu.* A Re-Evaluation of Taiwan Domestic Economic Policy: A Political-Economy Approach, *Pai-Hsien Pang and Shih-Ming Chen.* China's Foreign Exchange Rate Policy, *Jizu Wang.* Trade and Investment Across the Taiwan Straits: Maintaining Competitive Advantage, Pursuing Complementarity, *Koong-lian Kao.* Privatization and Productivity Growth in China: 1979-1990, *Chi-Chu Chou.* Japan's ODA and Its Role in China's Economic Reform, *David C. Cheng.* A Comparative Study of Economic Development: The Case of Shanghai, *Hong Kong and Taiwan, Chang-Hsien Chang and Peter Koveos.* Economic Relationships between Taiwan and China, *M. Jan Dutta.* Globalization of the Taiwanese Economy and U.S. - Taiwan Trade Relations, *Frank S. T. Hsiao.* The Pattern of U.S. - Asian Pacific Rim Trade, 1965-1987, *Ira N. Gang, Catherine Y. Co.* PART B: BUSINESS, FINANCE AND ACCOUNTING. An International Comparison of the Accuracy of Analysts' Forecasts of Earnings, *Jang Youn Cho and Andrew Pitcher.* Earnings Forecasting in Efficient Japanese Portfolios, *John B. Guerard Jr., Suzuki Makoto and Unmesh Bhide.* A Comparative Study of the Weekend Effects in the United States, British and the Pacific Rim Stock Markets: An Application of the ARCH Model, *Bwo-Nung Huang, Yu-Jane Liu and Chin W. Yang.* Corporate Ownership Structure and Corporate Governance Mechanism: With Experience of Korean Firms, *Ungki Lim.* On the Pricing of the Deposit Insurance Liabilities of the CDIC of Taiwan, *Jin-Chuan Duan, Mao-Wei Hung and Thomas Liaw.* The US, Japan and the Emerging Stock Markets of the Pacific Basin: A Test of Regional and Intertemporal Stability, *Richard Ajayi, Jongmoo Jay Choi and Seyed M. Mehdian.* Excess Returns of Unseasoned New Issues in Taiwan: An Institutional Perspective, *Gili Yen, E.C. Yen and S. Chen.* An Analysis of Mergers Between Mutual Banks and Credit Cooperatives in Japan, *Yasuo Hoshino.*

J A I P R E S S

Advances in Pacific Basin Financial Markets

Edited by **Theodore Bos** and **Thomas A. Fetherston**, *University of Alabama, Birmingham*

Volume 1, 1995, 376 pp. $78.75
ISBN 1-55938-861-7

CONTENTS: Advances in Pacific Basin Financial Markets: Introduction and Overview, *Theodore Bos and Thomas A. Fetherston.* Volume and Price Relationships in Three Yen Futures Markets, *Jonathan Batten and Ram Bhar.* Bidders' Initial Stake in Target Companies and Premiums Paid to Remaining Target Shareholders in New Zealand Full Takeover Offers: Could It Justify a Mandatory Offer Rule?, *Amnon Mandelbaum.* The Inflation-Stock Returns Puzzle: A Comparison of The United States and Japan, 1970-1992, *Susan Belden.* Equity Price Variation in Pacific Basin Countries. Thai Stock Market Volatility, *Don Dayananda and Kevin Fagg.* Using Interest Rate Swaps to Manage Corporate Bonds, *Zhenmin Fang.* The Cost of Capital in Japan and the United States: A Comparative Analysis, *Benton E. Gup.* Market Integration in the Four Newly Industrialized Economies of Asia, *Raymond H. F. Kwok.* "News" and the Volatility of The Foreign Exchange Market, *John Hin Hock Lee.* Large Operating Efficiency of Malaysian Banks, *Ming-Hua Liu, Nanda K. Rangan and Kah Hwa Ng.* The Impact of Price Limits on Market Volatility in Taiwan, *Soushan Wu and Tony Naughton.* The Relationship Between Accounting Returns and Stock Market Returns: Australian Evidence, *David E. Allen, Paul Kwang-Pore Lim and Gary MacDonald.* Equity Price Variation in Pacific Basin Countries, *Yin Wong Cheung and Lilian Ng.* The Stochastic Structure of Official and Black-Market Exchange Rates in the Pacific-Basin Economies, *Pochara Theerathorn and T. Chotigeat.* Diversification and Intervalling Effects on Stock: Returns Across Industrial Sectors: Evidence from Hong Kong, *Gordon Y. N. Tang.* Stochastic Behavior of Interest Rates in Singapore, *Y.K. Tse.* Measuring the Hedging Contribution of Futures Trading and Futures Contracts, *Soushan Wu, Her-Jiun Sheu, Yang-Cheng Lu and Raymond Chiang.* Response of Country Fund Returns, Premiums, and Trading Volume to News: The Case of the Korea Fund, *Chan-Wung Kim and Young-Kyu Kim.* The Long-Term Performance of IPO's and Non-IPO's: Evidence from the Firms Listed on the Tokyo Stock Exchange, *Chuan Yang Hwang and Narayanan Jayaraman.* The Tail Index of Asian Exchange Rate Returns, *Kees Koedjik and Fred Nieuwland.* Correlation Structure Forecasting of Ex-Ante Portfolio Selection Strategies in Emerging Asia Markets, *Richard Y. K. Ho and Raymond Siu-Kuen Lee.* Foreign Exchange Risk Strategies of Australian Firms, *Tony Naughton and Teoh Hai Yap.* Nonstationarity of the Market Model, Outliers, and Choice of the Market Rate of Return, *Theodore Bos and Thomas A. Fetherston.*